Cornelia Baltes

Dingbats

Paintings & Exhibitions 2012 – 2023

Index
Inhalt

Alexander Klar

The Picture as Object and Agent

Das Bild als Gegenstand und Akteur

To begin with a generality: a picture or image is the representation of an idea or a perception of something (of the world?) on a flat surface or ground. A picture is created in order to be seen; it is made, and it is looked at. For centuries, the picture was first and foremost a "likeness", only thereafter was it the bearer of a personal "handwriting"—out of the amalgam of the two emerged style. Then came the twentieth century, in the middle of which the picture became an object, a document of artistic activity. The withdrawal from the picture began with the recognition that a painting can overcome its centuries-old, tried and tested adherence to likeness if it becomes the pictorial imprint of the artist's personality, the document of the artistic act. The chance-based experiments of the Surrealists in the 1920s, Jackson Pollock's "drips" in the 1940s, and Emilio Vedova's "Plurimi" from the 1960s onwards mark at double-decade intervals the swift development of painting that was set in motion by the new departure of modernism in the twentieth century. The development began with the involvement of chance, whose lack of intentionality liberated the painting of surrealism; it continued in the painting of abstract expressionism, in which the traces left by artists as they worked on their canvases became a document of the composition itself; and it finally left the wall, thus conclusively making the painting into the object that it actually is. The result of this development is painting that, as a picture, reports on itself, and pictures that as painterly (not painted) objects can lead an independent existence in the exhibition space. The withdrawal from the picture as a phenomenon of art history is now more than half a century old: behind us lie the stages—outlined above in highly summary form—of a development whose future is just dawning.

In order to take a look at the current position of painting, a large-scale survey exhibition of young painting in Germany was staged in 2017. Its aim was to bring together and to present tendencies in contemporary art. Among the artists selected was Cornelia Baltes, whose powerfully lyrical paintings left a lasting impression on me. In the exhibition, titled *Jetzt* [Now] (pp. 98–108), it became manifestly clear that the outstanding feature of the present generation of painters is a liberated polystylistics, whose ostensible multilingualism, however, revolves essentially around the core question as to how ideas (both artistic and extra-artistic) are to be translated into form. A characteristic of the artist generation to which Cornelia Baltes belongs is the act of choosing between a wide variety of pictorial modes, for example geometrical or gestural painting, representational or narrative. Cornelia Baltes' oeuvre emancipates itself from concepts such as 'representational' or 'narrative': her pictures are in fact "object-like", but go clearly beyond this category. Her works are objects with a character of their own—works such as *Fla* (p. 17), *Taa* (p. 20) and *Jag* (p. 25) have not only a personality of their own but develop also a life of their own on the wall and in the room, because, even if the panel painting has not finally outlived its usefulness, the actual theatre-stage for Baltes' works is the surrounding roomspace. The wall itself, the traditional site of a painting, regularly becomes the performing area for the painting over

Um generell anzufangen: Ein Bild ist die Wiedergabe einer Idee oder einer Vorstellung von etwas (der Welt?) auf einem flachen Untergrund. Ein Bild wird geschaffen, um gesehen zu werden, es wird gemacht, und es wird betrachtet. Über Jahrhunderte war das Bild zuallererst „Abbild", danach erst „Handschrift", aus dem Amalgam beider entstand Stil. Dann kam das 20. Jahrhundert, in dessen Mitte das Bild zum Objekt wurde, zum Dokument künstlerischer Betätigung. Der Ausstieg aus dem Bild begann mit der Erkenntnis, dass ein Gemälde seine über Jahrhunderte erprobte Abbildhaftigkeit überwinden kann, wenn es zum bildlichen Abdruck der Künstlerpersönlichkeit, zum Dokument der künstlerischen Handlung wird. Die Zufallsexperimente des Surrealismus in den Zwanzigerjahren, Jackson Pollocks „Drips" in den Vierziger- und Emilio Vedovas „Plurimi" ab den Sechzigerjahren markieren in doppelten Dekadenabständen die rasche Entwicklung der Malerei, die der Aufbruch in die Moderne im 20. Jahrhundert losgetreten hatte. Die Entwicklung begann mit dem Einbezug des Zufalls, dessen Intentionslosigkeit die Malerei des Surrealismus befreite, sie führte sich fort in der Malerei des Abstrakten Expressionismus, in der die Spur der ihre Leinwände bearbeitenden Künstler*innen zum Dokument der Komposition selbst wurde, und verließ schließlich die Wand, um das Gemälde endgültig zu dem Objekt zu machen, das es eigentlich ist. Malerei, die als Bild über sich selbst berichtet, und Bilder, die als malerische (nicht bemalte!) Objekte eine unabhängige Existenz im Raum führen können, sind das Ergebnis dieser Entwicklung. Der Ausstieg aus dem Bild als kunsthistorisches Phänomen ist nun über ein halbes Jahrhundert alt, hinter uns liegen die hiermit sehr summarisch angerissenen Stadien einer Entwicklung, deren Zukunft gerade anbricht.

Um einen Blick auf den gegenwärtigen Stand der Malerei zu werfen, entstand 2017 eine groß angelegte Überblicksausstellung zur jungen Malerei in Deutschland, deren Ziel es war, Tendenzen der Gegenwartskunst zusammenzufassen und vorzustellen. Zur Auswahl der dort gezeigten Künstler*innen gehörte auch Cornelia Baltes, deren kraftvoll-lyrische Gemälde bei mir einen bleibenden Eindruck hinterließen. In der *Jetzt* (S. 98 – 108) betitelten Ausstellung wurde sichtbar: Das herausragende Merkmal der gegenwärtigen Maler*innengeneration ist eine befreite Polystilistik, deren vermeintliche Vielsprachigkeit aber im Wesentlichen um den Kern der Frage kreist, wie man Ideen (künstlerische wie außerkünstlerische) in Form überführt. Das Wählen zwischen den unterschiedlichsten Bildmodi, also etwa dem geometrischen oder dem gestischen Malen, dem abbildlichen oder narrativen, ist ein Charakteristikum der Maler*innengeneration, der Cornelia Baltes angehört. Cornelia Baltes' Arbeit emanzipiert sich von Begriffen wie *abbildlich* oder *narrativ*, ihre Bilder sind tatsächlich „objekthaft", sie gehen dabei aber deutlich über diese Kategorie hinaus: Ihre Werke sind Objekte mit eigenem Charakter: *Fla* (S. 17), *Taa* (S. 20) und *Jag* (S. 25) haben dabei nicht nur eine eigene Persönlichkeit, sie entwickeln auch ein Eigenleben an der Wand und im Raum. Denn der umgebende Raum ist die eigentliche Bühne von Baltes' Werken, wenn auch das Tafelbild nicht völlig ausgedient hat. Die Wand selbst, der angestammte Ort eines Gemäldes, wird regelmäßig zum Spielort des Bildes über die Leinwand hinaus; die Malerei verlässt die Leinwand, und neben der Wand werden auch Objekte, Sitzwürfel, Teppiche oder Vorhänge, verbunden durch Farbe, Teil der Komposition.

and beyond the canvas. The painting leaves the canvas, and not only the wall but also objects, cube seats, carpets or curtains—linked by colour—become part of the composition. Her painting consists of coloured surfaces whose boundaries are clearly distinguished from one another and whose forms have a playful effect—not least because the stylistic hallmarks of Cornelia Baltes are jet black lines, colour contrasts and vibrant colourfulness.

These were the characteristics I had in mind when, in 2022, I was looking for a selection of artists whose painting distances itself from the canvas and expands onto the wall, into the roomspace, and into speculation. Baltes' contribution was a group of works whose interplay with the painted exhibition wall redefined the latter into the object of painting and at the same time raised the question as to what then was the picture—the painted canvas, the painted wall, or both together. The correct answer, "both ... and", poses in its turn a question, namely as to where the picture's boundary (which got lost in the twentieth century through the demise of the frame) might be. In Baltes' wall-pictures, the composition on the canvas and the composition on the wall are mostly related to one another in terms of a contrast: regularly, the surfaces or forms of the wall-picture touch the canvas optically, come up against it, end beside it, or comment on its motifs. The room-space becomes the picture, the beholders discover themselves to be variable parts of the composition and hence inside the picture, and the purported immobility of the picture is moved. The pictures of Cornelia Baltes (we remember: they are individuals) populate this space just as much as they define it. They are simultaneously subjects and objects.

Ihre Malerei, das sind farbige Flächen, deren Grenzen sich klar voneinander abheben, deren Formen spielerisch wirken, spielerisch auch, weil tiefschwarze Linien, Farbkontraste und leuchtende Buntheit das stilistische Merkmal der Malerei von Cornelia Baltes sind.

Ebendiese Eigenschaften hatte ich 2022 im Kopf, als ich nach einer Auswahl von Künstler*innen suchte, deren Malerei sich von der Leinwand entfernt und auf die Wand, in den Raum und in die Spekulation hinein expandiert. Baltes' Beitrag war eine Gruppe von Werken, deren Zusammenspiel mit der bemalten Ausstellungswand diese zum Objekt der Malerei umdefinierte und gleichzeitig die Frage aufwarf, was denn nun das Bild sei, die bemalte Leinwand, die bemalte Wand oder beides zusammen. Die korrekte Antwort „sowohl als auch" wirft wiederum eine Frage auf, nämlich wo die (im 20. Jahrhundert durch die Demise des Rahmens verloren gegangene) Grenze des Bildes sei: In Baltes' Wandbildern beziehen sich die Komposition auf der Leinwand und die Komposition auf der Wand meistens kontrastierend aufeinander: Regelmäßig touchieren die Flächen oder Formen des Wandbildes optisch die Leinwand, treffen auf sie, enden an ihr oder kommentieren die Motive der Leinwand. Der Raum wird zum Bild, die Betrachter*innen finden sich als variabler Teil der Komposition und damit im Bild wieder, und das vorgeblich Immobile des Bildes wird bewegt. Die Bilder von Cornelia Baltes bevölkern diesen Raum ebenso (wir erinnern uns: Es sind Individuen), wie sie ihn definieren. Sie sind Subjekte und Objekte zugleich.

Larissa Kikol

Farewell to the Pathos of Gesture

Abschied vom Pathos der Geste

The first things that stand out in Cornelia Baltes' works are the lines—short curves, longer, crooked lines, comma-like tangles, and lopsided outlines. The colours seem to give them a world, a biotope, in which they grow, rear up, hover, dangle, or again fall down. Fall off. And then decide otherwise, making their way back, self-willed but whistling, onto the playing field. The lines not only enact the main motif: they also put on an act. The words 'play' and 'act' will take on several further meanings, for example in the painterly actingout of non-serious gestures. But more on this later.

The line as such is a subject of art history and one that, through a great variety of painting eras, has prompted ever-new, but ever-important reflections—no matter whether the line was adduced as a contour for the distinguishing of architectural and cultural eras, for stylistic analyses or for the beginning or the continuation of modernism and the castingoff of the respective previous academic conventions. In 1855, the neo-classical artist Jean-Auguste-Dominique Ingres gave the young Edgar Degas the following advice: "Draw lines, young man, and then yet more lines, both in situ and from memory, and you will become a good artist." And although painters who revolutionized art, like Édouard Manet for example, also fought against many ideas of their predecessors such as Ingres, his advice can, from the vantage point of today, also be interpreted more universally. Be it abstract or figurative, individual work on the line helps the painter to develop and

Es sind die Linien, kurze Kurven, längere krumme, kommaartige Knäule und schiefe Umrisse, die in Cornelia Baltes Arbeiten als Erstes hervortreten. Die Farben scheinen ihnen eine Welt zu geben, ein Biotop, in denen sie wachsen, sich aufbäumen, schweben, baumeln oder wieder herunterfallen. Abfallen. Und dann entscheiden sie sich wieder anders, begeben sich eigenwillig, aber pfeifend zurück ins Spielfeld. Die Linien spielen nicht nur das Hauptmotiv, sie spielen auch etwas vor. Das Wort „Spielen" wird noch mehrere Bedeutungen bekommen, etwa beim malerischen Ausspielen der unernsten Gesten. Doch dazu später mehr.

Die Linie an sich ist ein kunsthistorischer Gegenstand, der durch die verschiedensten Malepochen immer neue, aber immer wichtige Reflexionen anstieß, ob nun die Linie als Kontur für das Ausmachen von architektonischen und kulturellen Epochen herangezogen wurde, für Stilanalysen oder für den Beginn bzw. das Fortschreiten der Moderne und die Loslösung der jeweils vorherigen akademischen Konventionen. 1855 gab der neoklassische Künstler Jean-Auguste-Dominique Ingres dem jungen Edgar Degas folgenden Rat: „Zeichnen Sie Linien, junger Mann, und dann noch mehr Linien, sowohl vor Ort als auch aus dem Gedächtnis, und Sie werden ein guter Künstler werden." Und obwohl auch Maler, die die Kunst revolutionierten, wie beispielsweise Édouard Manet, gegen viele Vorstellungen ihrer Vorgänger wie Ingres ankämpften, kann sein Rat aus heutiger Sicht auch universaler gedeutet werden. Ob abstrakt oder figurativ, die individuelle Arbeit an der Linie hilft dem Maler beim Herausbilden und Festigen seines Ansatzes, egal in welchem Stil er arbeitet.

establish their approach, irrespective of the style in which they are working.

Through modernism, the line released itself from its purely naturalistic purpose of serving a precise form, i.e. of being subordinate and submissive, and through the avant-gardists, it achieved more and more a life of its own. It was granted freedom from constraint, self-confidence and emotions—the line acquired a soul. Thus the line developed more and more into a gesture—and thereby into the basis for expressive, gestural painting. When interpretation was *en vogue*, for instance in the heyday of abstract expressionism in America, the gesture was accredited with the ability to lay a direct trail into an artist's subconscious, disclosing artists' temperaments, their concerns, afflictions, and impulses—at least, that was what the art reception of those days longed for.

This is the point from which the painting of Cornelia Baltes starts—but does not give in to the aforementioned longing.

Baltes' works can be read as abstract or figurative. Some clearly show motifs, such as hairy posteriors or chickens; feet and hands also interest the artist. Other paintings merely allow things to be possibly recognizable, but not necessarily so. There is always the option of devoting oneself to the line, the surfaces and the colours. The pictures lose nothing thereby—on the contrary: they do not need to hide themselves in their abstractness, have no need of any figure to catch and hold the eye.

Whether one believes that in the mural *Glen* (p. 73), painted on the wall of a school sports hall, one can make out—perhaps this is too obvious—someone playing a ballgame, is not in the final analysis the unfailing key to Baltes' painting. It is much more fascinating to study the black line, the gesture, more closely. Twice it gains élan from below, tries several times to work its way up, and finally at a height falls away to the left in a somewhat askew closed form, while to the right, another, smaller length supports its temperament or sails nonchalantly around it in the air. Most of Baltes' pictures have these gestural scribbles, done very swiftly, spontaneously and authentically in oil stick, brush or chalks on paper or canvas. One thinks of the nervous, scribbly drawings of Ernst Ludwig Kirchner or of Cy Twombly—Baltes' paintings could be cutouts and enlargements of these scribbling phenomena, as painterly research work, as it were. It is a playing-through of pictorial solutions, without the pressure of finding a perfect definitive solution. In a game, it is a question first of all only of possibilities, of the gathering of findings by trying out as many things as possible uncoerced. "Overambition", Baltes lets it be known, "can also lead to weaker works". Children too play for the sake of playing, and not so that the result fulfils certain (external) expectations. In this way, their play does not become boring and remains fun. With Cornelia Baltes, it is not a question of the gesture as emotion-charged poignancy: she prefers the non-serious gesture, addressing herself tongue-in-cheek to the male "heroes" of solemn abstraction.

Durch die Moderne löste sich die Linie von ihrem rein naturalistischen Zweck, einer genauen Form zu dienen, also sich unterzuordnen, und kam durch die Avantgardisten mehr und mehr zu einem Eigenleben. Dazu wurden ihr Lockerheit verliehen, Selbstvertrauen, Emotionen, die Linie wurde beseelt. So entwickelte sich die Linie mehr und mehr zur Geste. Und damit zur Grundlage einer expressiven, gestischen Malerei. Zu Deutungshochzeiten, etwa während der Blütezeit des amerikanischen abstrakten Expressionismus, gestand man der Geste zu, eine direkte Spur ins Unterbewusstsein des Künstlers zu legen. Sie verrät sein Temperament, seine Sorgen, seine Verletzungen, seine Impulse; so zumindest die damalige Rezeptionssehnsucht.

Die Malerei von Cornelia Baltes setzt an diesem Punkt an, gibt aber jener angesprochenen Sehnsucht nicht nach.

Baltes' Arbeiten können abstrakt oder figurativ gelesen werden. Einige zeigen deutlich Motive, wie behaarte Hintern oder Hühner, auch Füße und Hände interessieren die Künstlerin. Andere Gemälde lassen lediglich zu, dass Erkennbarkeiten möglich sind, aber auch nicht sein müssen. Immer ist die Option gegeben, sich alleine der Linie, den Flächen und den Farben zu widmen. Die Bilder verlieren dadurch nichts, im Gegenteil, sie brauchen sich in ihrer Abstraktheit nicht zu verstecken, brauchen keine Figur, um den Blick länger an sich zu binden.

Ob man auf dem Wandgemälde *Glen* (S. 73) in einer Sporthalle – vielleicht zu naheliegend – einen Ballspieler zu erkennen glaubt, ist letzten Endes nicht der unbedingte Schlüssel zu Baltes' Malerei. Viel spannender ist es, die schwarze Linie, die Geste näher zu betrachten. Zweimal nimmt sie von unten her Schwung, versucht sich mehrmals hochzuarbeiten und fällt schließlich in der Höhe in einer etwas schiefen geschlossenen Form nach links ab, während rechts noch eine kleinere Bahn ihr Temperament unterstützt, oder locker in der Luft um sie herumsegelt. Die meisten Bilder von Baltes weisen diese gestischen Kritzel auf, die durch Stifte, Pinsel oder Kreiden sehr schnell, spontan und authentisch ihren Niederschlag auf Papier oder Leinwand finden. Man denkt an die nervösen, kritzeligen Zeichnungen von Ernst Ludwig Kirchner oder von Cy Twombly – so könnten Baltes' Gemälde Ausschnitte und Vergrößerungen dieser Kritzelphänomene darstellen, quasi als malerische Forschungsarbeit. Es ist das Durchspielen von Bildlösungen, ohne den Druck, eine perfekte Endlösung zu finden. Beim Spiel geht es erst einmal nur um Möglichkeiten, um das Sammeln von Erkenntnissen, indem man ungezwungen so viel wie möglich ausprobiert. „Überambition kann auch zu schwächeren Arbeiten führen", verrät Baltes. Auch Kinder spielen um des Spielens willen, nicht damit das Ergebnis bestimmte (Außen-)Erwartungen erfüllt. So wird ihr Spiel nicht langweilig und bleibt ein Spaß. Bei Cornelia Baltes geht es nicht um die Geste als Pathos, sie bevorzugt die unernste Geste und richtet sich dabei augenzwinkernd an die männlichen „Helden" der feierlichen Abstraktion.

Die Geste ist kein dramaturgisches Psychogramm mehr, sie soll nicht mehr den geniehaften Ausdrucksimpuls unter Beweis stellen, sie repräsentiert nicht mehr die einstigen Cowboys des Action-Paintings. Baltes' Gesten zeigen die Geste zwar überdimensional wie ein *Bravo*-Starschnitt die Spice Girls, aber eben auch

The gesture is no longer a dramaturgic psychogram: it is no longer to offer proof of the expressive impulse of a genius, no longer represents the one-time cowboys of Action painting. Baltes' gestures admittedly show the gesture in monumental supersize like a mega-poster from the *Bravo* magazine showed the Spice Girls, but precisely also as a playful understatement, as a line that represents nothing but itself.

Cornelia Baltes' lines are not averse to having imperfect details: double lines or short starts and stabs that give the impression as if the hand were correcting itself in a quick reaction as in *Ko Au* (p. 77) or *Jeg* (p. 81). These elements also, however, are planned like this from the very start.

Yet is it then still a gesture? Or is it rather a gesture without a gesticular hand, i.e. a gesture without any gesticulating creator? Is it a gesture in its purest form, detached from all the intimate promises of interpretation with which gestures normally come? Cornelia Baltes frees herself from the compulsion of the gesticular psychogram and turns to this category of line in all unconstrainedness, indeed with an unafraid enjoyment of exploration.

In her pictorial world she says farewell to the pathos of abstract expressivity in the cowboy male art history of the postwar years. If her art were a game of poker, she would throw her fellow players off-balance by sending a few canvases with feet (*Dingbats*, p. 212) or some luscious chickens (*CooCoo, Headless Chicken*, p. 222) walking over the card table. And then she would lay out faked cards that simulate the really grand gestures. Cornelia Baltes' game manoeuvres—one could also say her painting style—could by all means be called Comic-Abstraction. In all levity, she shows that even a posterior (*Twiste wo ich swinge I*, p. 184), yes, buttocks, whose hairs are set to flee in all directions, might have the pathos of abstraction.

als spielerisches Understatement, als Linie, die nichts anderes repräsentiert als sich selbst.

Cornelia Baltes' Linien tragen gerne unperfekte Details in sich: doppelte Striche oder kurze Ansätze und Hiebe, die so wirken, als korrigiere sich die Hand in einer schnellen Reaktion selbst, wie in *Ko Au* (S. 77) oder *Jeg* (S. 81). Allerdings sind aber auch diese Elemente von vornherein so geplant.

Aber ist es dann noch eine Geste? Oder ist es vielmehr eine Geste ohne gestische Hand, also eine Geste ohne gestikulierenden Urheber? Ist es eine Geste in Reinform, losgelöst von all den intimen Deutungsversprechen, mit denen Gesten normalerweise daherkommen? Cornelia Baltes befreit sich von dem Zwang des Gestenpsychogramms und wendet sich dieser Linienkategorie in aller Lockerheit, ja in unerschrockener Erkundungslust zu.

In ihrer Bildwelt verabschiedet sie das Pathos der abstrakten Expressivität der männlichen Cowboy-Kunstgeschichte der Nachkriegszeit. Wäre ihre Kunst ein Pokerspiel, würde sie ihre Mitspieler aus dem Gleichgewicht bringen, indem sie ein paar Leinwände mit Füßen (*Dingbats*, S. 212) oder leckere Hühner (*CooCoo, Headless Chicken*, S. 222) über den Spieltisch laufen ließe. Und dann legte sie gefakte Karten aus, welche die ganz großen Gesten vorspielten. Cornelia Baltes' Spielmanöver, man könnte auch Malstil sagen, ließe sich durchaus als Comicabstraktion benennen. In aller Leichtigkeit zeigt sie, dass auch ein Hintern (*Twiste wo ich swinge I*, S. 184), ja ein Gesäß, dessen Haare nach allen Seiten zu fliehen versuchen, ein Pathos des Abstrakten sein könnte.

George Vasey

Seesawing the world

Schaukelnd die Welt sehen

We see the world upside down. We perceive the ground beneath the sky because our visual cortex flips it. Seeing is temporal and somatic, crafted in conversational play between our retina, nervous system and brain. Seeing is also social and cultural. We see what we want to see. See what we're told to see. We look for things that aren't there. Seeing is a signal we decipher. Our brains are predictive—framed by memories, undermined by biases, and wired by belief systems that shape how we respond to what is in front of us. The colour yellow may alarm some, soothe others and trigger horrific flashbacks in a few.

Cornelia Baltes is an image intervener: an image underminer if you will. If seeing is a conversational process, her works trade in disfluency. Baltes hacks seeing's efficient flow. She nudges and pokes the world with her paint brush, disrupting the neat work of the visual cortex. Don't let the pristine surfaces and coolly expressed canvases fool you—this work is messy, meddling with your eyes and messing with your head.

In her works, the errant is simplified and essentialized. The paintings are animatedly indefinable. Baltes is a sponge, her images absorbent to the incidental. She draws often and the paintings are based on memories rather than direct observation. The works on paper create a loose scaffolding for the later work. Everything is fragmented, zoomed in on. In many of the paintings, minutiae are scrutinized. Details emerge, glimpses of things are subject to forensic analysis. Her work is an act of seesawing, oscillating between recognition and abstraction, thinginess and metaphor, smallness and bigness. Baltes doesn't see the world, she seesaws it: up and down, left and right. Mobile and roving, her eyes scan the environment; her head, hovering and drone-like.

While her iconography is diverse, recurrent interests can be traced: figures are tightly cropped and curtly edited. The outline of a rotund head appears. A torso. A thigh. An armpit. Knotted hair. Latticed hands embrace. A shirt cuff.

Wir sehen die Welt, als stünde sie auf dem Kopf. Wir erkennen nur deshalb, dass der Himmel oben und die Erde unten ist, weil unser visueller Kortex – unser Sehzentrum – das Gesehene umdreht. Das Sehen ist somit ein zeitlich-somatischer Prozess, es kommt in einem dialogischen Zusammenspiel zwischen Netzhaut, Nervensystem und Gehirn zustande. Unser Sehen ist indes auch soziokulturell bedingt. Wir sehen das, was wir sehen möchten, sehen das, was wir sehen sollen. Wir suchen nach Dingen, die gar nicht da sind. Sehen heißt: ein empfangenes Signal dechiffrieren. Dabei fungiert das Gehirn prädiktiv, d.h., es ist von Erinnerungen konditioniert, von Vorurteilen und Vorlieben unterminiert, durch Glaubenssysteme quasi verdrahtet, die alle zusammen mit beeinflussen, wie wir auf das, was uns begegnet, reagieren. Die Farbe Gelb etwa mag auf einige erschreckend und auf andere besänftigend wirken, bei wiederum anderen hingegen kann sie horrend-verstörende Flashbacks auslösen.

Cornelia Baltes greift in gegebene Bilder ein. Sie untergräbt Bilder, höhlt sie quasi aus. Wenn das Sehen ein dialogischer Prozess ist, so reden ihre Arbeiten mit den Sprachmitteln der Kommunikationsstörung. Baltes hackt in den sonst reibungslos-effizienten Fluss des Sehens hinein. Mit ihrem Pinsel stupst und stößt sie die Welt an, wobei sie das ordentliche Fungieren des visuellen Kortexes empfindlich stört. Lassen Sie sich ja nicht von den makellosen Oberflächen und der kühlen Ausführung und Ausstrahlung ihrer Leinwände hinters Licht führen! Diese Kunstwerke sind Störenfriede, sie machen sich an Ihren Augen zu schaffen und legen sich mit Ihrem Kopf an.

In Baltes' Arbeiten wird das In-die-Irre-Geführte vereinfacht und auf seinen Kern reduziert. So sind ihre Gemälde anregend undefinierbar. Die Künstlerin fungiert quasi wie ein Schwamm, wobei ihre Bilder gerade das Beiläufige, Nebensächliche aufsaugen. Baltes zeichnet viel und vieles, ihre Gemälde basieren eher auf Erinnerungen als auf unmittelbarer Beobachtung. Die Papierarbeiten bilden dabei ein loses Baugerüst für das spätere Werk. Alles ist fragmentiert und herangezoomt – in vielen Gemälden werden auch kleinste Details unter die Lupe genommen. Einzelheiten treten hervor, flüchtig erblickte Dinge werden einer forensischen

The incidental is exalted and glacially contoured. Simplification as a form of amplification. The artist asks us to focus our attention, editing out the noise to re-see (or seesaw) the world anew.

Baltes' paintings are perched between semi-figurative and partially abstract, encompassing a broad sweep of painterly gestures. There are big fat painterly lines as well as thin, scrawny ones. Her images often convene incongruous juxtapositions: smooth calligraphic marks and the occasionally hastilydrawn oil pastel scrawl. The edges of things come up against each other, forming a pictorial jigsaw.

First impressions can be misleading. While the paintings appear strifeless, their extended gestation and reworking is, in fact, concealed under smooth layers of paint. The paintings' elegance is anything but carefree. I've seen the artist working up close, making her endless cups of tea, while she repeatedly reworks the image until every line is flawless. These are hard-won and deceptively stubborn images. This concealment is both formal and metaphoric. The effortlessness is part of their performance. Baltes' labour is one of looking and thinking, the ratio of making and pondering weighted very much in favour of the latter. This approach can be easy to dismiss.

While generations of artists have interrogated the policed boundaries of aesthetic hierarchies, many biases still permeate the ways in which we see. Descriptive words such as 'sublime', 'critical', 'interrogative', and 'hard-won' pepper conversations around serious art, while terms such as 'cute', 'pretty', 'funny', 'pleasurable', and 'colourful' often elicit a sense of superficiality. Issues of taste and judgment are deeply fraught. How we see and what we do with what we see is freighted with social and cultural biases framed by issues of race, gender and class. My questions are: why can't pleasure play in tandem with criticism? Why does seriousness have to be, well, so po-faced? What's so wrong with sentimentalism?

Painting is similarly hamstrung by these assumptions. The model of intelligence (shrewd, wry, inauthentic, detached) vs brawn (impulsive, intuitive, emotionally open, intimate) plays out in myriad ways across social archetypes. In this dichotomy, intellect is often viewed as easy and brawn as hard-won. In many ways, these stereotypes are nothing more than that: social narratives that offer dead-end metaphors, and yet they permeate the cultural landscape. The cultural theorist and literary critic Sianne Ngai has written about words such as 'pretty', 'cute', and 'interesting' as minor aesthetic categories that act as equivocal terms, existing in thresholds.

In this sense, we can frame Baltes' painterly strategies—the performed easiness, the use of humour and word-play—as further acts of artistic seesawing, putting the world out of kilter and off balance. Her work operates in a minor key, resistant to settling: poking at and subtly undermining policed aesthetic boundaries.

Analyse unterzogen. Dabei wird ihre Arbeit zu einem Hin- und Herschaukeln, zu einem Oszillieren zwischen Erkennen und Abstrahieren, Dinghaftigkeit und Metapher, dem Klein- und dem Großdimensionierten. Baltes sieht die Welt nicht, sie schaukelt sie: auf und ab, nach links und nach rechts. Ihre – stets mobilen, umherblickenden – Augen suchen das sie Umgebende ab. Ihr Kopf schwebt – einer Drohne ähnlich – über dem zu Sehenden.

Obwohl ihre Ikonografie recht vielfältig ist, lassen sich wiederkehrende Motive und Interessen durchaus erkennen. So werden gemalte Formen eng beschnitten und kurzerhand bearbeitet. Der Umriss eines rundlichen Kopfes erscheint. Ein Oberkörper. Ein Oberschenkel. Eine Achselhöhle. Verknotete Haare. Verschränkte, innig verschlungene Hände. Eine Hemdmanschette. Das Beiläufige wird gefeiert, aber mit weichen, abgerundeten Konturen versehen. Eine Vereinfachung als Form der Amplifizierung. Die Künstlerin fordert uns auf, unseren Blick zu fokussieren, etwaige Sehstörungen auszublenden, um die Welt mit frischen Augen schaukelnd neu zu sehen.

Baltes' Gemälde, die zwischen dem Halbfigurativen und dem Teilabstrakten angesiedelt sind, umfassen eine breite Palette an malerischen Gesten. Man findet große, dicke, malerische Linien sowie auch dünne, dürre Striche. Ihre Bilder inszenieren häufig unpassende Nebeneinandersetzungen: glatte kalligrafische Zeichen etwa neben mitunter hastig gezeichneten Kritzeleien in Ölkreide. Die Ränder der gemalten Objekte stoßen aneinander und ergeben ein Bilderpuzzle.

Der erste Eindruck kann täuschen. Während die Gemälde wirken, als seien sie ohne Kampf und Konflikt zustande gekommen, verdecken ihre glatten Farbschichten in Wirklichkeit einen längeren Entstehungs- und Bearbeitungsprozess. Die Eleganz der Gemälde ist alles andere als ein Produkt der Sorglosigkeit. Ich habe die Künstlerin bei der Arbeit aus der Nähe beobachten können: wie sie wiederholt das Bild überarbeitet, dabei sich endlose Tassen Tee machend, bis jede einzelne Linie makellos-perfekt ist. Es sind hart erkämpfte Arbeiten, gewonnen aus täuschend zähem, störrischem Bildmaterial. Das Verbergen dieses Tatbestands ist sowohl formal als auch metaphorisch zu verstehen. Die scheinbare Mühelosigkeit ist Teil der Performanz. Die von Baltes praktizierte Arbeitsweise ist eine schauend-reflektierende, wobei das Verhältnis Kreieren : Sinnieren stark zugunsten des Letzteren gewichtet ist. Ein solcher Arbeitsaufwand lässt sich allzu leicht als unwesentlich oder unerheblich abtun.

Obwohl Generationen von Künstler:innen die stark patrouillierten Grenzen der ästhetischen Hierarchien infrage gestellt haben, sind unsere Sehweisen nach wie vor von Voreingenommenheiten durchsetzt. In Gesprächen über seriöse Kunst wimmelt es von deskriptiven Vokabeln wie etwa „grandios", „zeitkritisch", „hinterfragend" oder „mühsam errungen", wohingegen Wörter wie „niedlich", „hübsch", „drollig", „angenehm" und „farbenfroh" oft Oberflächlichkeit suggerieren. Fragen des Geschmacks und des Urteilens sind ein äußerst heikles Thema – wie wir sehen und wie wir mit dem Gesehenen umgehen, ist von soziokulturellen Vorurteilen behaftet, die in Fragen der Herkunft und des Genders wurzeln. In diesem Zusammenhang möchte ich fragen: Warum kann das Vergnügliche nicht mit dem Gesellschaftskritischen

As Baltes utilises a full array of painterly marks, her work also draws from a broad chromatic range: lemon yellow, cobalt blue, hot pinks, full-bodied oranges and myriad pastels. While gradients appear frequently, colour is predominantly flat, recalling the visual language of cartoons, children's toys, design and commercial imagery. These objects share a wish to be interacted with and desired.

Baltes' formal inventiveness extends through the gallery. Her canvases appear at odd angles, installed in corners and adjacent to walls to cast irregular shadows. The paintings often crouch on the floor and stand tall on pedestals and at wonky angles on crutches. This spatial dynamic is crucial as the gallery's windows, doors and walls edit and frame the imagery further. The installation becomes a *mise-en-scène* with the artist choreographing the viewer's feet as much as their eyes. We dance around these paintings as our eyes pirouette.

An exhibition of Baltes' work that I curated at Northern Gallery for Contemporary Art, Sunderland, in 2015 characterises many of these exemplary tropes. The paintings—encompassing routed painted MDF panels with imagery drawn from the artist's sketchbook—were displayed on the gallery floor on wheels. The show's title, *Turner* (pp. 172–180)—a typical Baltes' pun—was a sly nod to one of Britain's most famous painters, to the German word for 'gymnast', and a reference to the paintings' wheels. The British sculptor Phyllida Barlow once said that if the gallery wall represented the institution, the floor was its anarchic mirror. *Turner* is a typical Baltes' gesture: embracing a certain unruliness that flips expectations.

Over the last 10 years, Baltes has pushed at her own practice, continually experimenting and expanding. In earlier works, canvases were cut and folded, breaching the boundaries of the stretcher bars and in some cases the gallery walls. In works such as *Deep Thought* (p. 211) and *Ghostowl* (p. 209), the canvas becomes both material and image. Incised holes become eyes, directing our looking to the gallery wall behind the painting. Baltes revels in the painter's ability to conjure imagery from an economical palette. Often the imagery in these earlier works, while simple, is more recognisable: birds and fragmented human anatomy frequently appear.

In works such as *Stoned* (p. 200), a canvas is propped in the middle of the gallery space with, you guessed it, a stone. An image of a large red full-stop-like shape is propped with skinny, crow-like hands. The work's precarity seems to poke fun at something monumental. Like many of Baltes' paintings of this era, the wonkiness emphasizes a certain slapstick quality, as if waiting for an overexcited visitor to careen into it.

Does the red dot represent the monolithic history of painting? Perhaps. Does the stone represent the myth of Sisyphus, the Greek king doomed to roll a heavy marble block up and down a hill for eternity? Maybe. Monumentality and

einhergehen? Warum muss Seriosität so, nun ja, so bierernst-humorlos sein? Was ist so schlimm an Sentimentalität?

Auch die Malerei leidet am Korsett dieser Annahmen. Das Modell Geisteskraft vs. Körperkraft (scharfsinnig, ironisch, uneigentlich, distanziert vs. impulsiv, intuitiv, offen emotional, intim) zeigt sich vielfach in einer ganzen Palette an sozialen Archetypen. In dieser Dichotomie wird die Intelligenz oft als die leichte Option, die Körperkraft hingegen als eine hart erkämpfte gesehen. In mehrfacher Hinsicht erweisen sich diese Stereotypen als ebendas: als gesellschaftliche Narrative, die in Sackgassenmetaphern münden. Trotzdem sind sie im heutigen Kulturwesen allgegenwärtig. Die Kulturtheoretikerin und Literaturkritikerin Sianne Ngai hat Wörter wie „hübsch", „niedlich" und „interessant" als untergeordnete ästhetische Kategorien bezeichnet, die als doppeldeutige, in Schwellenlagen zu findende Begriffe operieren.

In dieser Hinsicht lassen sich Baltes' malerische Strategien – die gespielte Leichtigkeit, die Verwendung von Humor und Wortspielen – als weitere Belege für eine künstlerische Schaukelstellung deuten, durch welche die Welt aus dem Gleichgewicht und aus dem Lot gebracht wird. Ihr Œuvre wird in einer Molltonart gespielt, die sich der Festlegung widersetzt. Mit subtil unterwandernder Geste stupst sie gegen streng kontrollierte ästhetische Grenzmarkierungen.

So wie Baltes ein ganzes Spektrum an malerischen Zeichen verwendet, so gedeiht ihr Werk ebenso an einer breiten chromatischen Palette: Zitronengelb, Kobaltblau, heiße Pinkfarben, kräftige Orangetöne, unzählige Pastellnoten. Obwohl Farbverläufe nicht selten vorkommen, ist die Farbsetzung vorwiegend flach, wobei sie an die visuellen Sprachen von Cartoons und Comics, Kinderspielzeug, Design und Werbung erinnert. All diesen Objekten und Sprachen gemeinsam ist der Wunsch nach Interaktion und Begehr.

Der formale Einfallsreichtum der Künstlerin erstreckt sich auch auf den Galerieraum. Ihre Leinwände werden in unerwarteten Blickwinkeln präsentiert, werden in Ecken installiert oder nah bei Wänden platziert, damit sie unregelmäßige Schatten werfen. Des Öfteren kauern die Gemälde auf dem Boden, stehen hoch auf Podesten oder schräg auf Stelzen. Die räumliche Dynamik ist dabei wesentlich, denn durch die Fenster, Türen und Wände der Galerie erfahren die Bilder eine zusätzliche Redaktion und Rahmung. Die Installation wird zu einer Mise en Scène, in der die Künstlerin die Füße der Besucher*innen ebenso choreografiert wie deren Augen. Wir tanzen um diese Gemälde herum, während unsere Augen Pirouetten drehen.

In einer Ausstellung zu Baltes' Werk, die ich 2015 in der Northern Gallery for Contemporary Art, Sunderland (UK), kuratiert habe, traten bereits viele der obengenannten exemplarischen Tropen in charakteristischer Form auf. Die Gemälde, deren Motive aus dem Skizzenbuch der Künstlerin stammten, wurden auf gefräste MDF-Platten (d. h. mitteldichte Holzfaserplatten) gemalt und, auf Rädern stehend, auf dem Galerieboden auf- und ausgestellt. Der Ausstellungstitel, *Turner* (S. 172-180) – ein typischer Baltes-Kalauer –, war eine gewitzte Anspielung auf einen der renommiertesten Maler Großbritanniens, auf das deutsche Wort „Turner",

futility; these are big, serious themes for painting, treated—of course—in Baltes' minor key. Whatever the symbolism, there is a slapstick quality to the work that betrays a broad set of influences. We could start with the artists who have trodden similar aesthetic terrain: Ellsworth Kelly, Monika Baer, Raoul De Keyser, as well as Patrick Caulfield and others. Yet it's in the visual inventiveness of cartoons such as Looney Tunes and Disney that I would draw much comparison to Baltes' work.

There is a similar economy of transformation. Movement and sound translated into forms that push at the boundaries of our seen world. Each painting creates its own language that seesaws between the world and our understanding of it; entangling itself in the retina, nervous system and our brain. Baltes gets involved in the mess, in her own inimitable and elegant way. She embraces it all—the incidental and the beautiful, the monumental and the miniscule—and seesaws it. Up and down, back and forth: persistently refusing to settle.

sowie auf die sich drehenden (engl.: *turning*) Räder unter den Gemälden. Die britische Bildhauerin Phyllida Barlow hat einmal gesagt, dass, wenn die Galeriewand für die Kunstinstitution stehe, der Boden ihr anarchischer Spiegel sei. *Turner* ist eine typisch Baltes'sche Geste: Sie ist Ausdruck einer gewissen regelmissachtenden Widerborstigkeit, die Erwartungen konterkariert.

Im Laufe der letzten zehn Jahre hat Baltes ihre künstlerische Praxis weiter vorangetrieben, indem sie unablässig experimentiert und neue Wege eingeschlagen hat. In ihren früheren Werken wurden Leinwände zerschnitten und gefaltet, um die Grenzen der Keilrahmenleisten – und in einigen Fällen auch der Galeriewände – zu sprengen. In Arbeiten wie *Deep Thought* (S. 211) und *Ghostowl* (S. 209) ist die Leinwand sowohl Gewebe als auch Bild. Eingeschnittene Löcher werden zu Augen, die unser Schauen auf die Galeriewand hinter dem Gemälde lenken. Baltes findet Gefallen an der Fähigkeit der Malerei, eine Bilderwelt auch mittels einer sparsamen Farbpalette hervorzuzaubern. In diesen früheren Werken ist die Bildsprache, obzwar einfach, erkennbarer: Vögel und Fragmente der menschlichen Anatomie treten vielfach in Erscheinung.

In Arbeiten wie *Stoned* (S. 200) steht eine Leinwand mitten im Galerieraum, aufgestützt mittels – Sie haben's wohl erraten – eines Steins. Das Bild einer großen, roten, satzschlusspunktähnlichen Form wird von dünnen, krähenartigen Händen aufgestützt. Das Prekäre der Arbeit scheint sich über etwas Monumentales lustig zu machen. Wie bei vielen von Baltes' Werken aus jener Zeit unterstreicht das Wackelige eine gewisse Slapstickqualität, als warte die Arbeit nur darauf, dass ein überaufgeregter Besucher in sie hineinschlittert.

Steht der rote Punkt für die monolithische Geschichte der Malerei? Vielleicht. Steht der Stein für den Mythos von Sisyphos, dem König aus der griechischen Mythologie, der von den Göttern dazu verdammt wurde, einen schweren Marmorblock immer wieder in alle Ewigkeit einen Berg hinaufzuwälzen? Eventuell. Monumentalität und Vergeblichkeit – das sind große, ernsthafte Themen für die Malerei, die – selbstredend – von Baltes in Moll behandelt werden. Was auch immer hier symbolisiert wird, der Arbeit haftet etwas Slapstickartiges an, das eine breite Palette an Einflüssen verrät. Man könnte bei den Künstler*innen anfangen, die auf ähnlichem ästhetischen Terrain unterwegs waren: bei Ellsworth Kelly, Monika Baer und Raoul De Keyser sowie bei Patrick Caulfield und anderen. Und dennoch: Vergleiche würde ich eher ziehen mit dem visuellen Erfindungsreichtum von Cartoons wie bei Looney Tunes und Disney.

Es gibt eine ähnliche Ökonomie der Überführung. Bewegung und Ton werden in Formen übersetzt, die an die Grenzen der von uns gesehenen Welt stoßen und sie überschreiten. Jedes Gemälde schafft eine eigene Sprache, die zwischen der Welt und unserem Verständnis von ihr schaukelt und sich in der Netzhaut, dem Nervensystem und dem Gehirn verfängt. Auf die ihr eigene unnachahmlich-elegante Art und Weise nimmt es Baltes mit dieser wirren Komplexität auf. Sie erfasst alles, das Beiläufige und das Schöne, das Monumentale und das Winzige – und schaukelt es. Schaukelt es auf und ab, hin und her, wobei sie sich konstant weigert, sich festzulegen oder niederzulassen.

No Illusions – Painting in Space, Hamburger Kunsthalle (DE), 2023

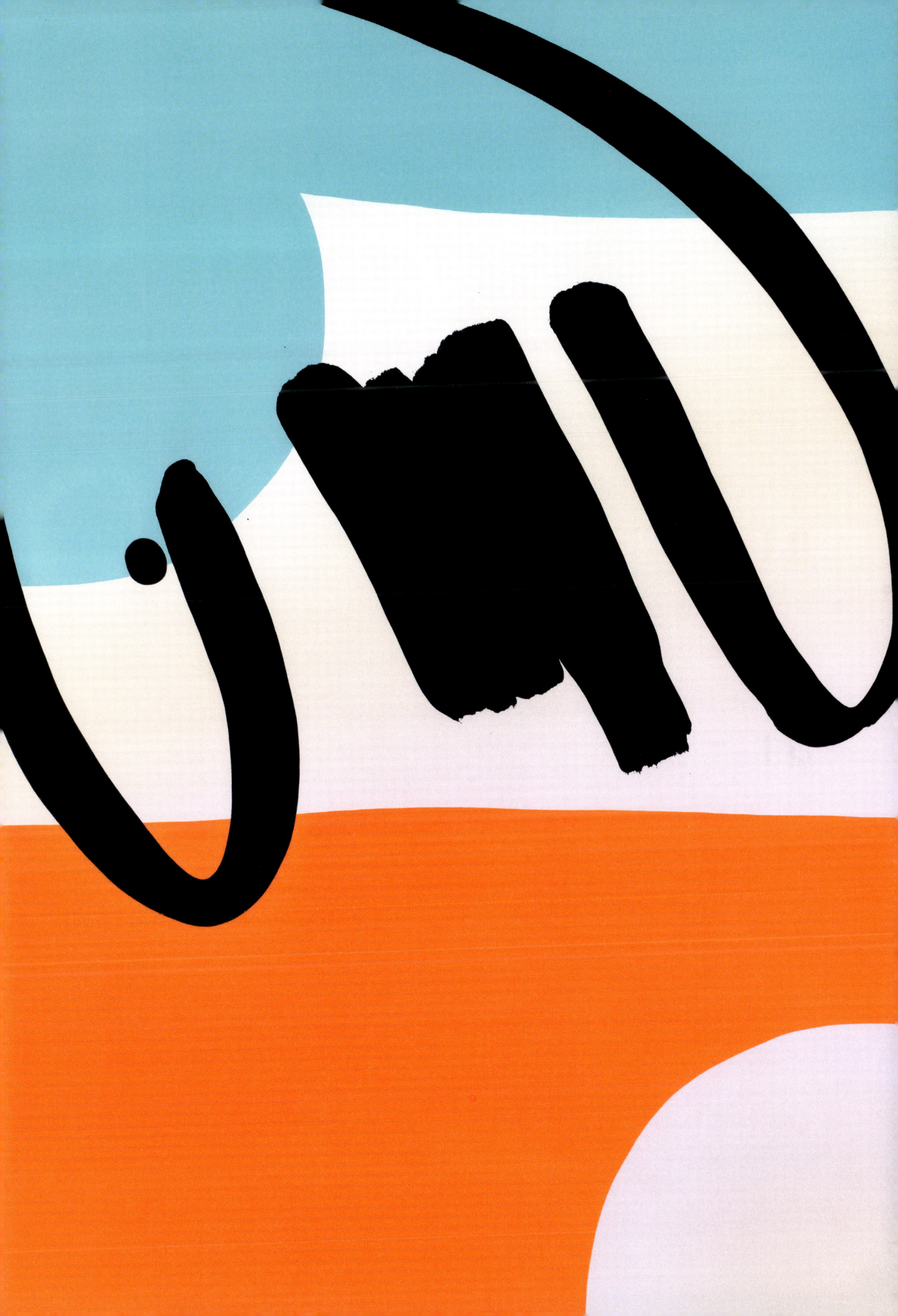

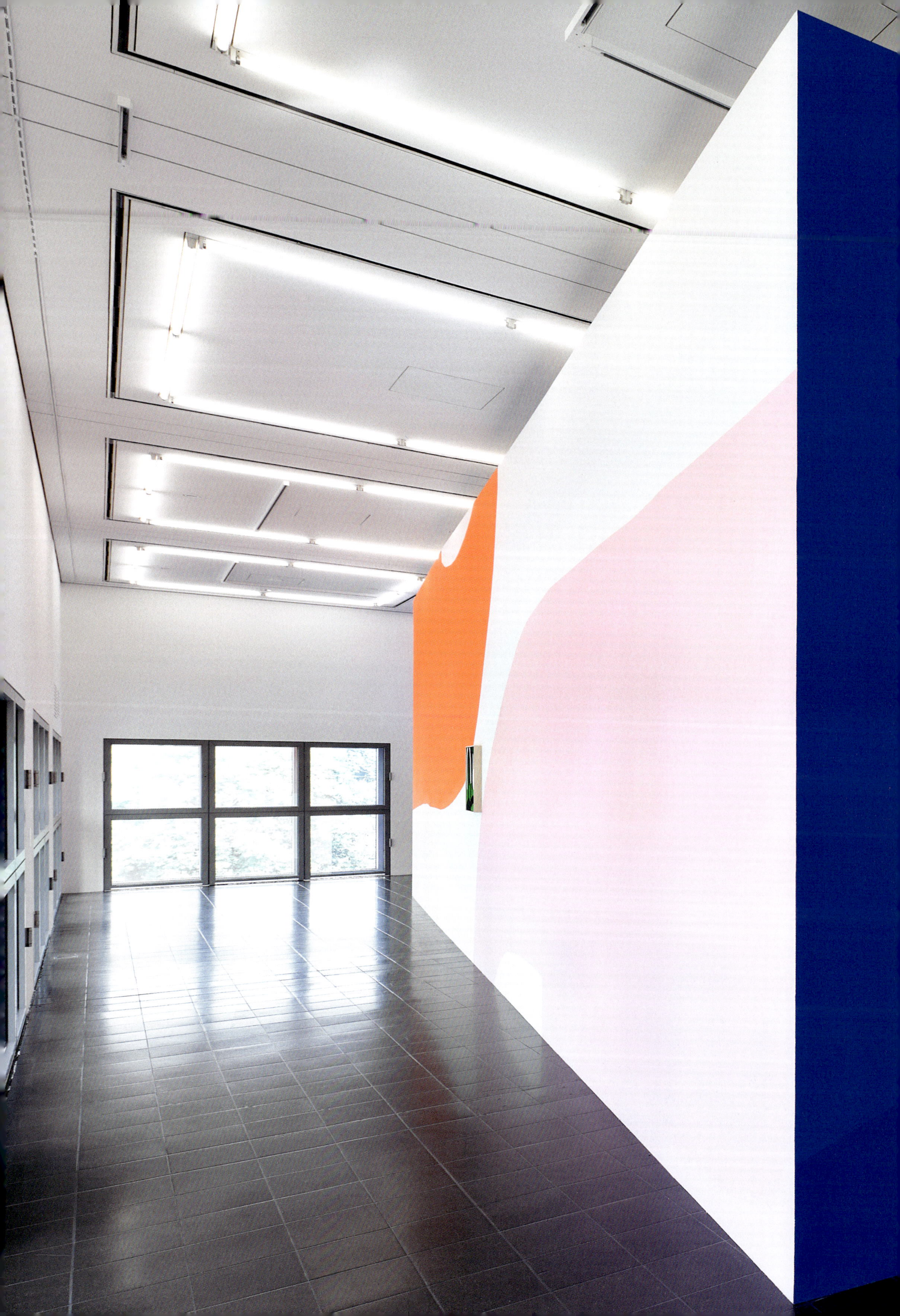

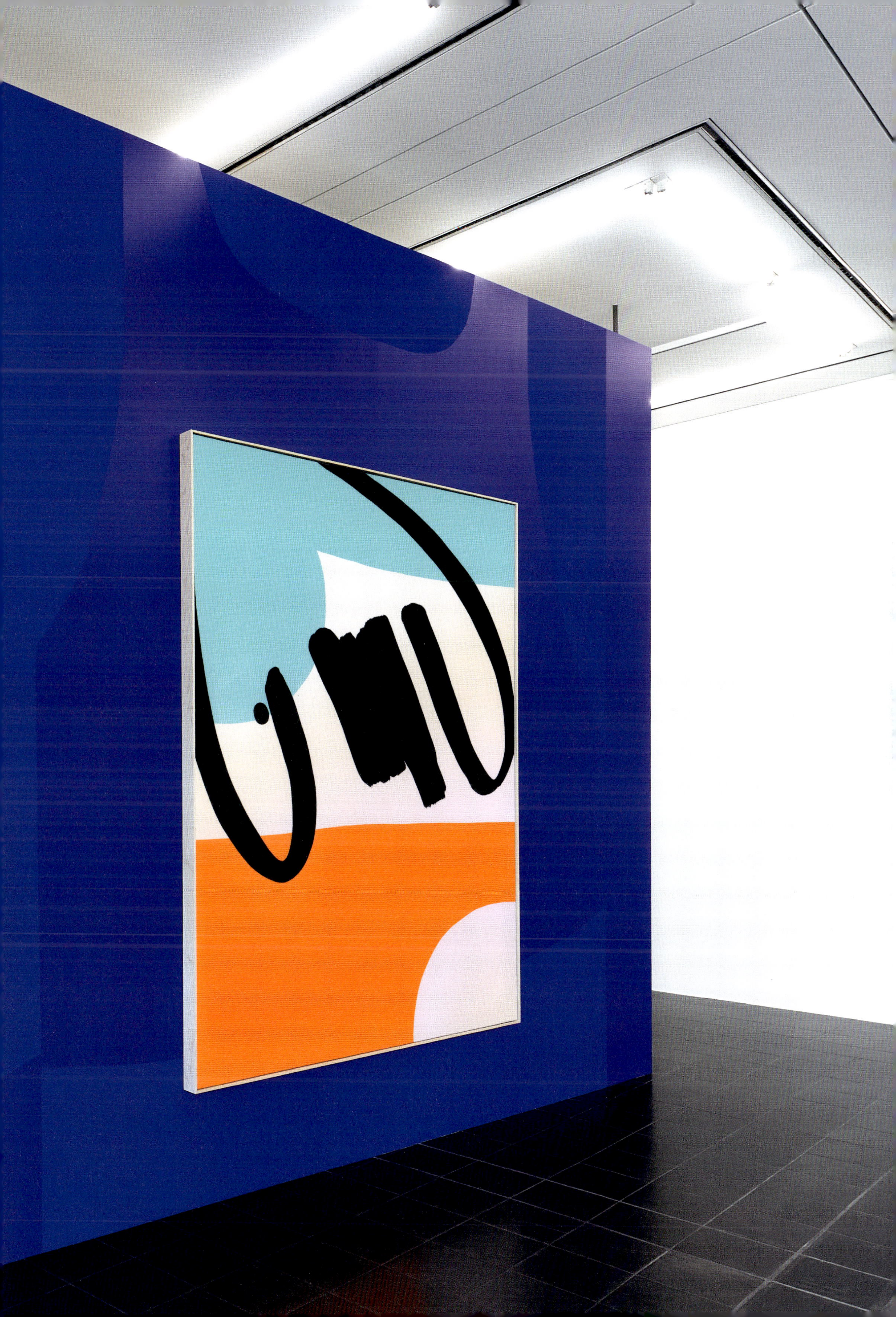

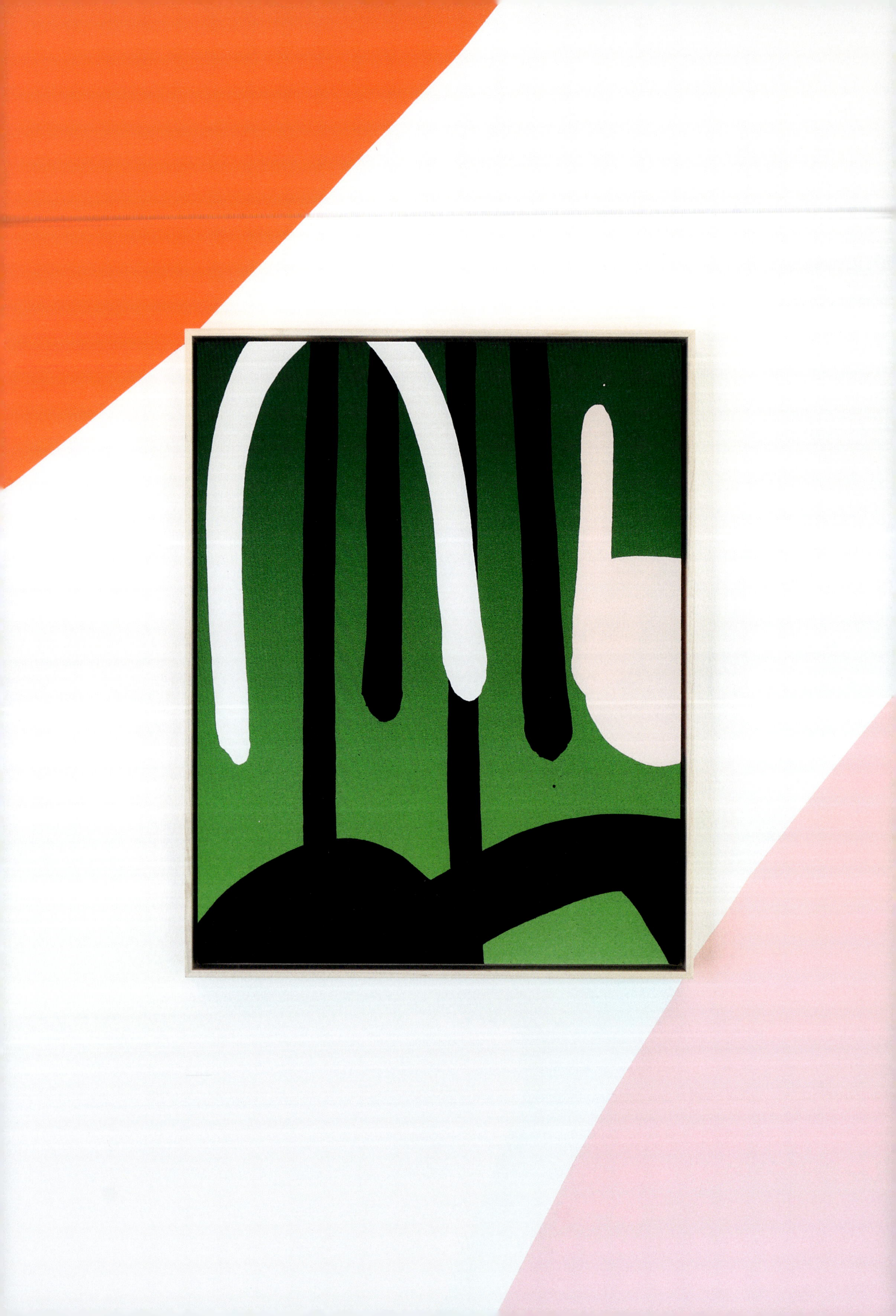

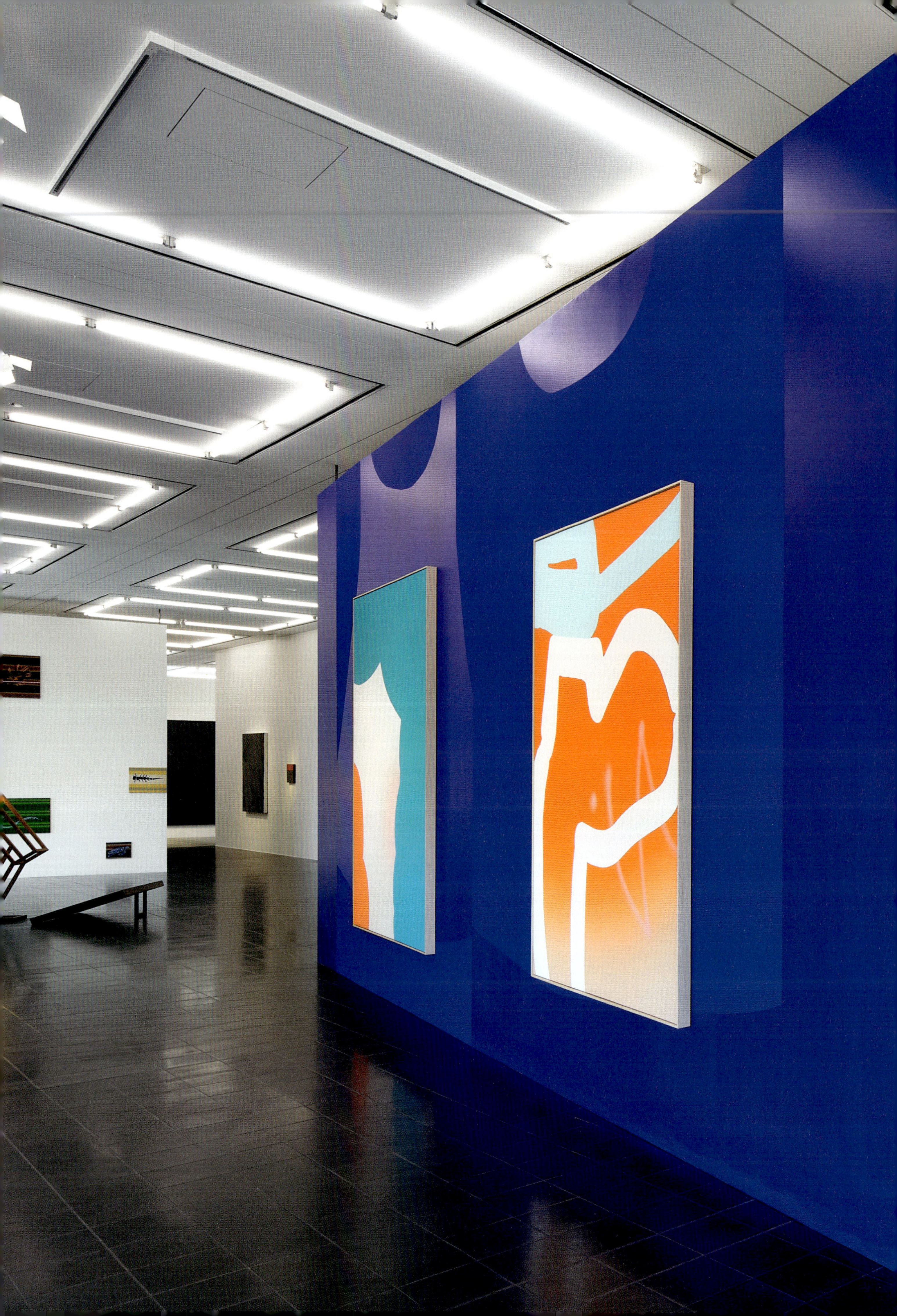

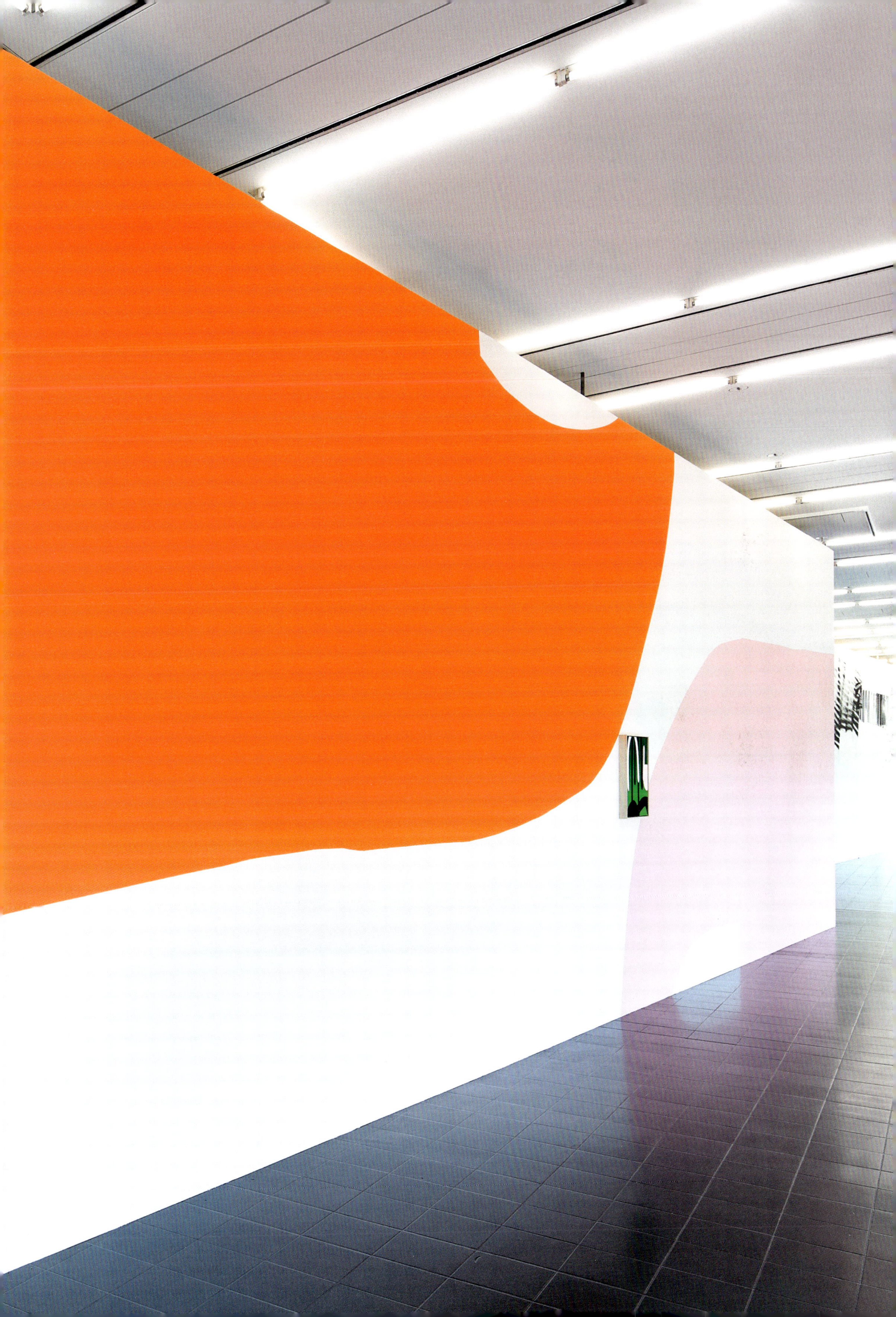

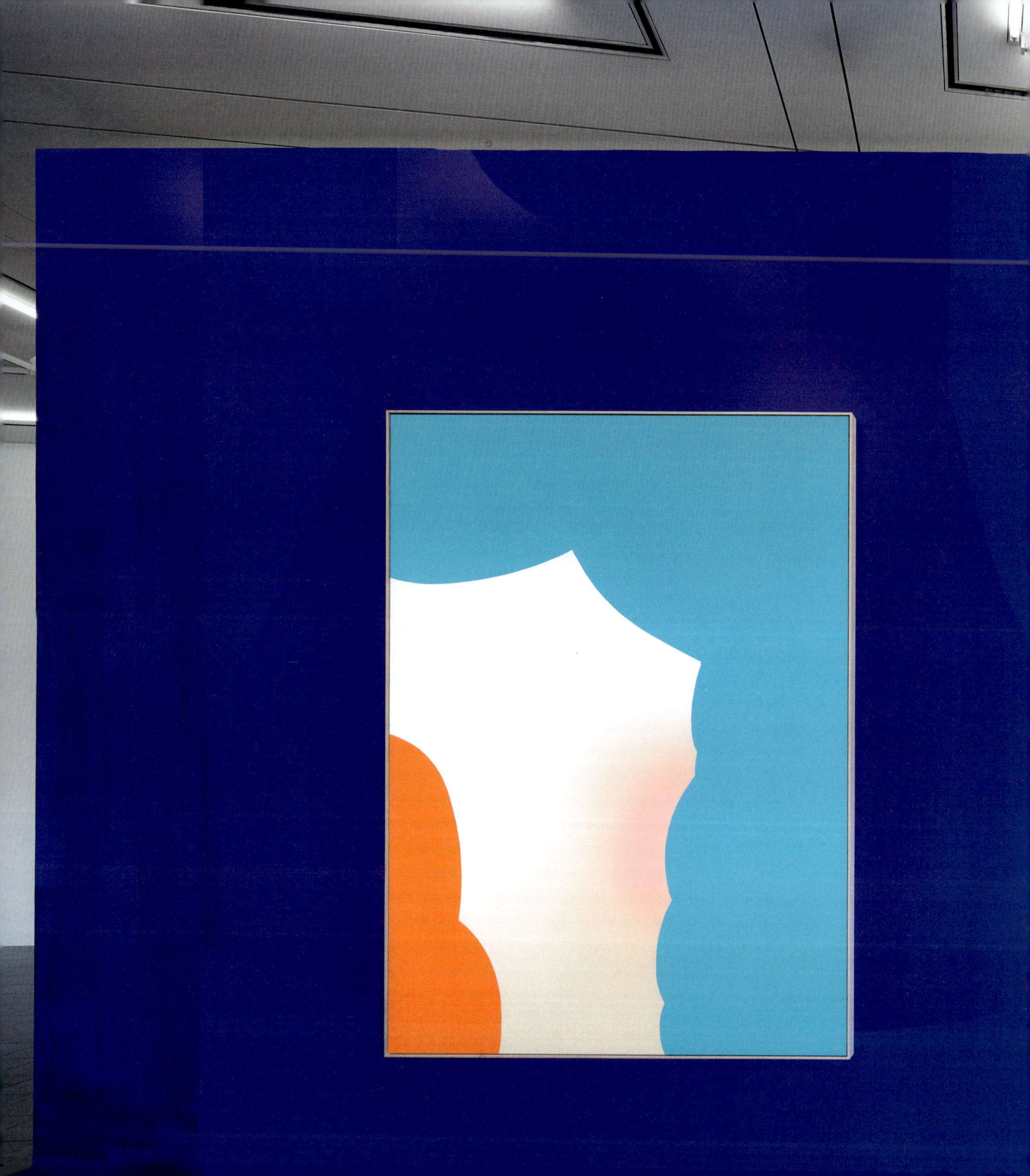

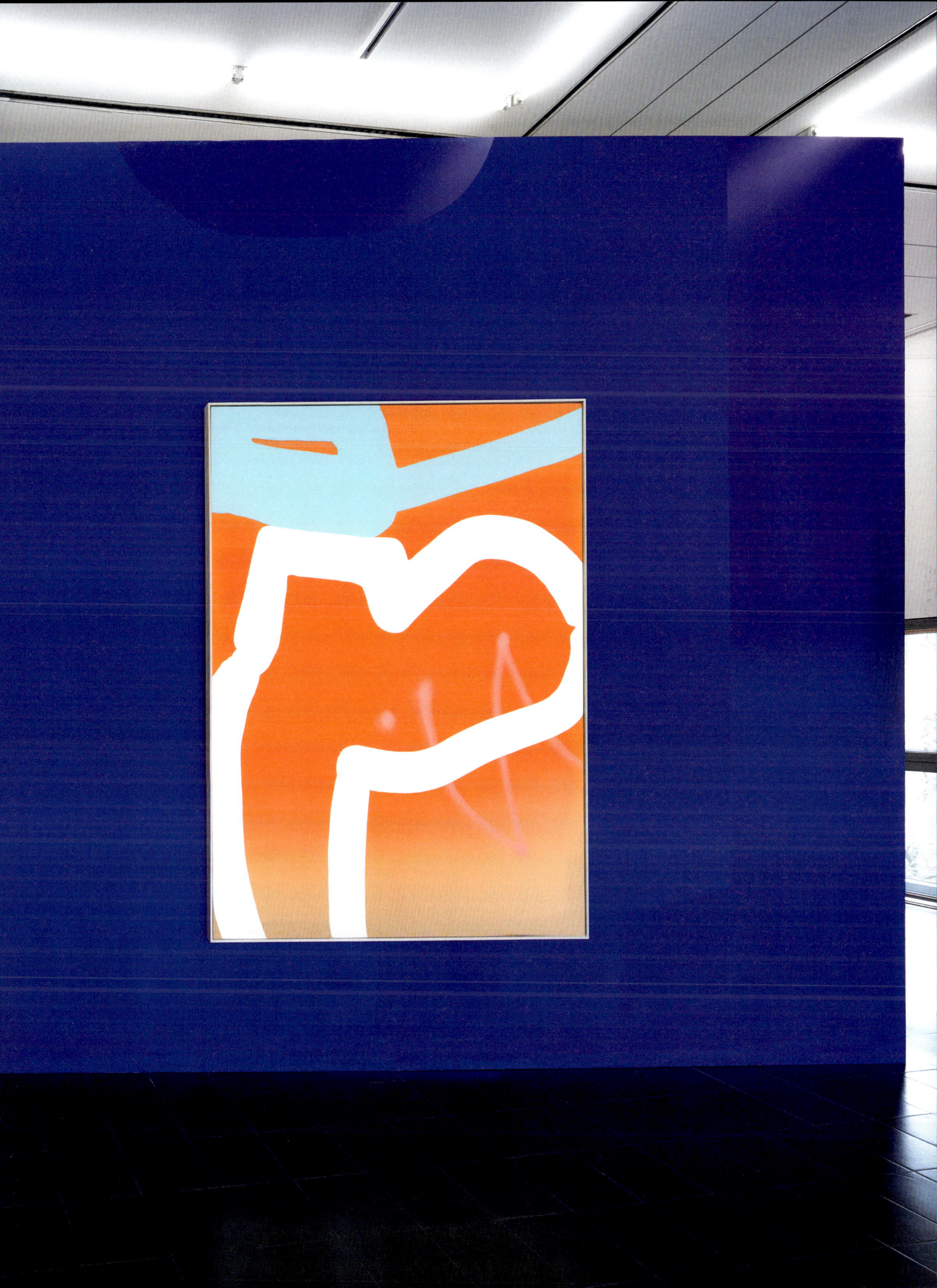

Hub Bub, Andréhn-Schiptjenko, Stockholm (SE), 2023

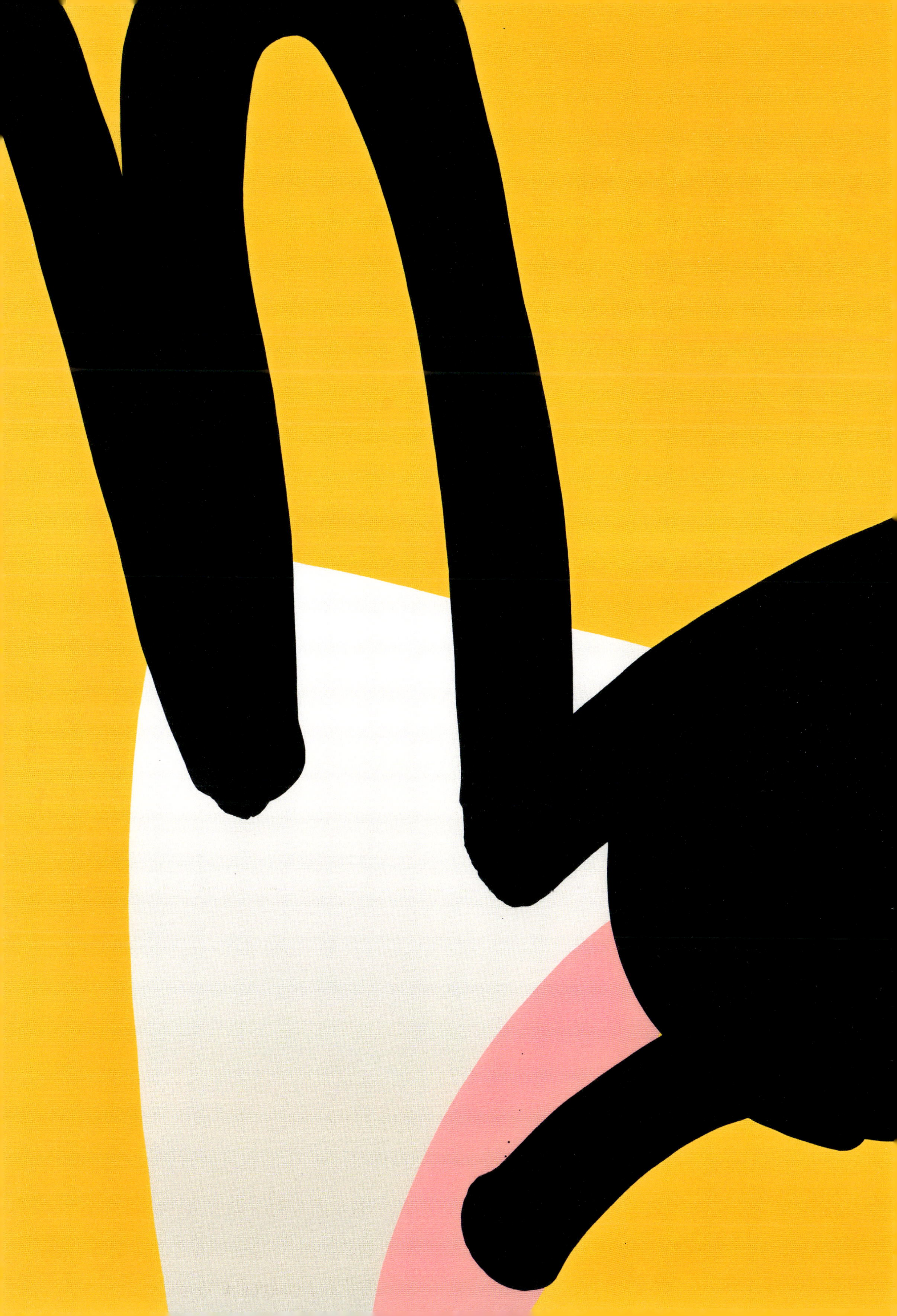

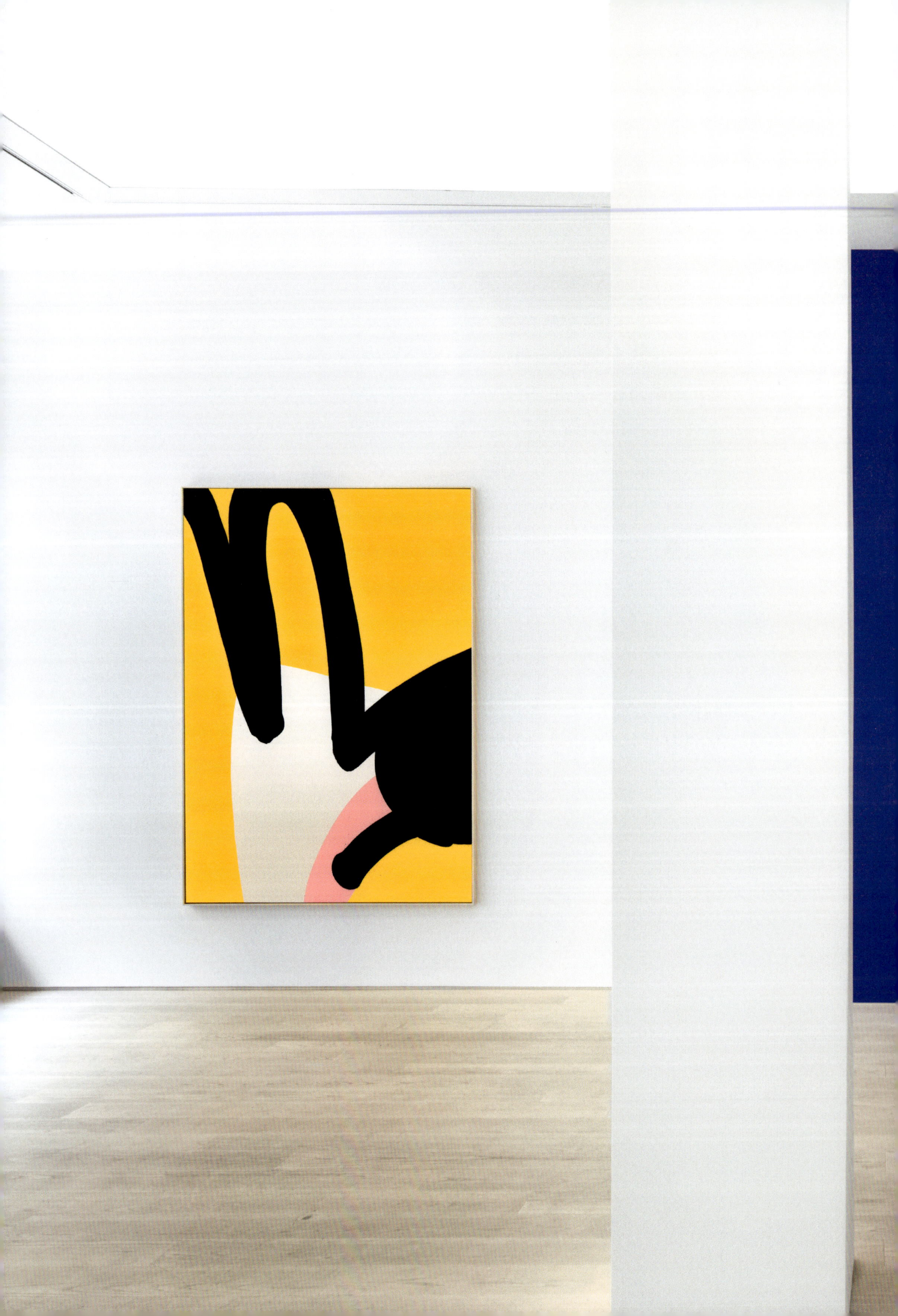

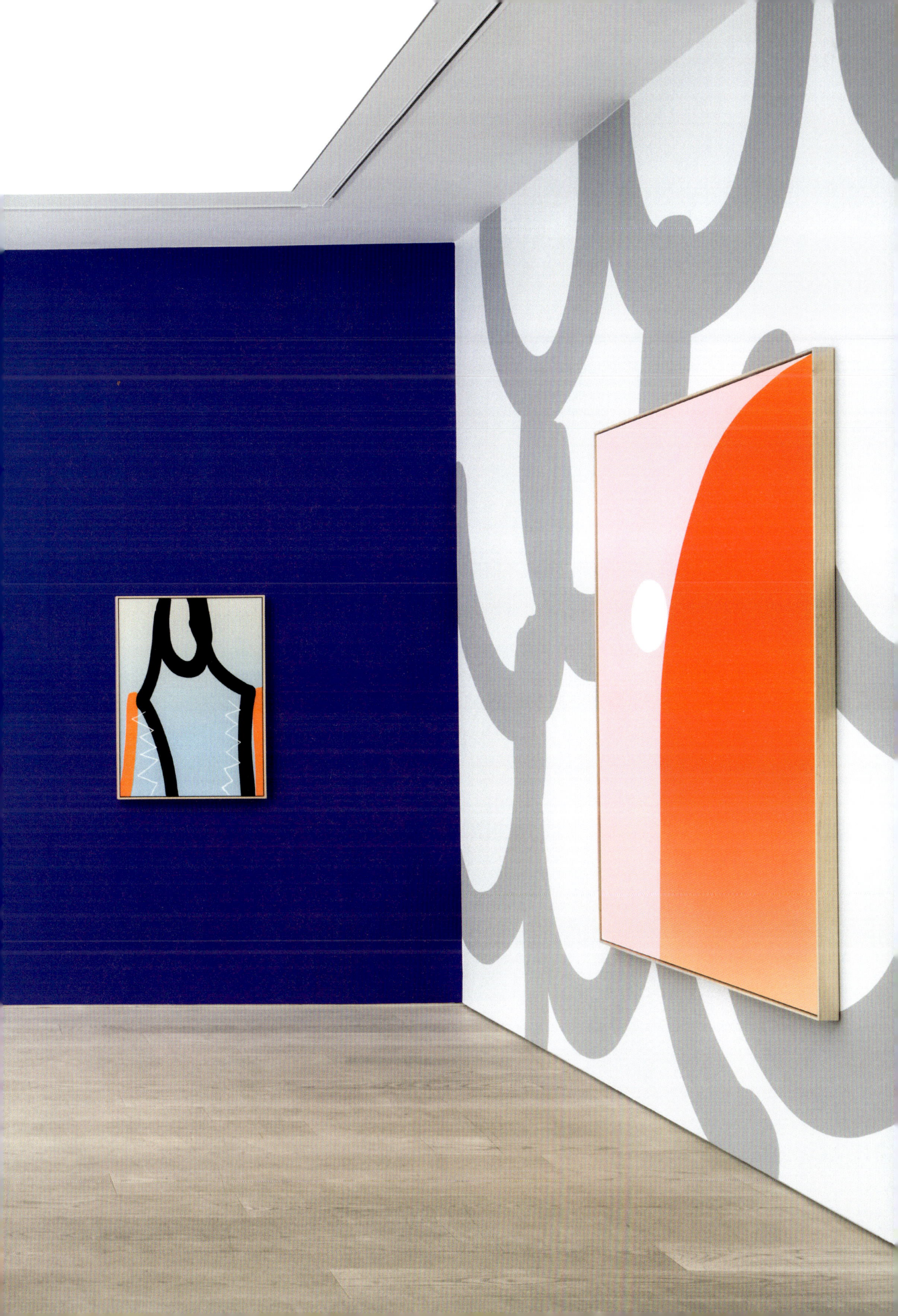

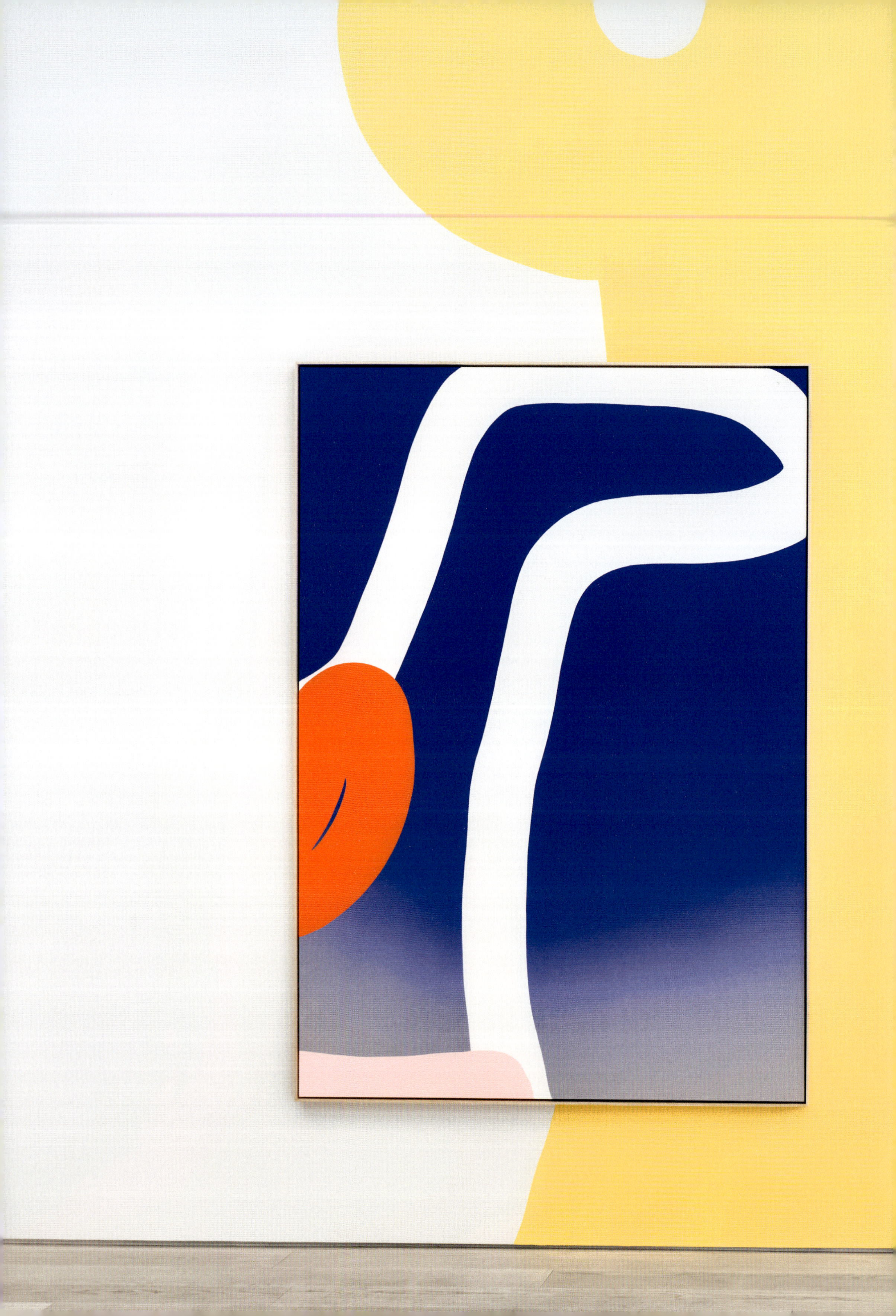

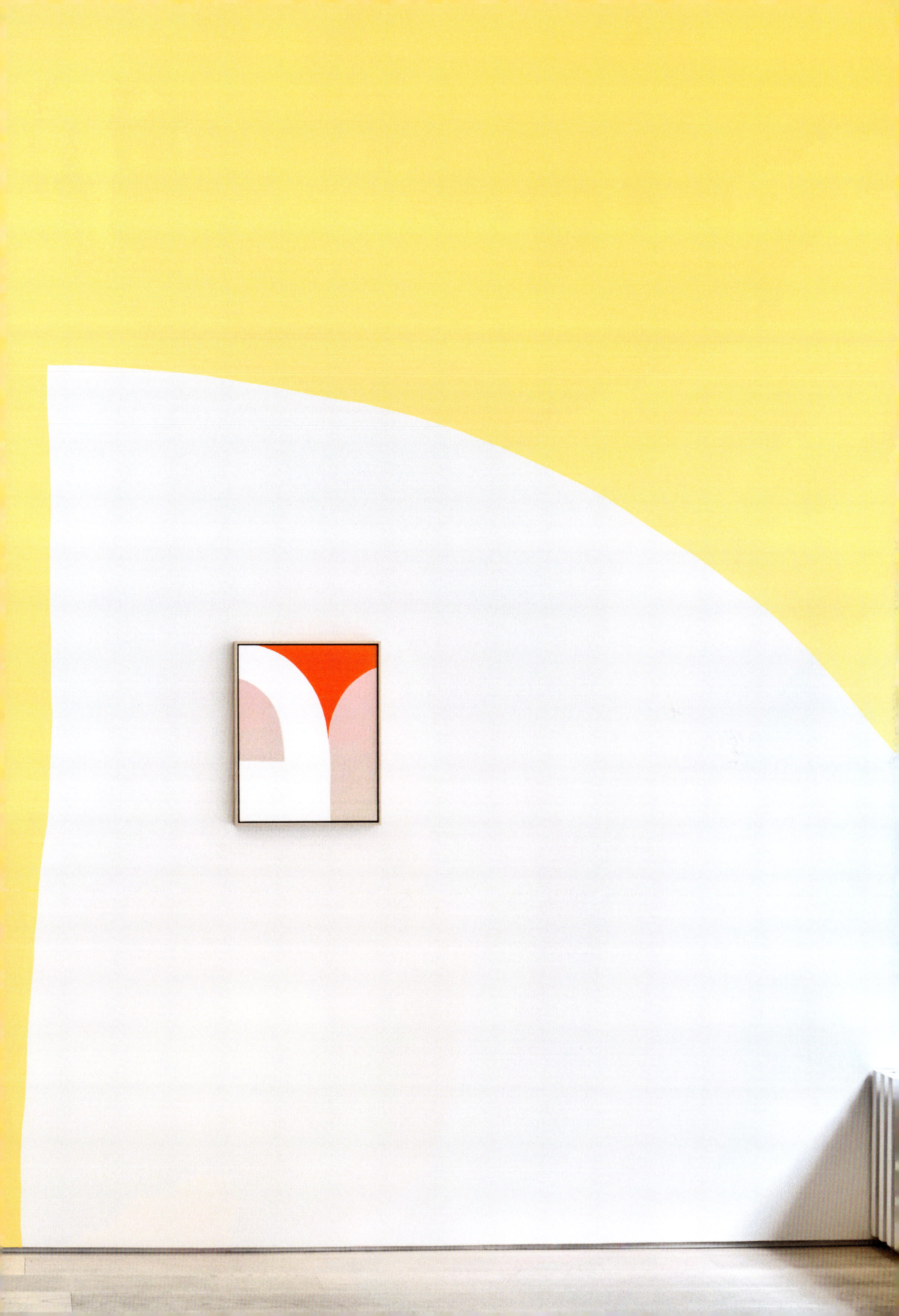

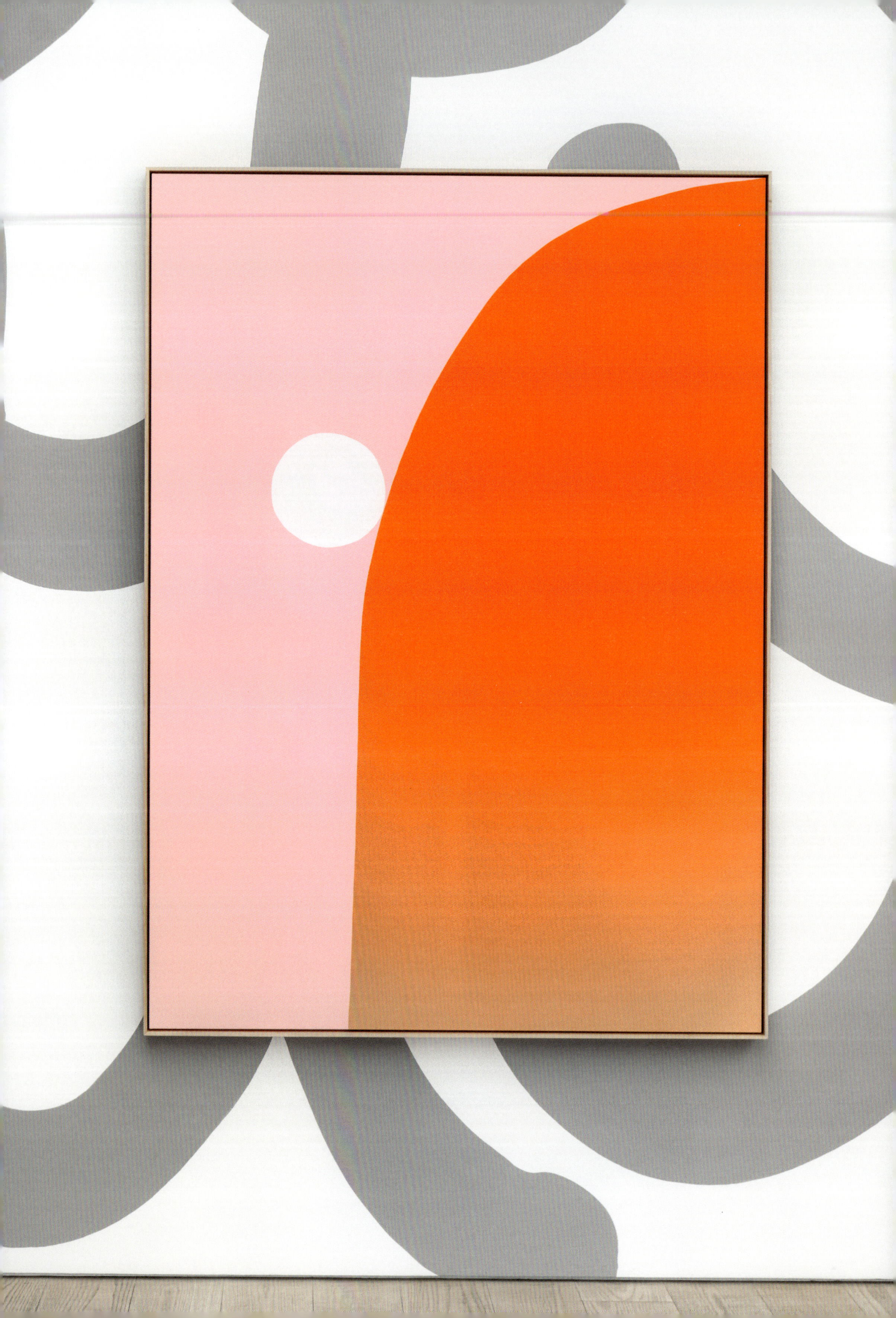

Bup Hup Tup Lup, Fort Worth (US), 2023

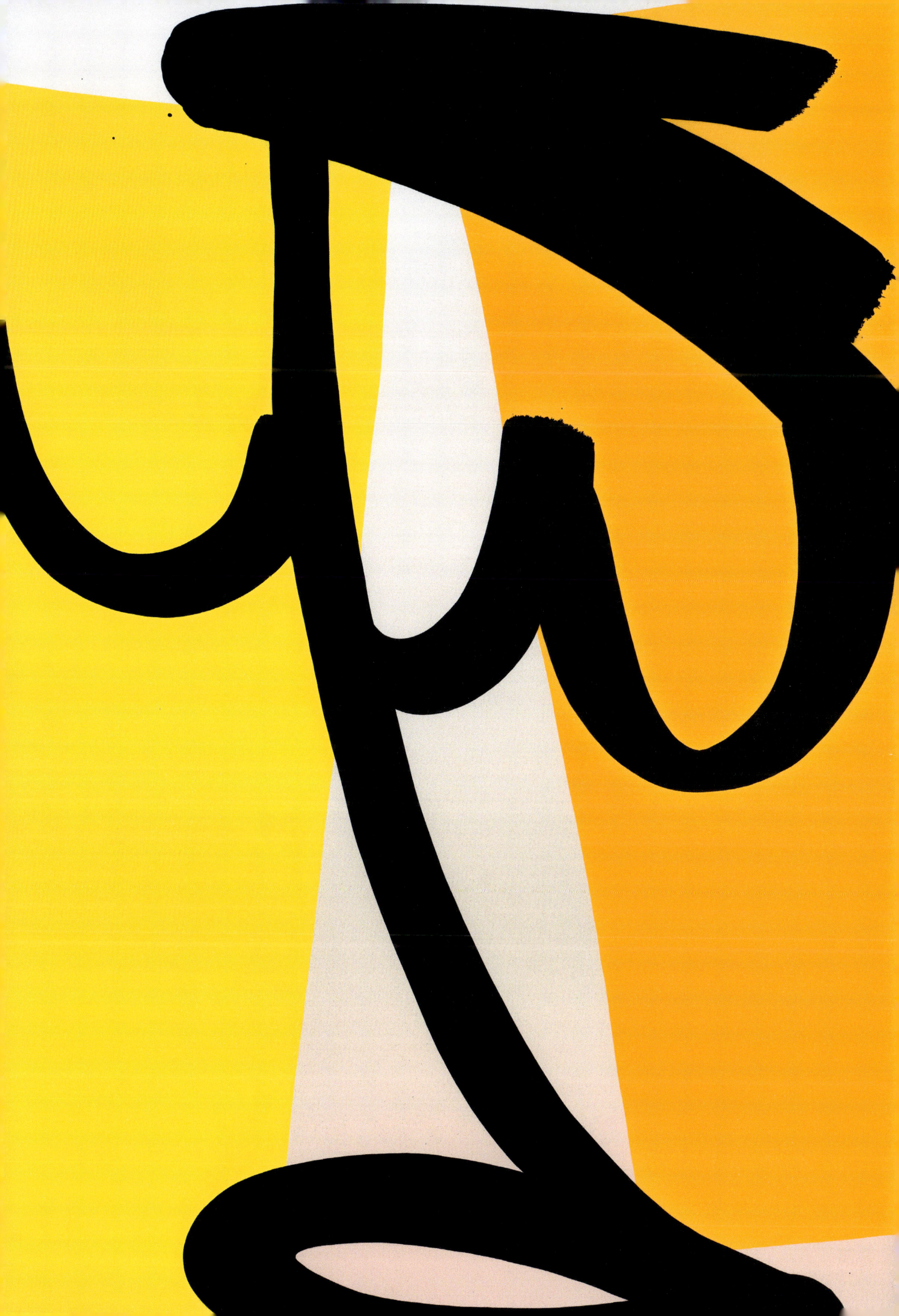

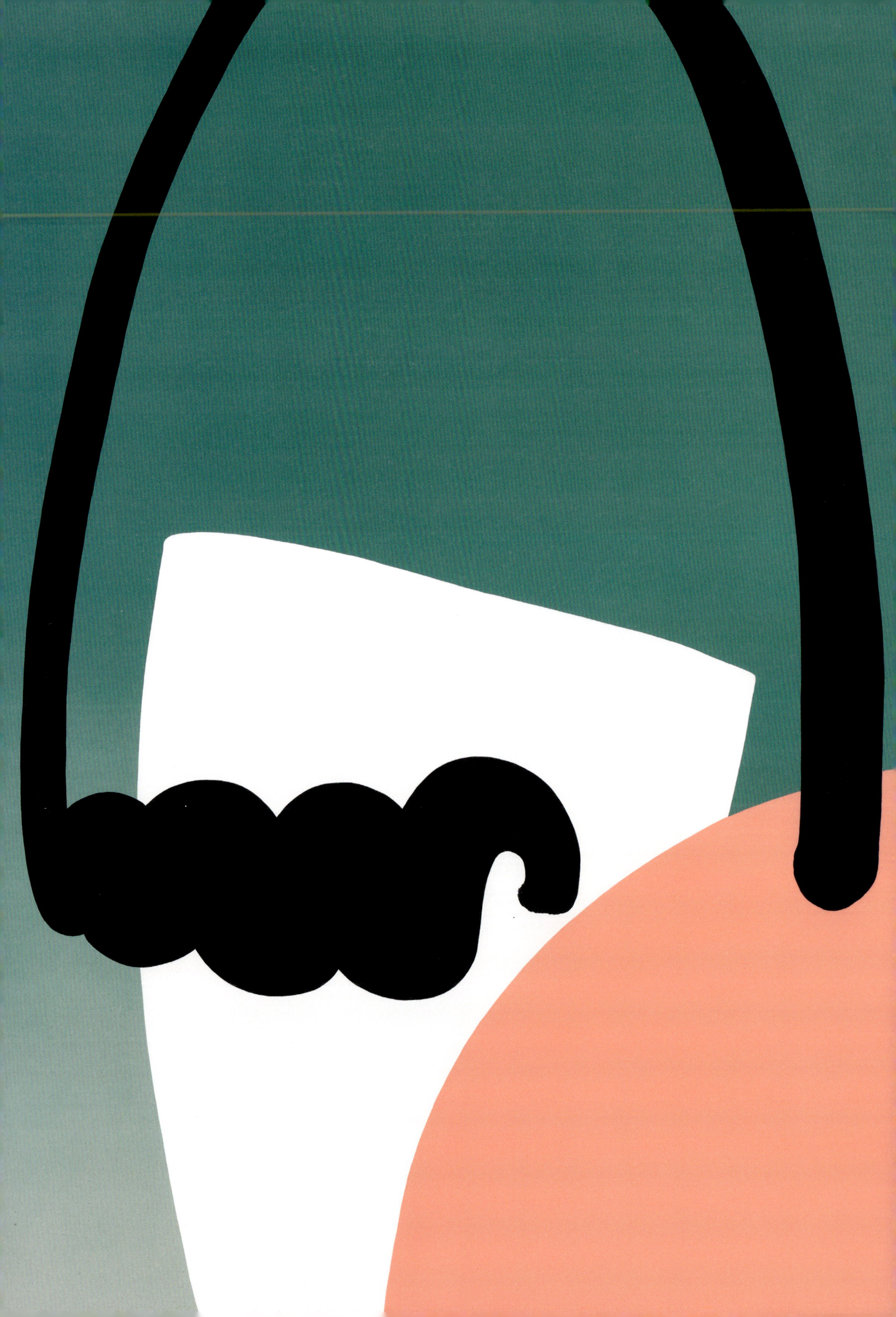

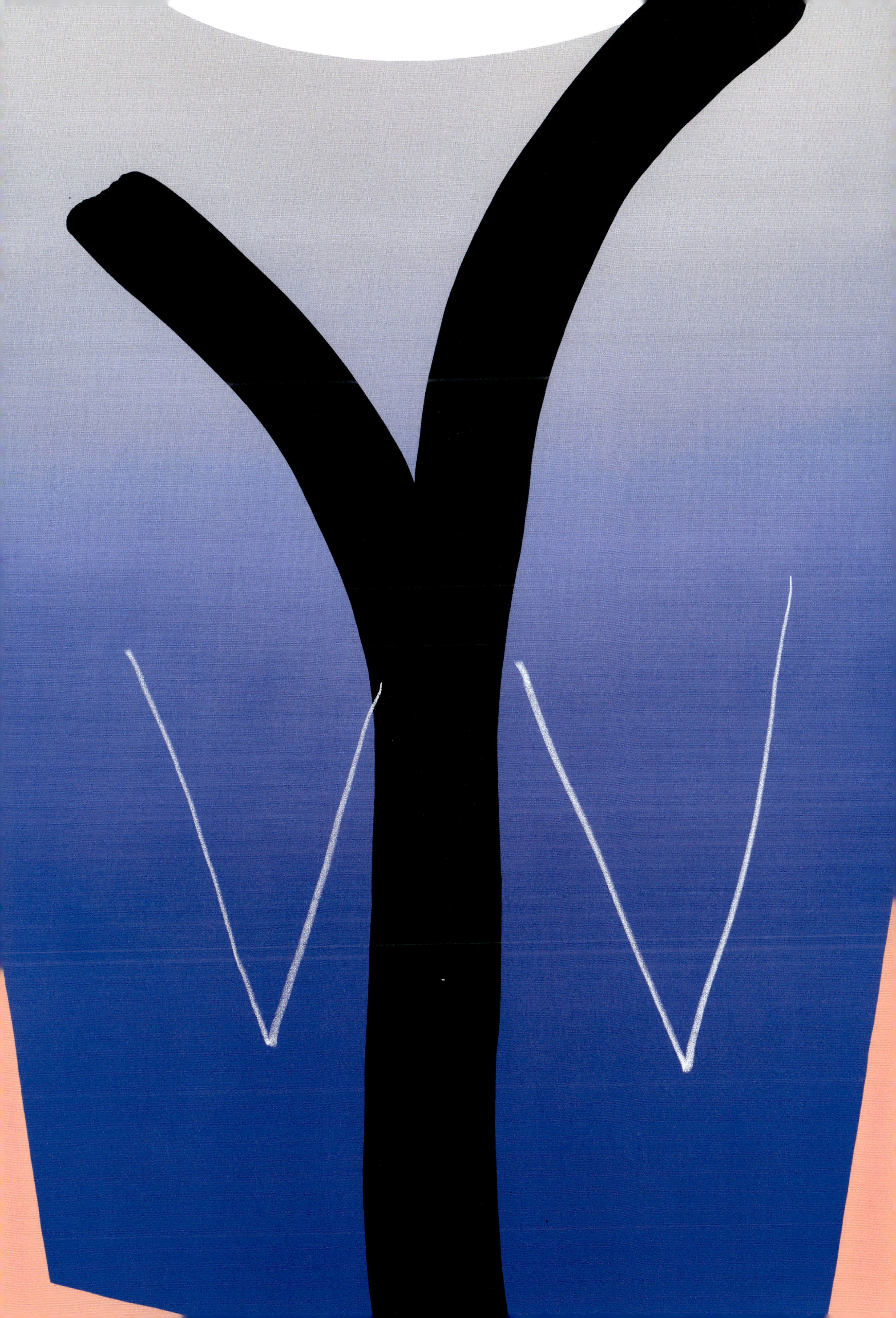

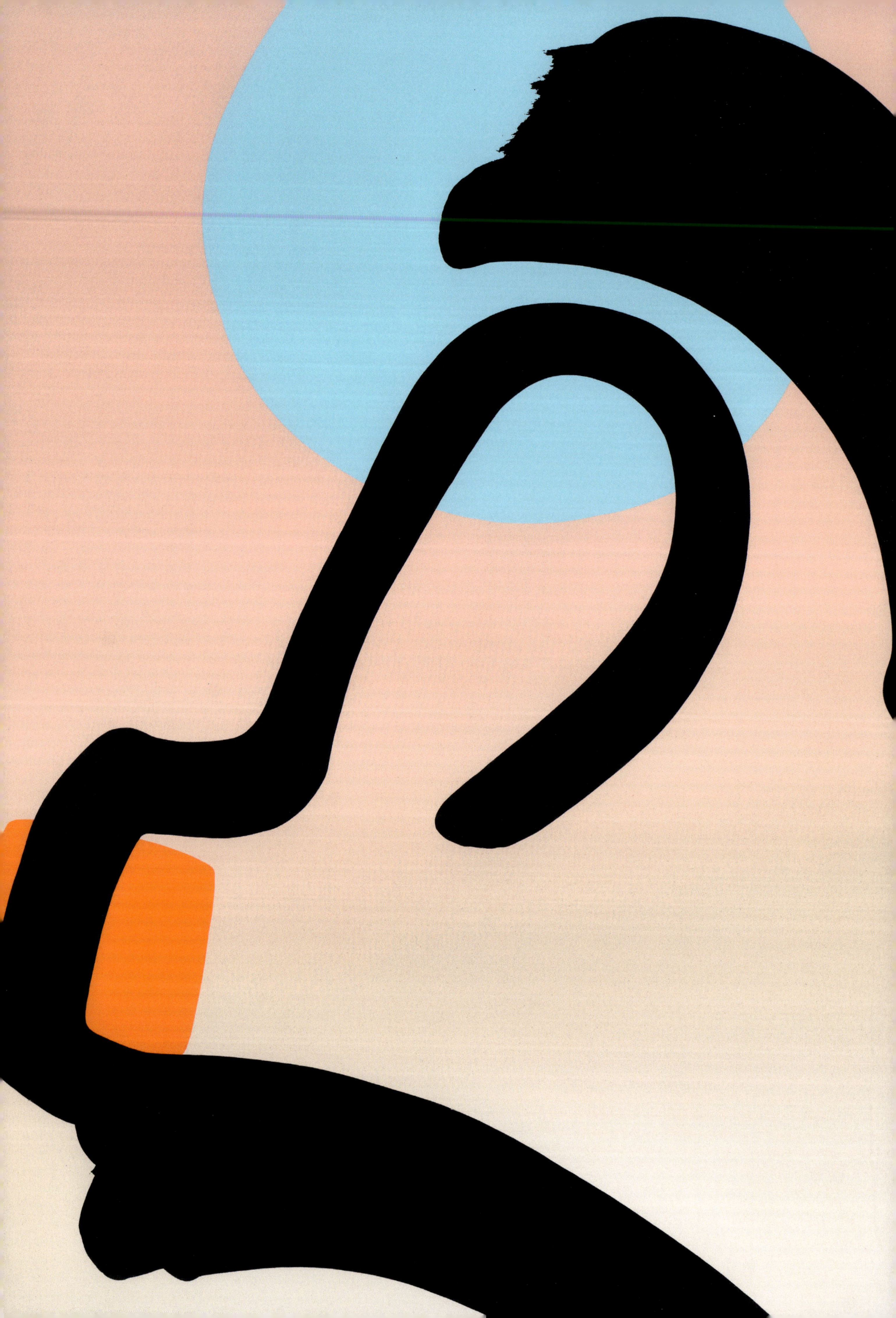

oh-HO, Contemporary Sculpture Fulmer, Buckinghamshire (UK), 2023

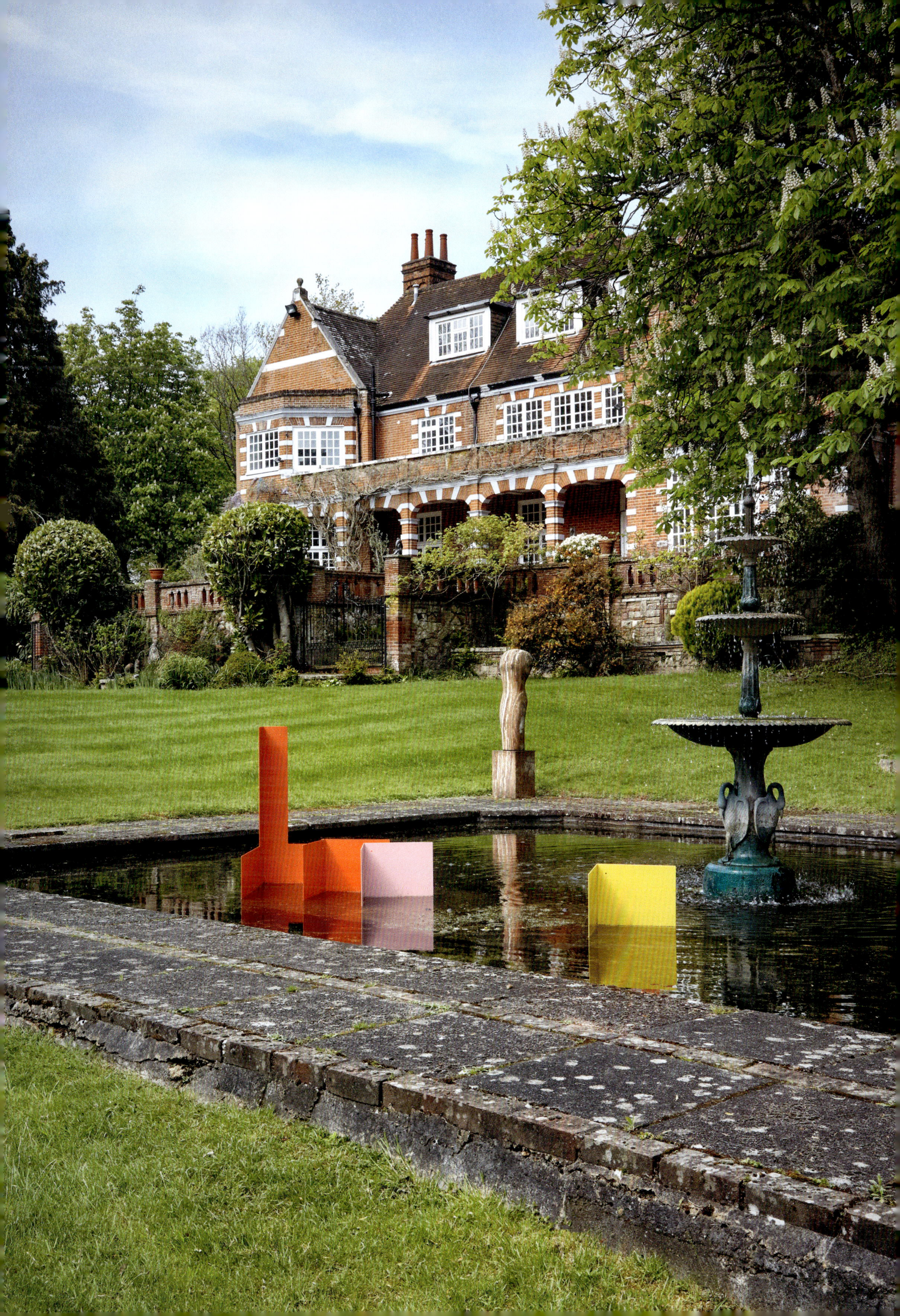

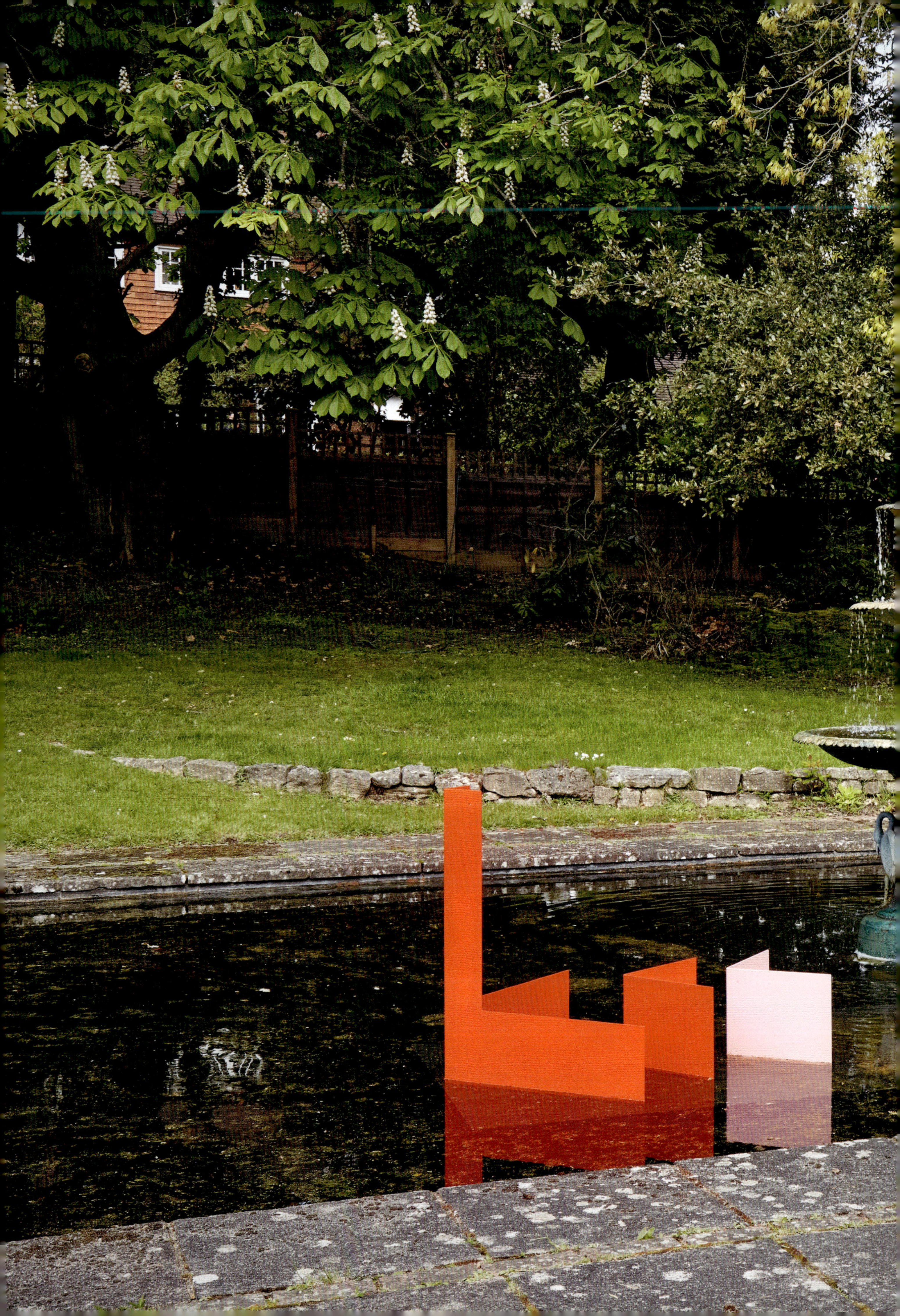

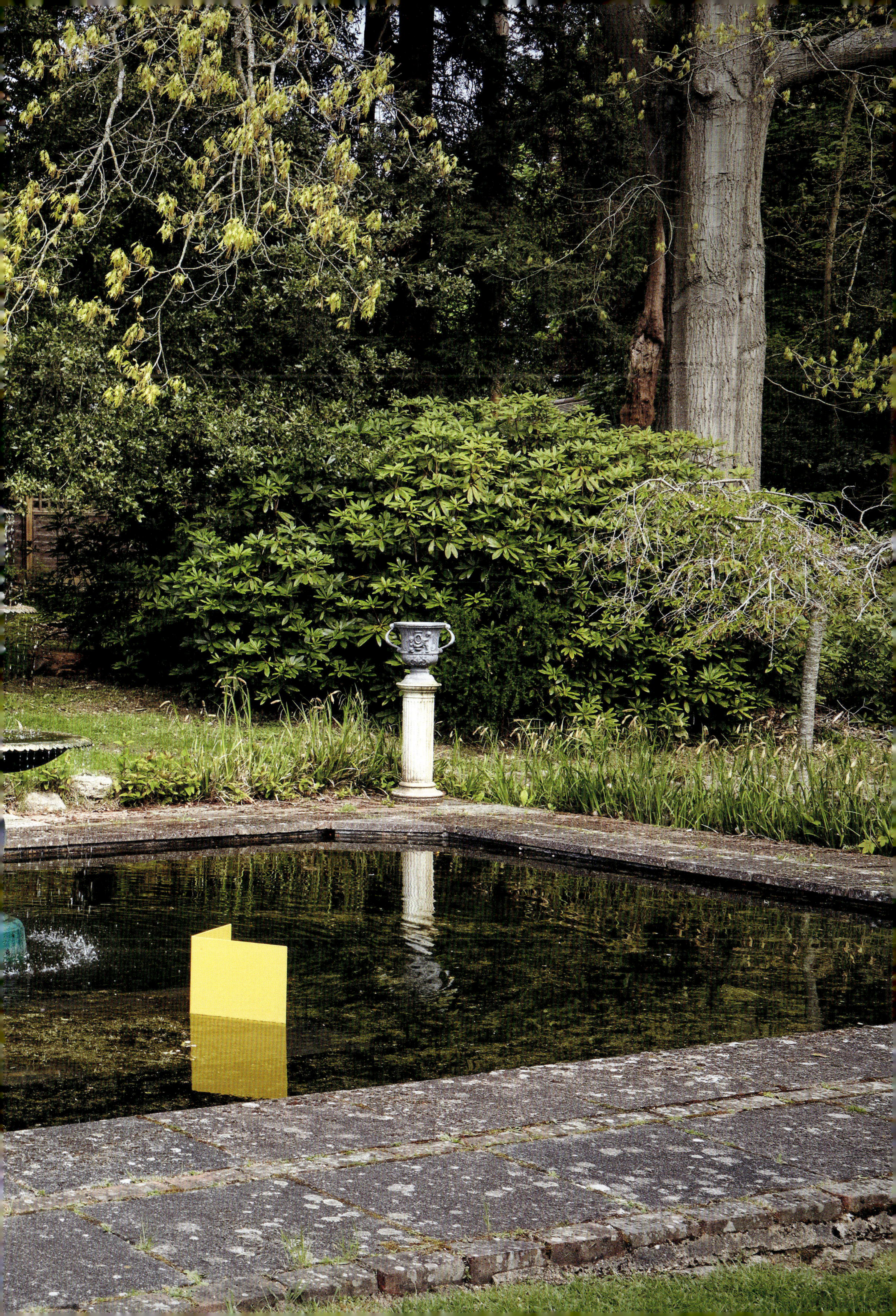

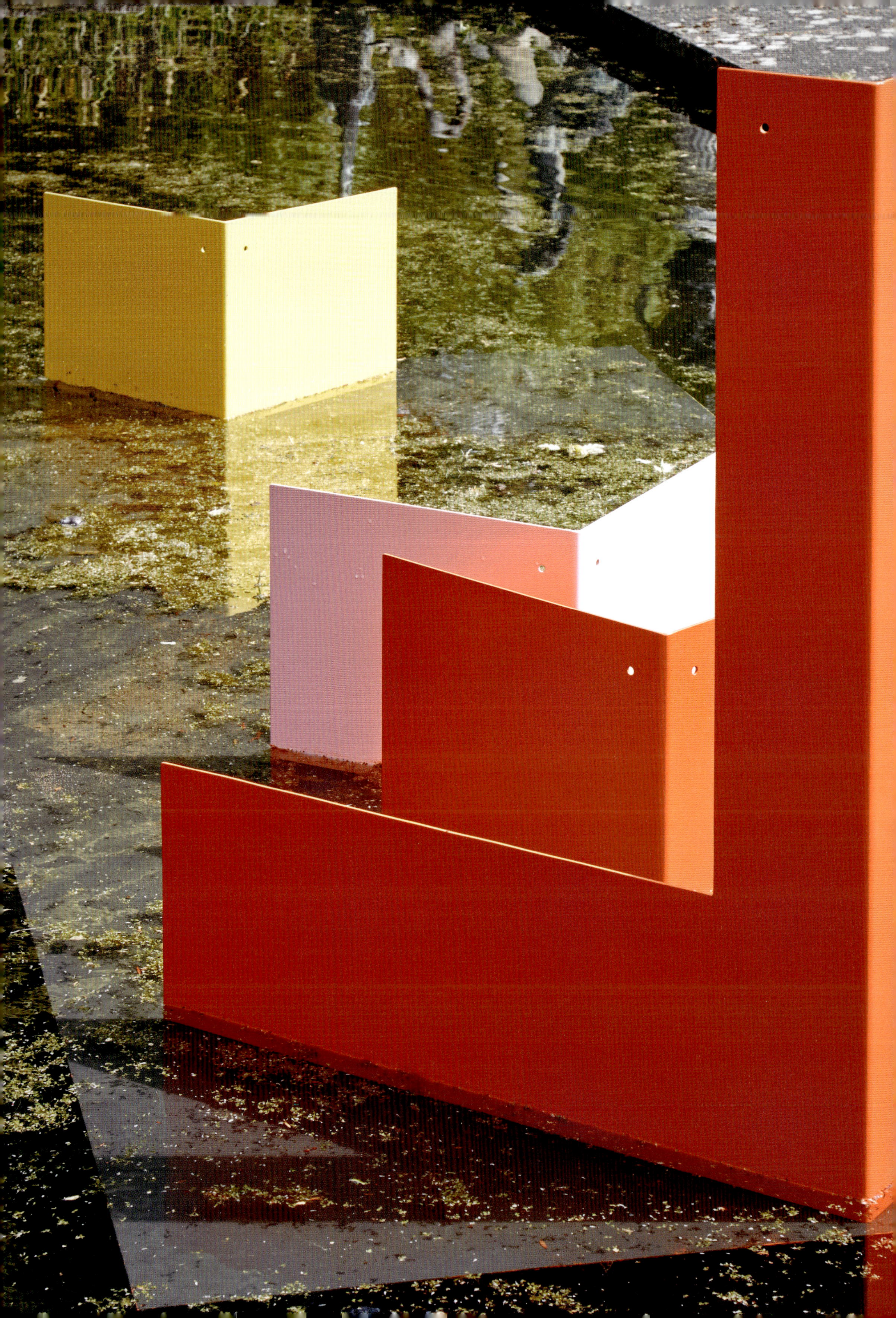

Waggle Dance, rodolphe janssen, Brussels (BE), 2022

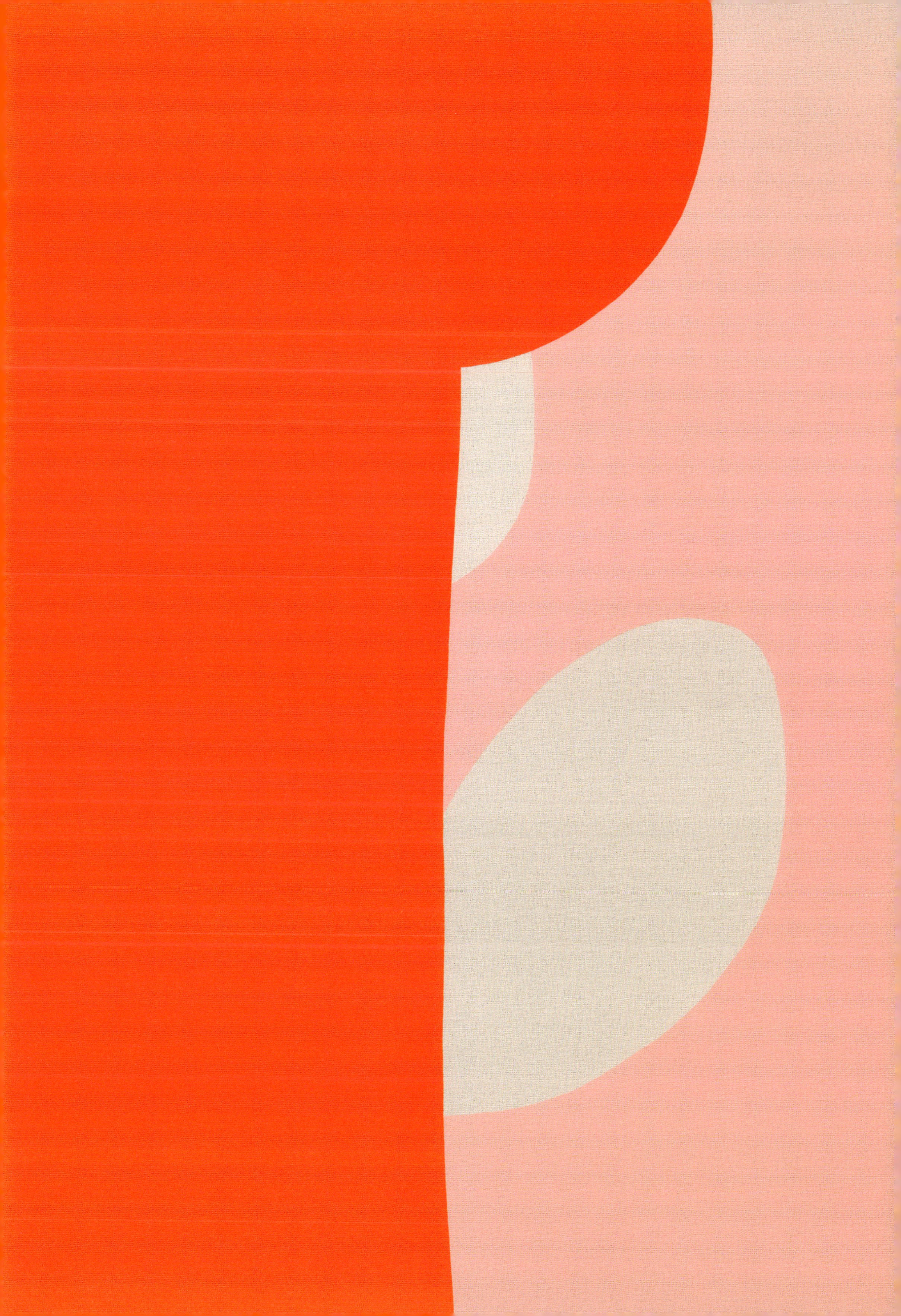

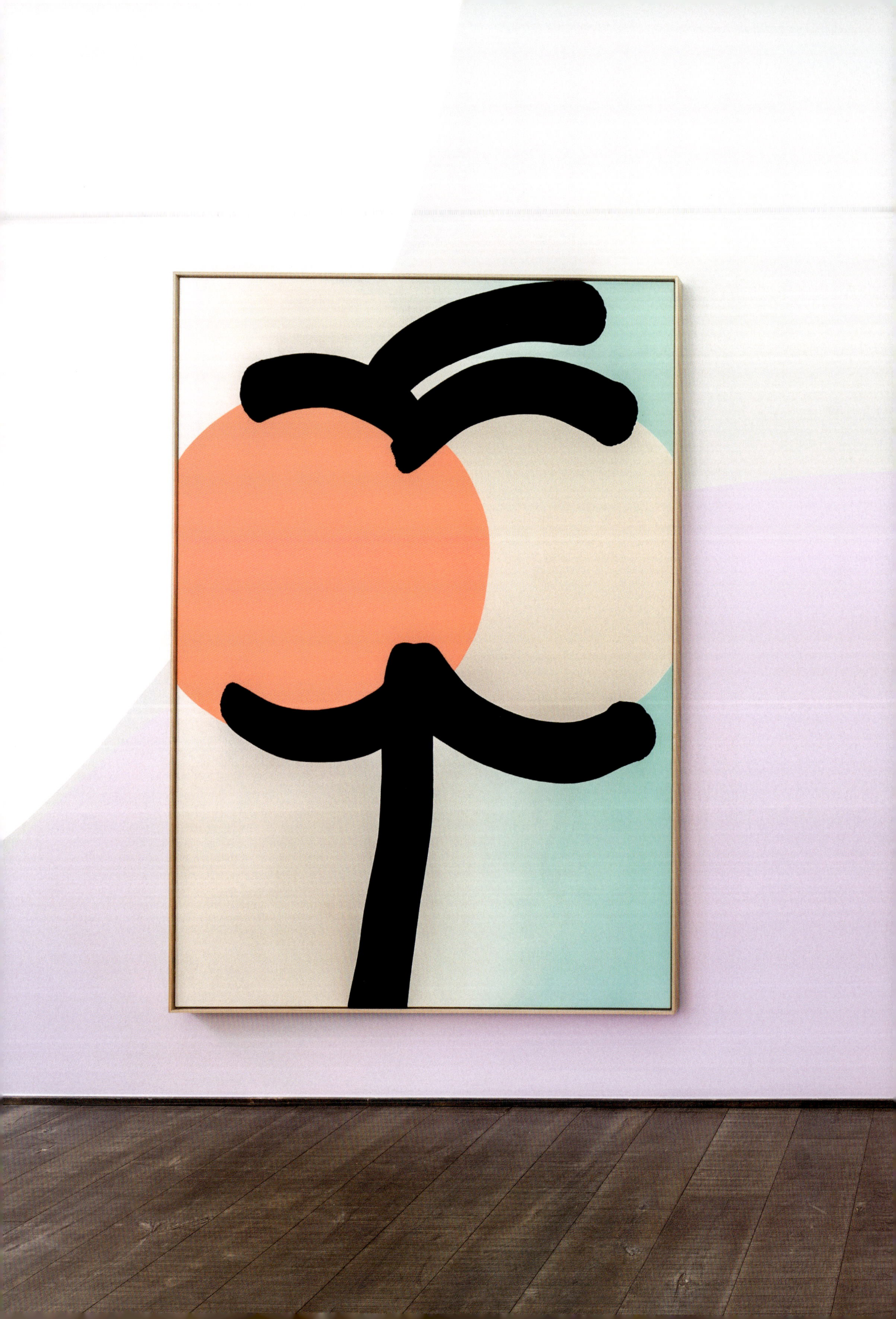

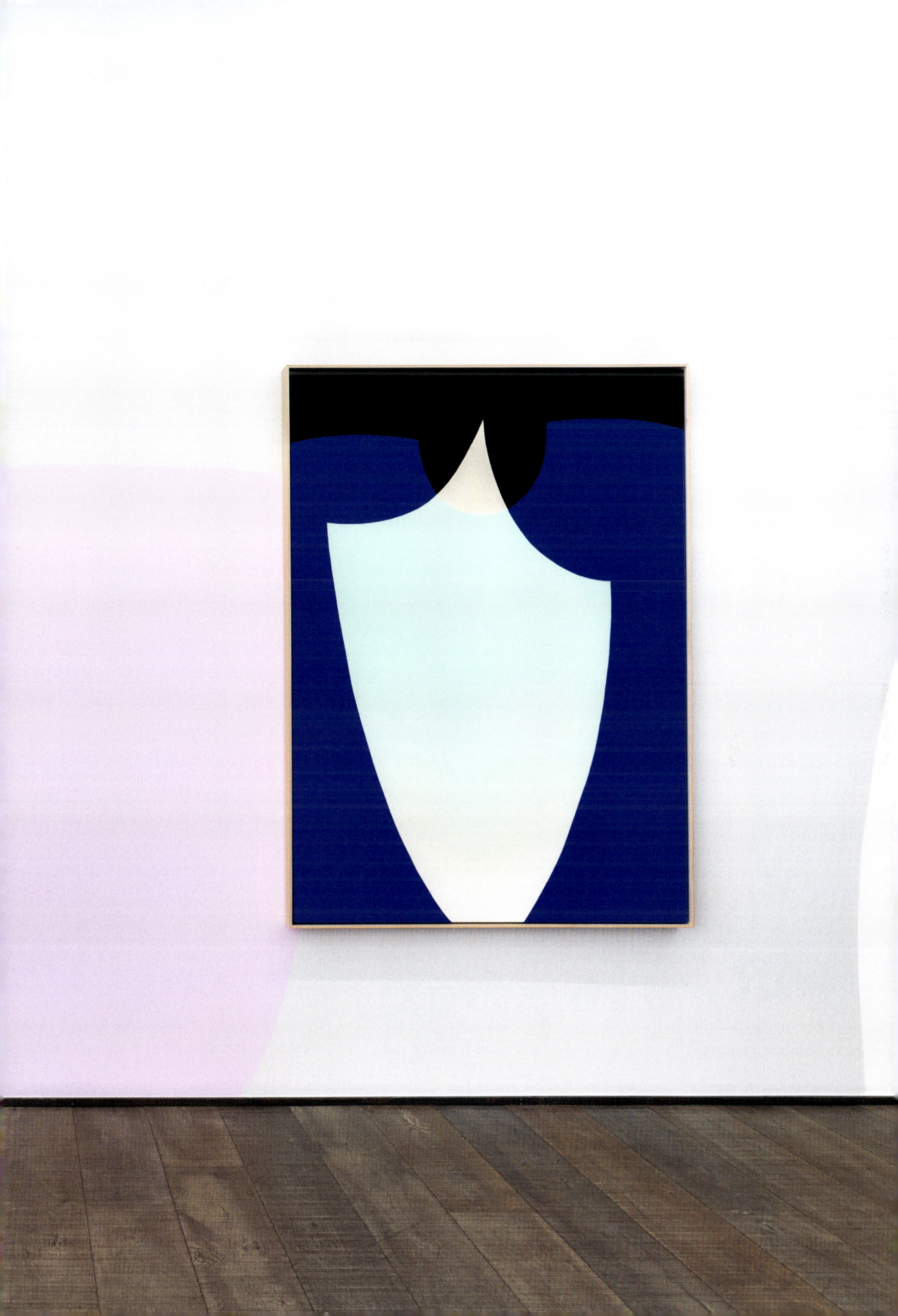

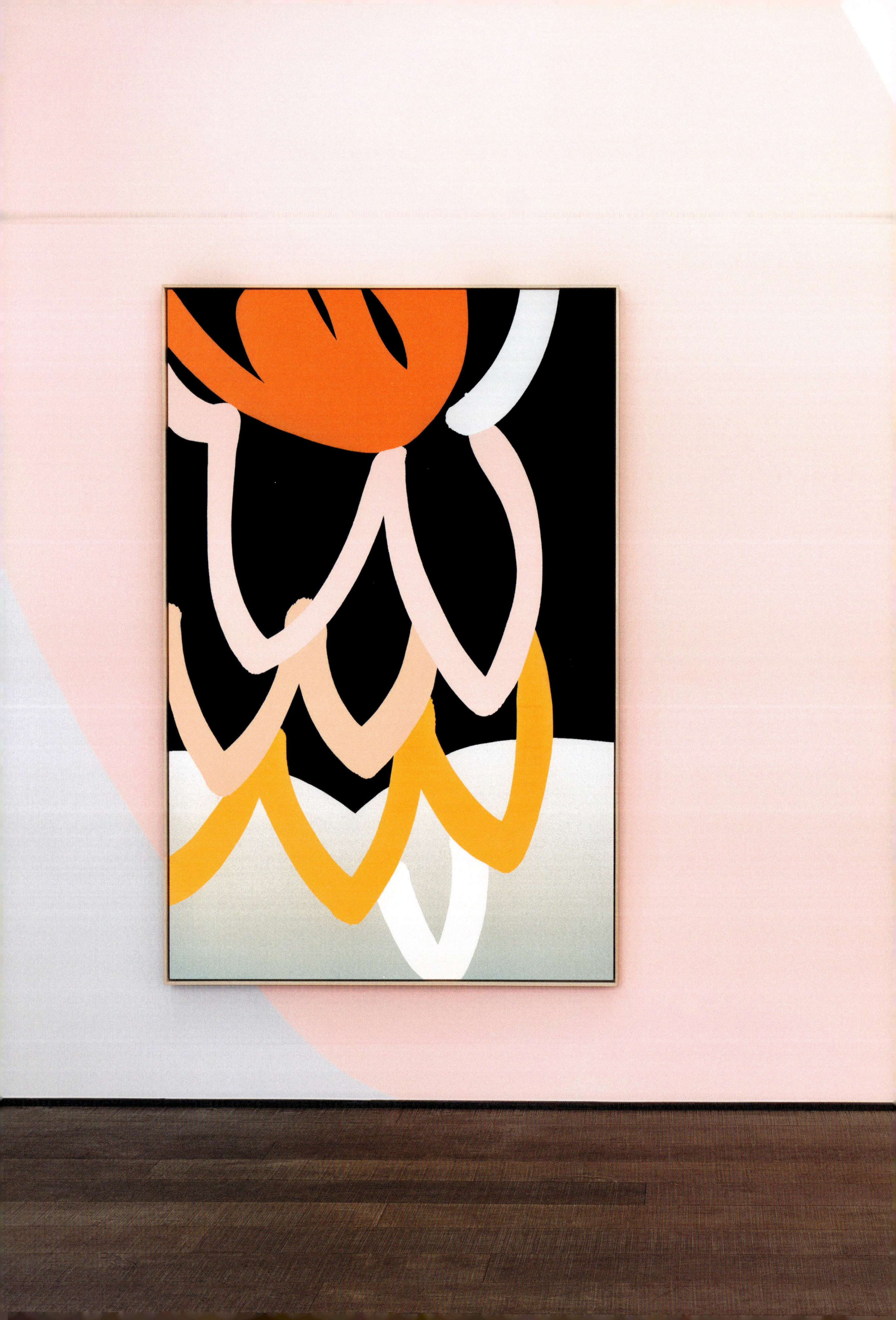

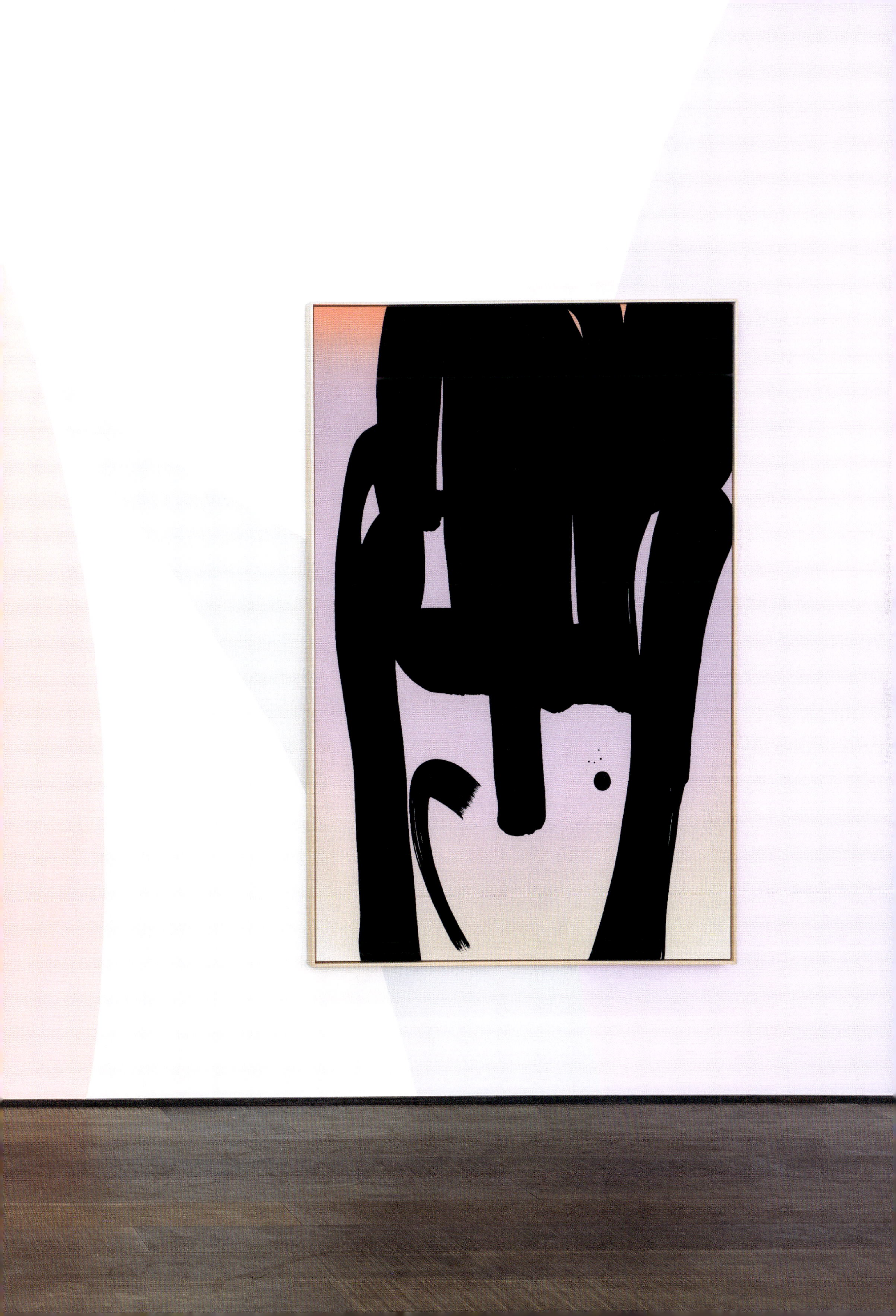

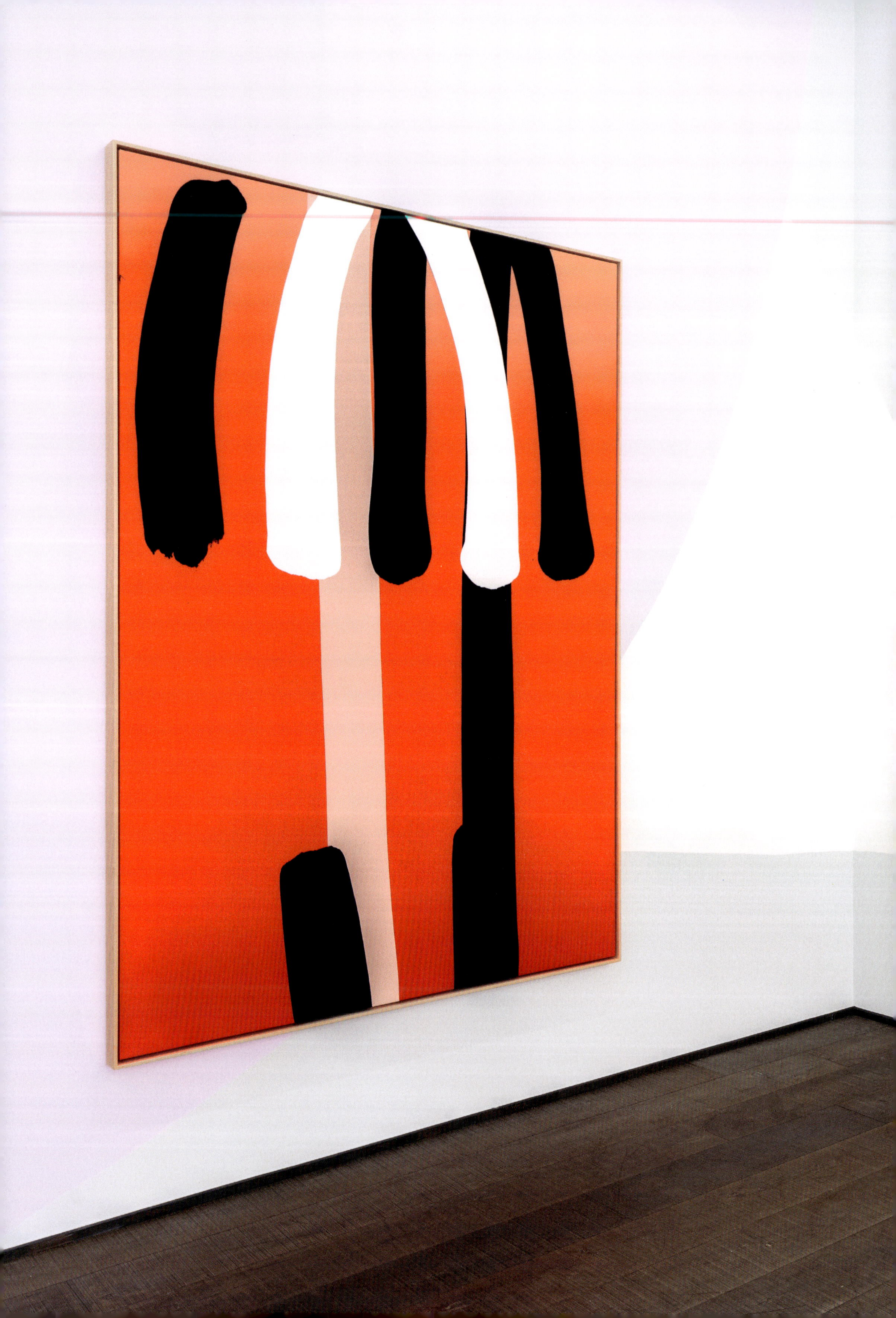

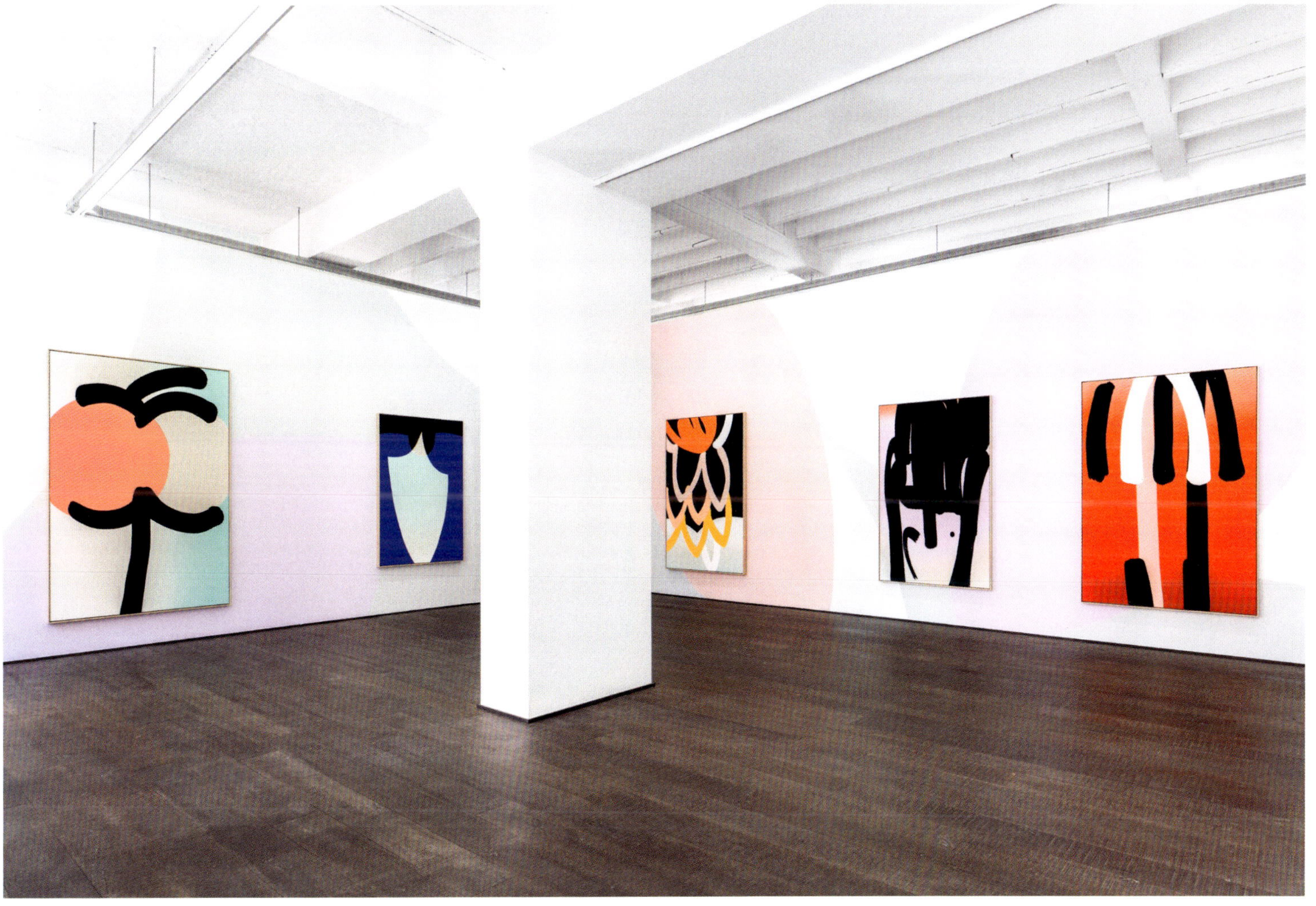

Lazybones, Nino Mier Gallery, Los Angeles (US), 2022

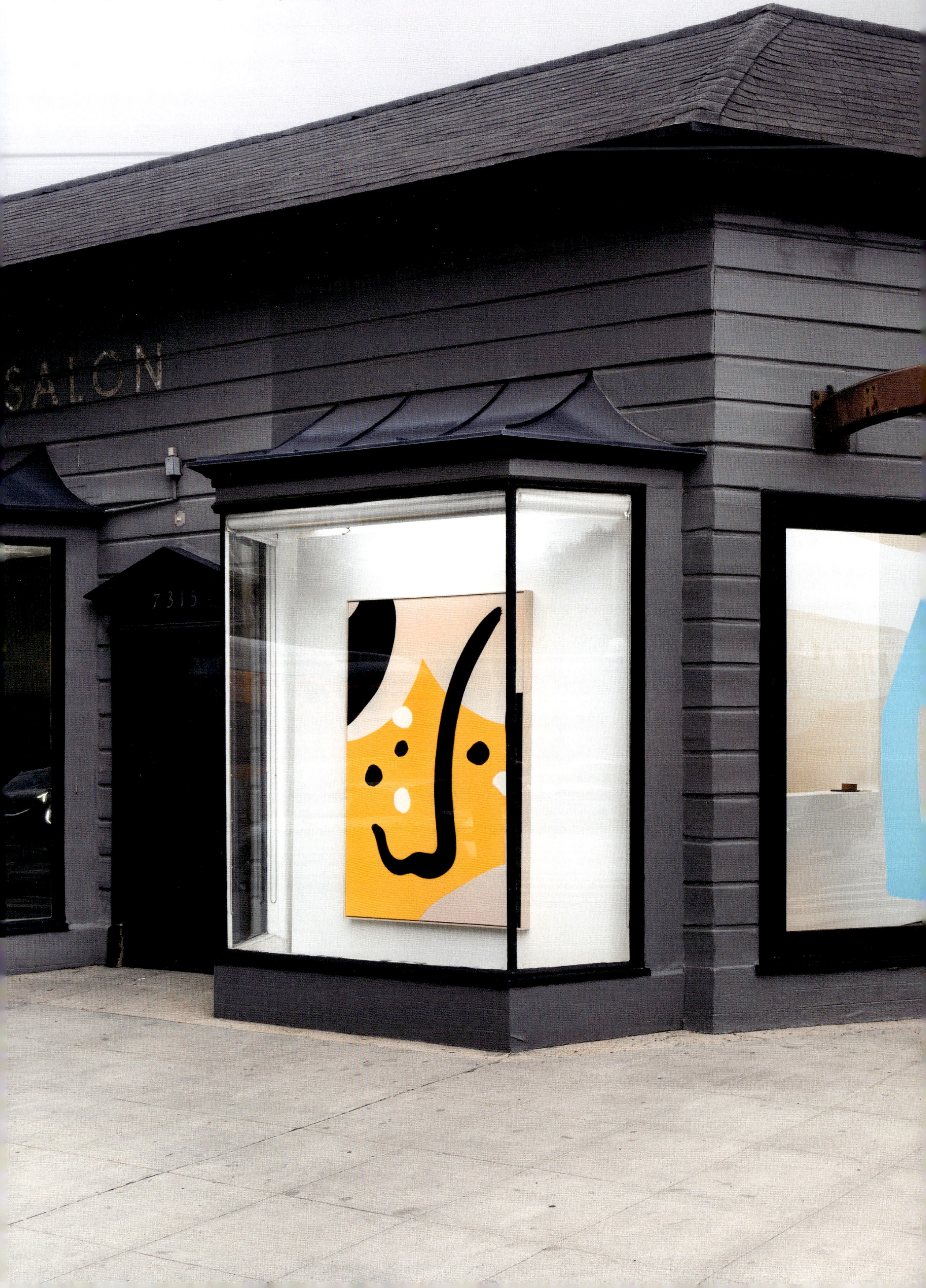

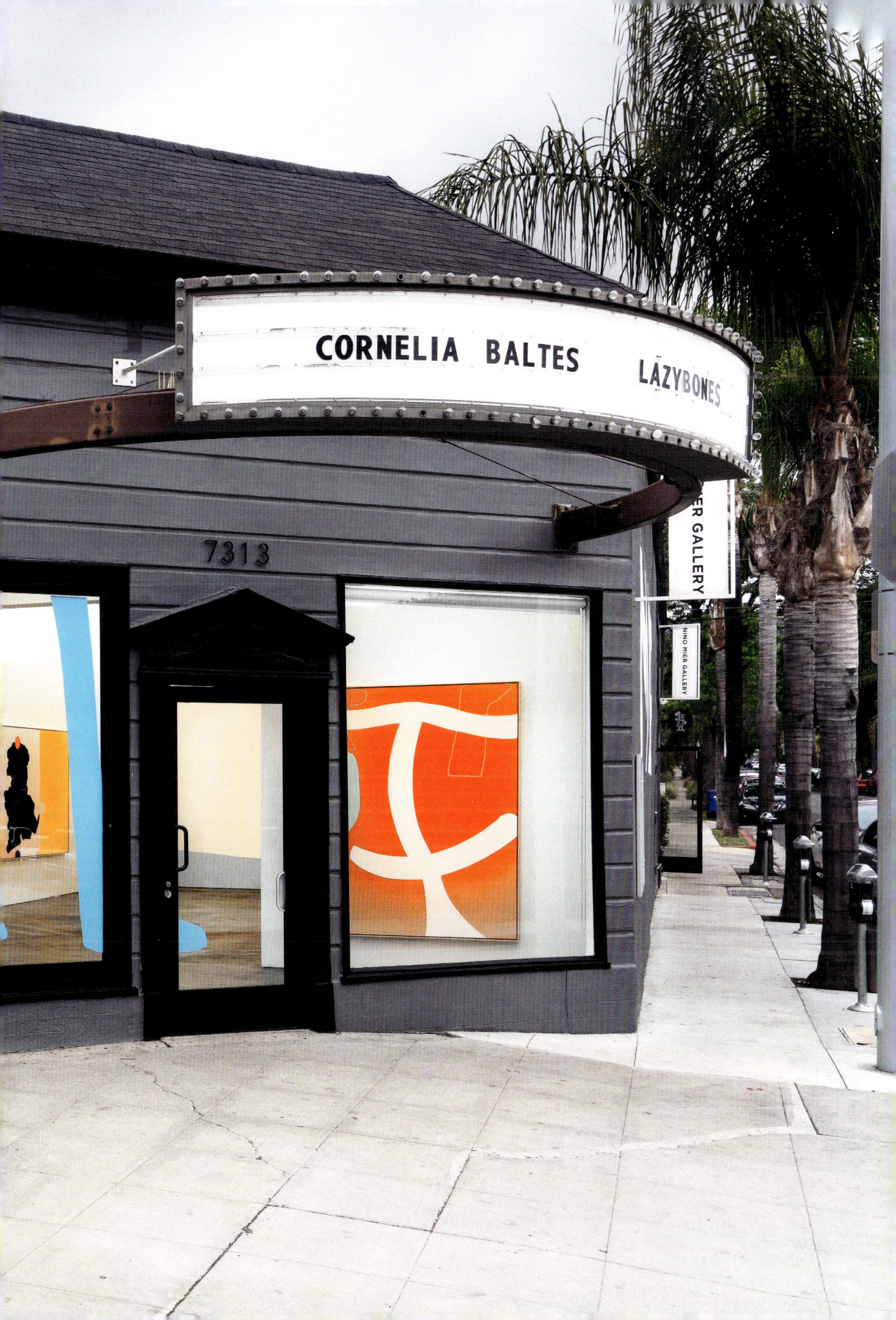
CORNELIA BALTES
LAZYBONES
7313
NINO MIER GALLERY

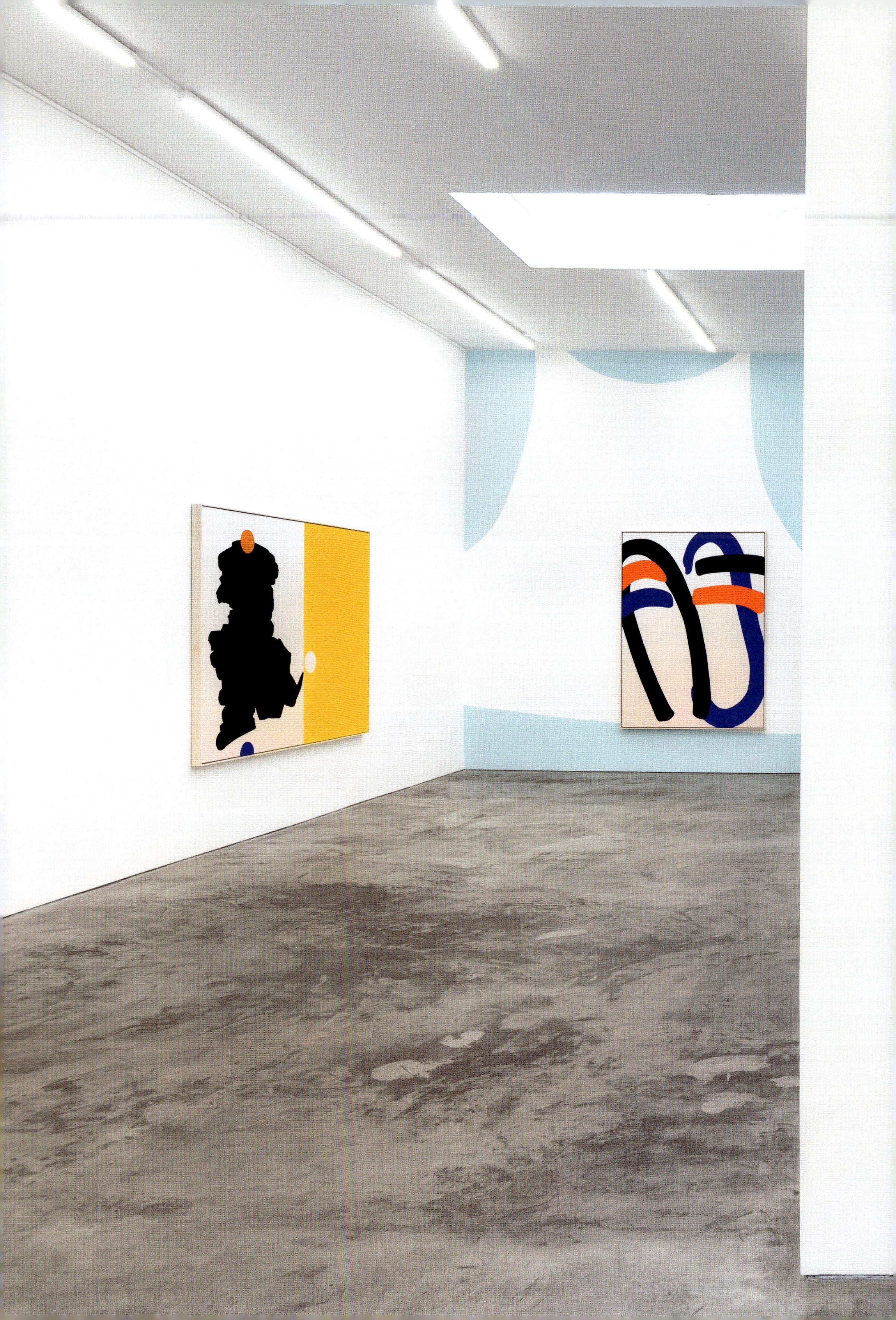

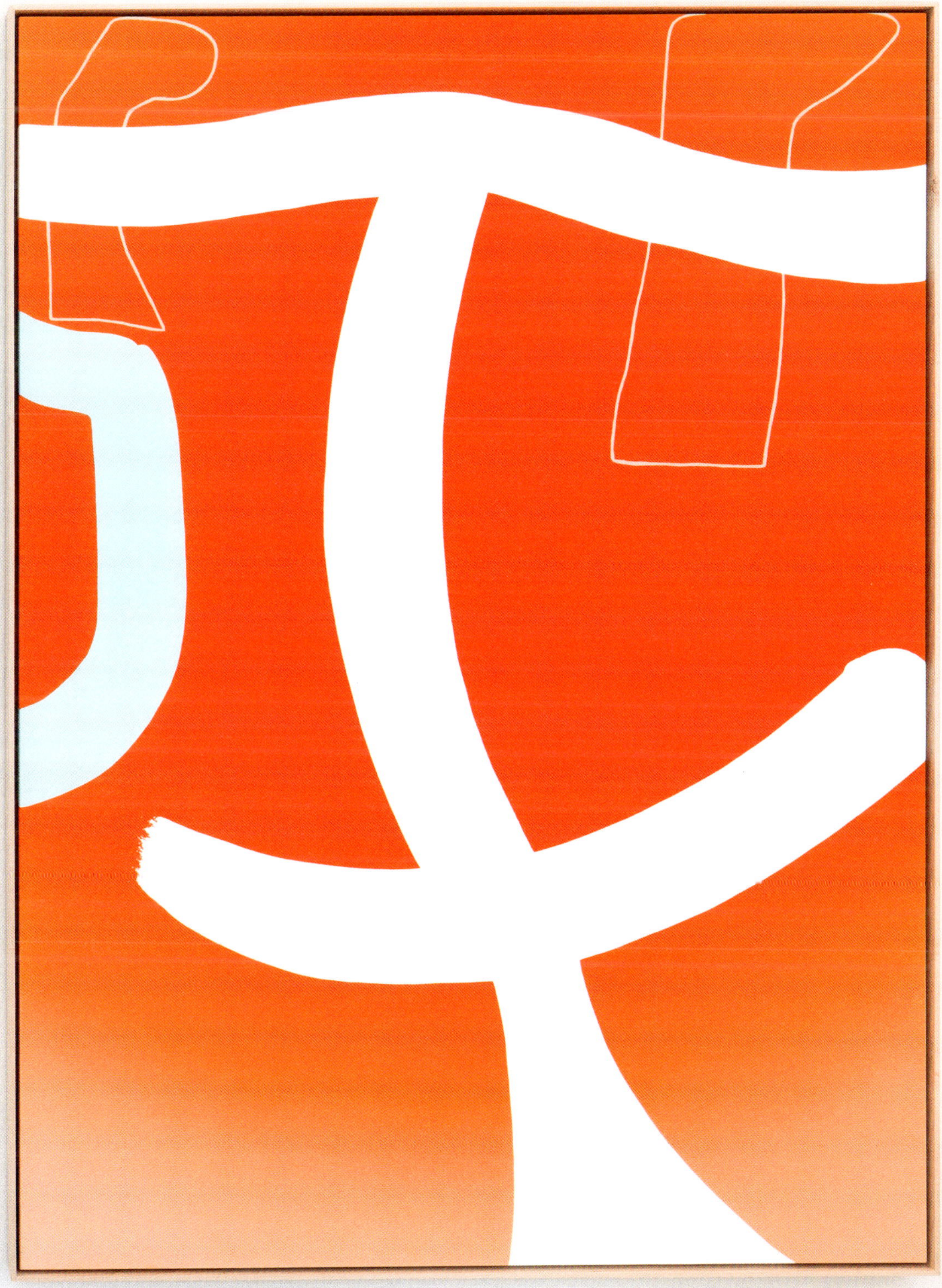

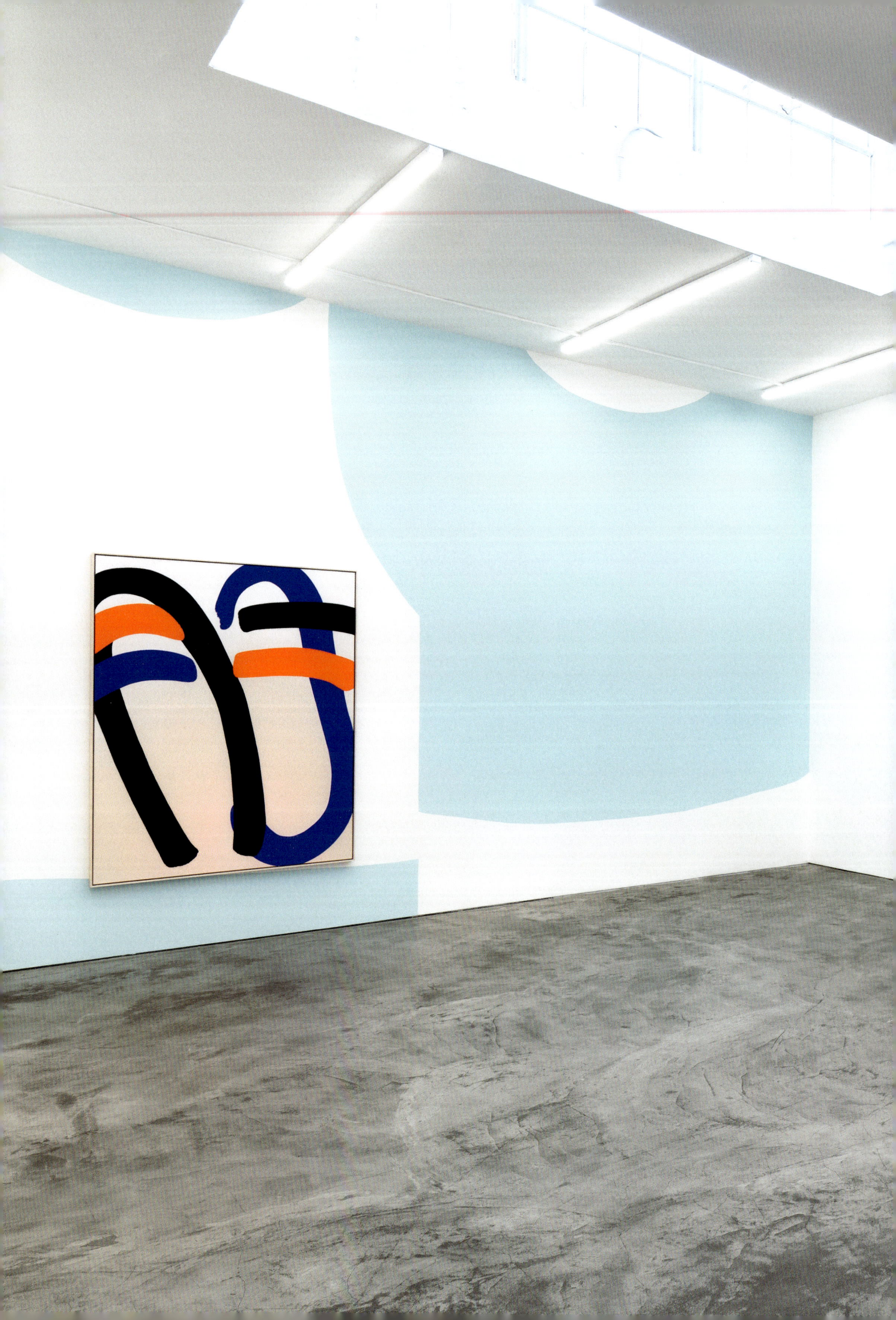

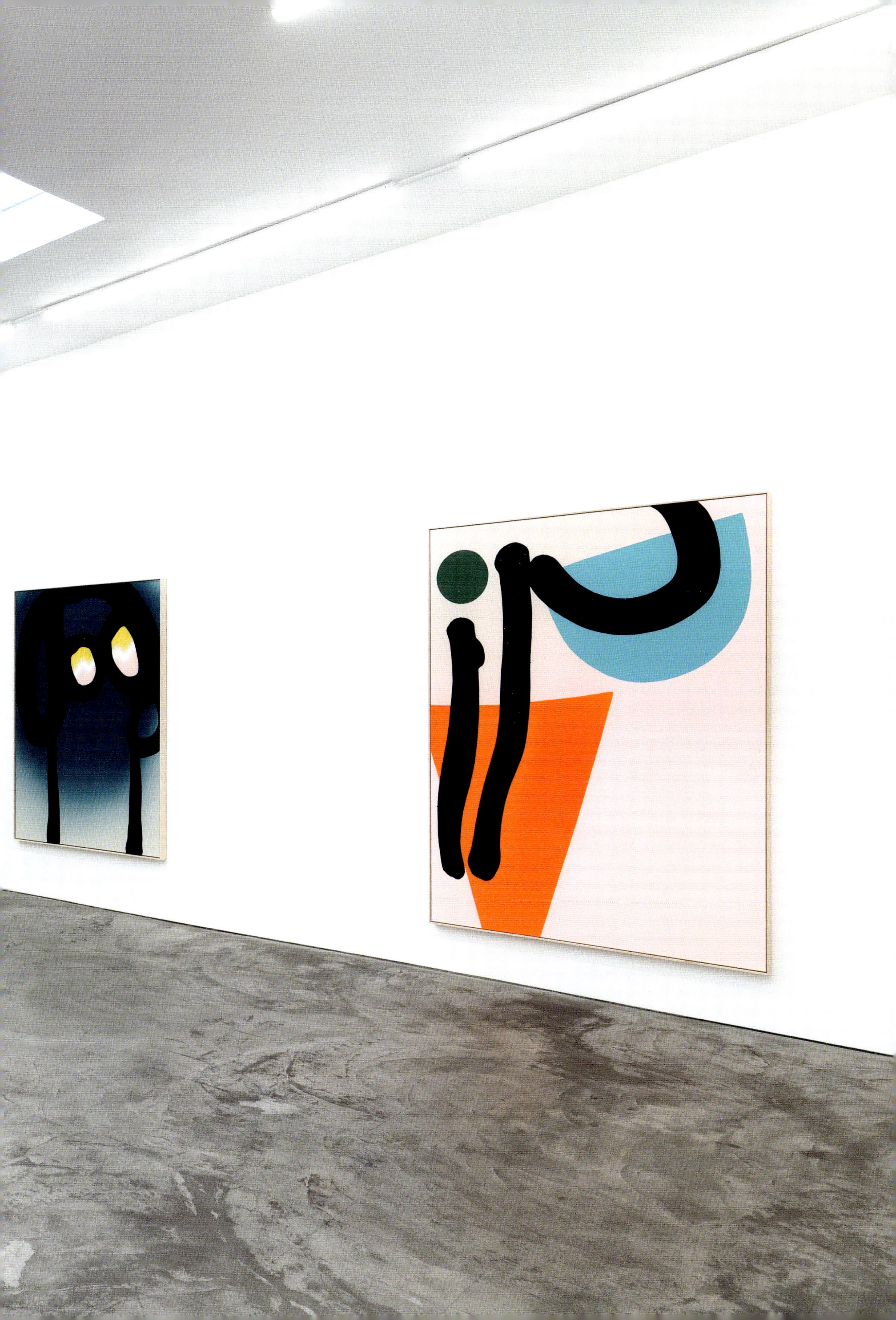

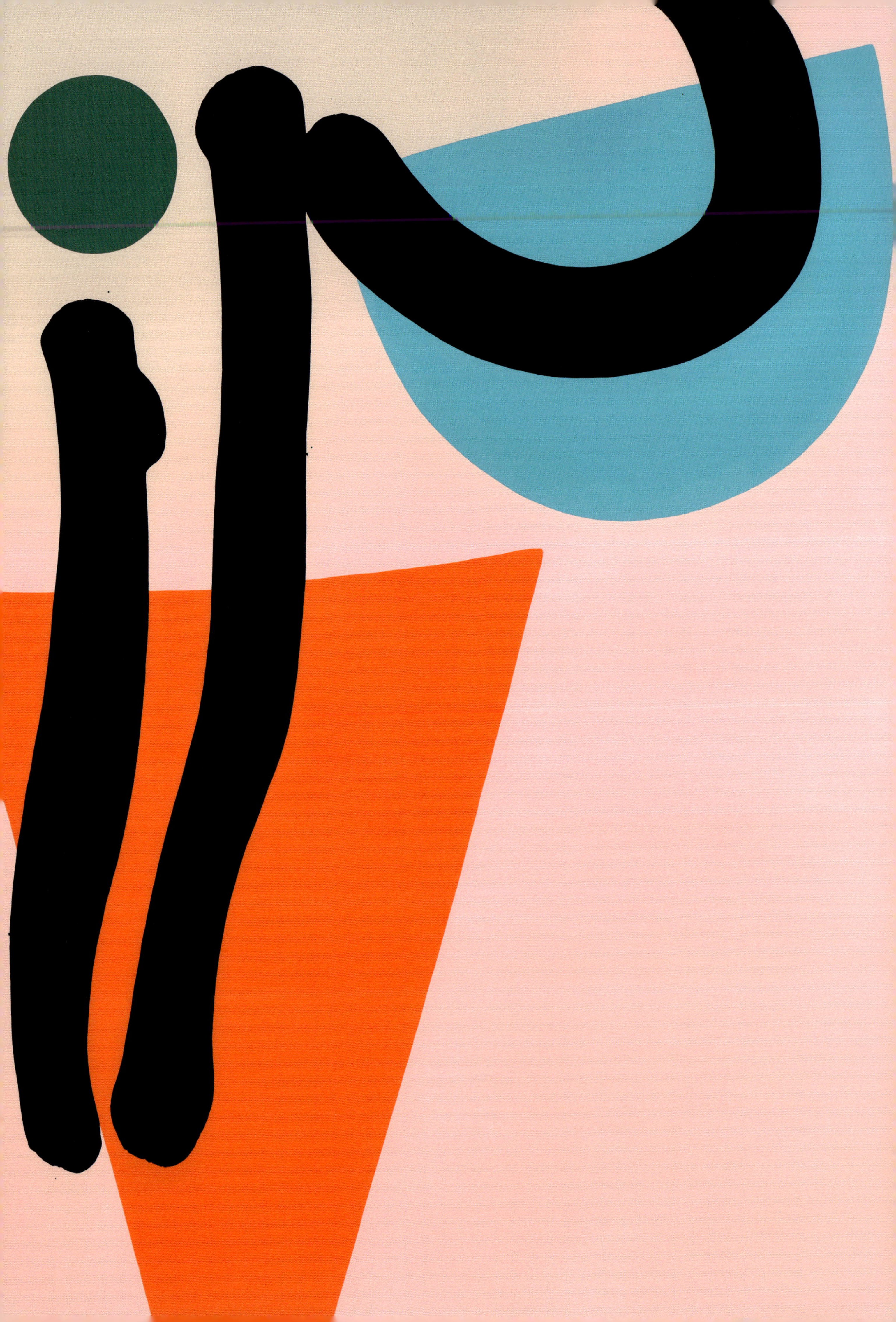

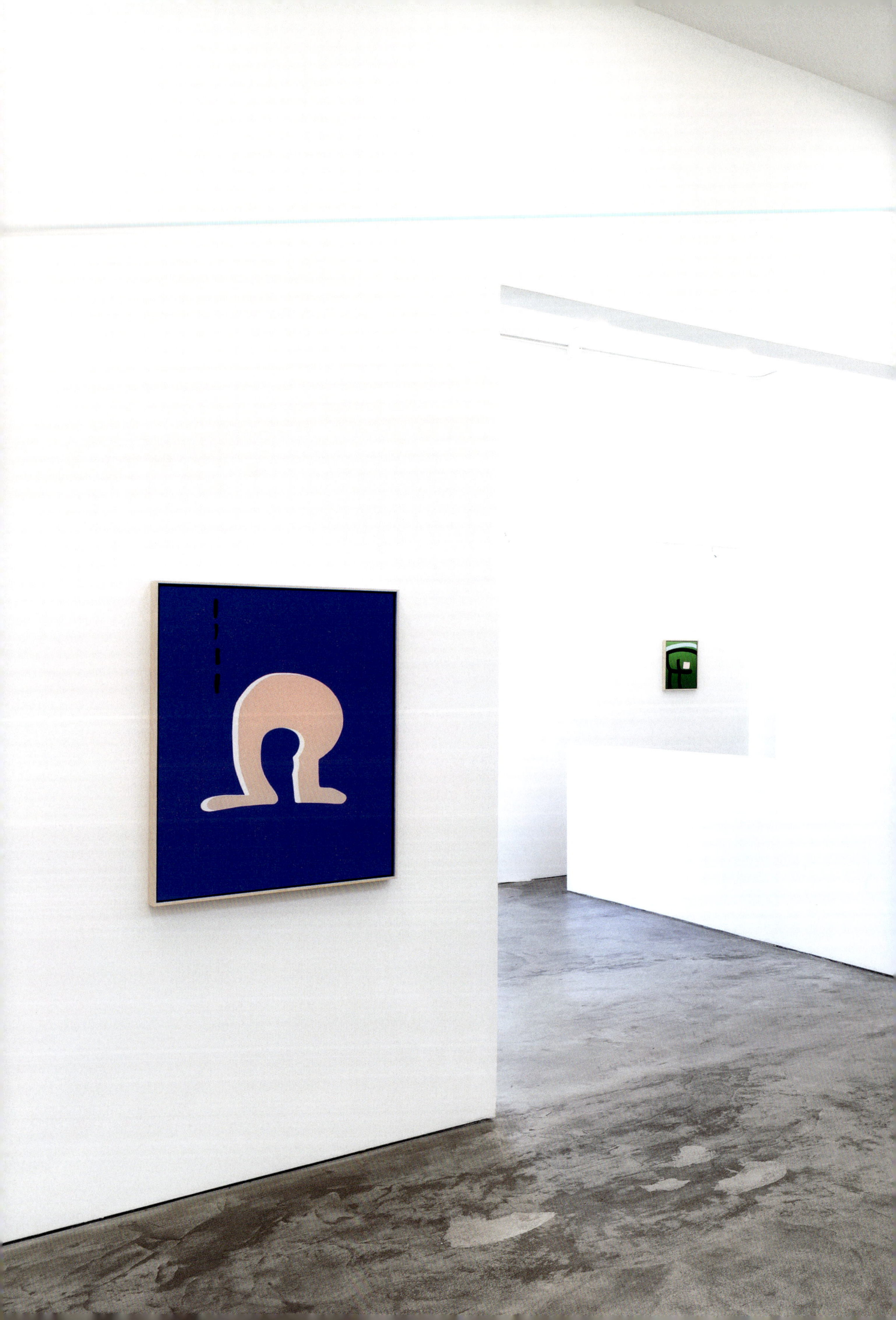

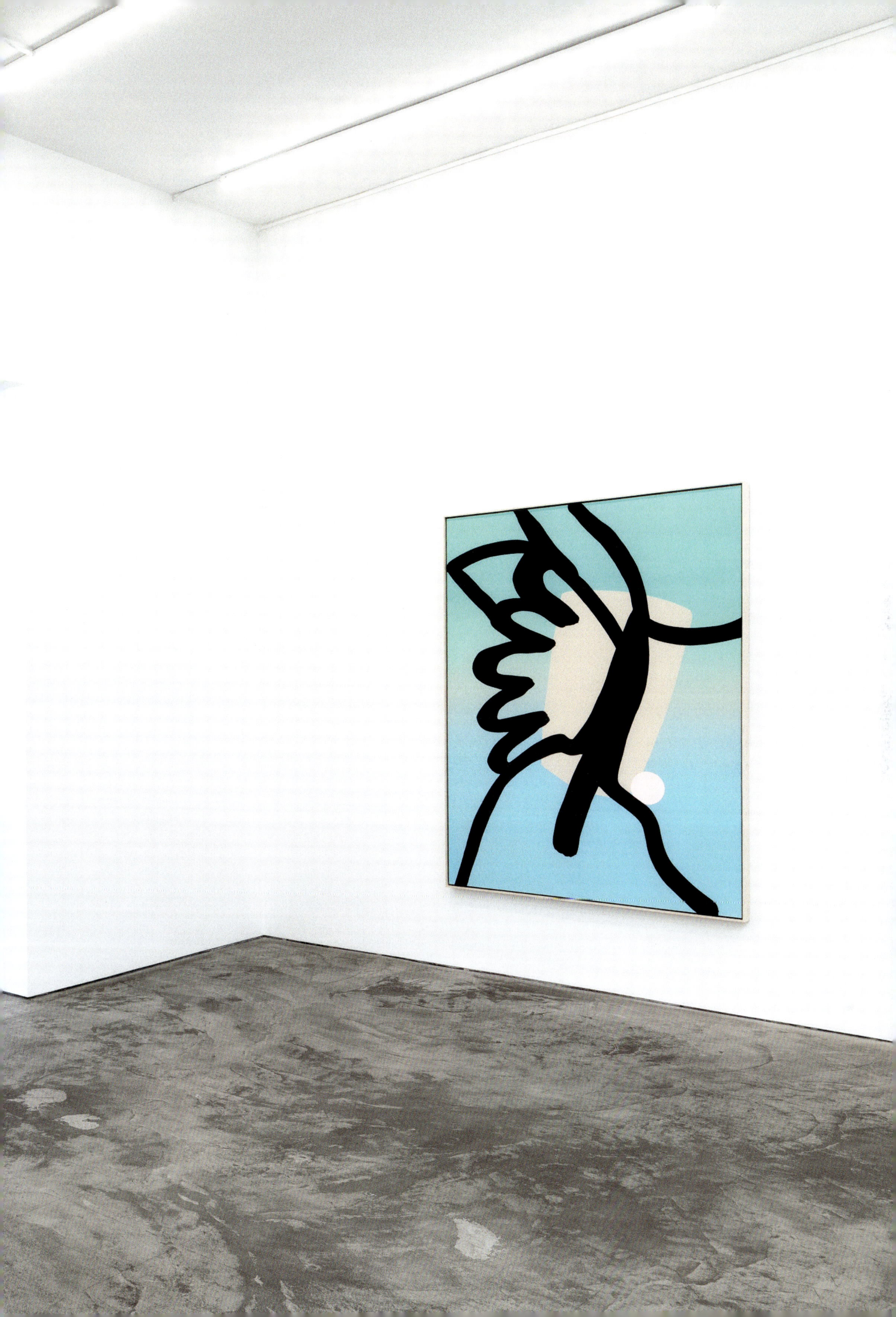

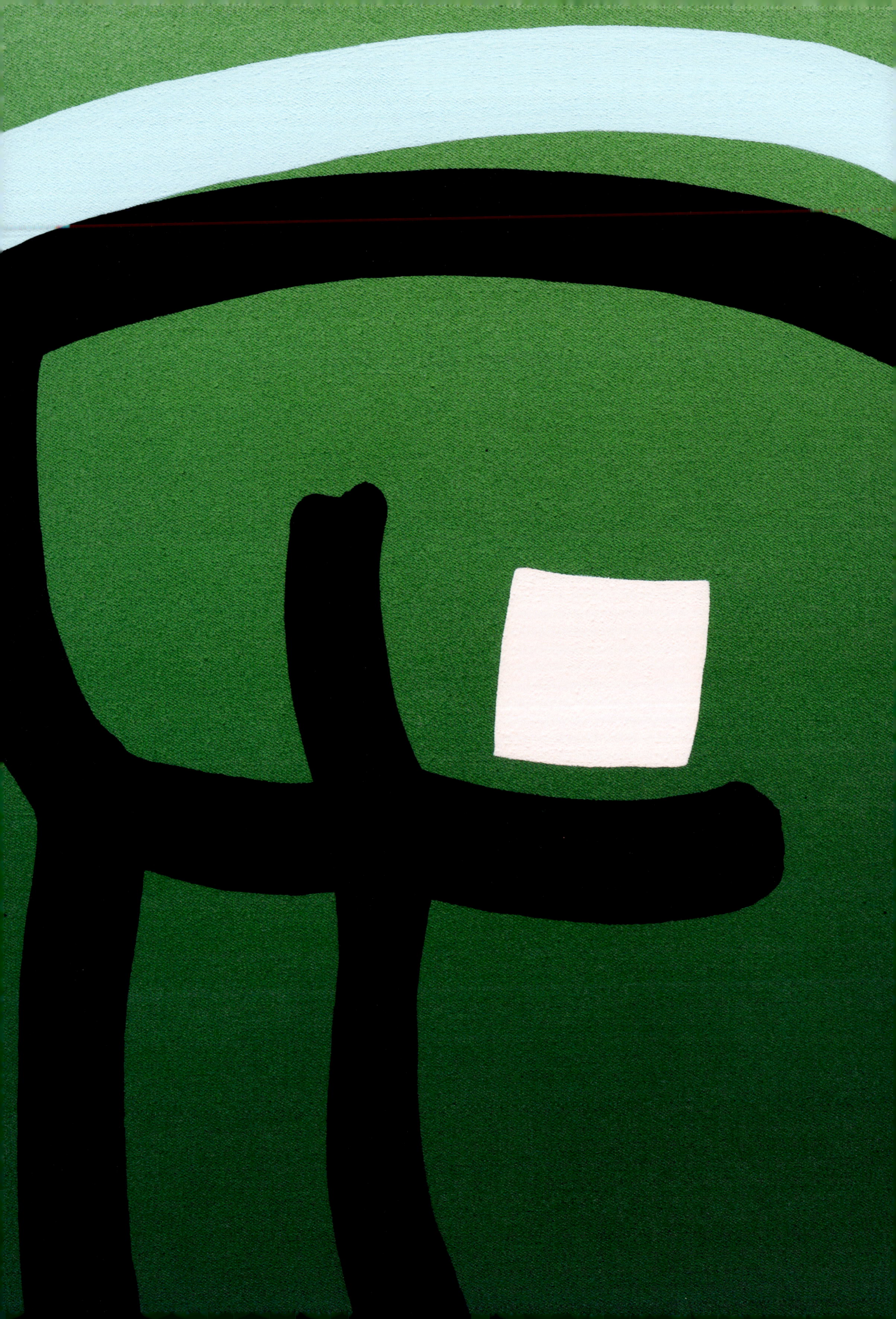

Art Cologne (DE), rodolphe janssen, 2022

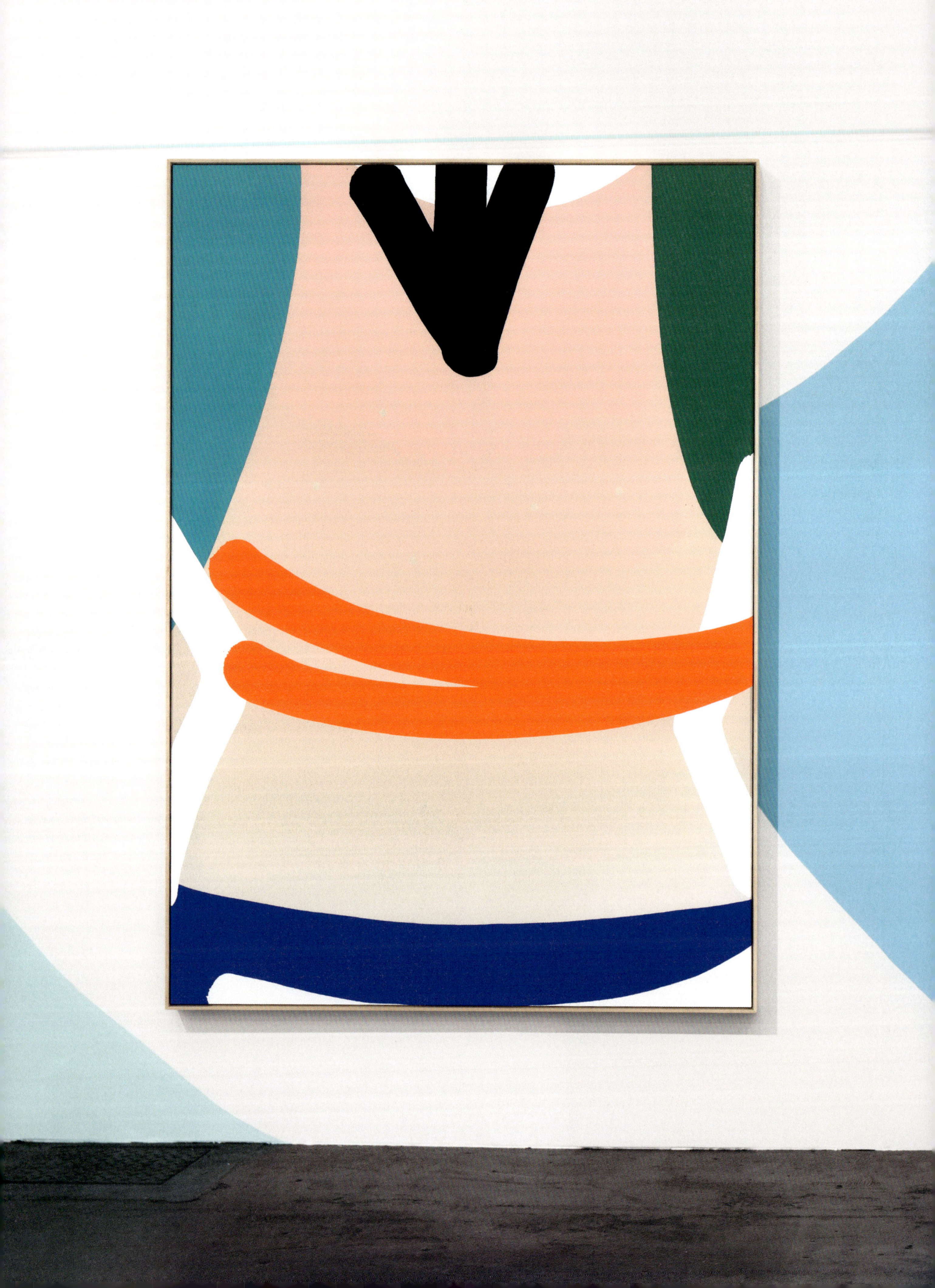

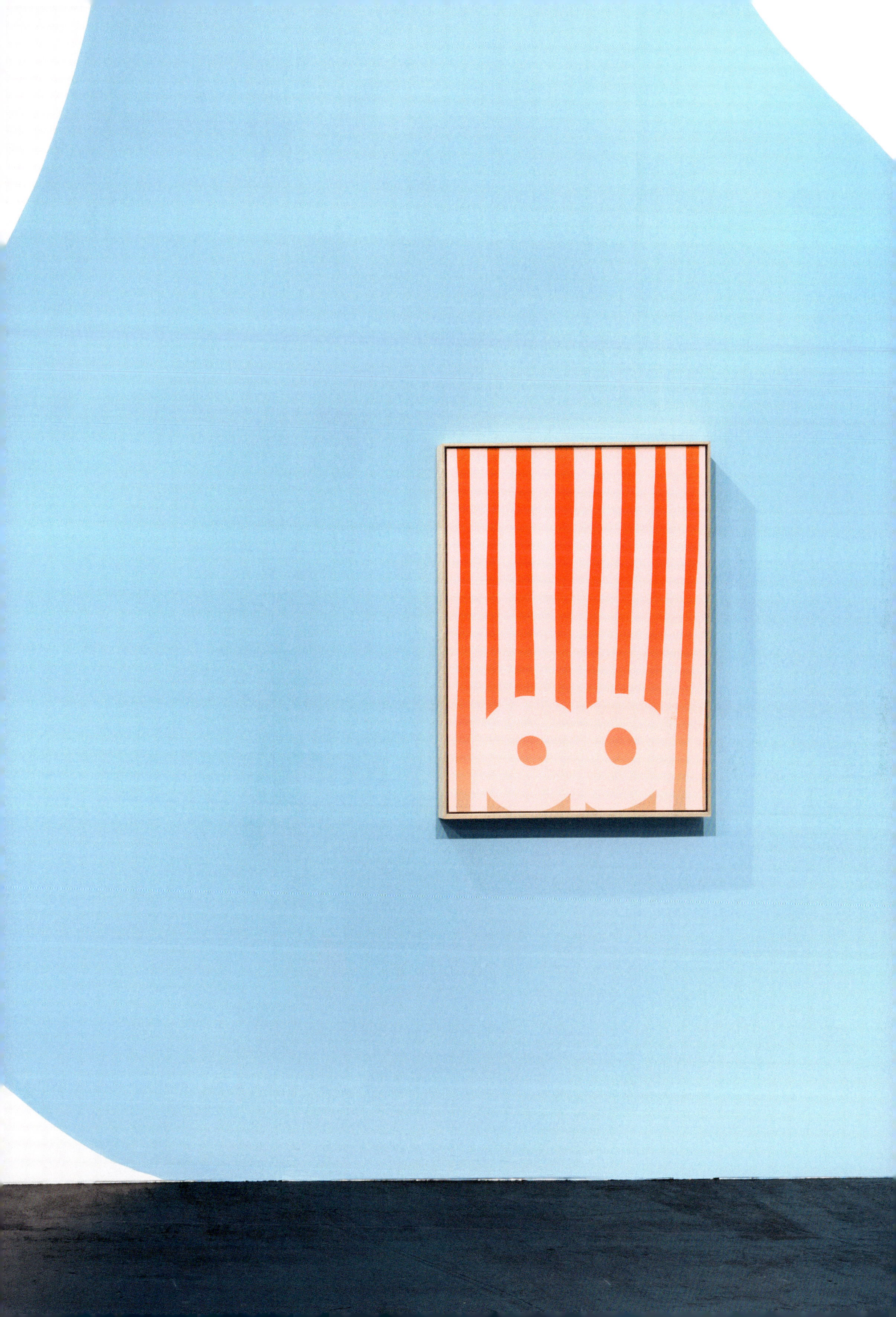

Glen, SOSU Østjylland, Aarhus (DK), 2021

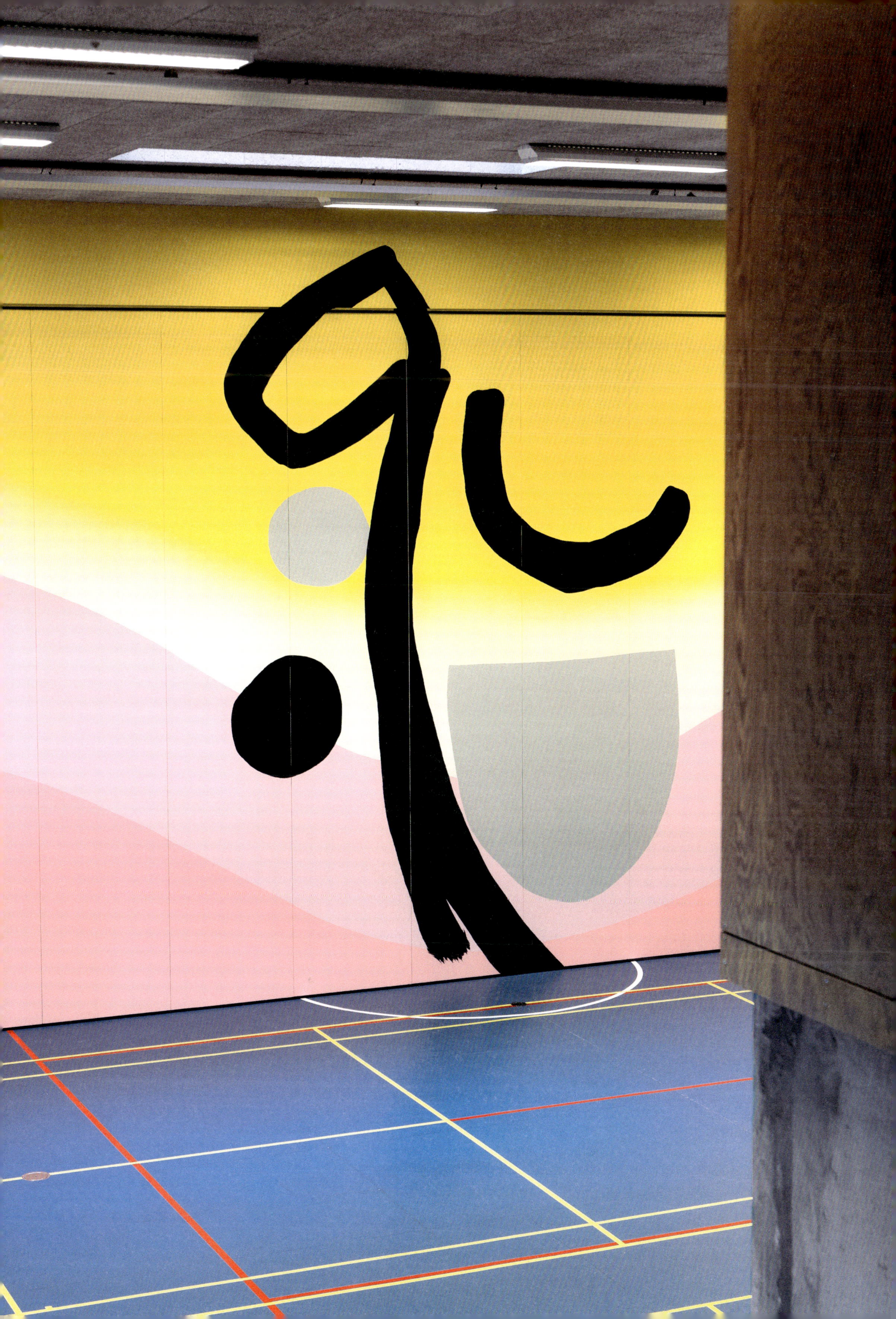

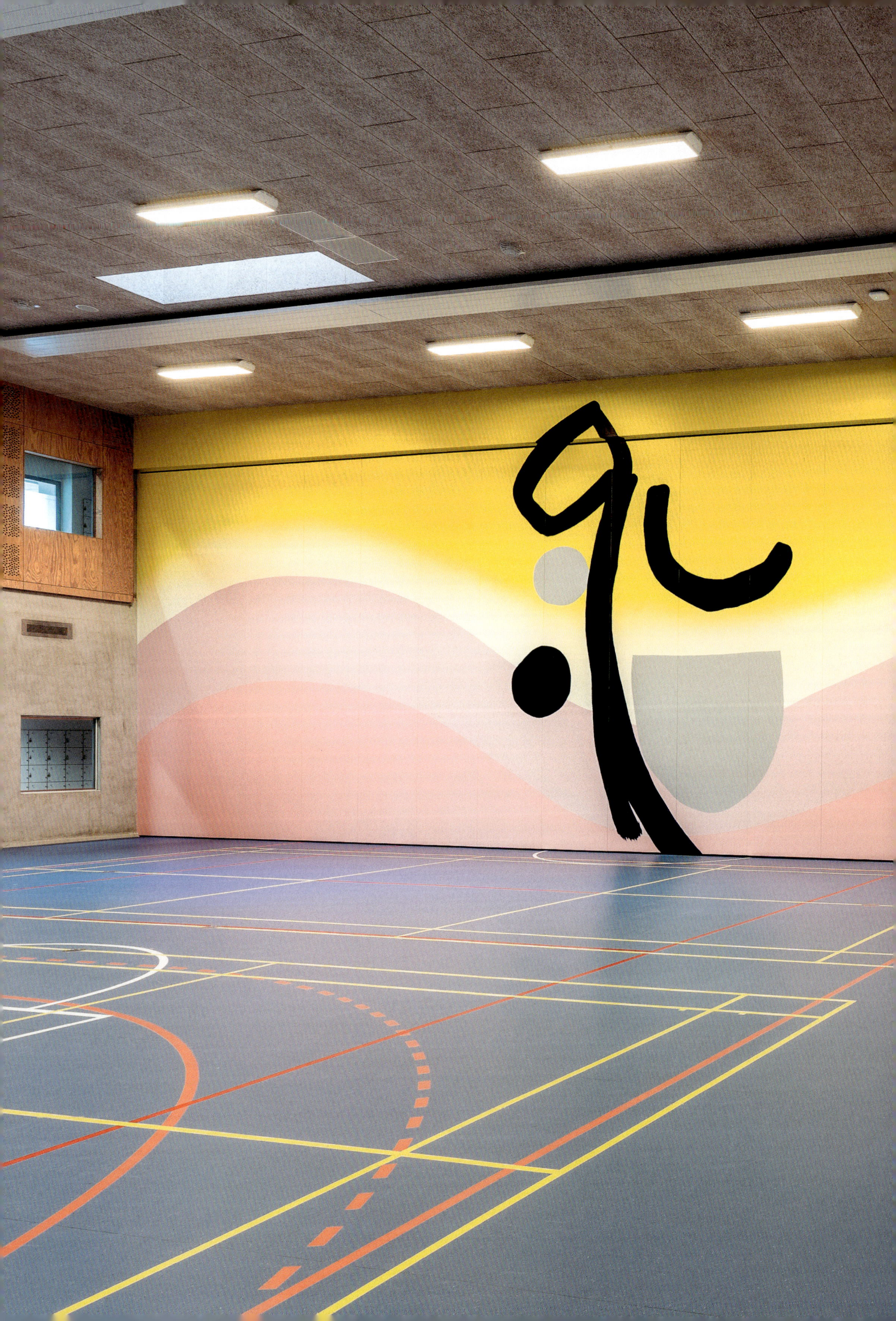

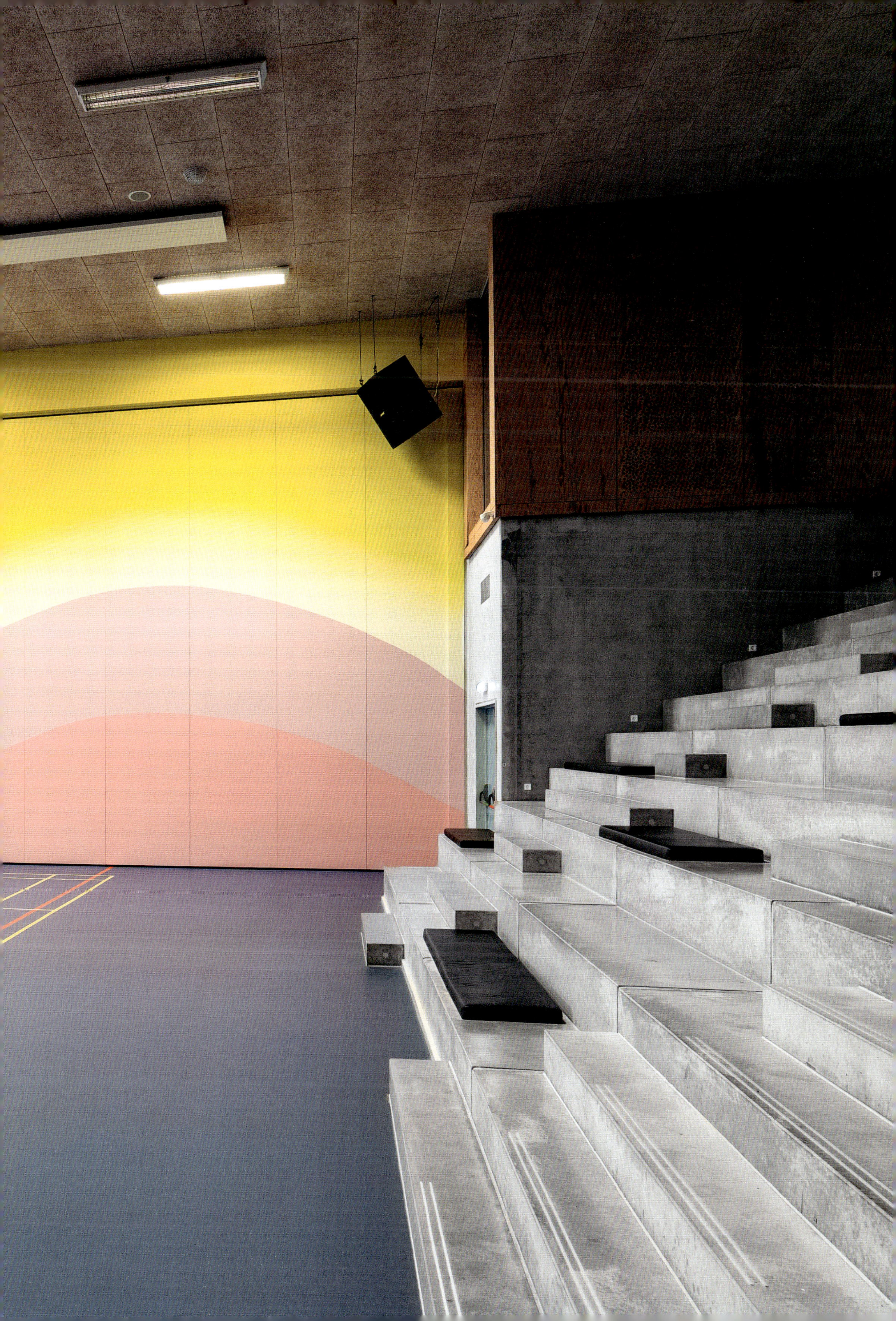

Eigenbrötler, EIGEN + ART Lab, Berlin (DE), 2021

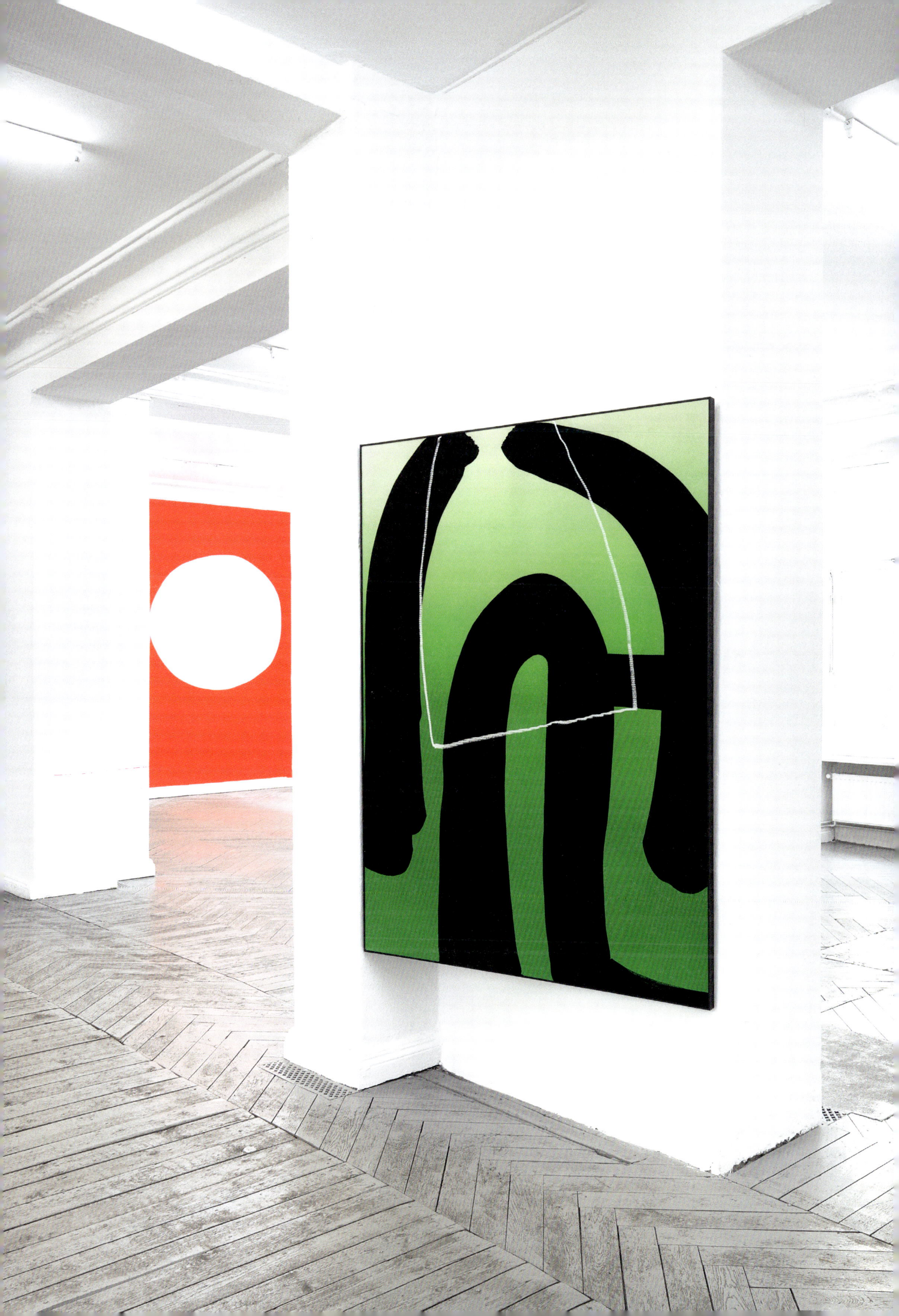

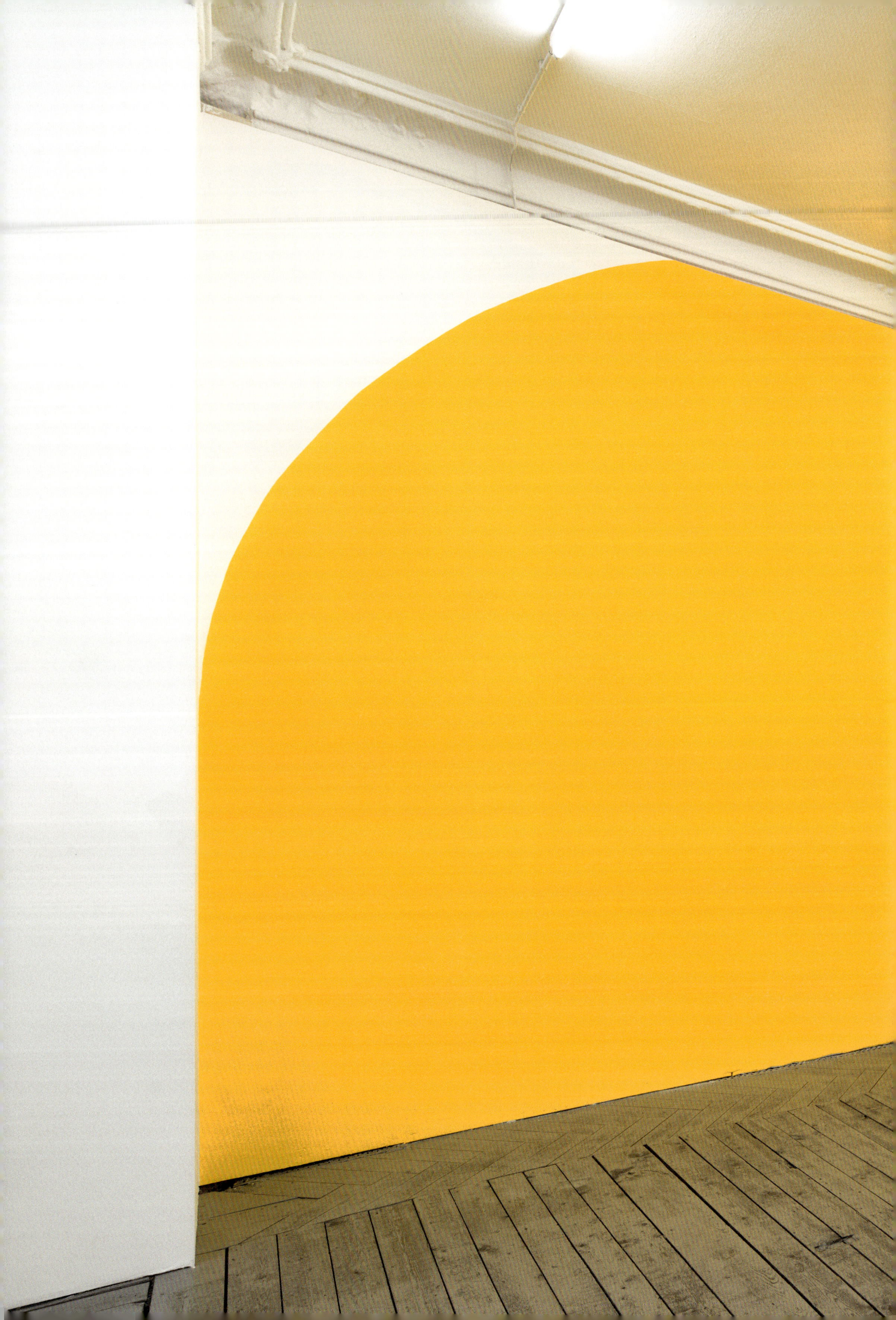

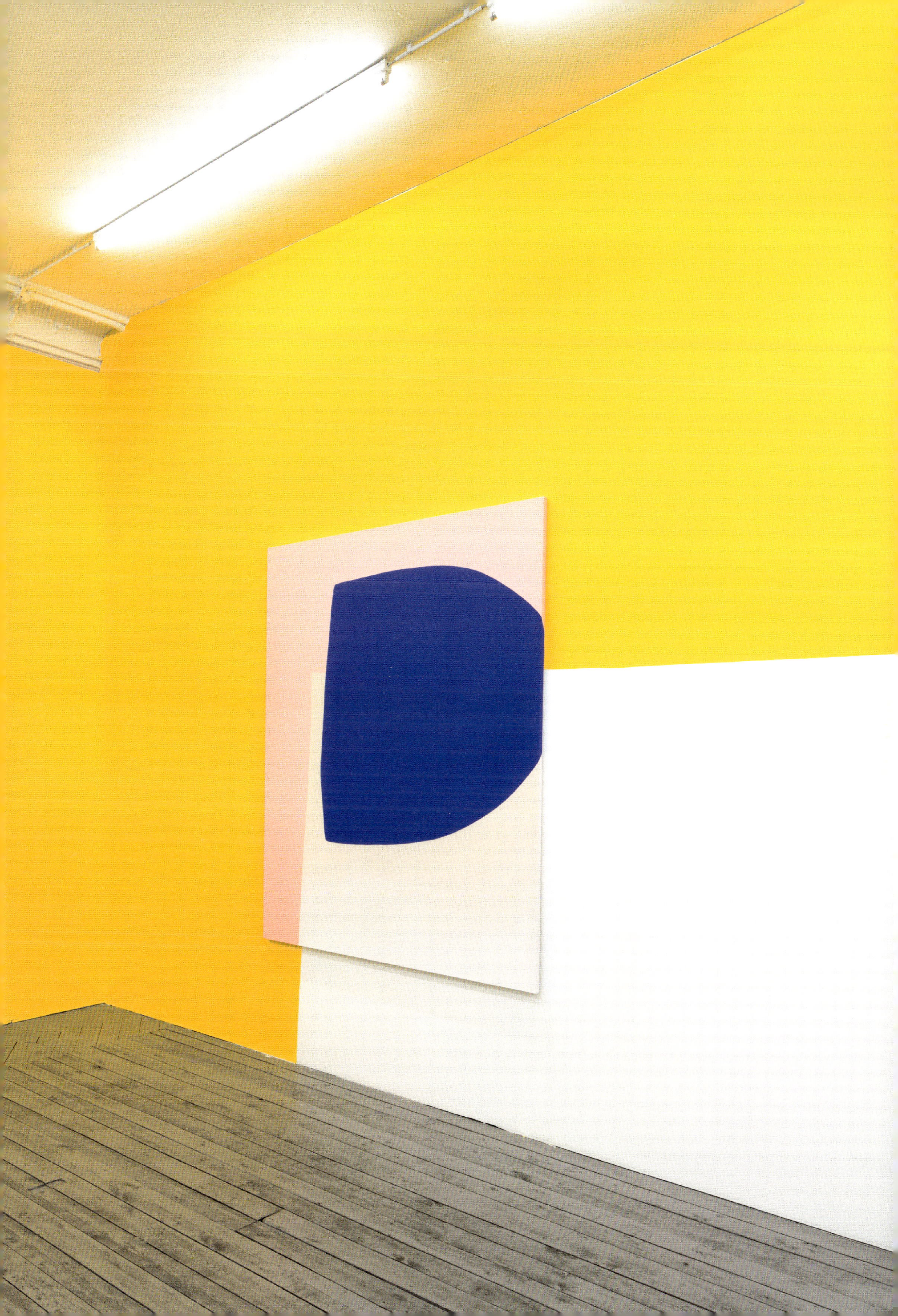

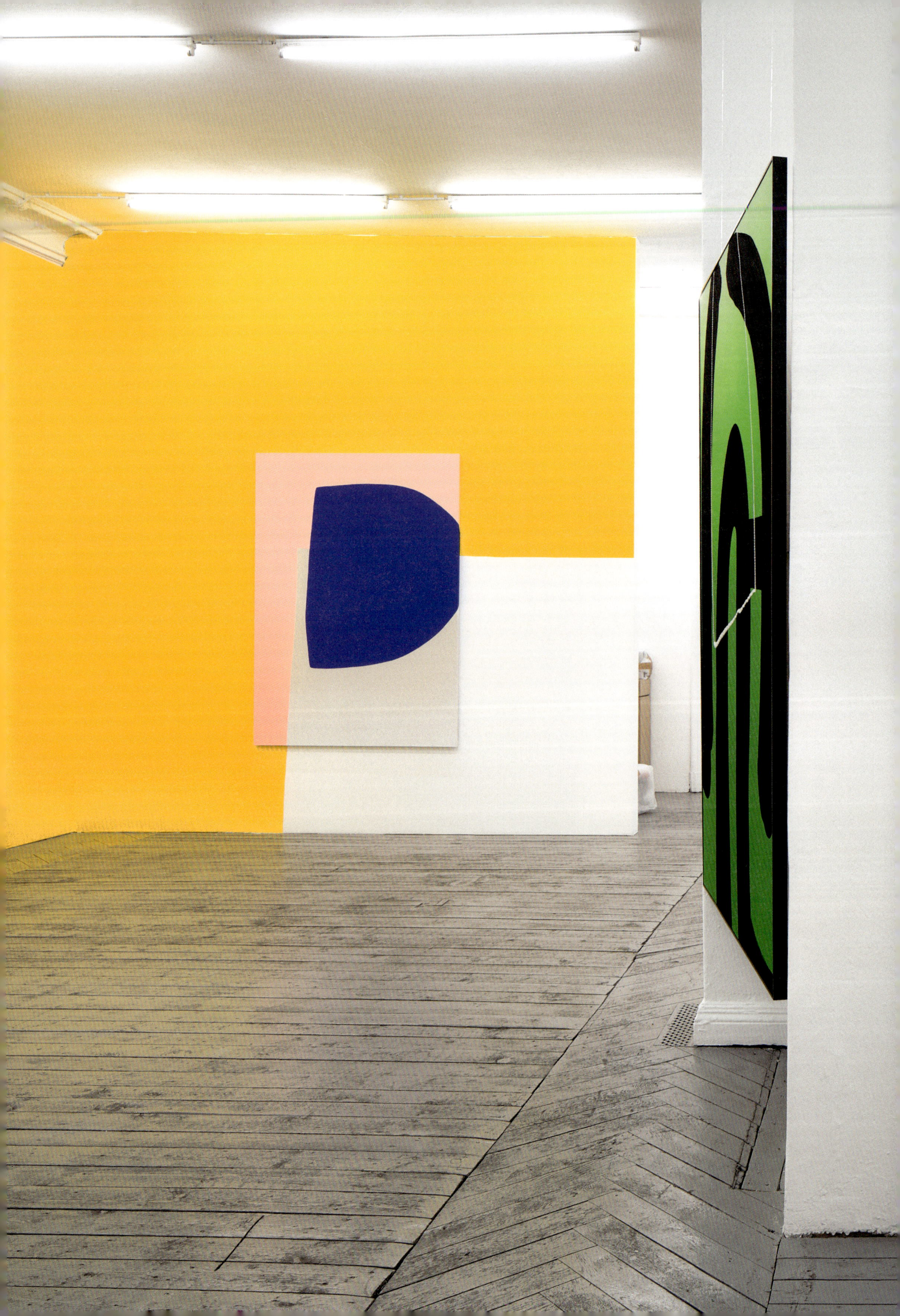

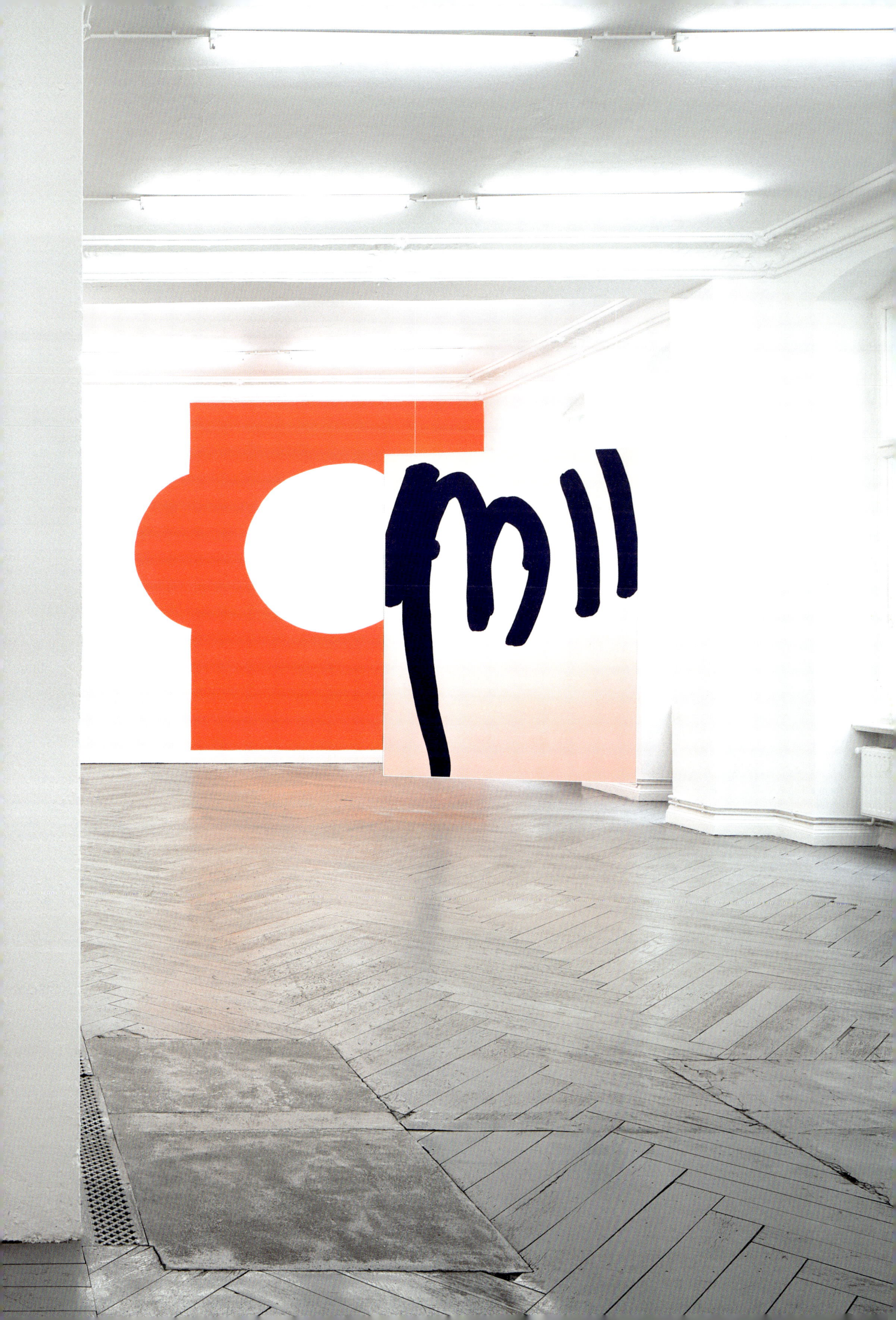

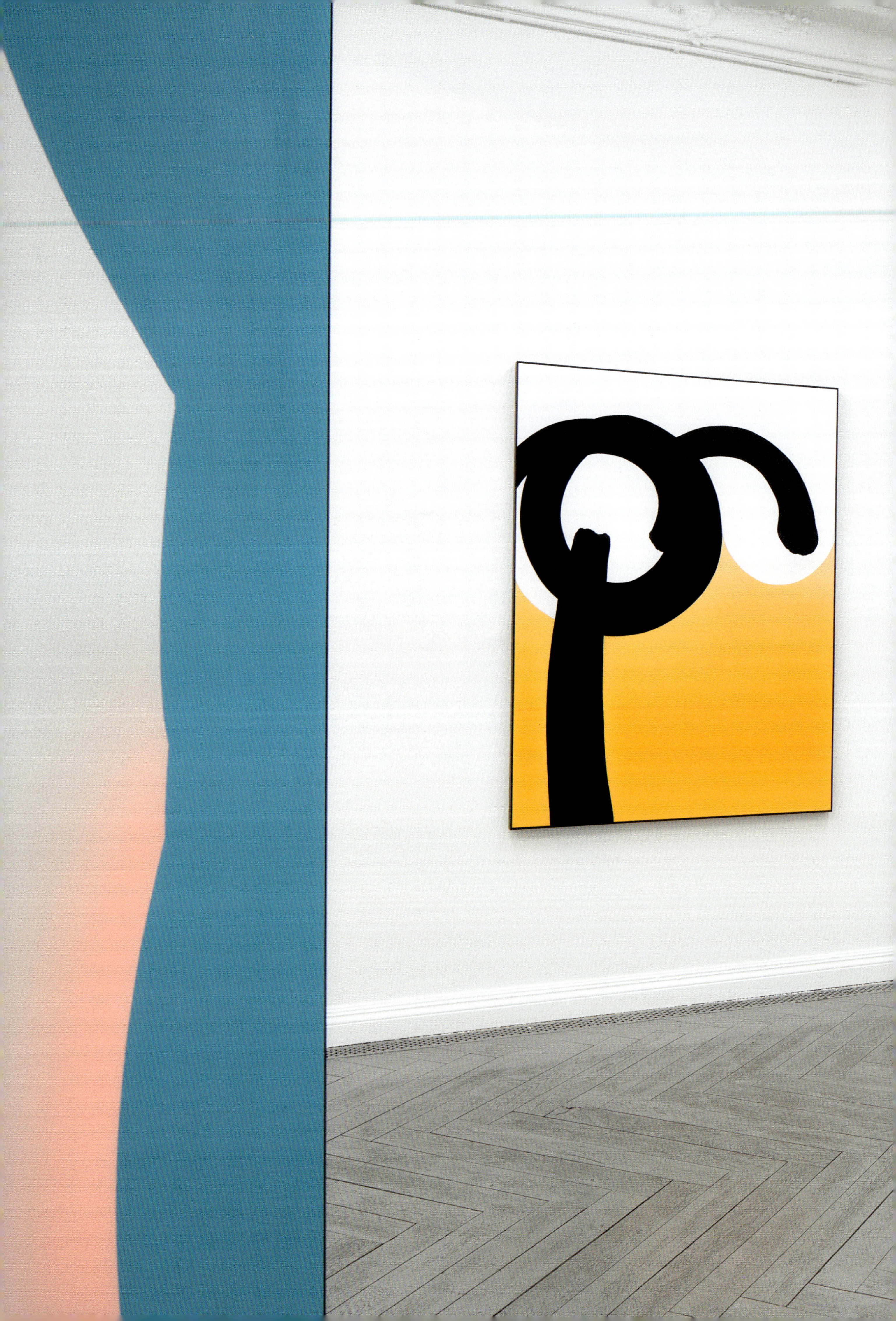

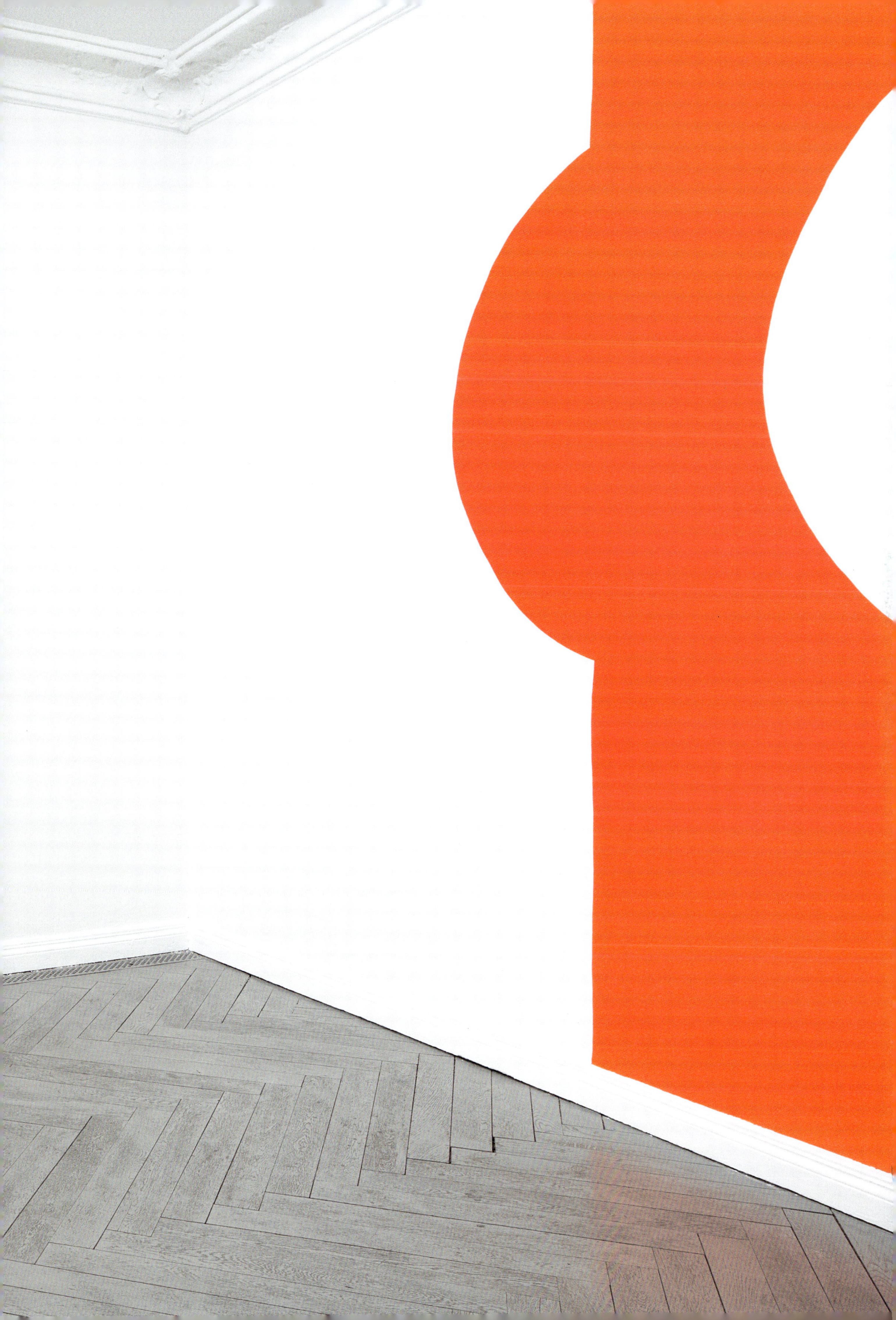

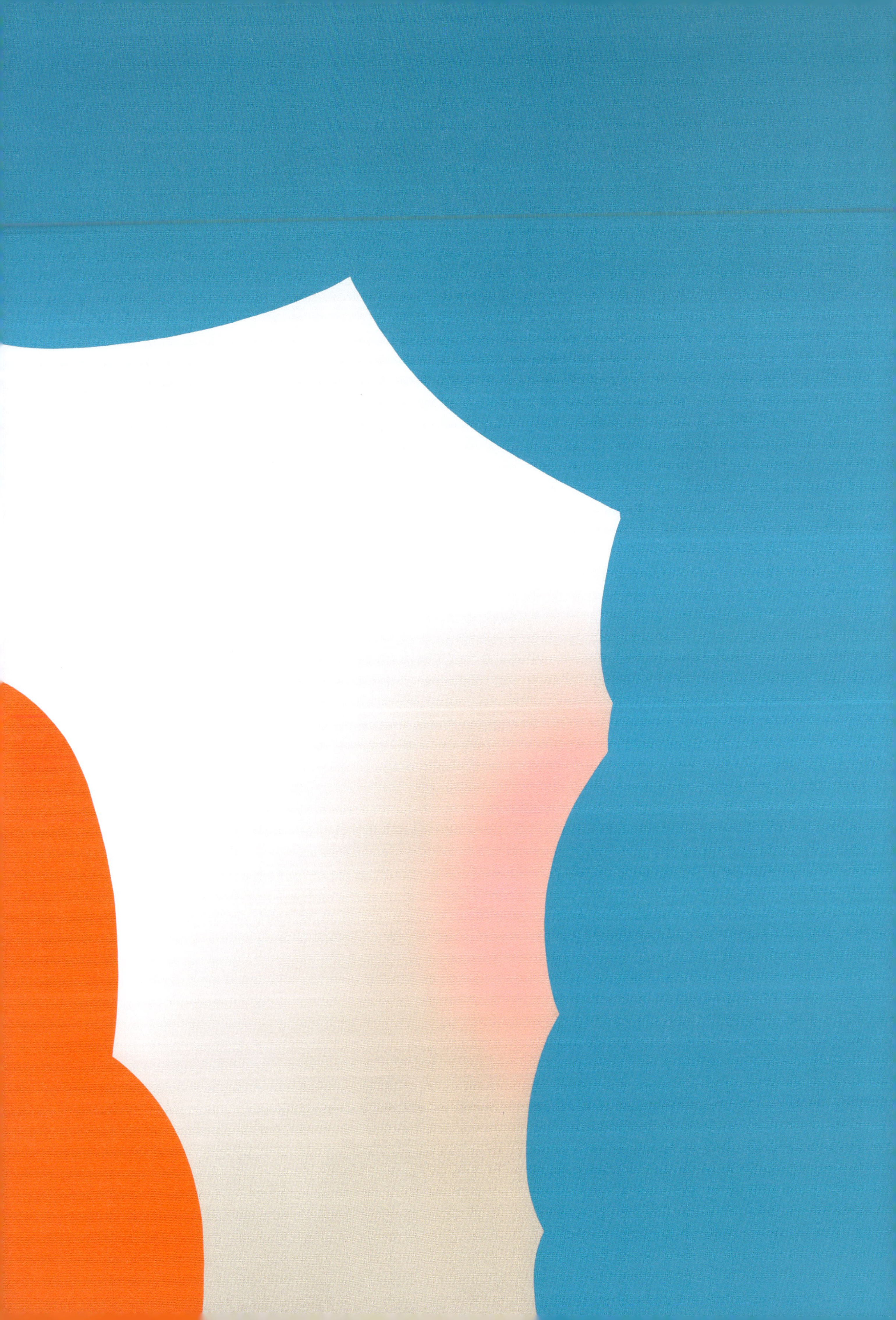

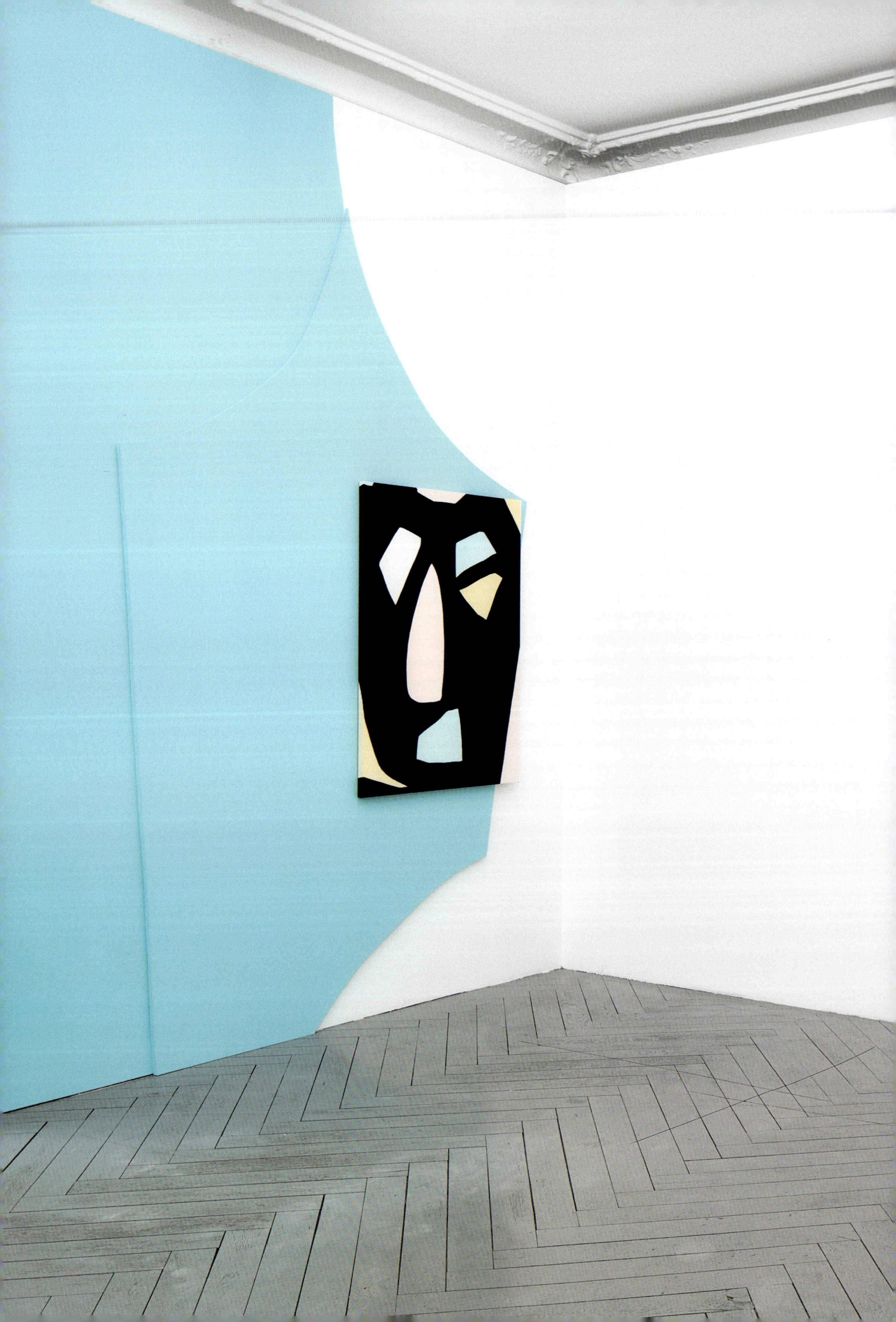

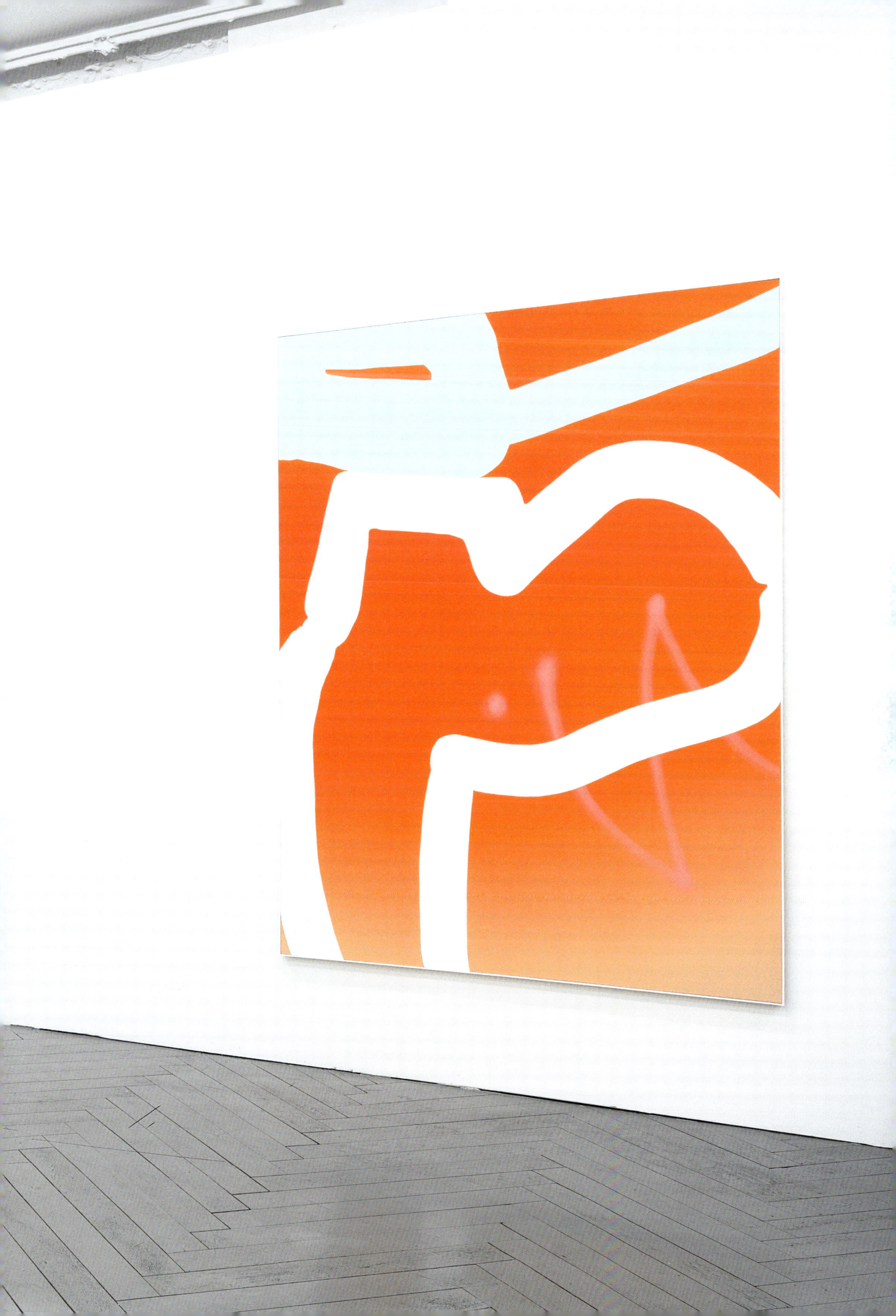

Tit for Tat, Galleri Nicolai Wallner, Copenhagen (DK), 2020

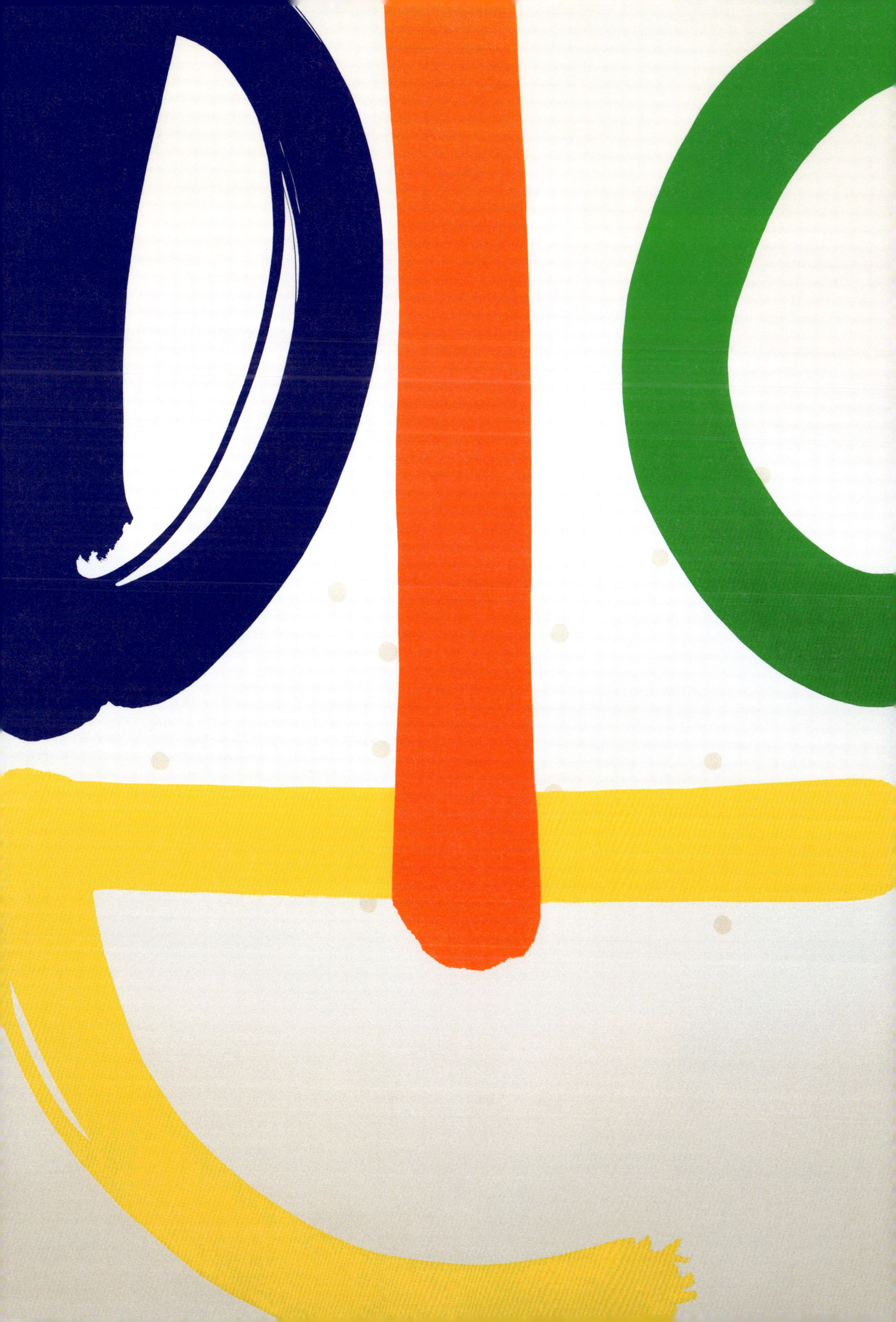

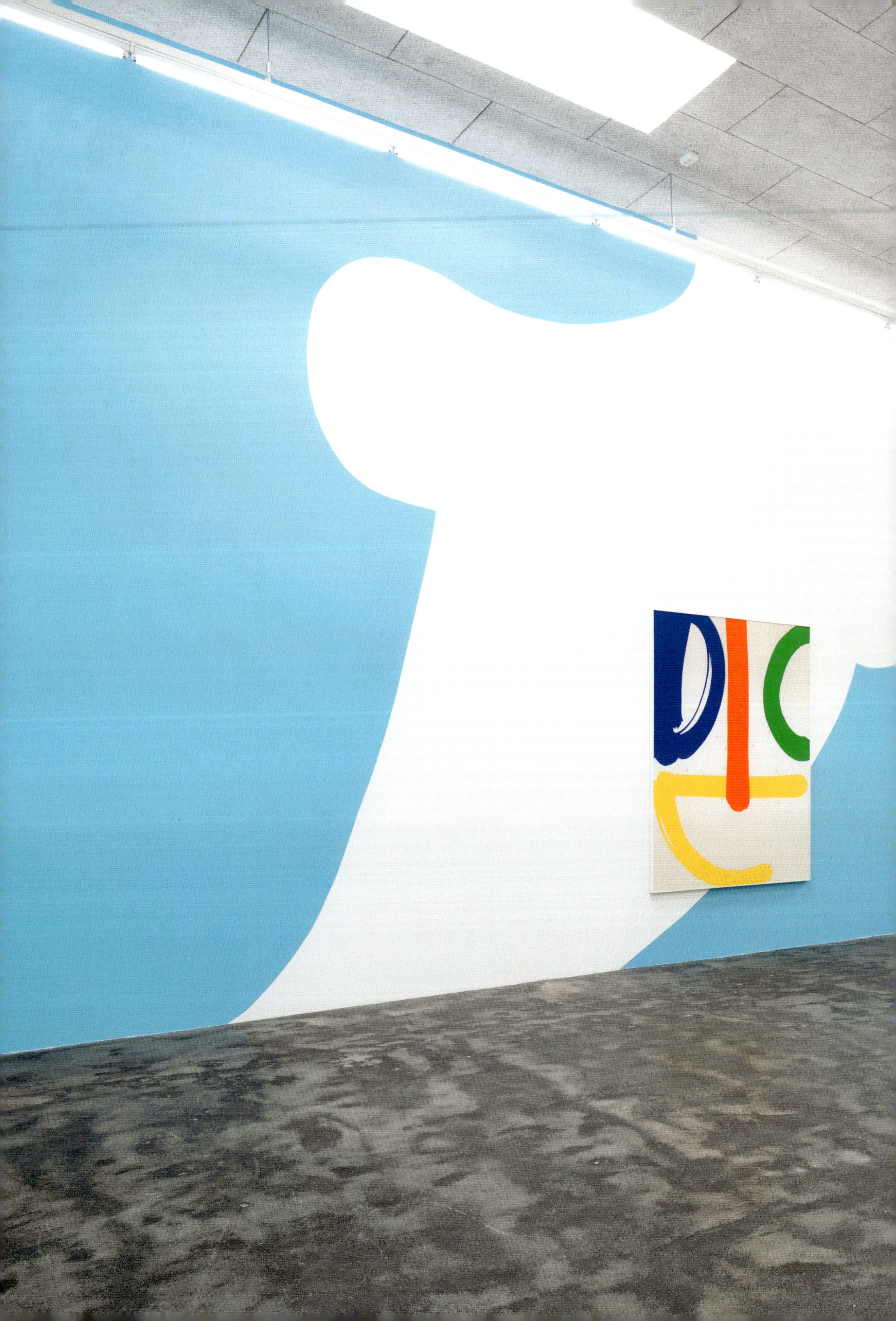

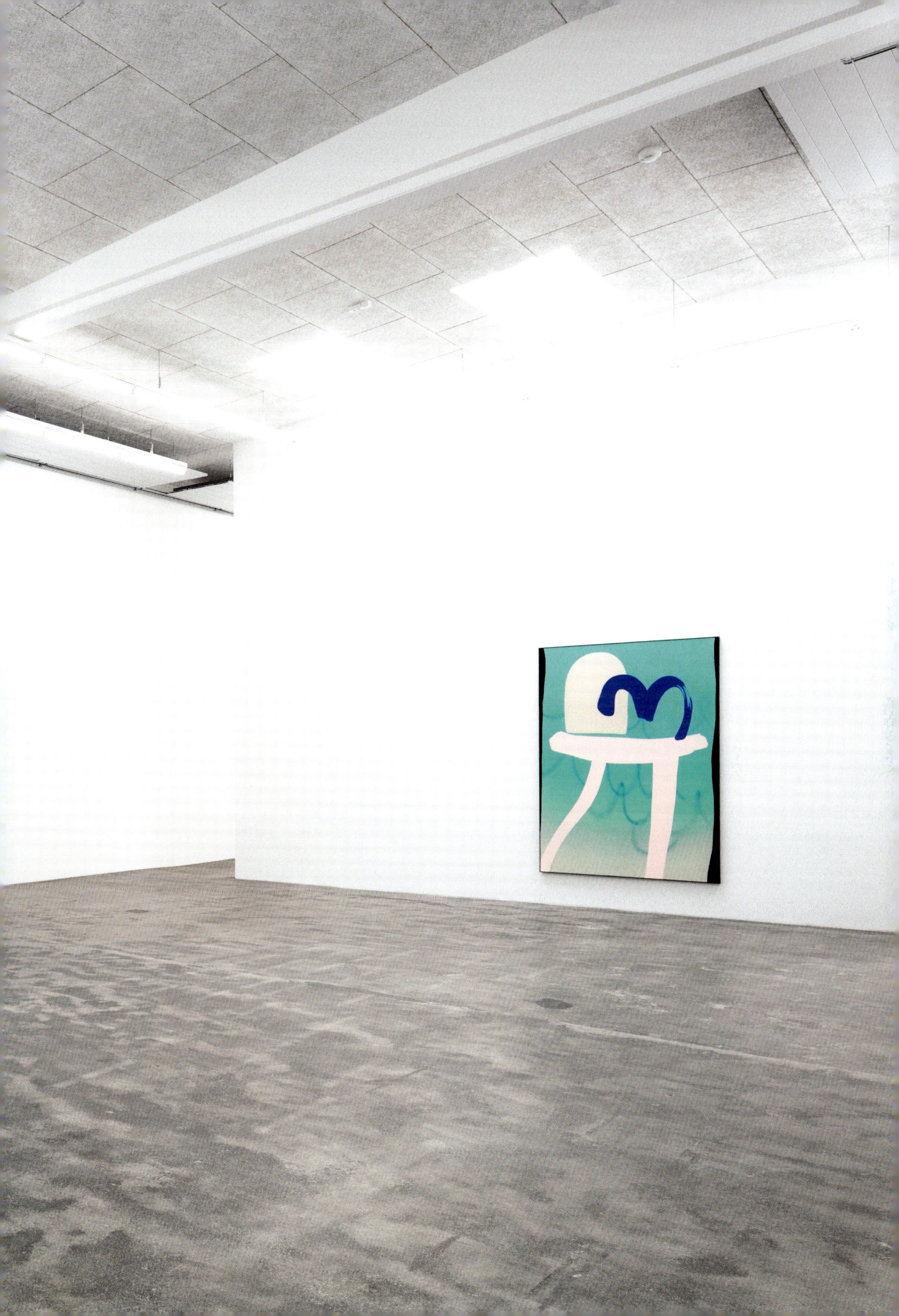

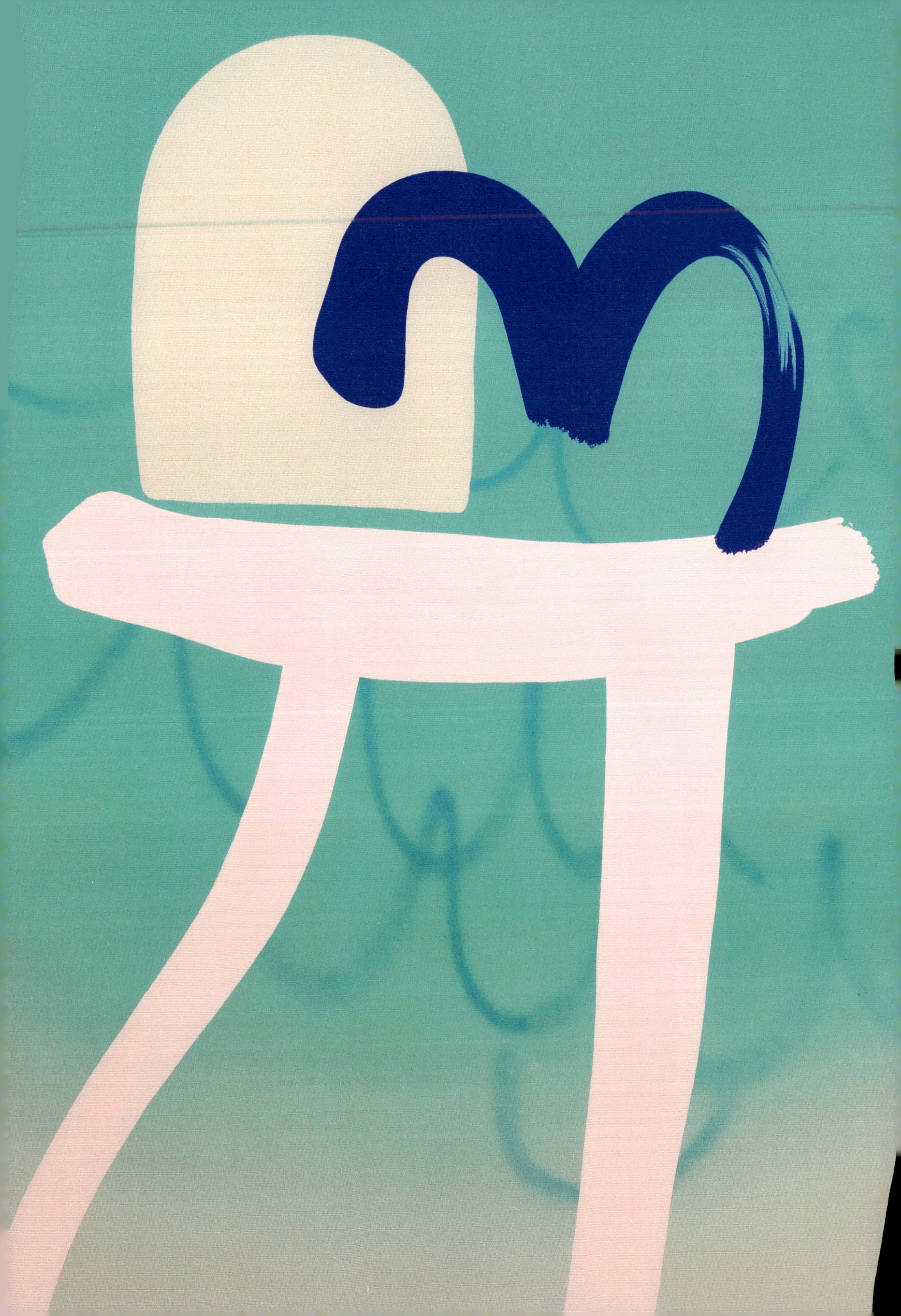

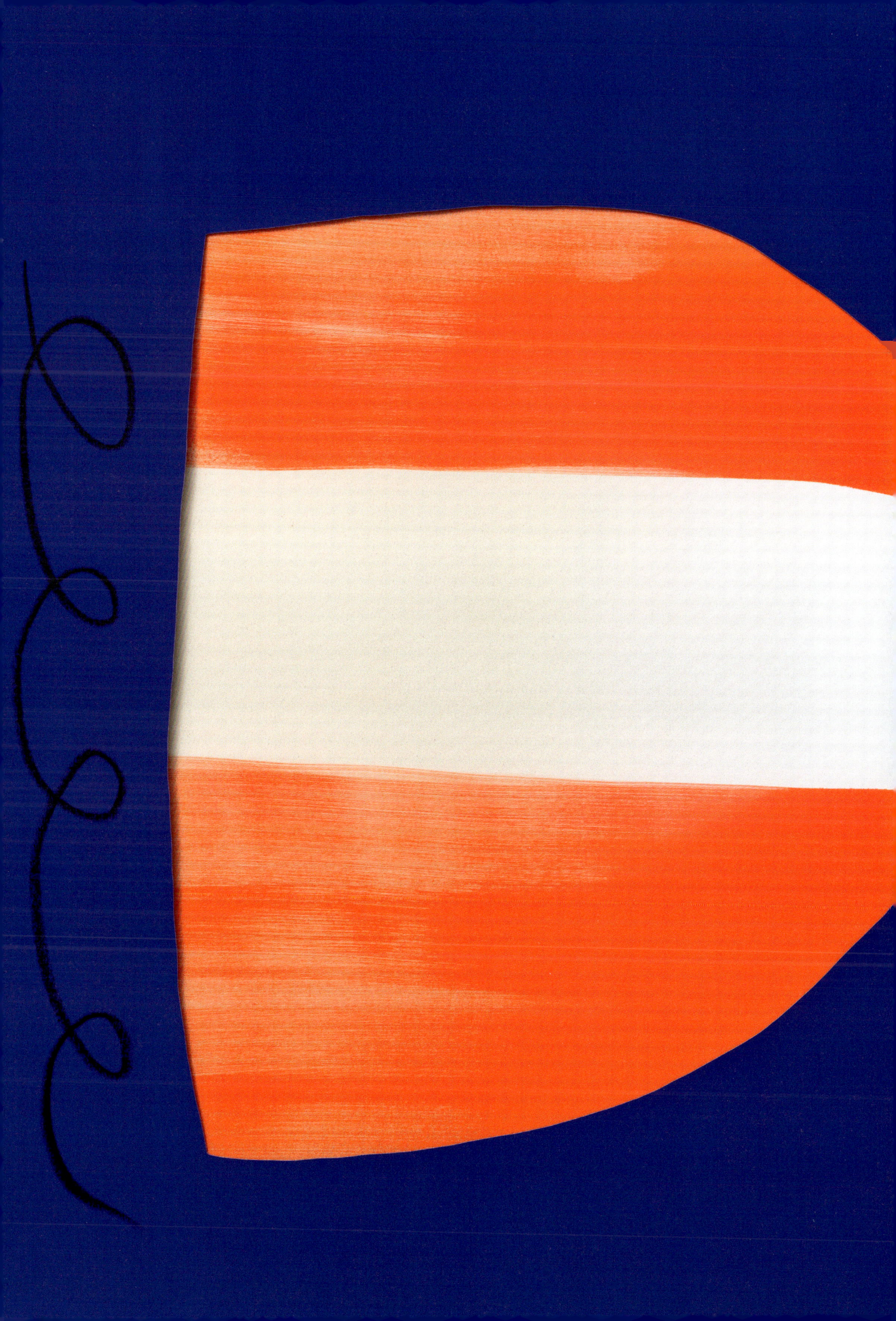

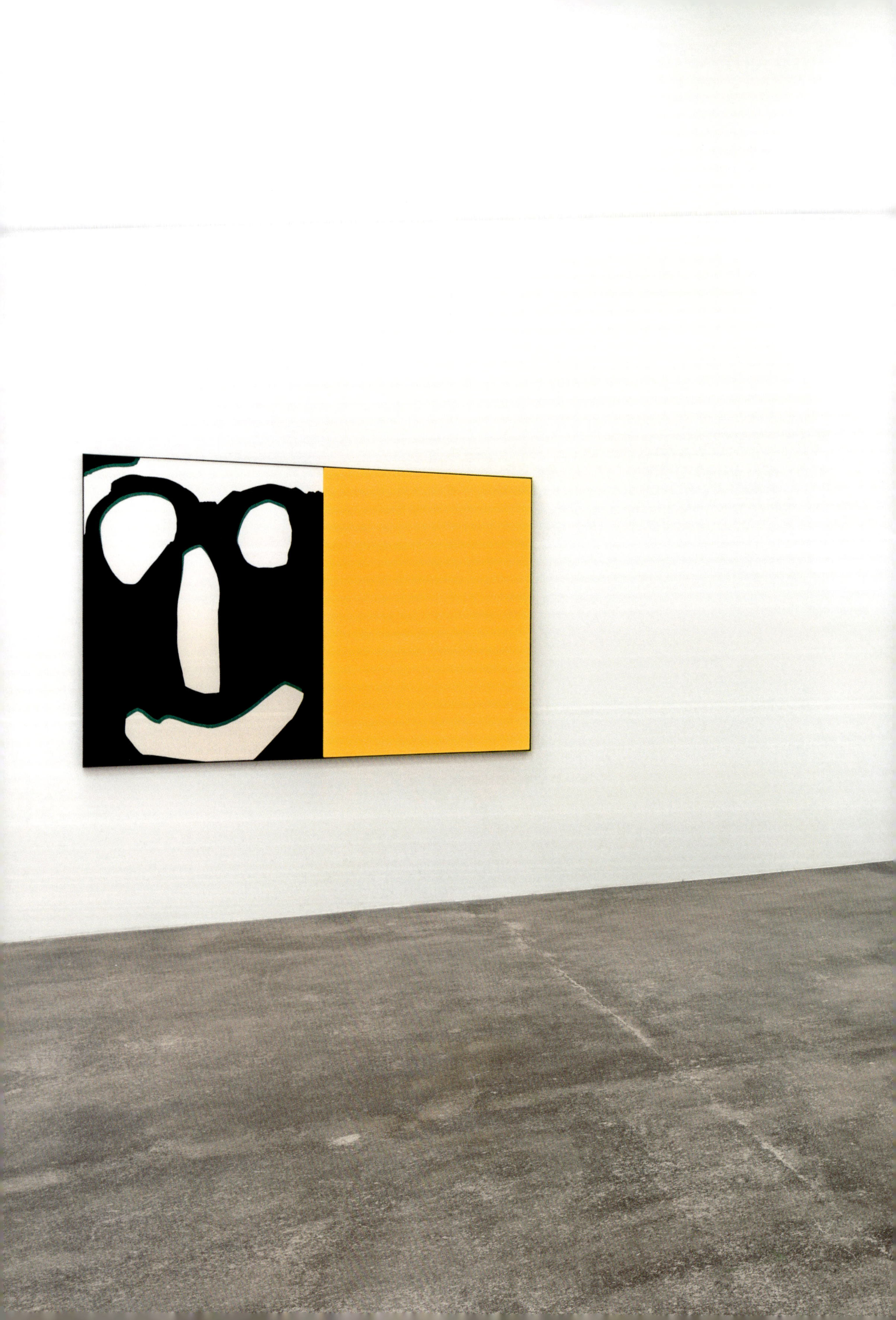

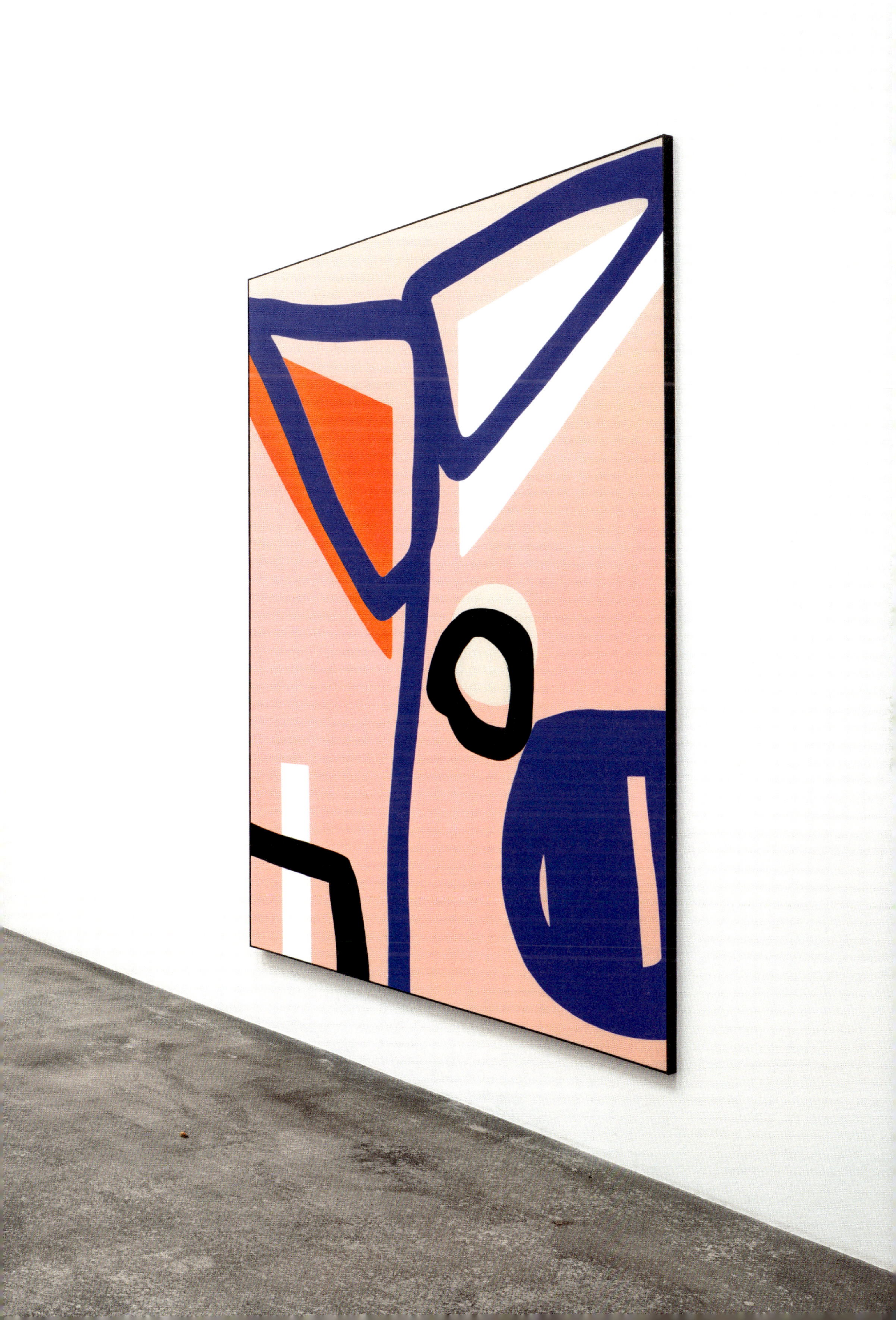

Now! Painting in Germany Today, Deichtorhallen Hamburg (DE), 2020 / Kunstmuseum Bonn (DE), 2019

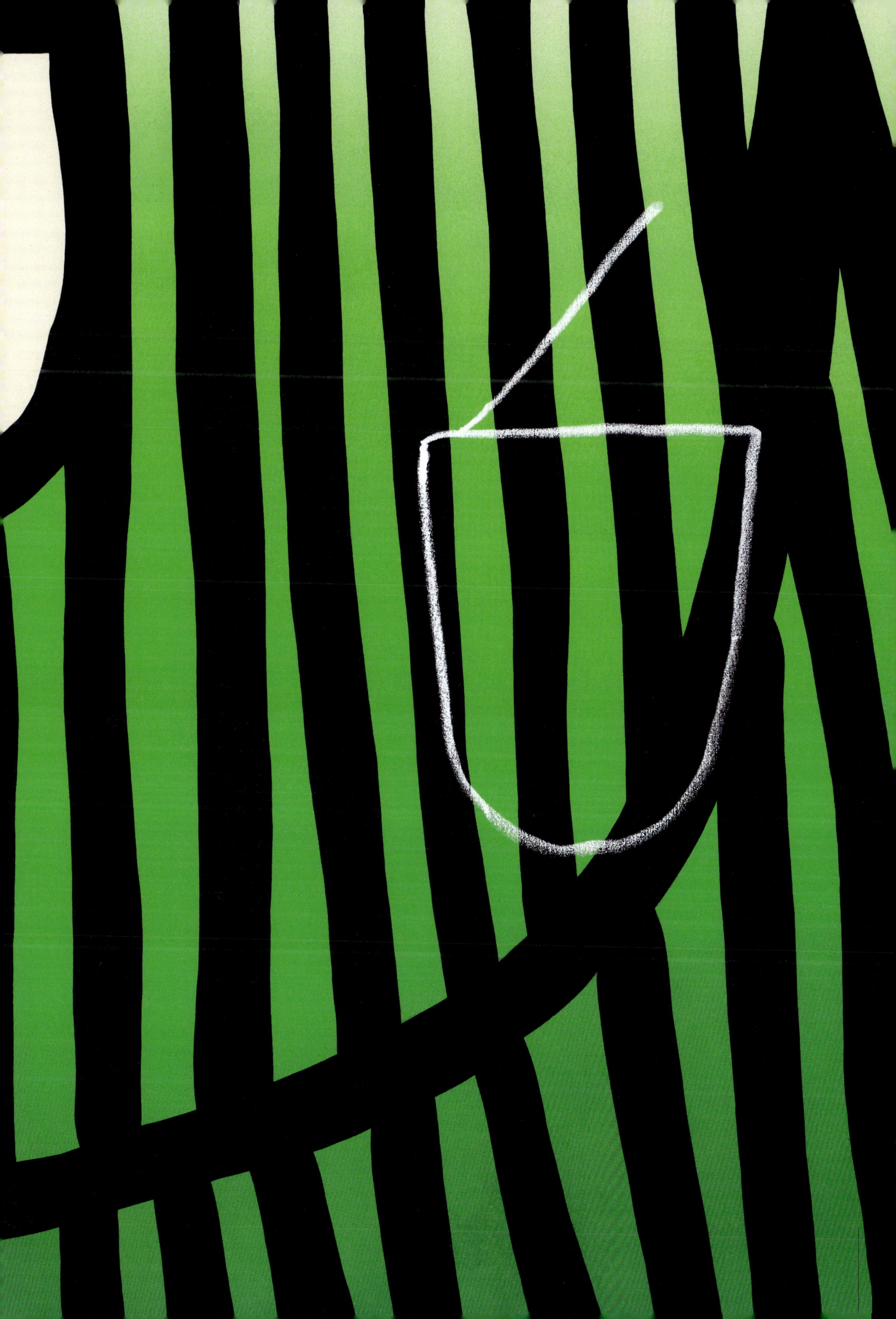

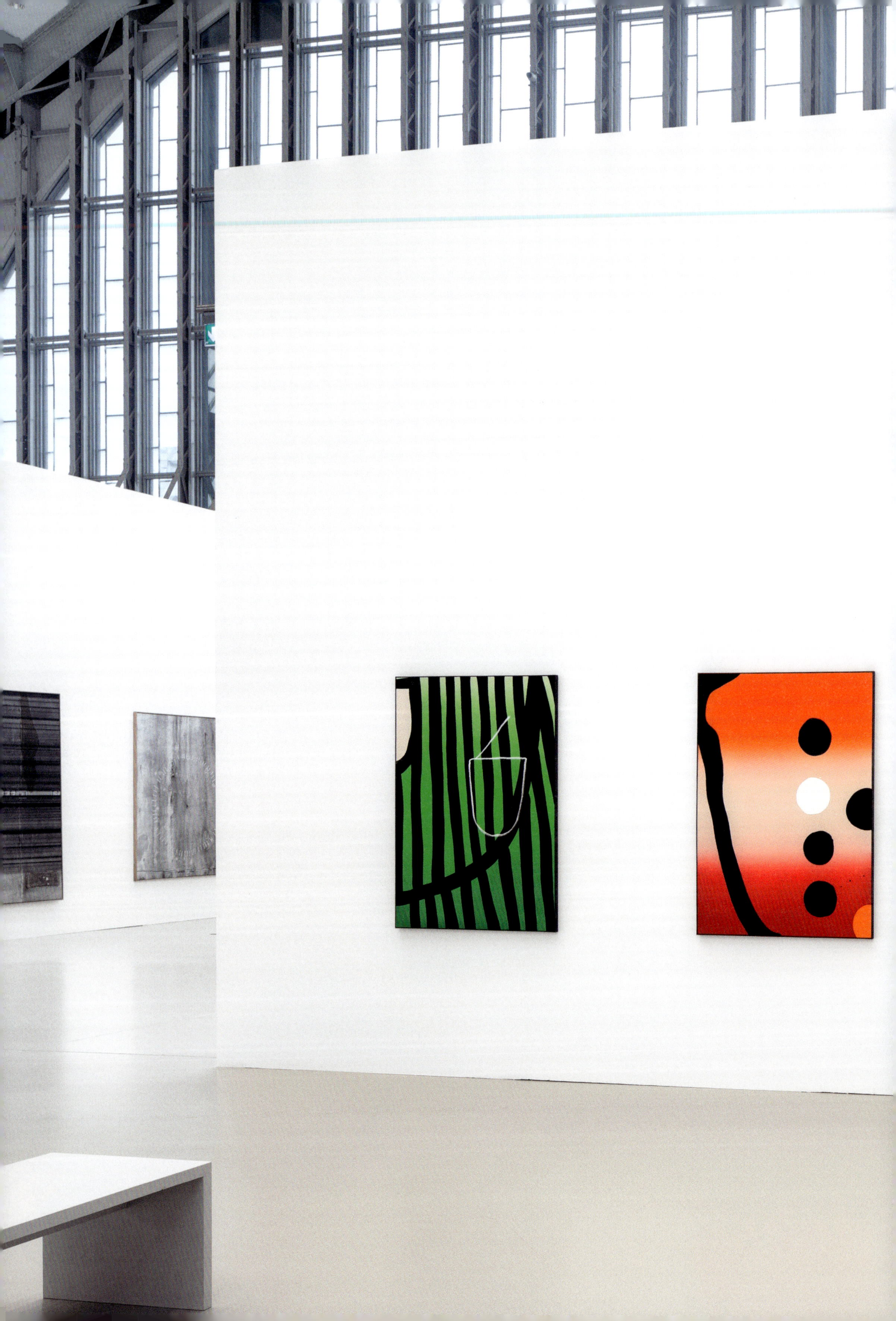

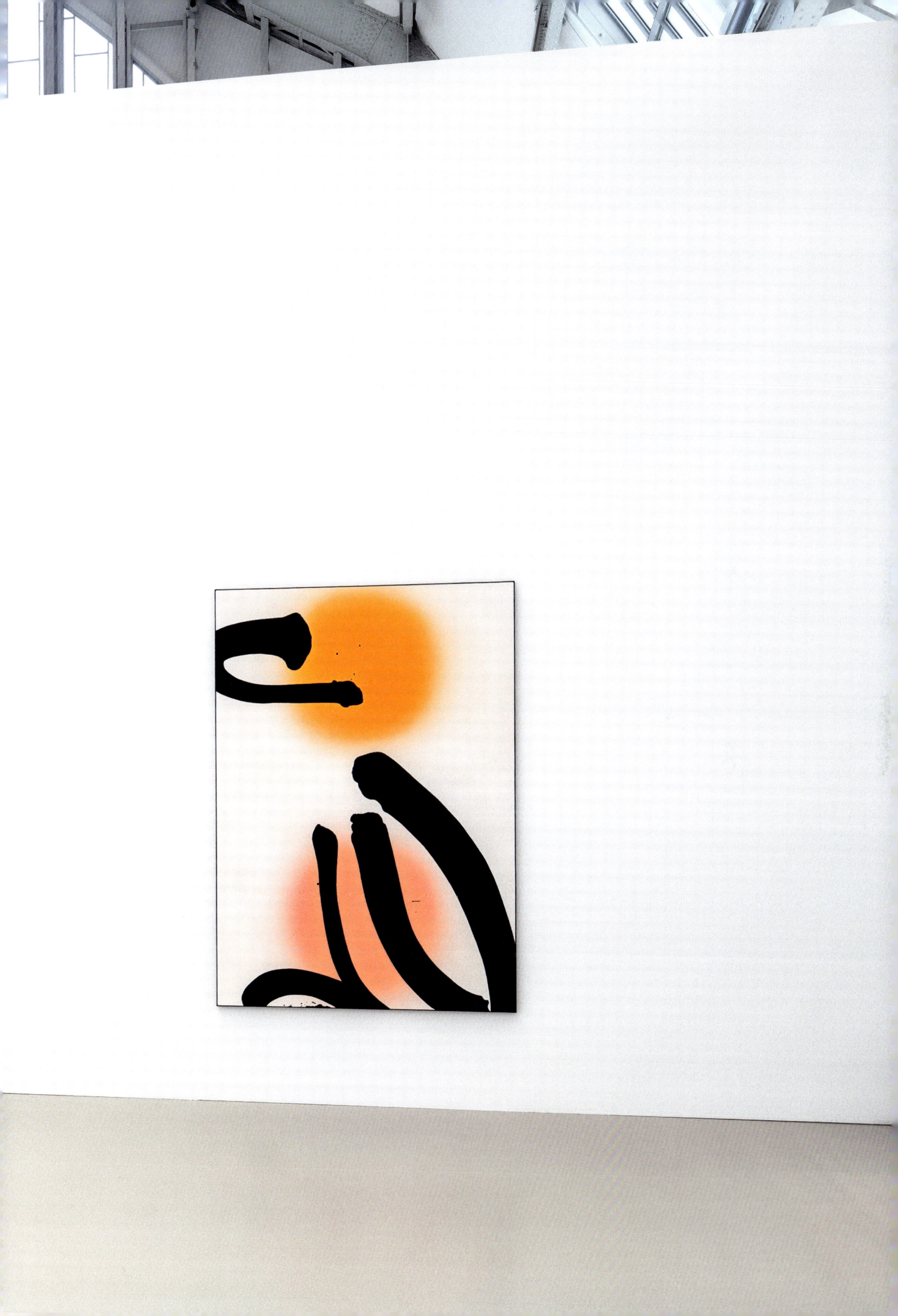

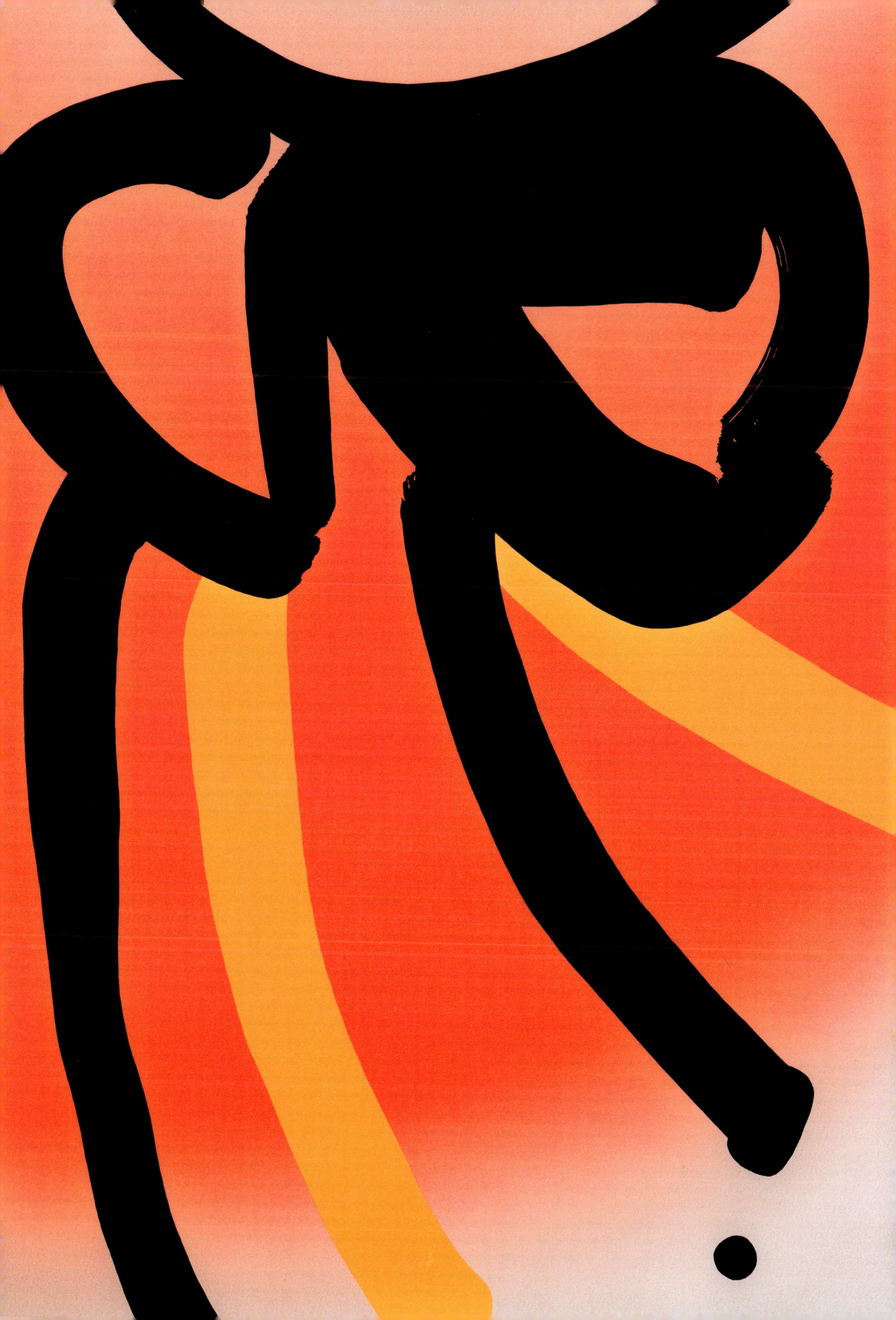

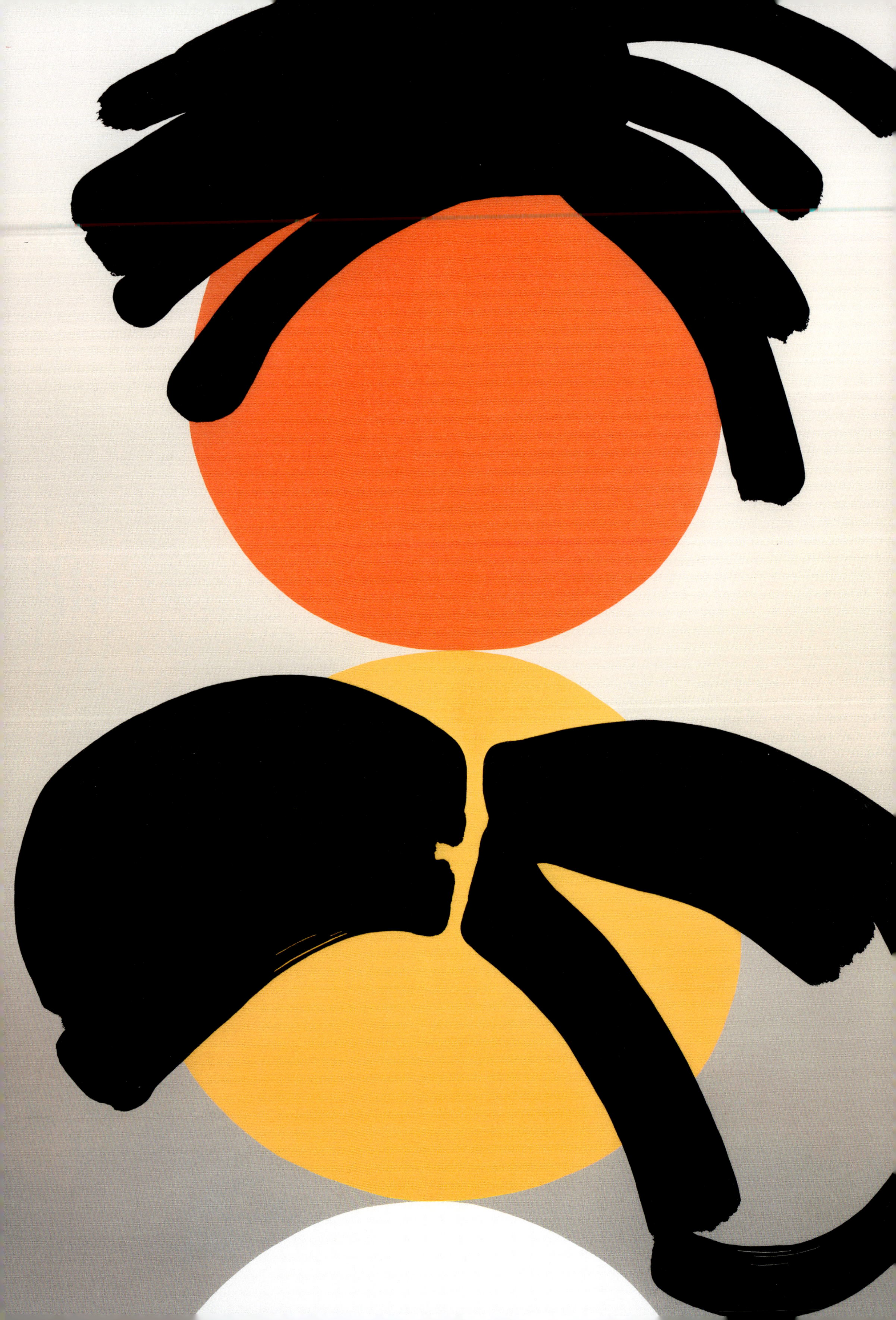

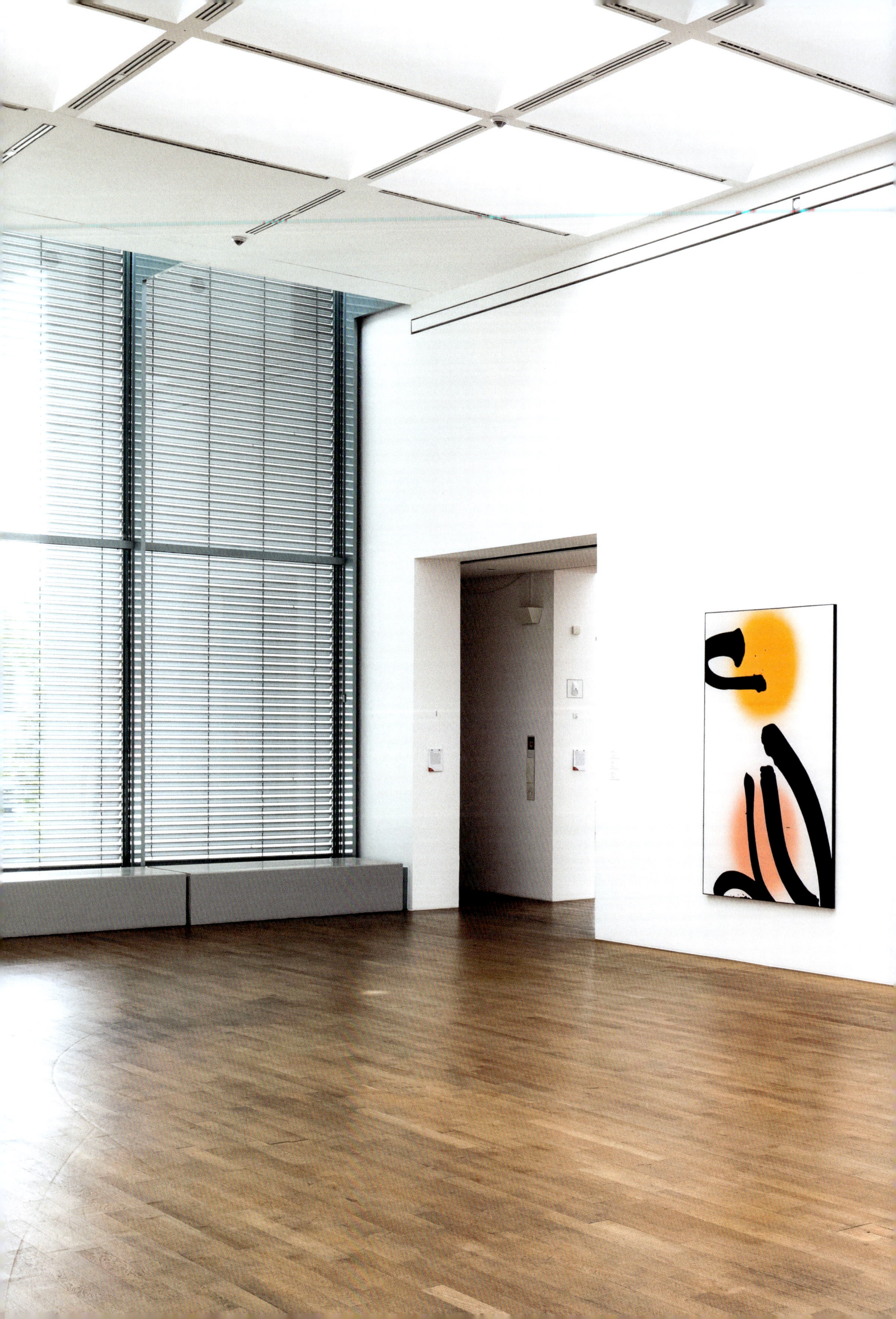

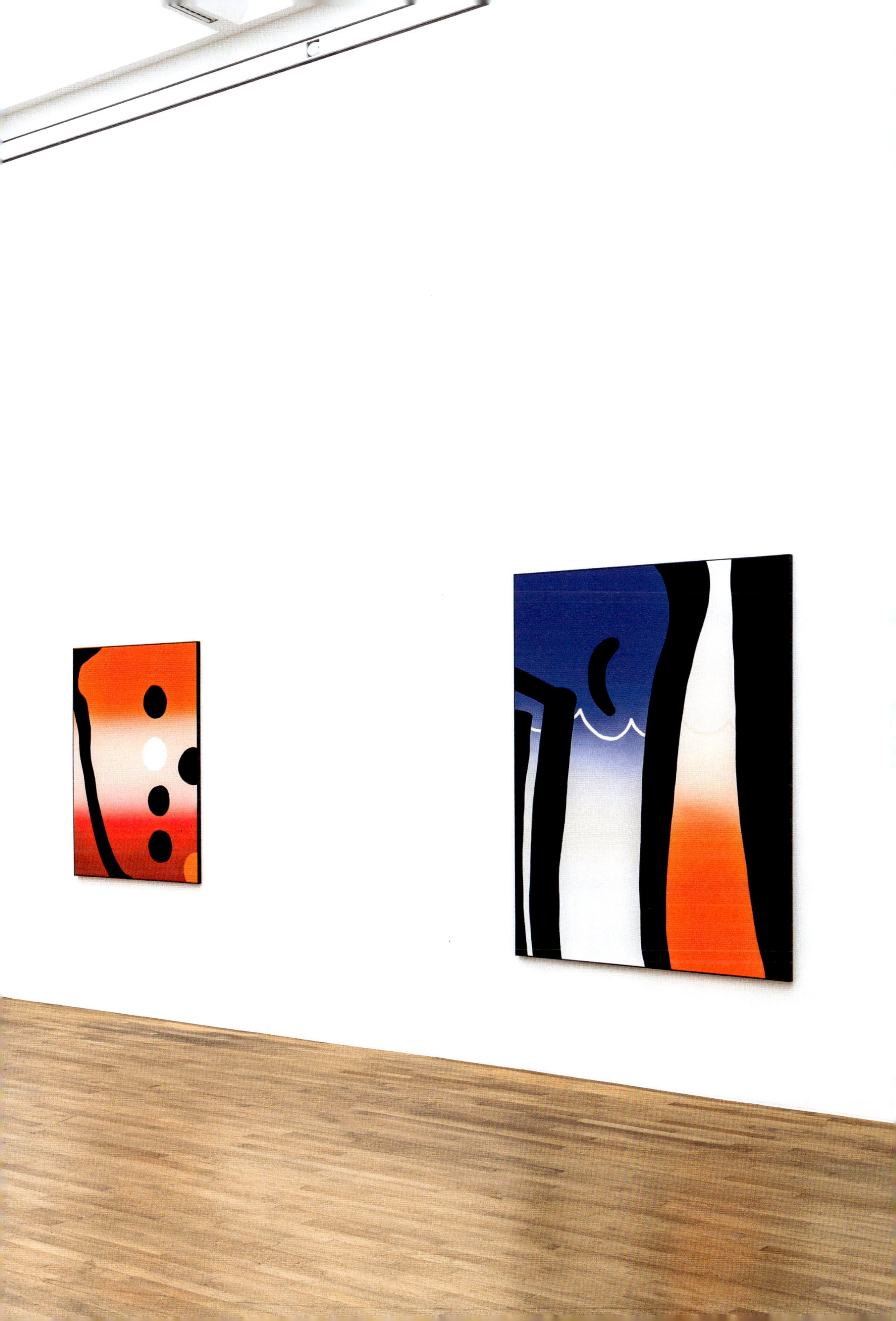

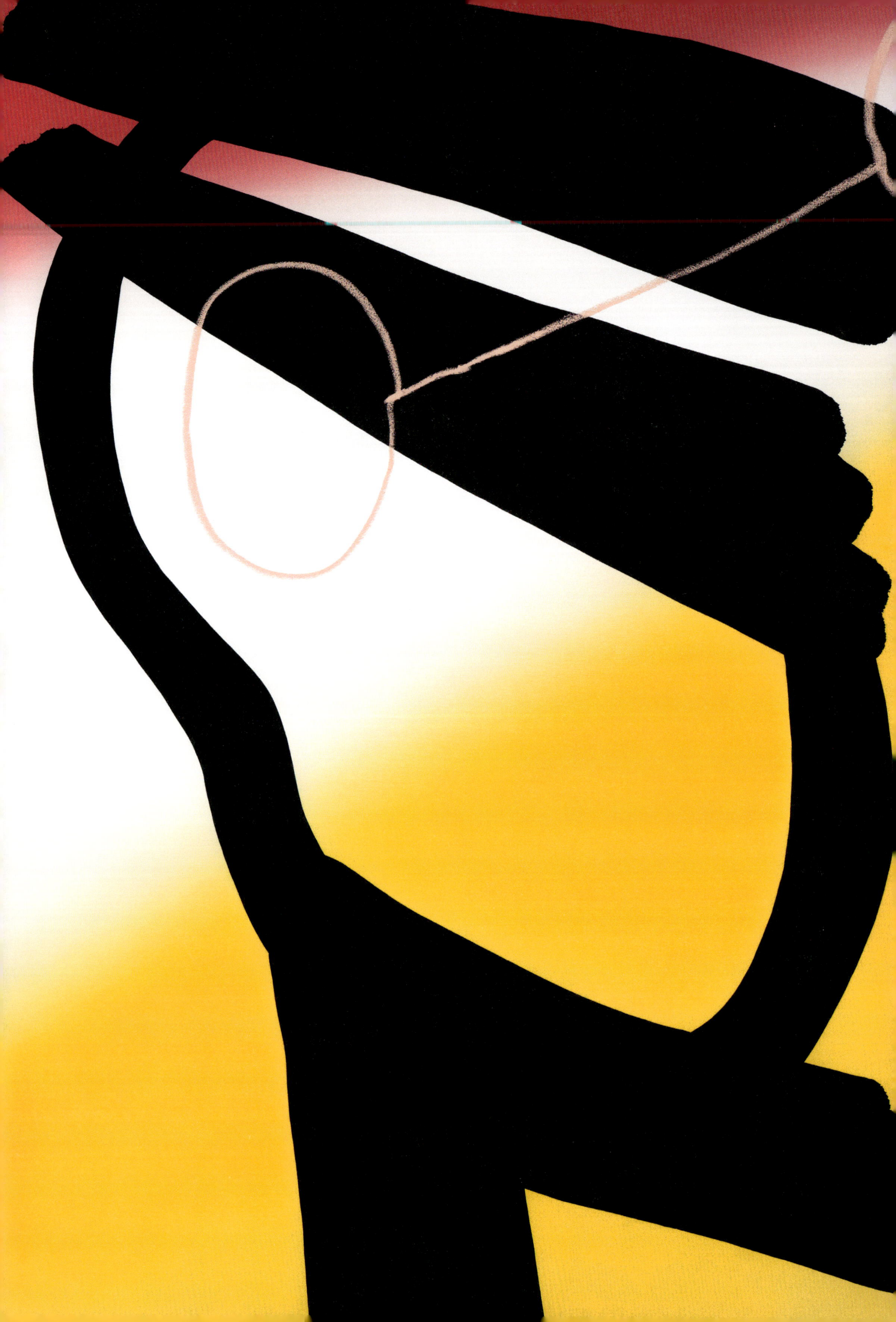

Teamwork, Frutta Gallery, Glasgow (UK), 2018

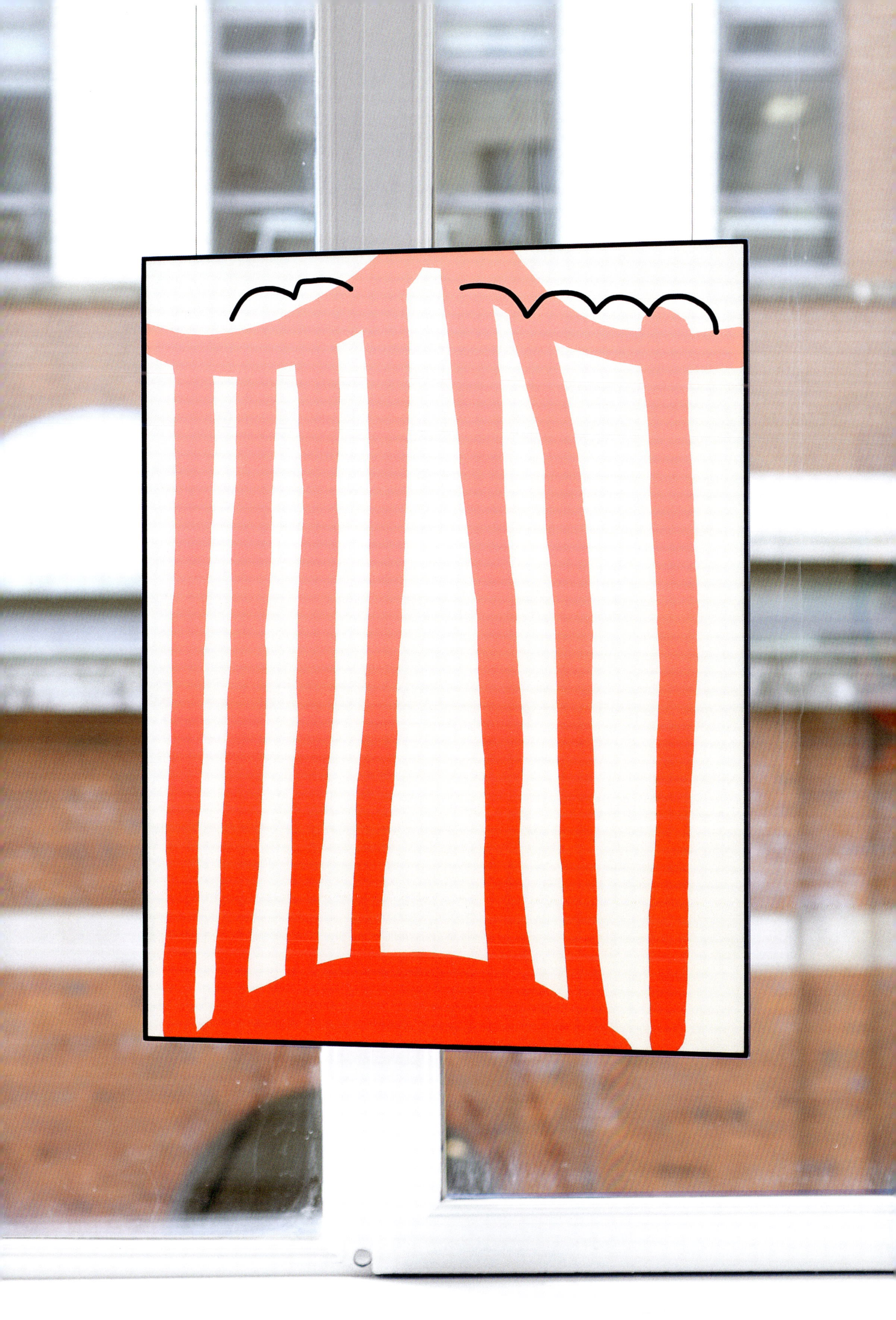

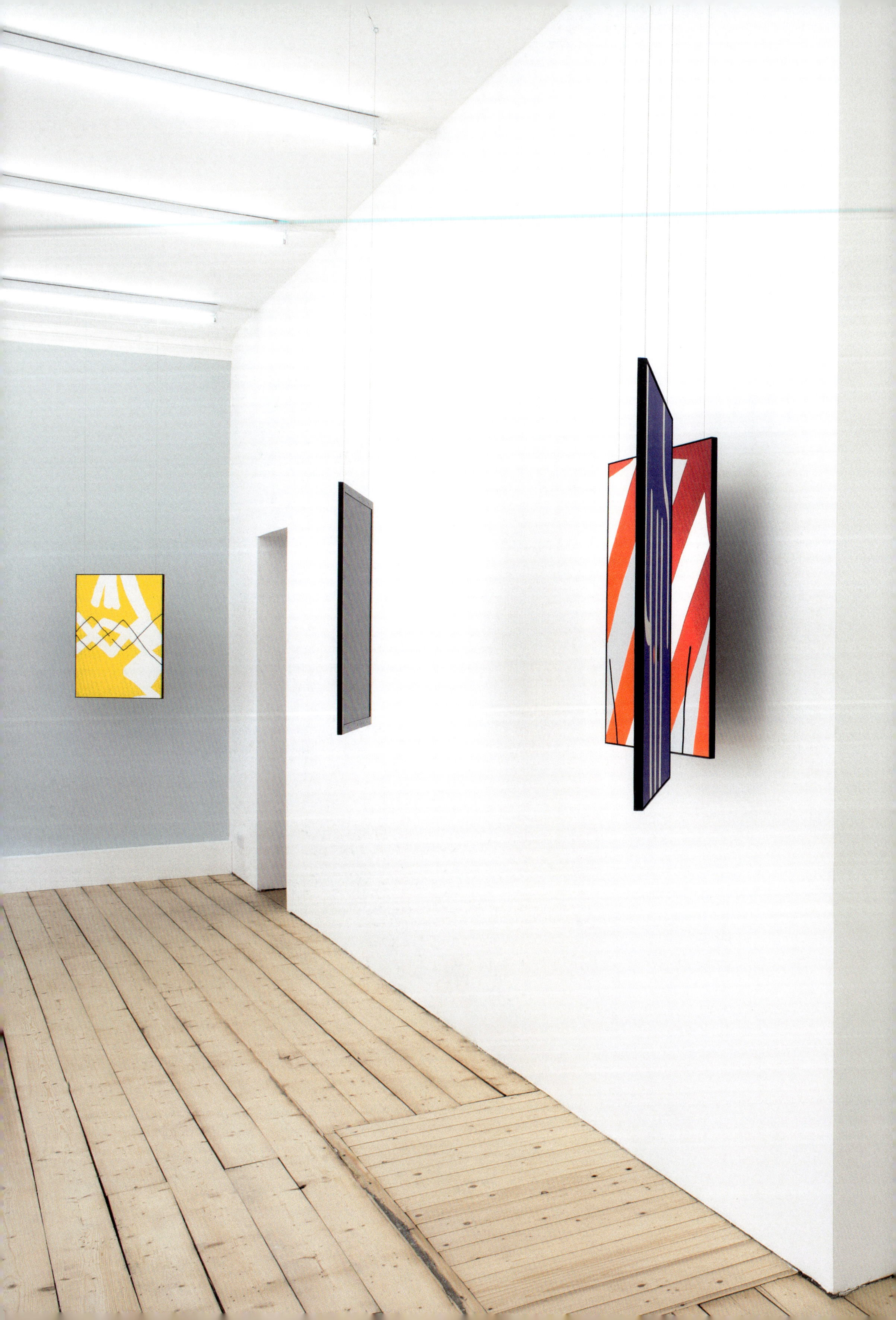

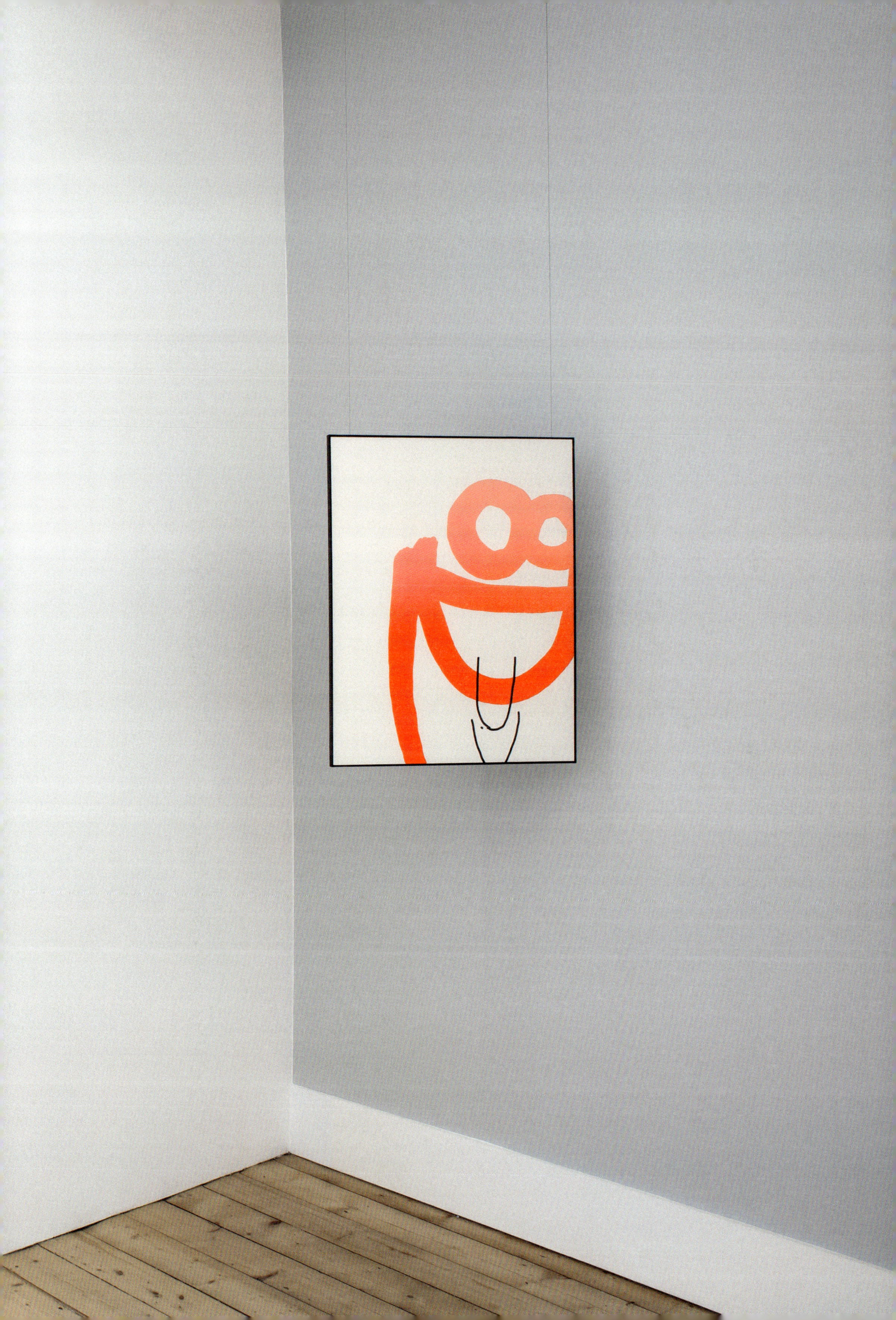

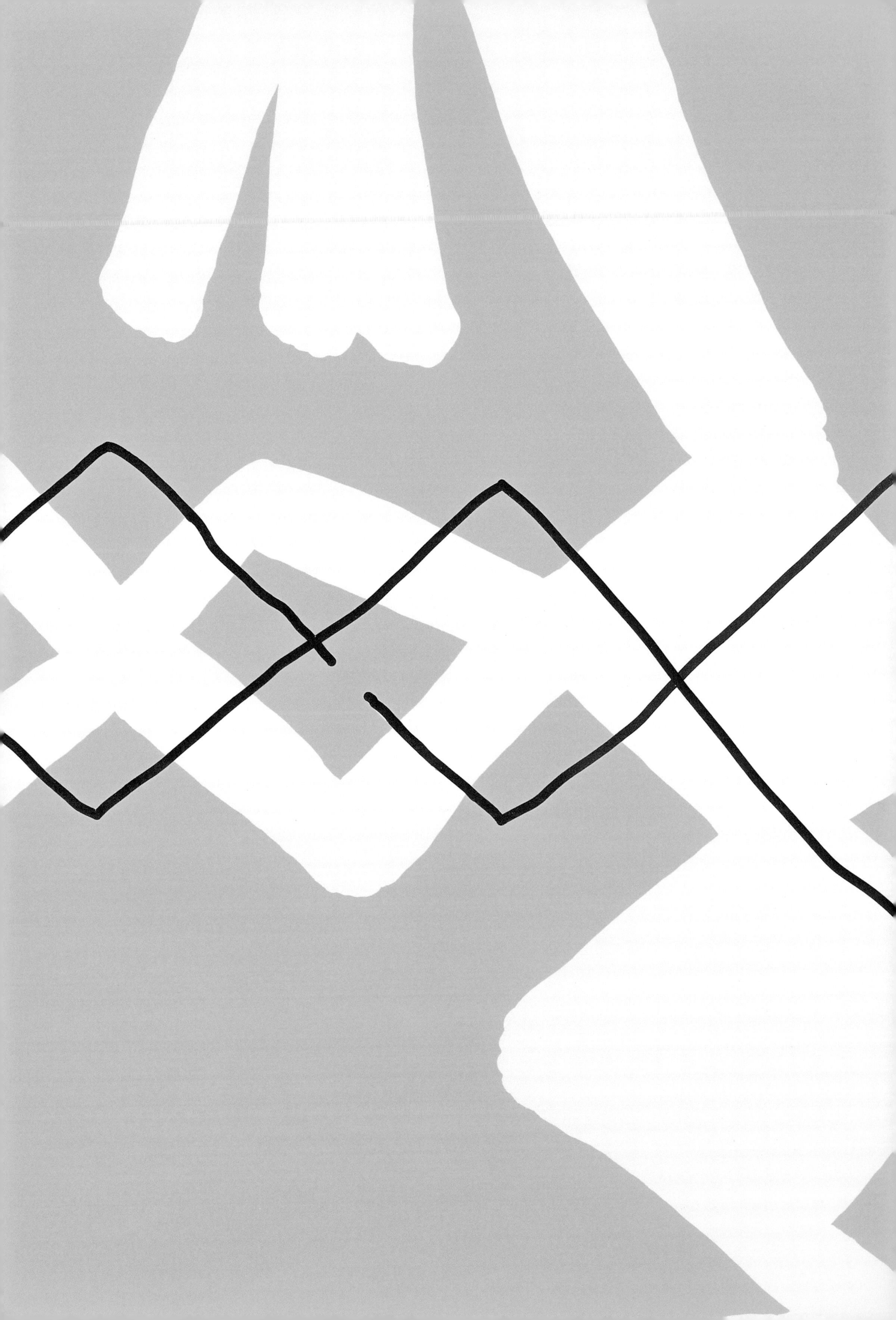

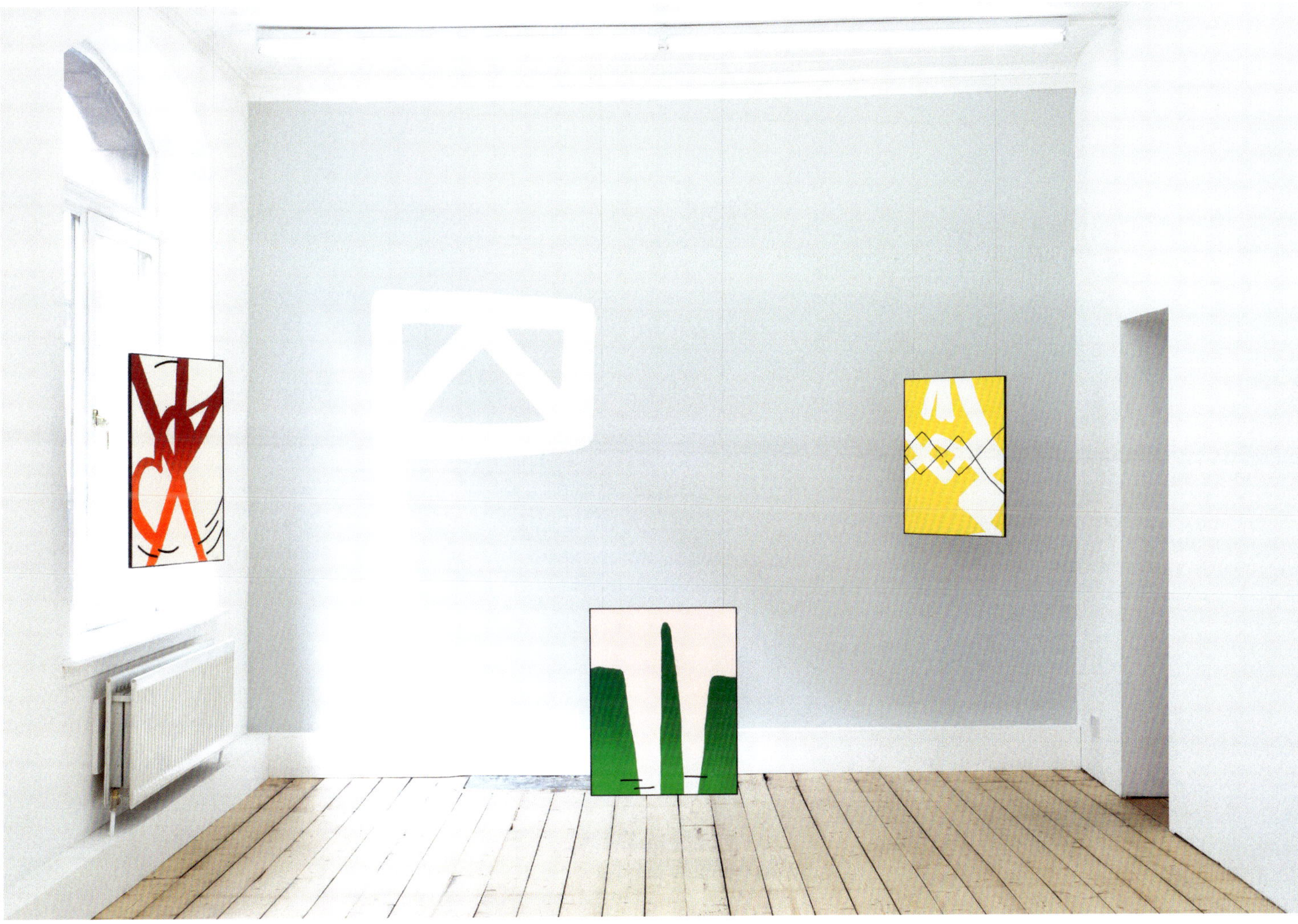

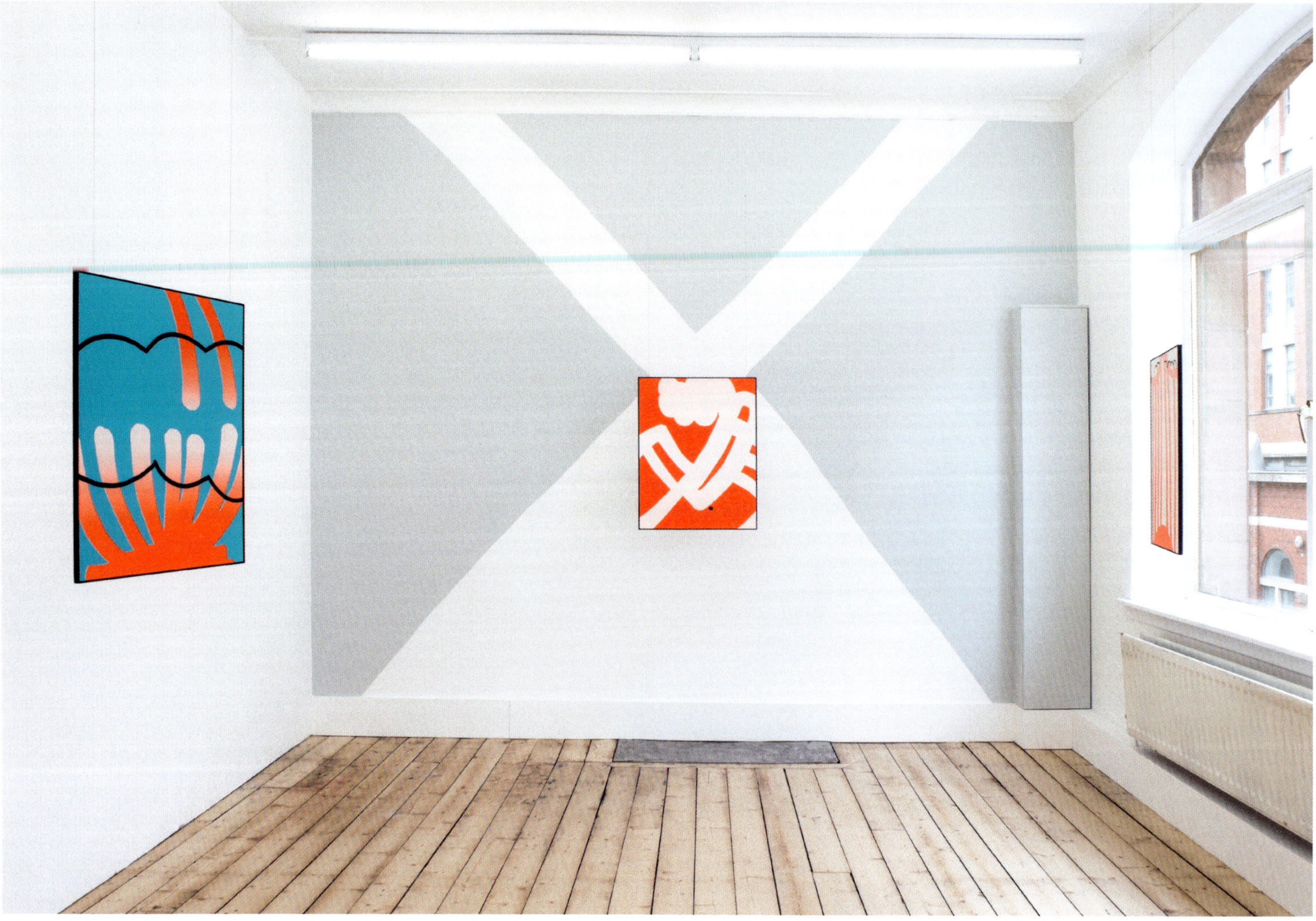

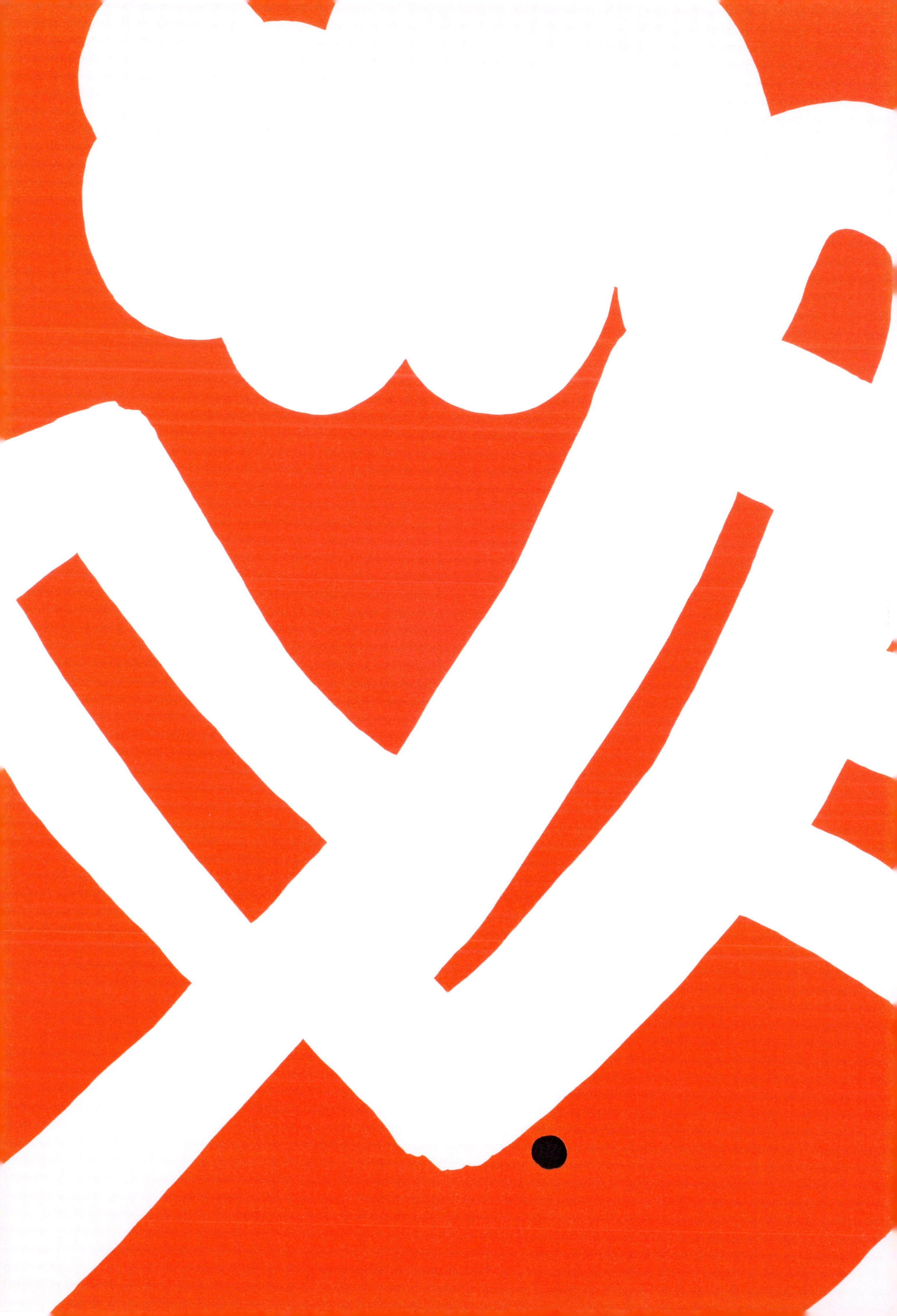

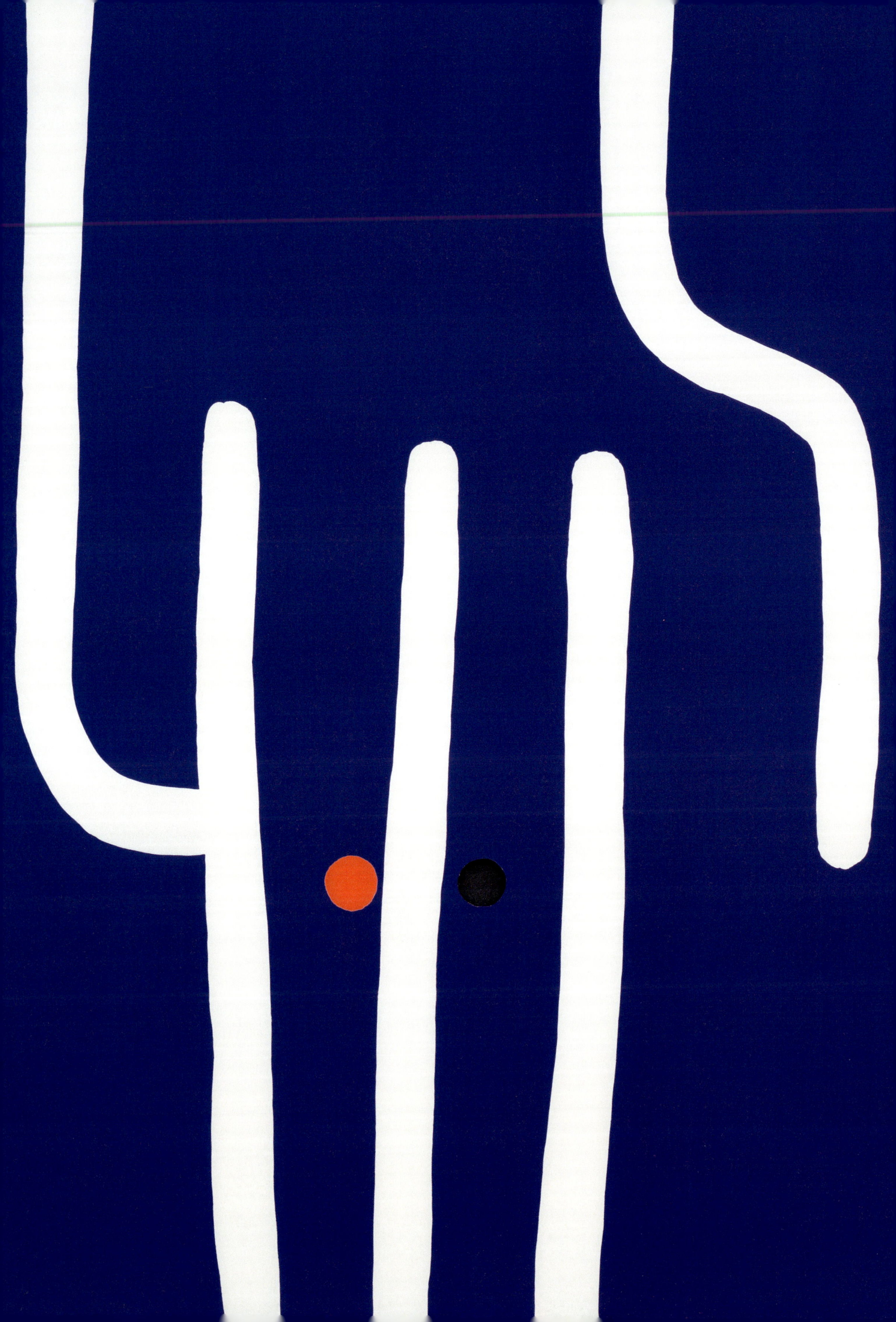

Chapter Arts Centre, Cardiff (UK), 2018

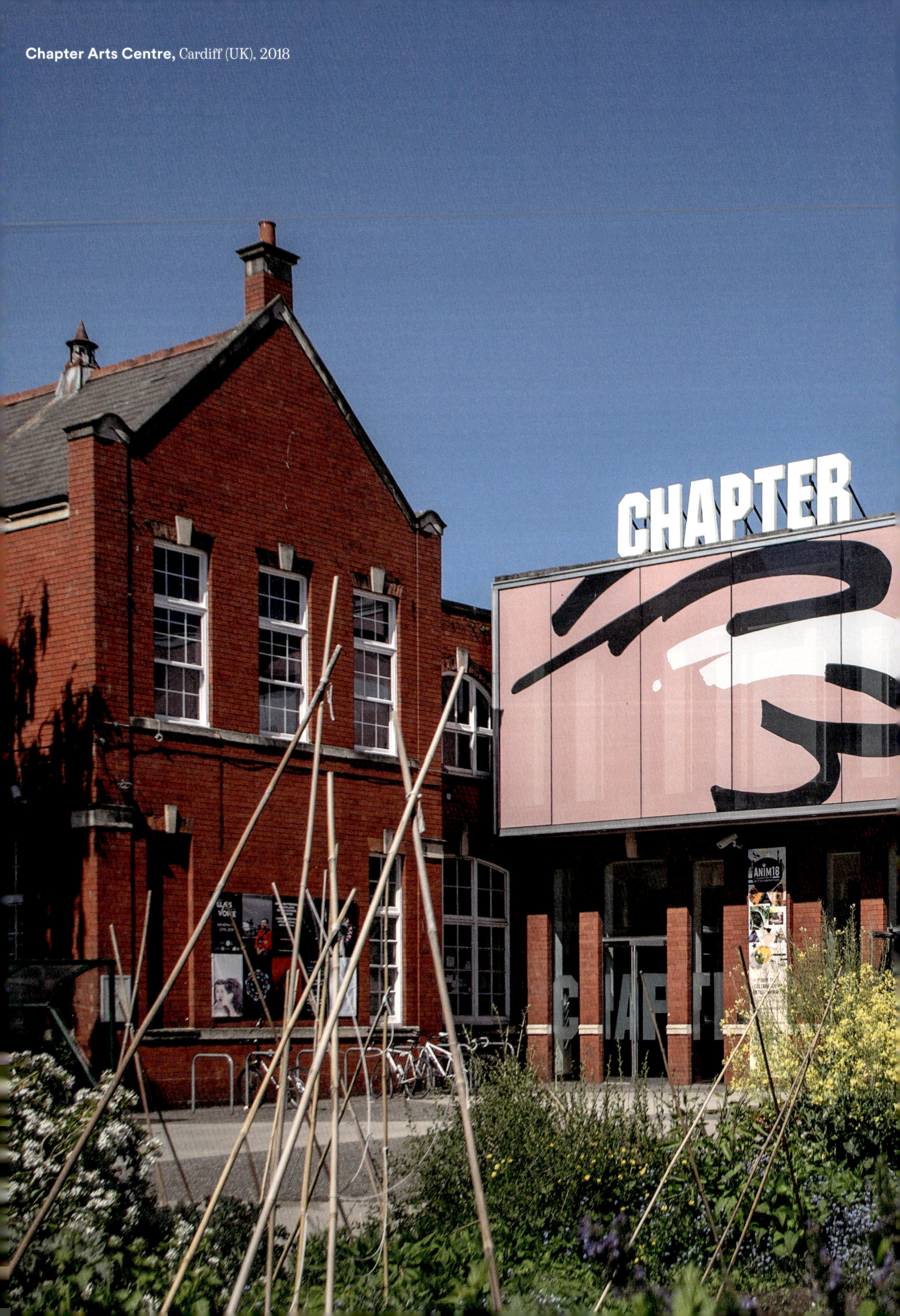

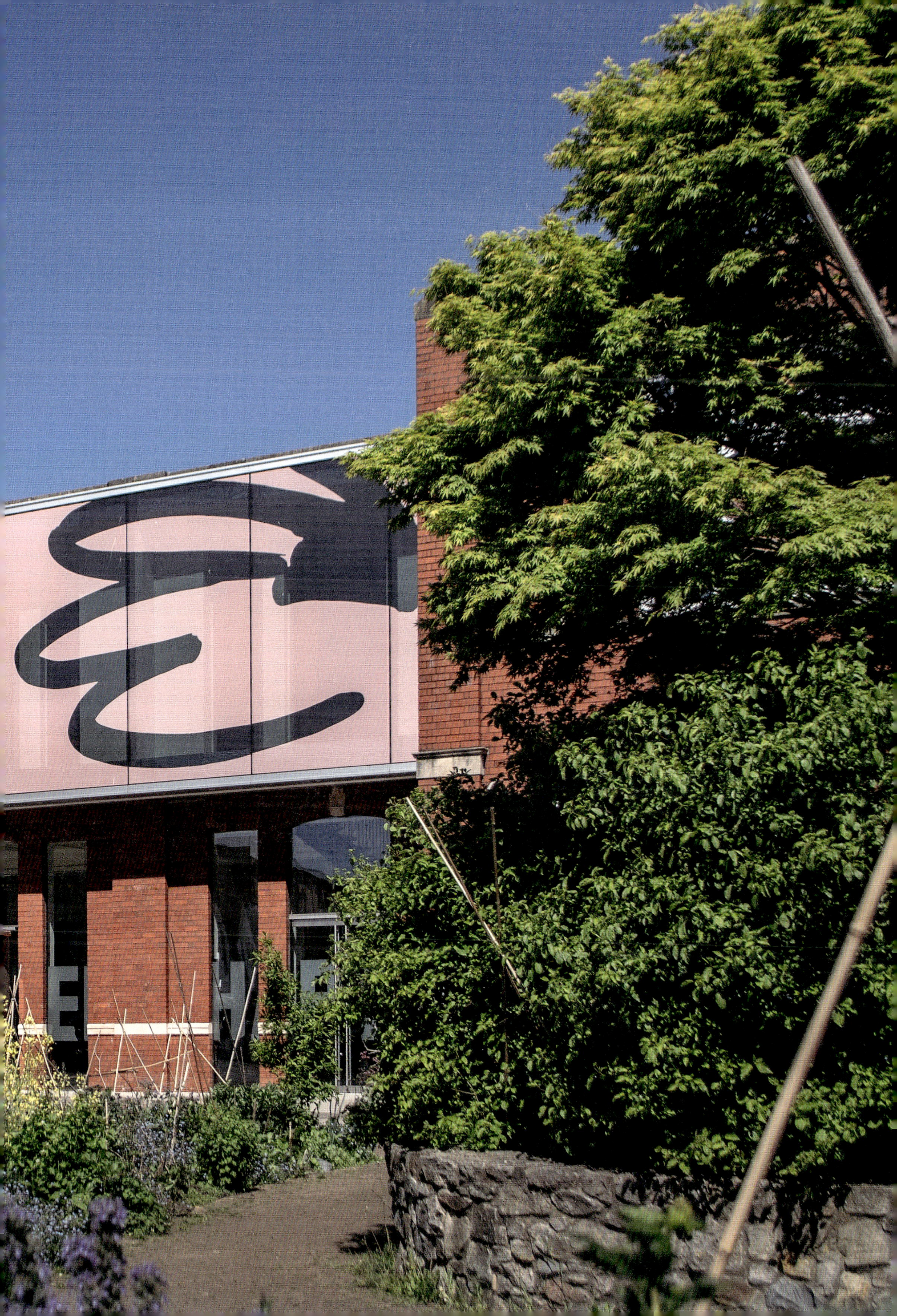

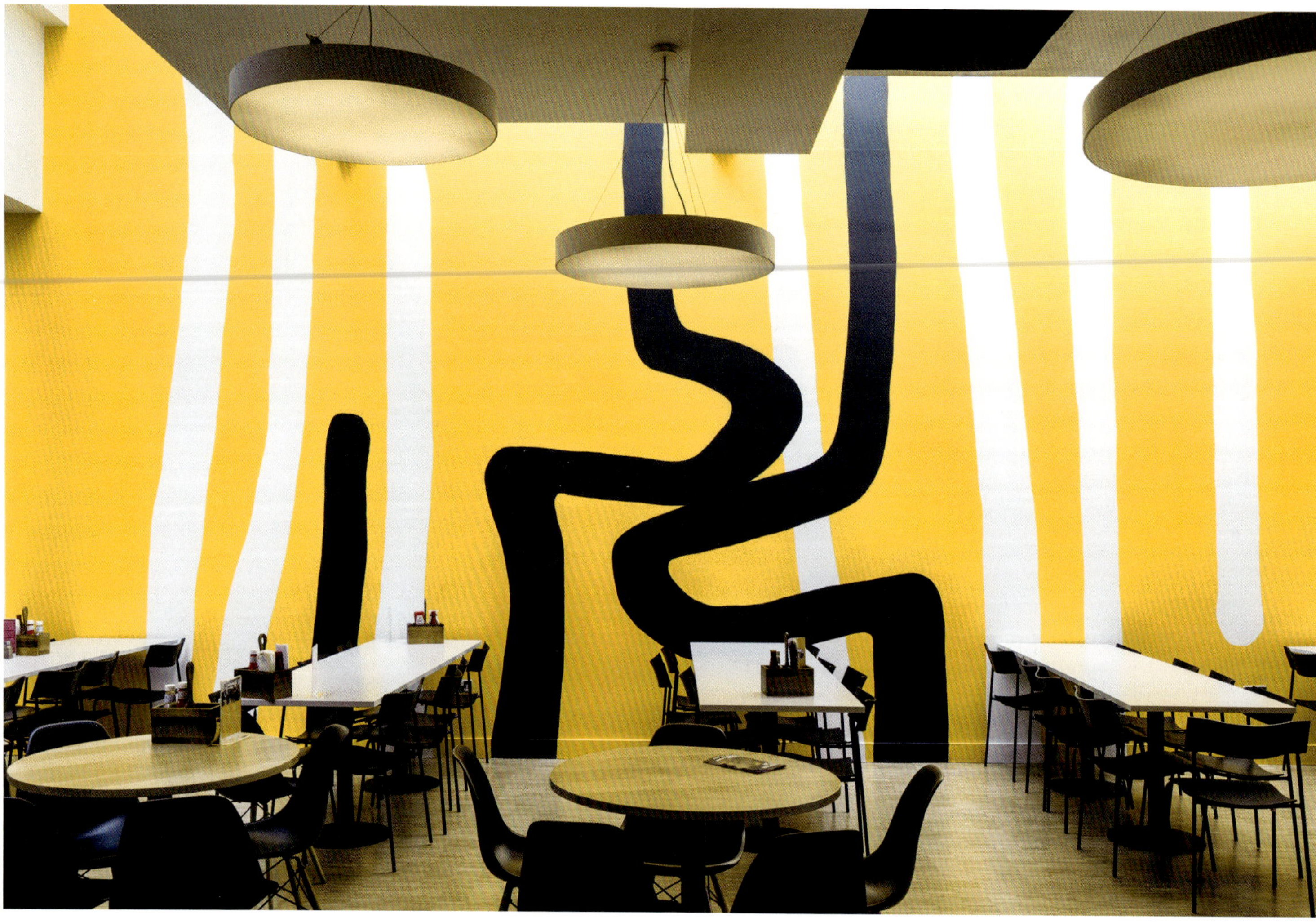

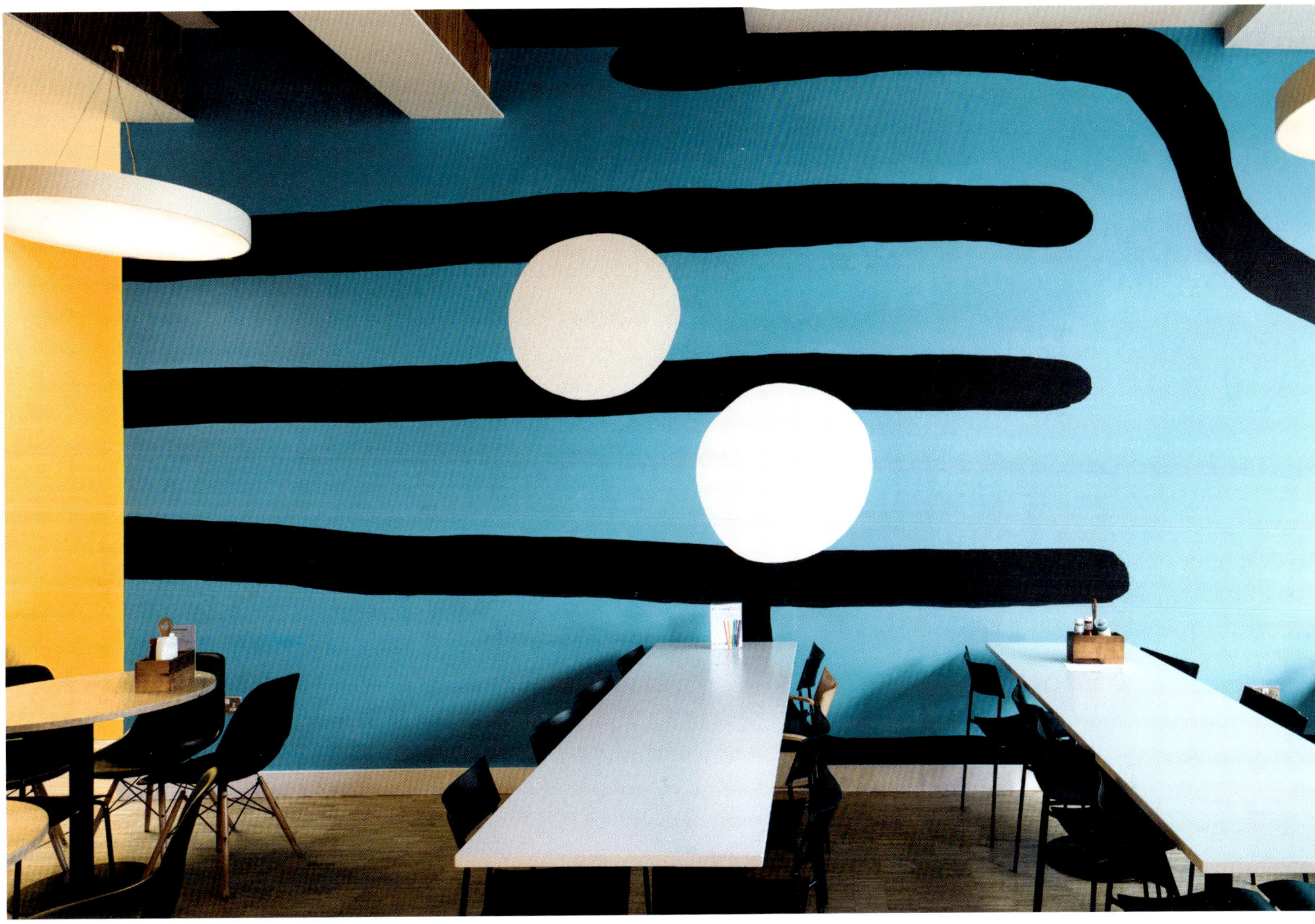

Mingle Mime, BolteLang, Zurich (CH), 2018

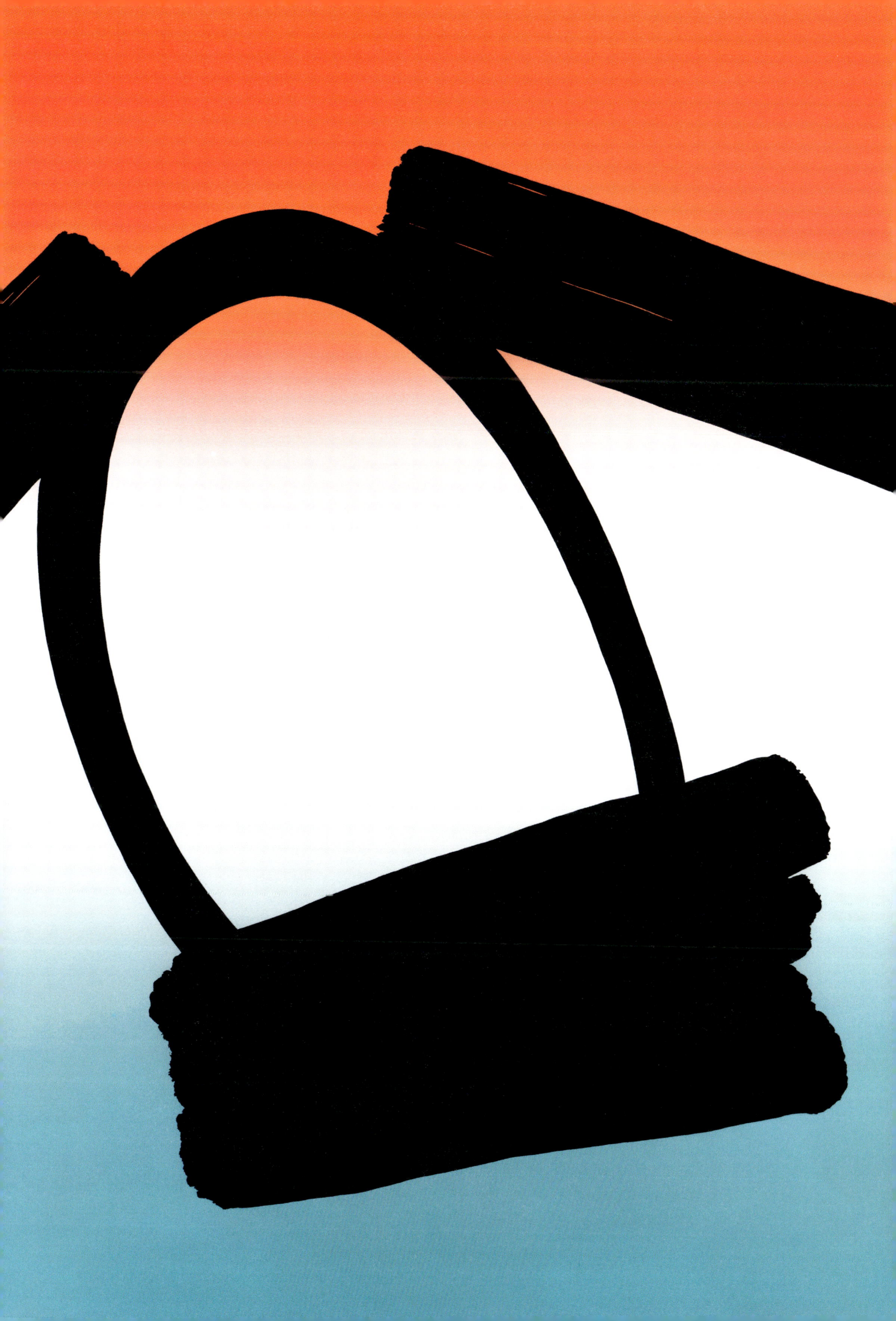

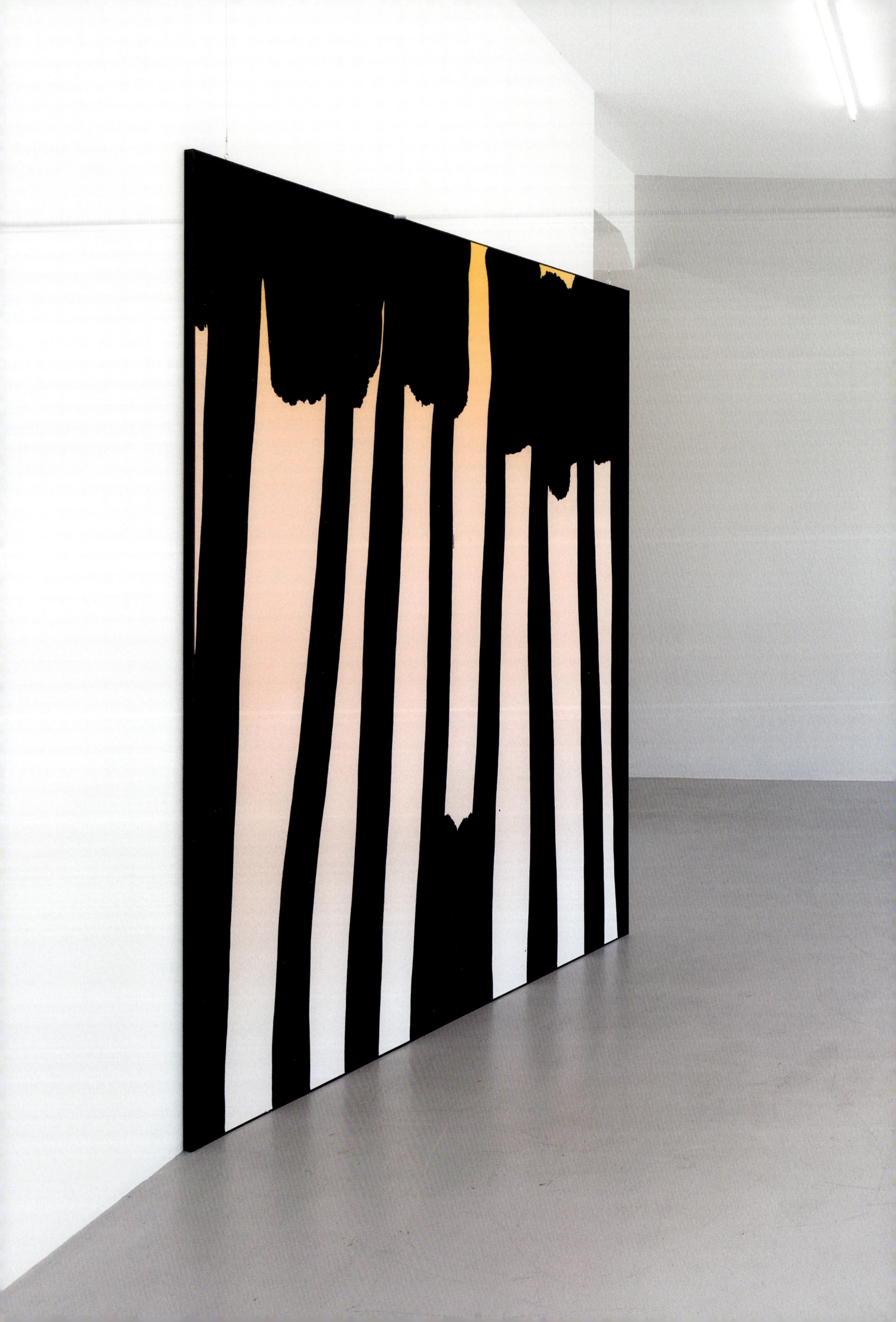

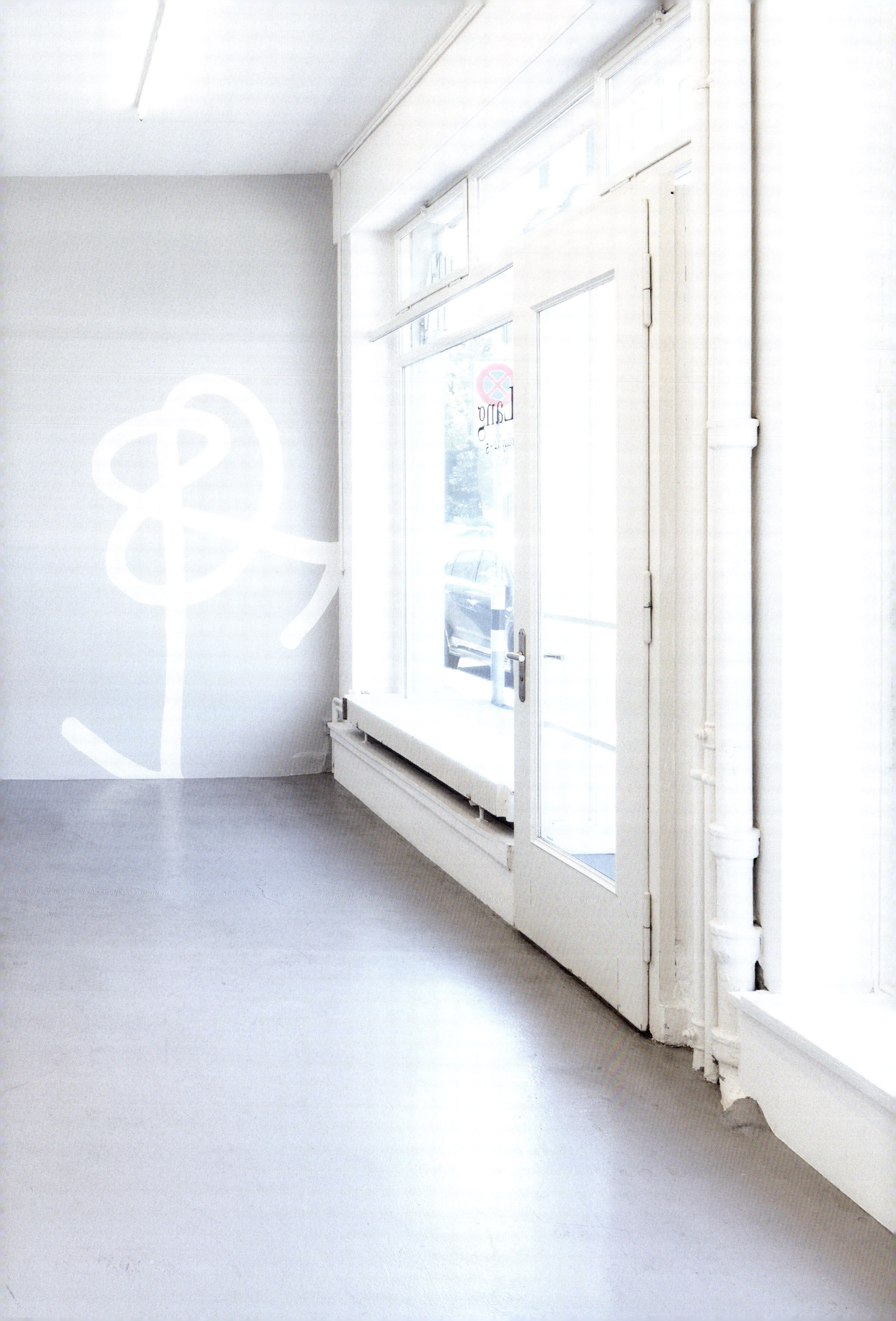

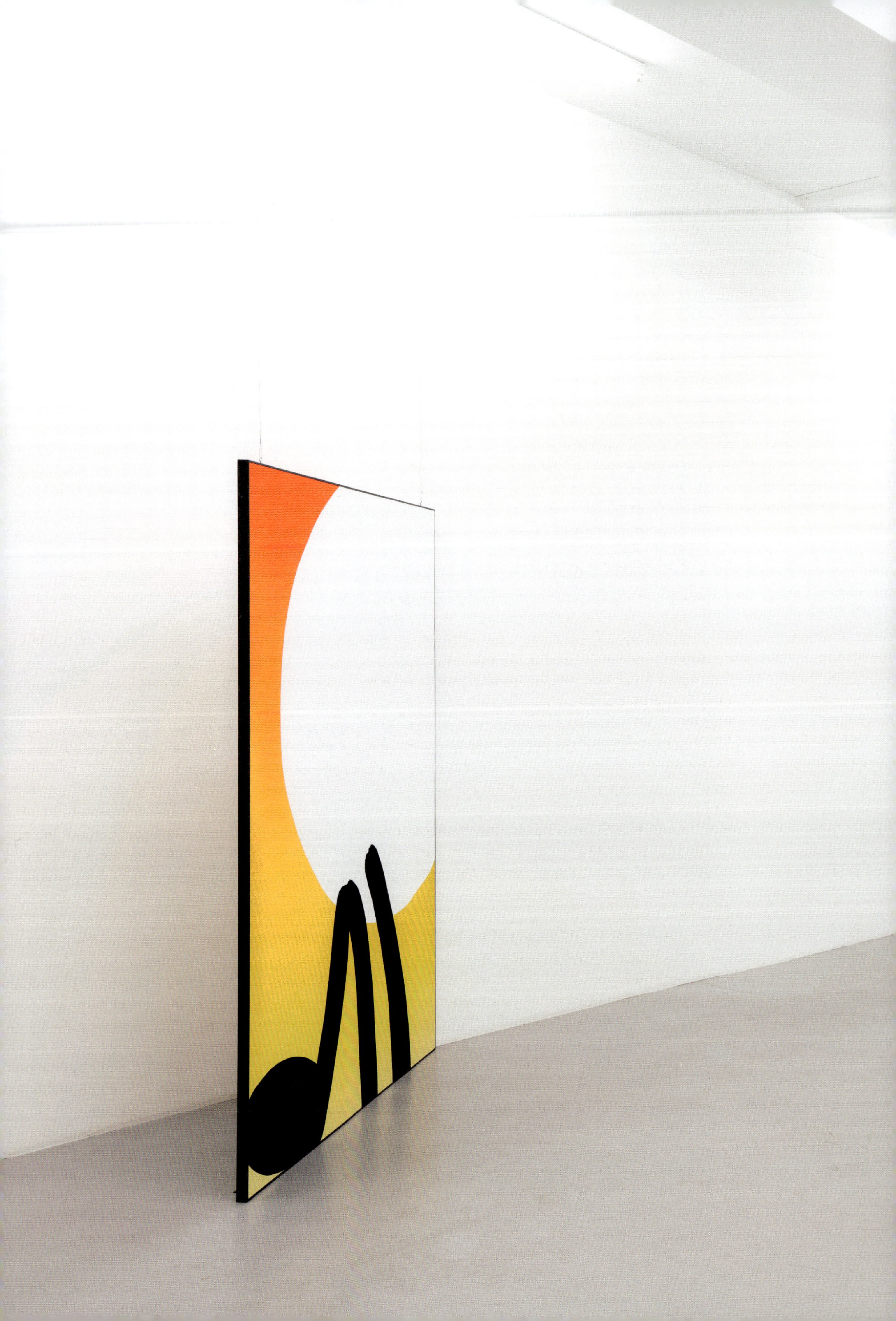

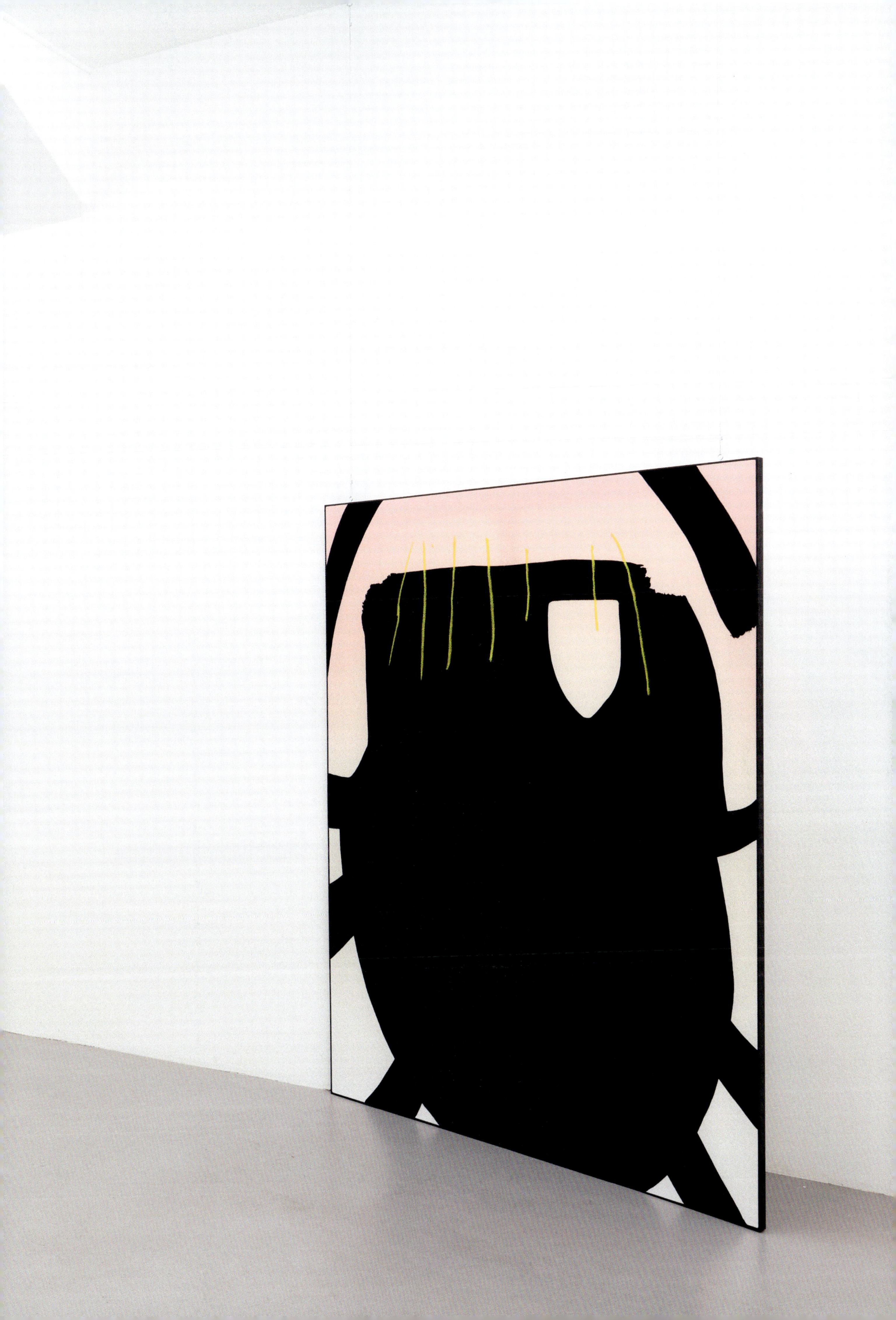

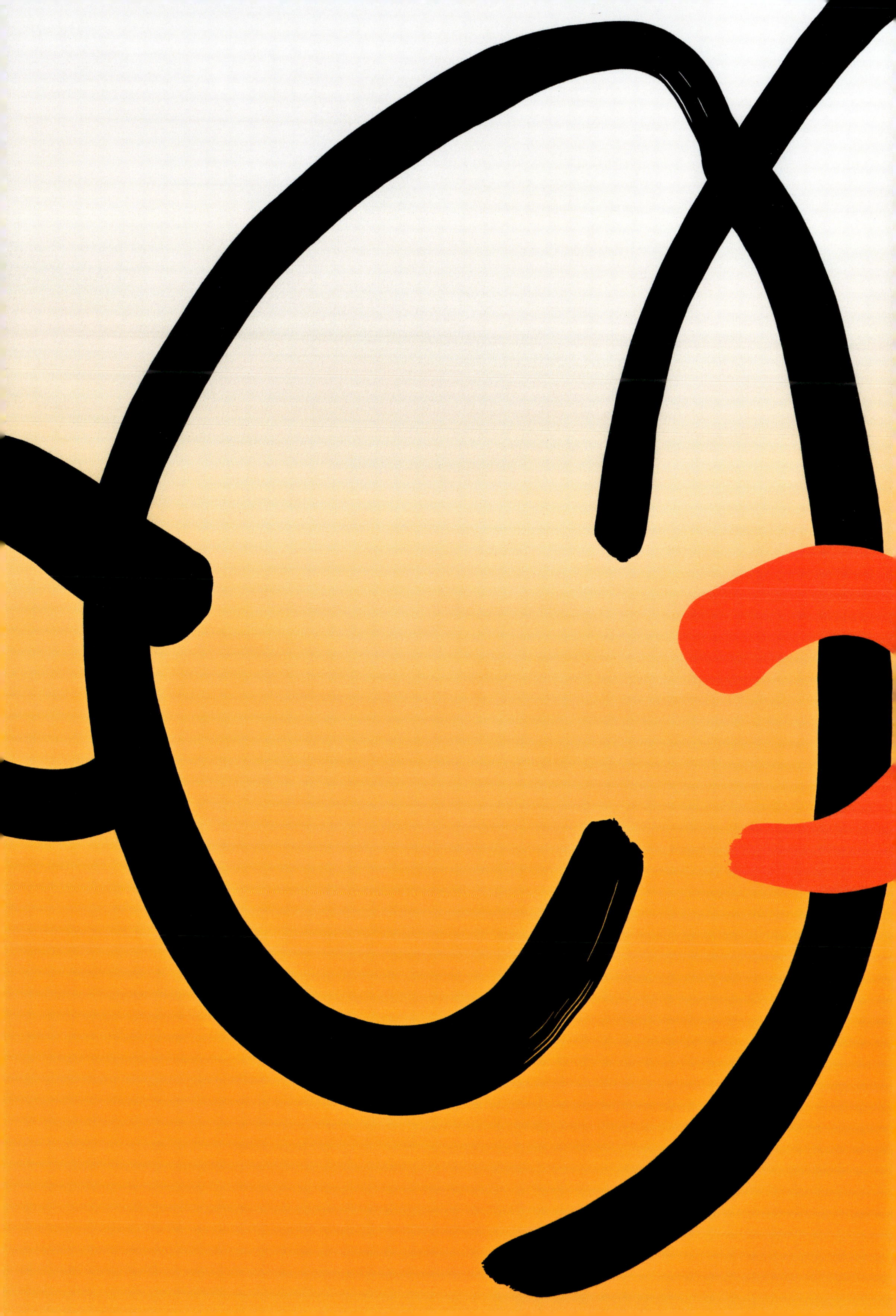

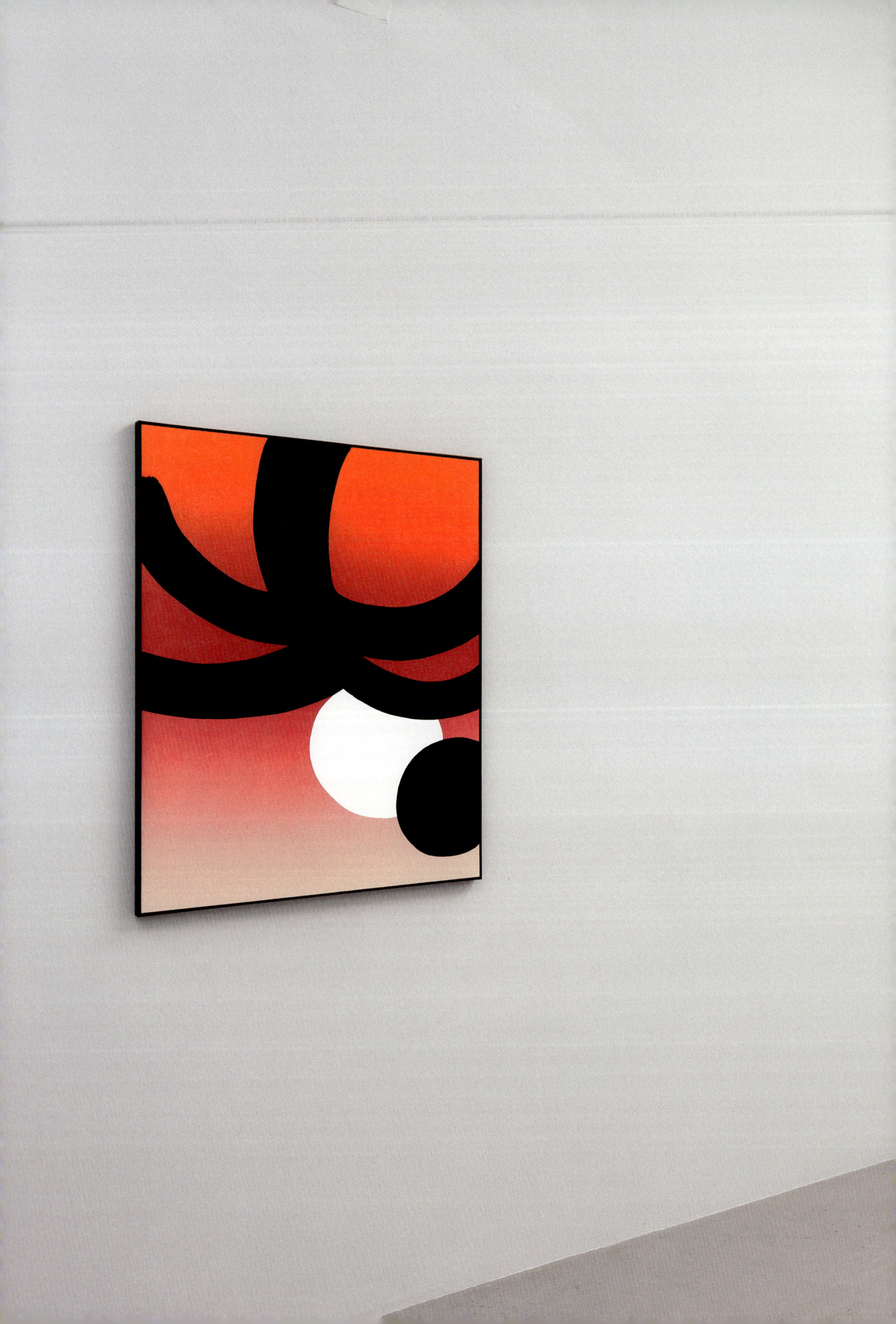

CAPRI, Galleri Nicolai Wallner, Copenhagen (DK), 2017

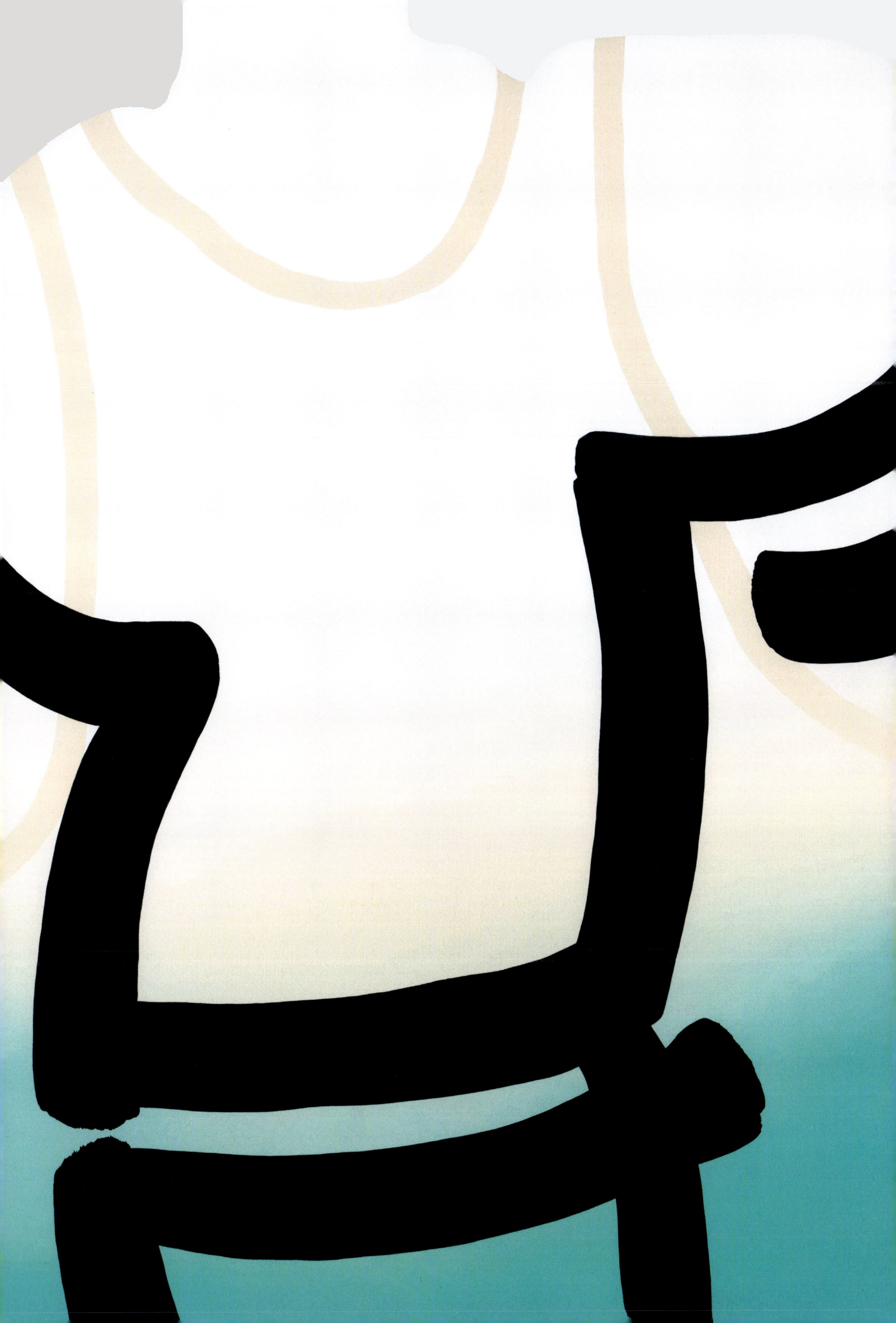

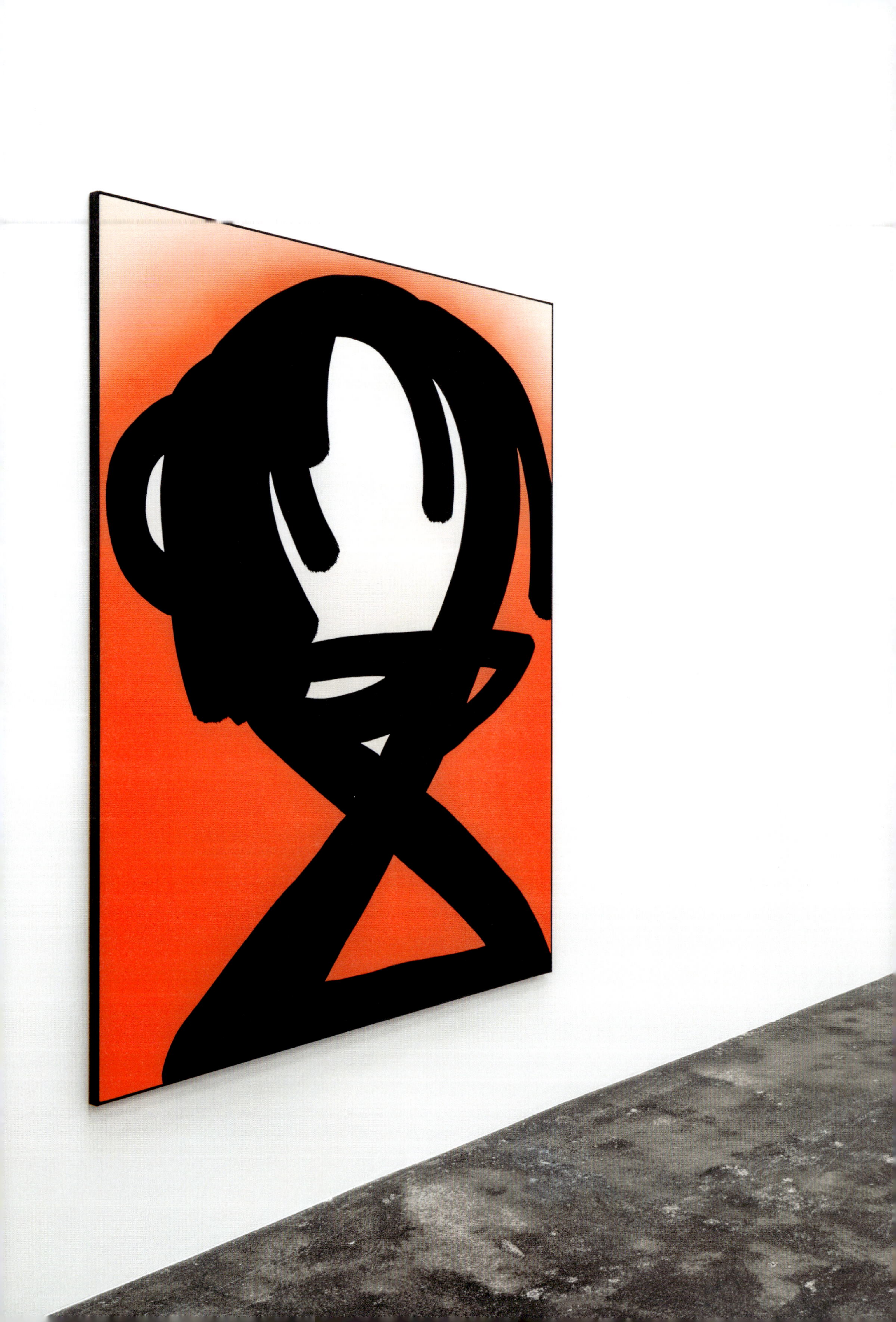

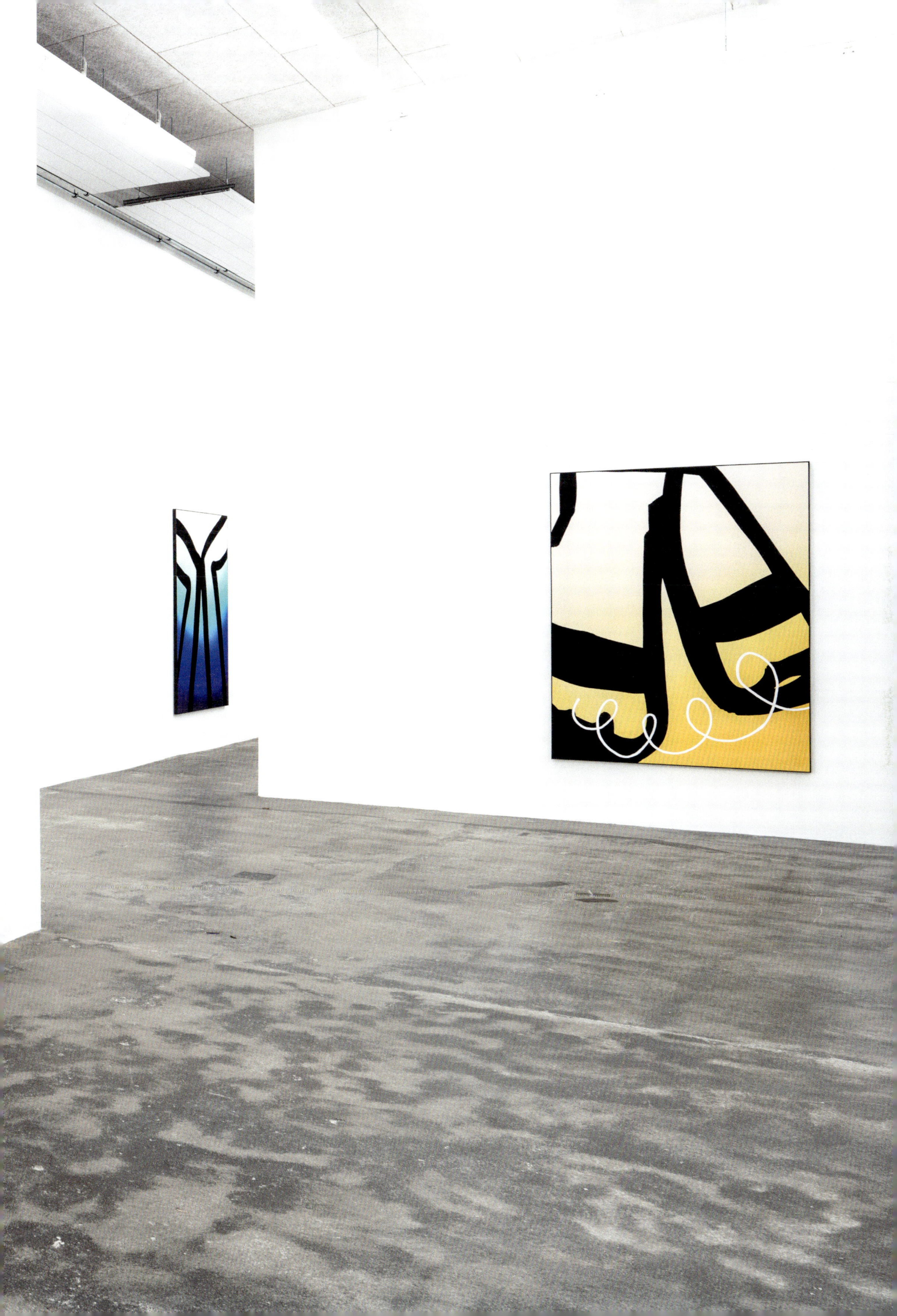

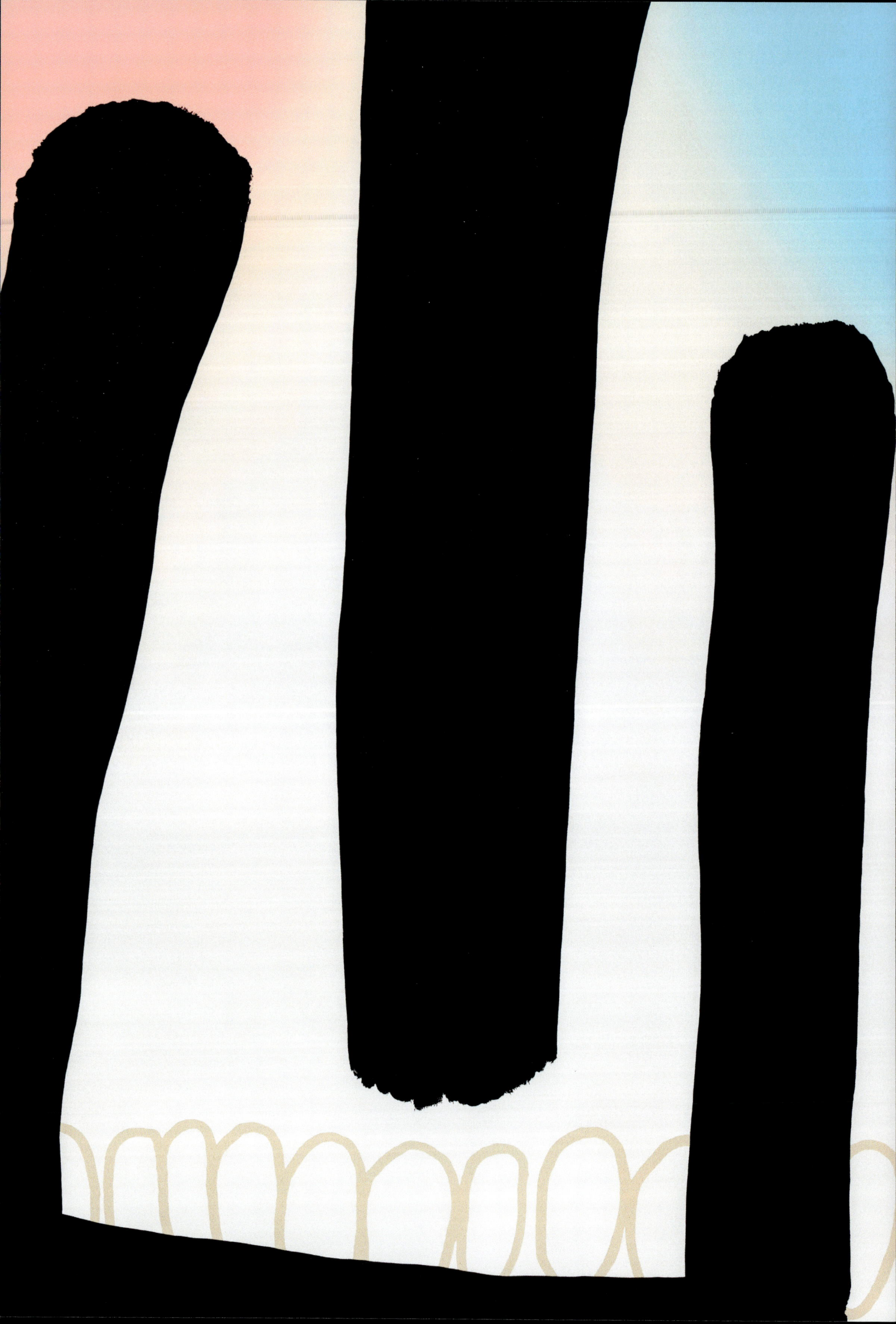

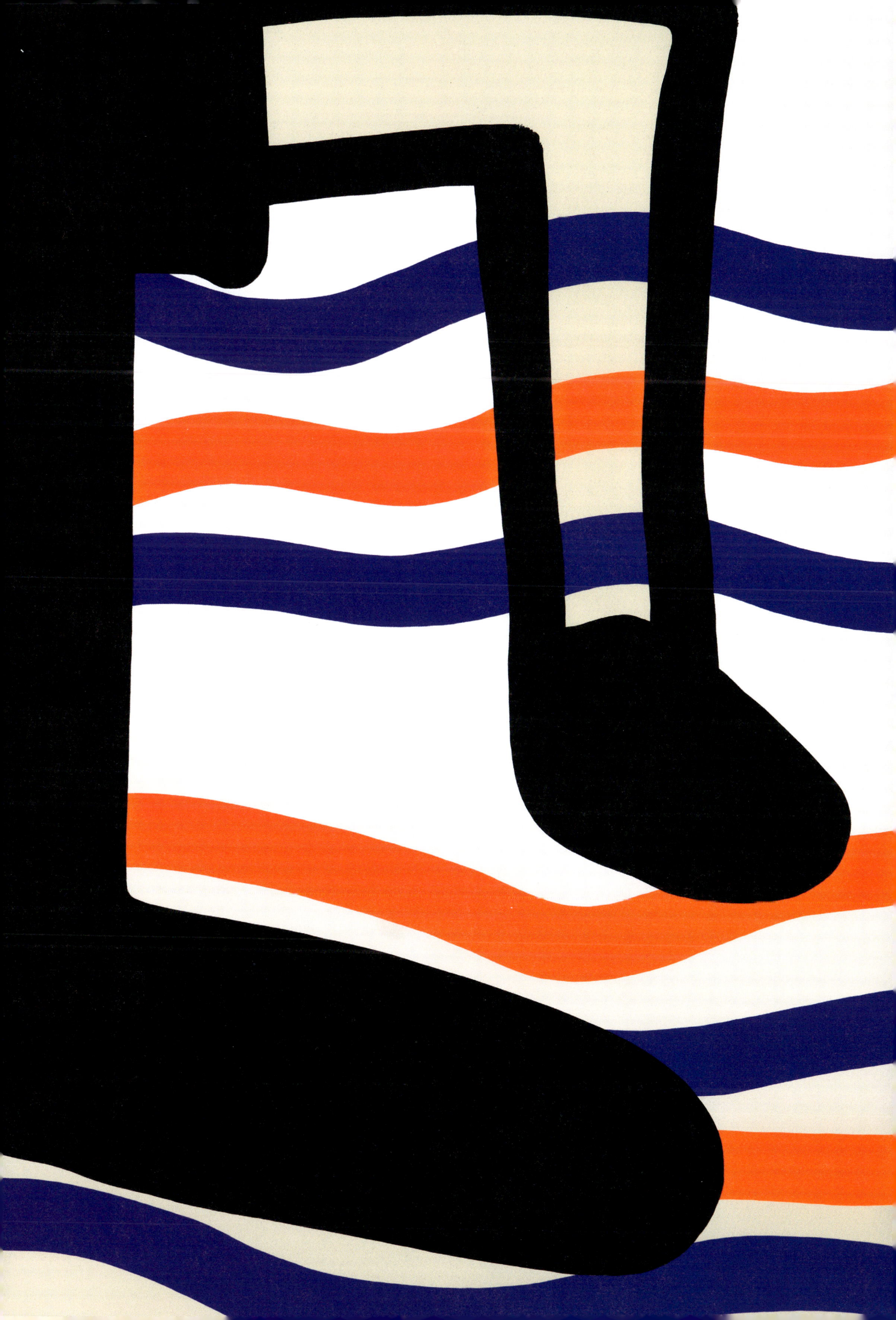

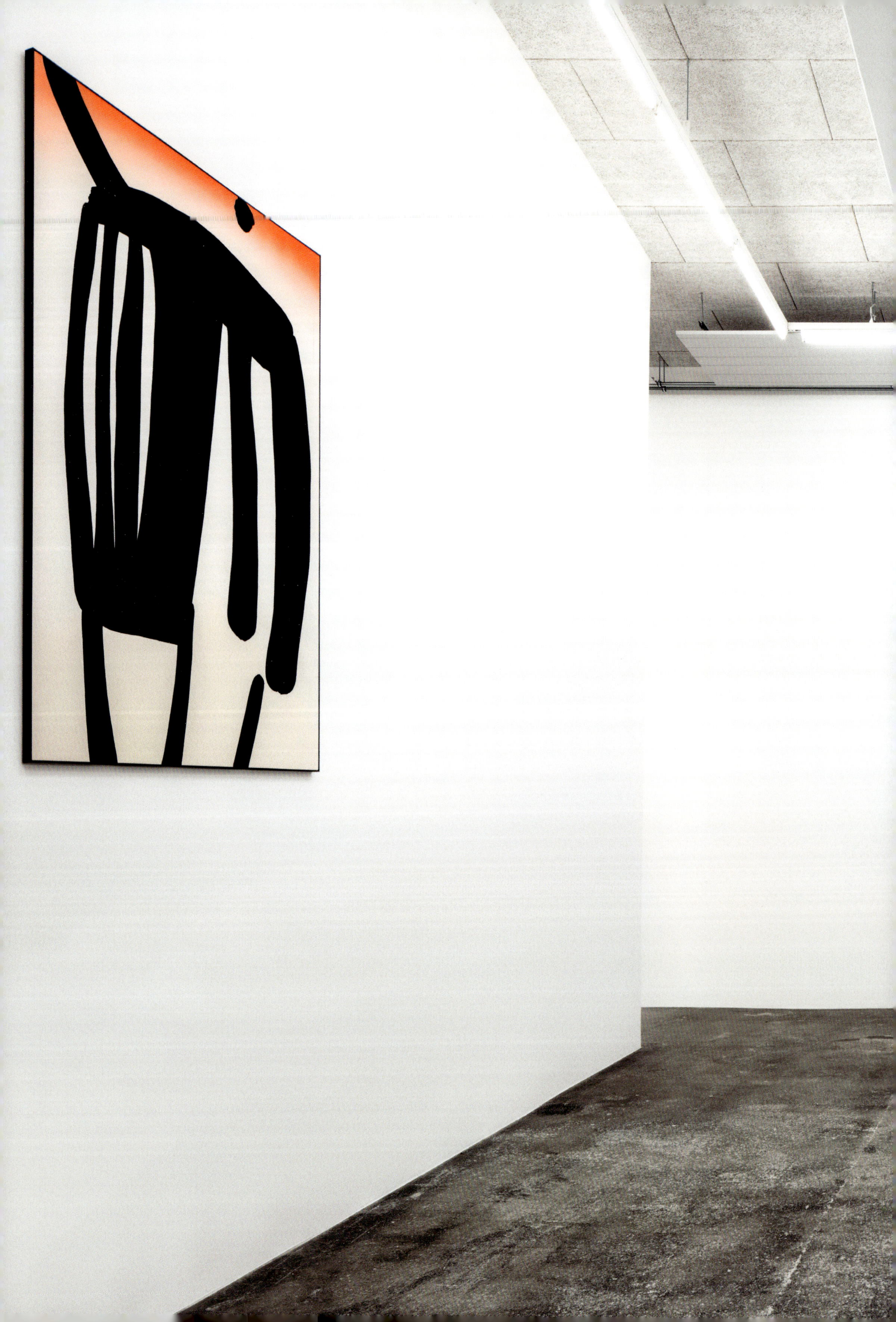

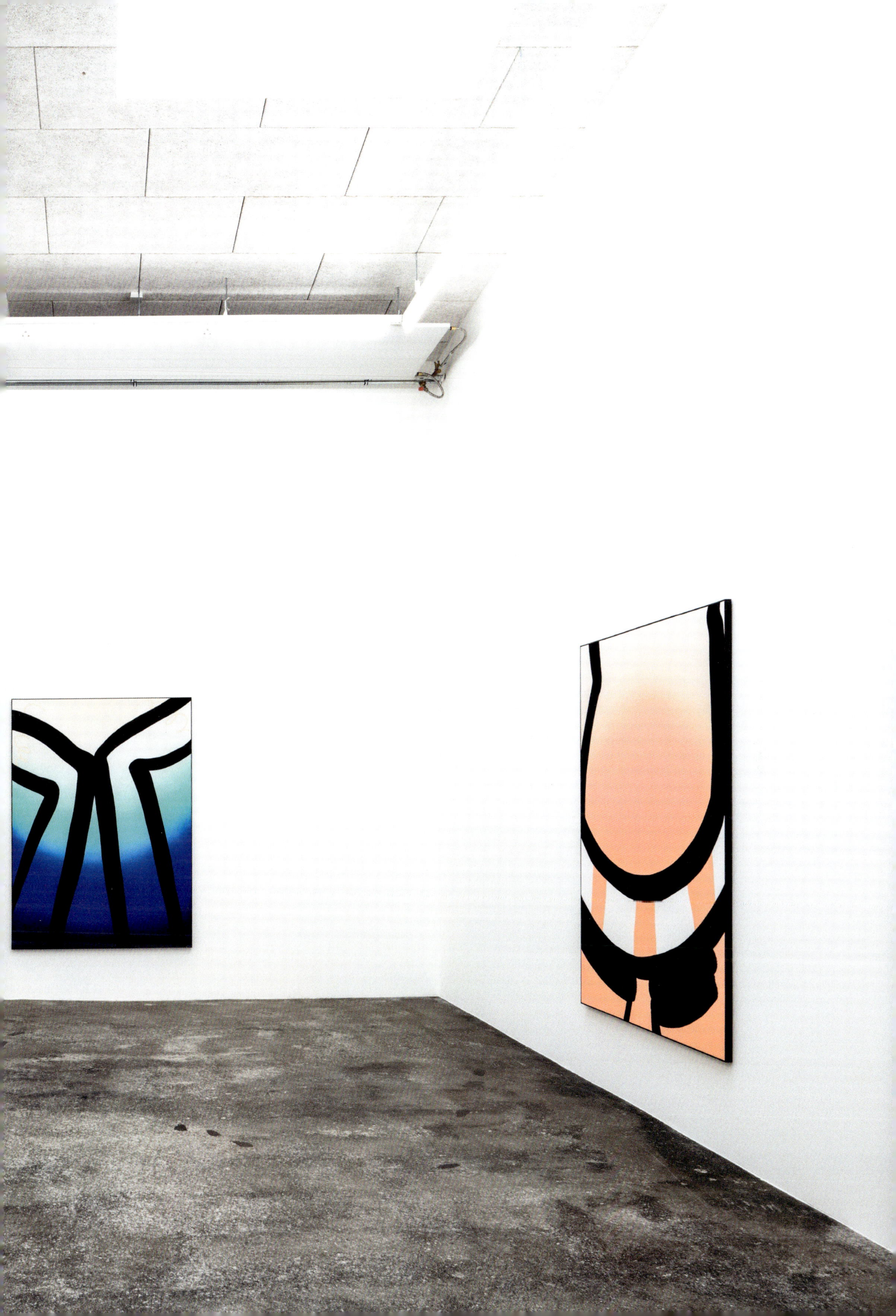

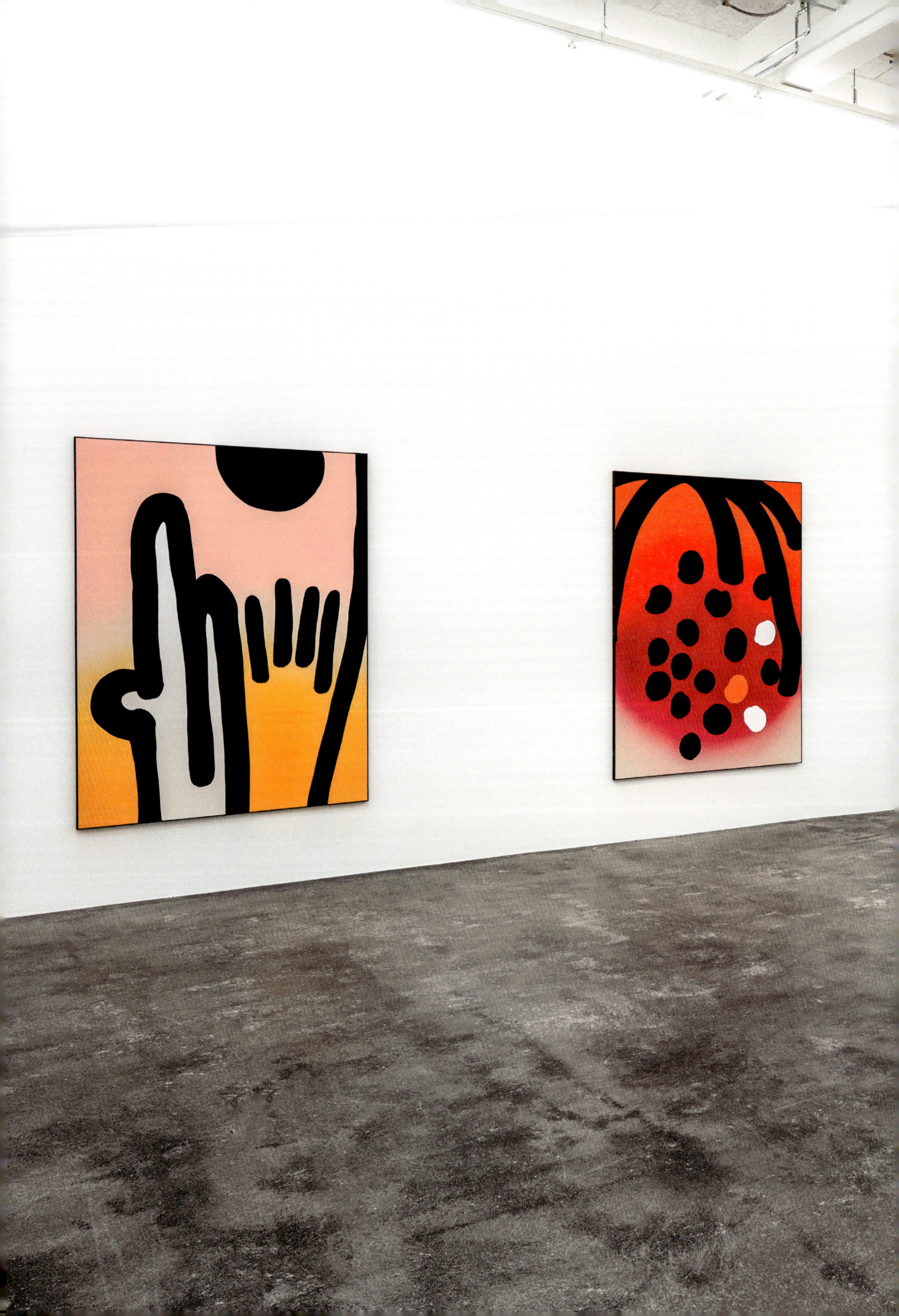

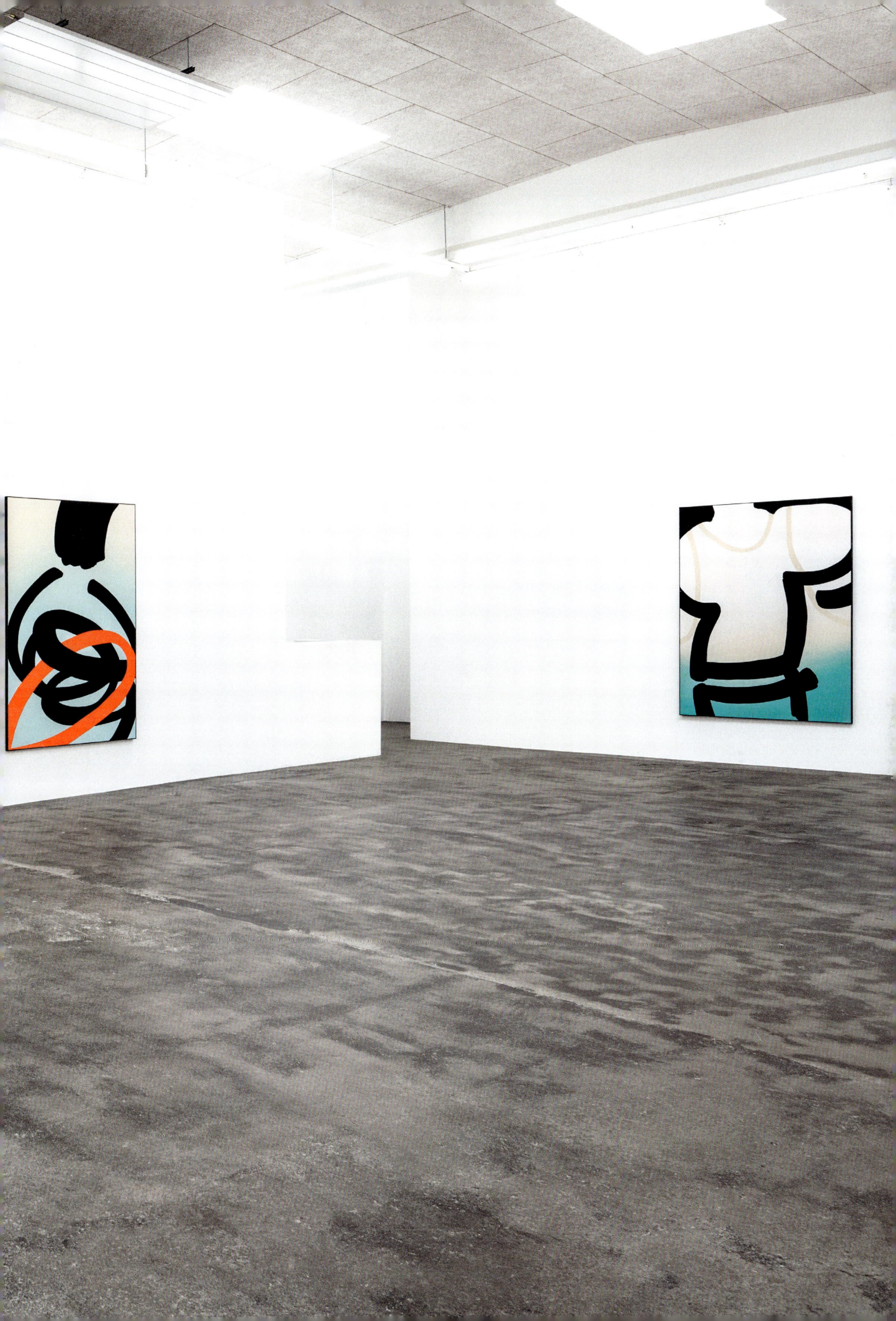

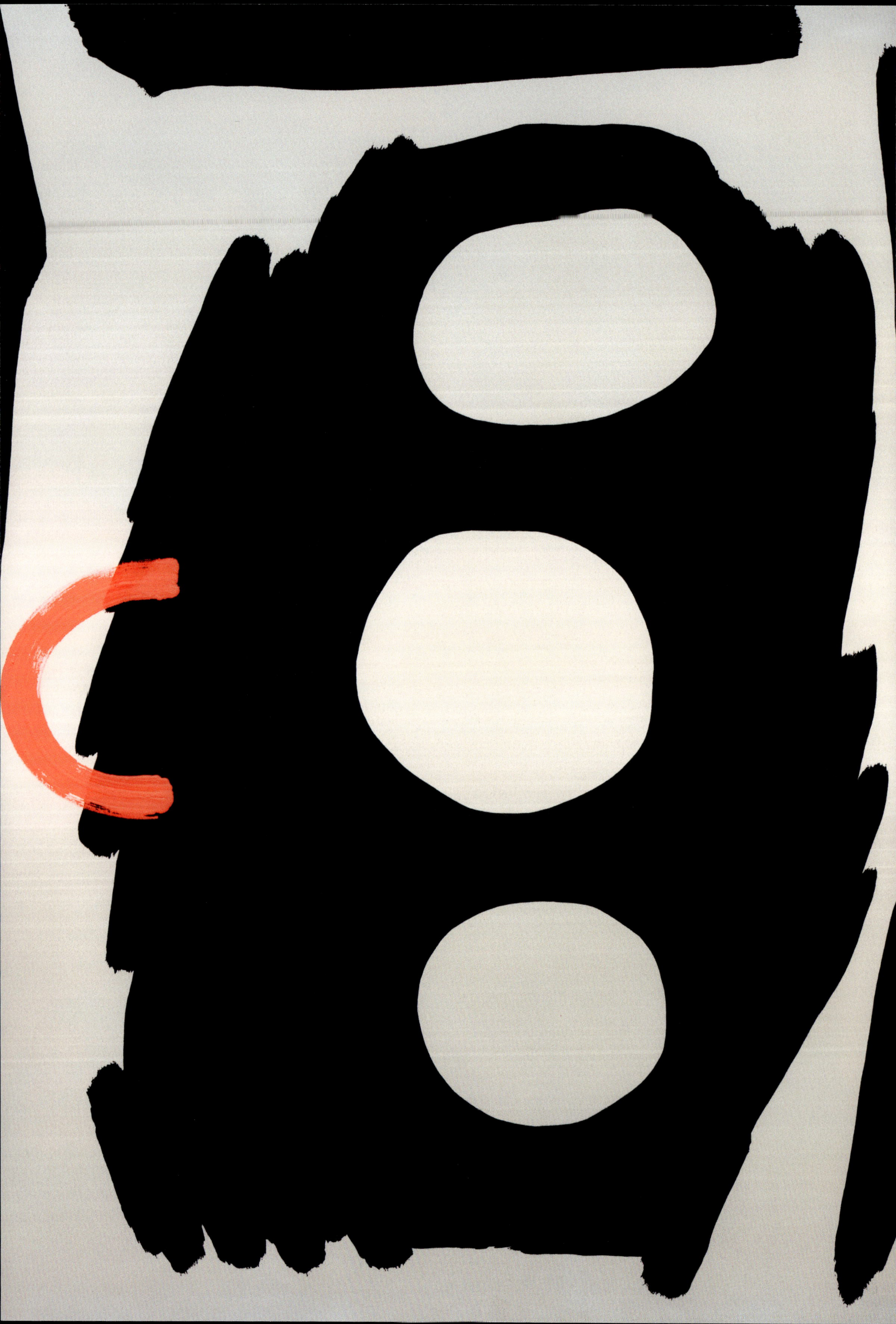

New Adventures in Vexillology 2, Kunstverein Amrum, Badestrand Nebel, Amrum (DE), 2016

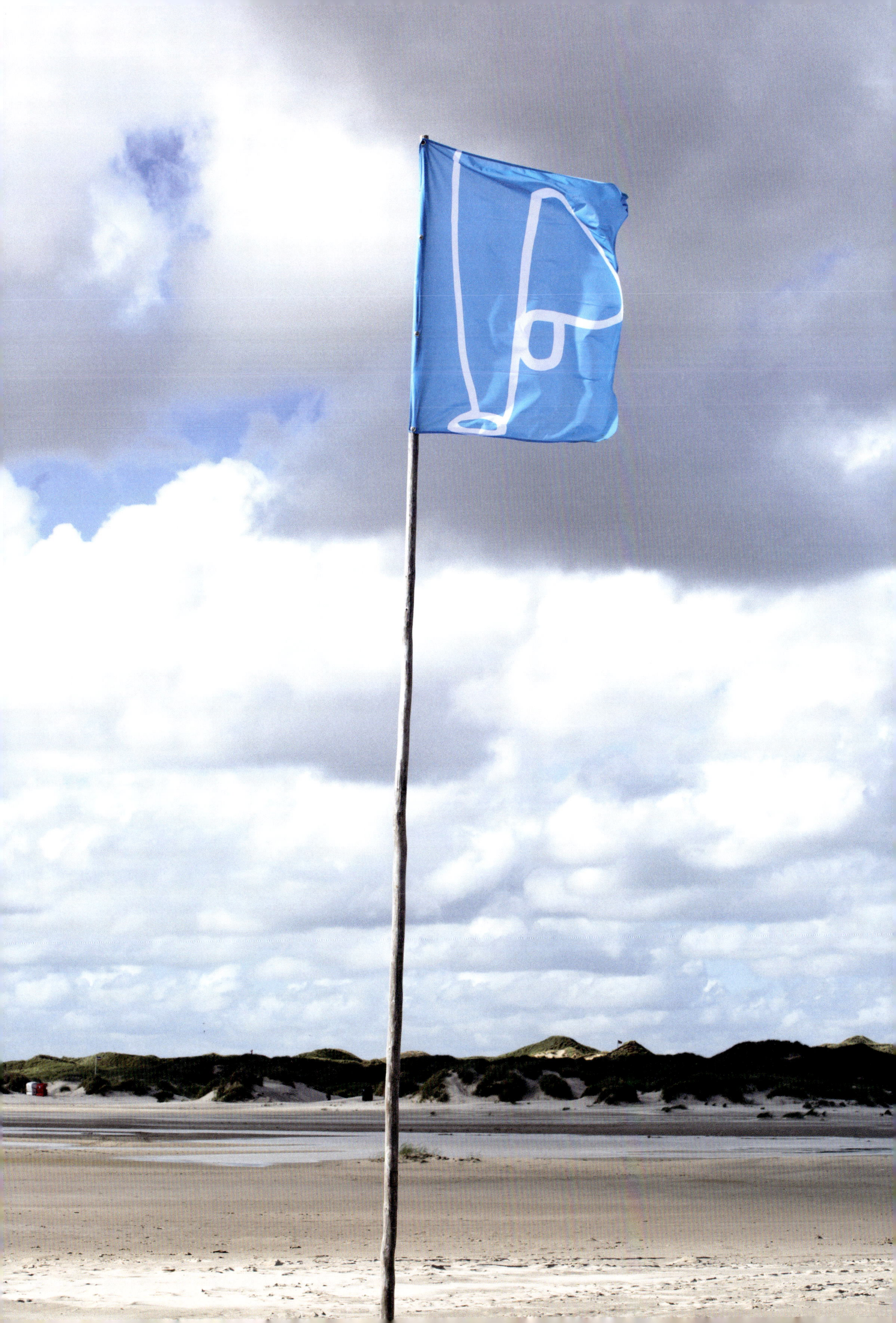

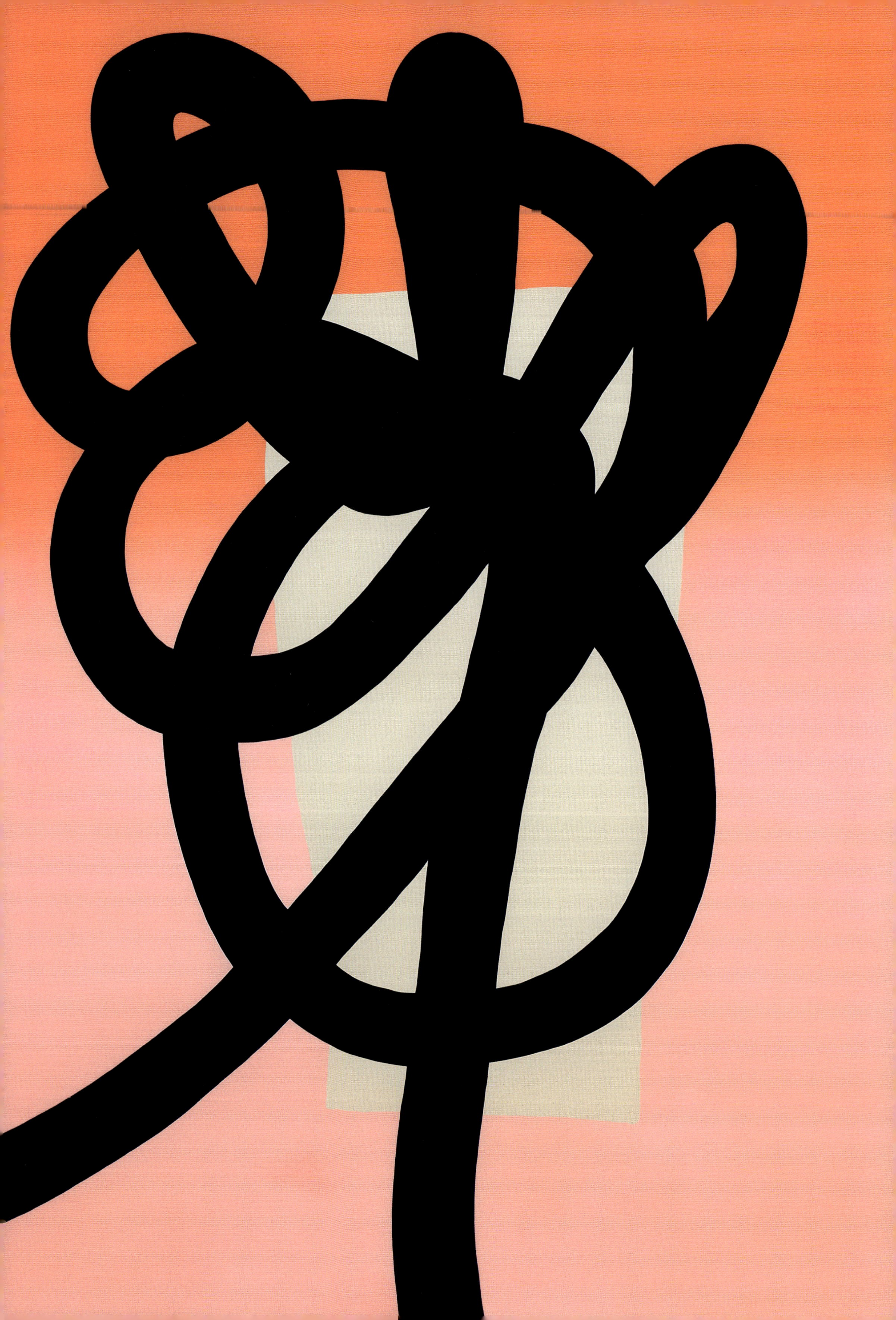

Eclipse, Projektraum ung5, Ebertplatz, Cologne (DE), 2016

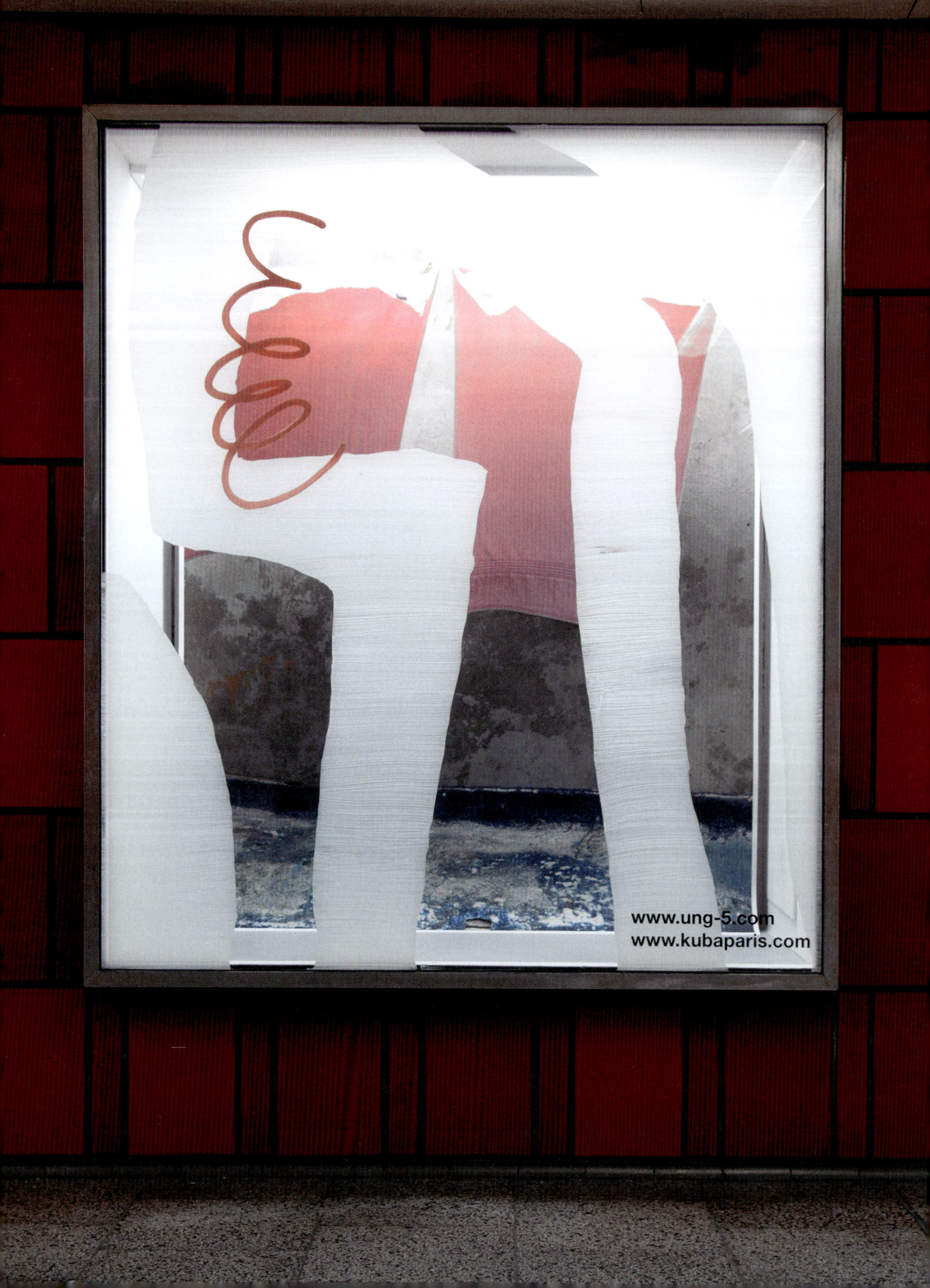

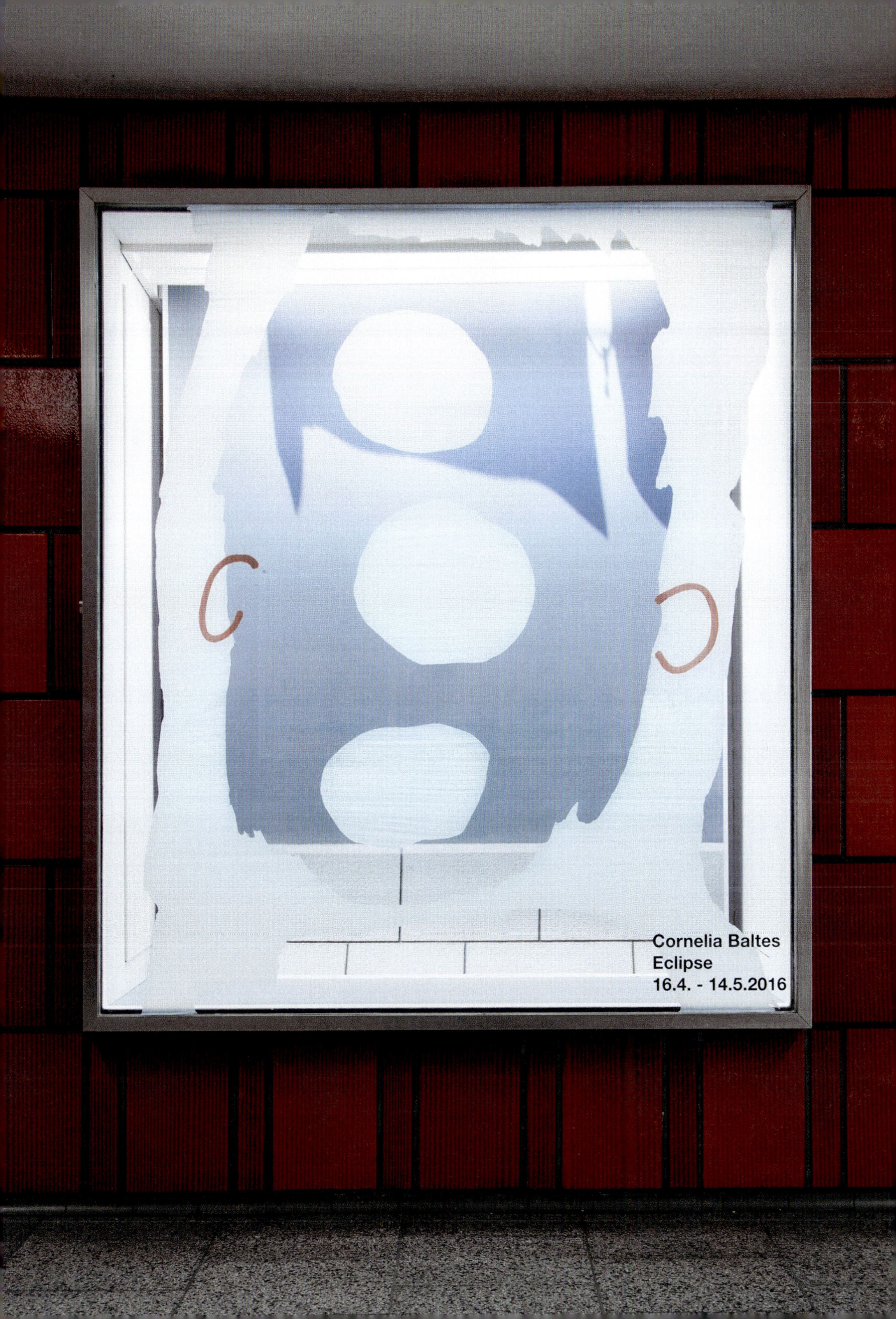
Cornelia Baltes
Eclipse
16.4. - 14.5.2016

Liste Art Fair, Limoncello, Basel (CH), 2016

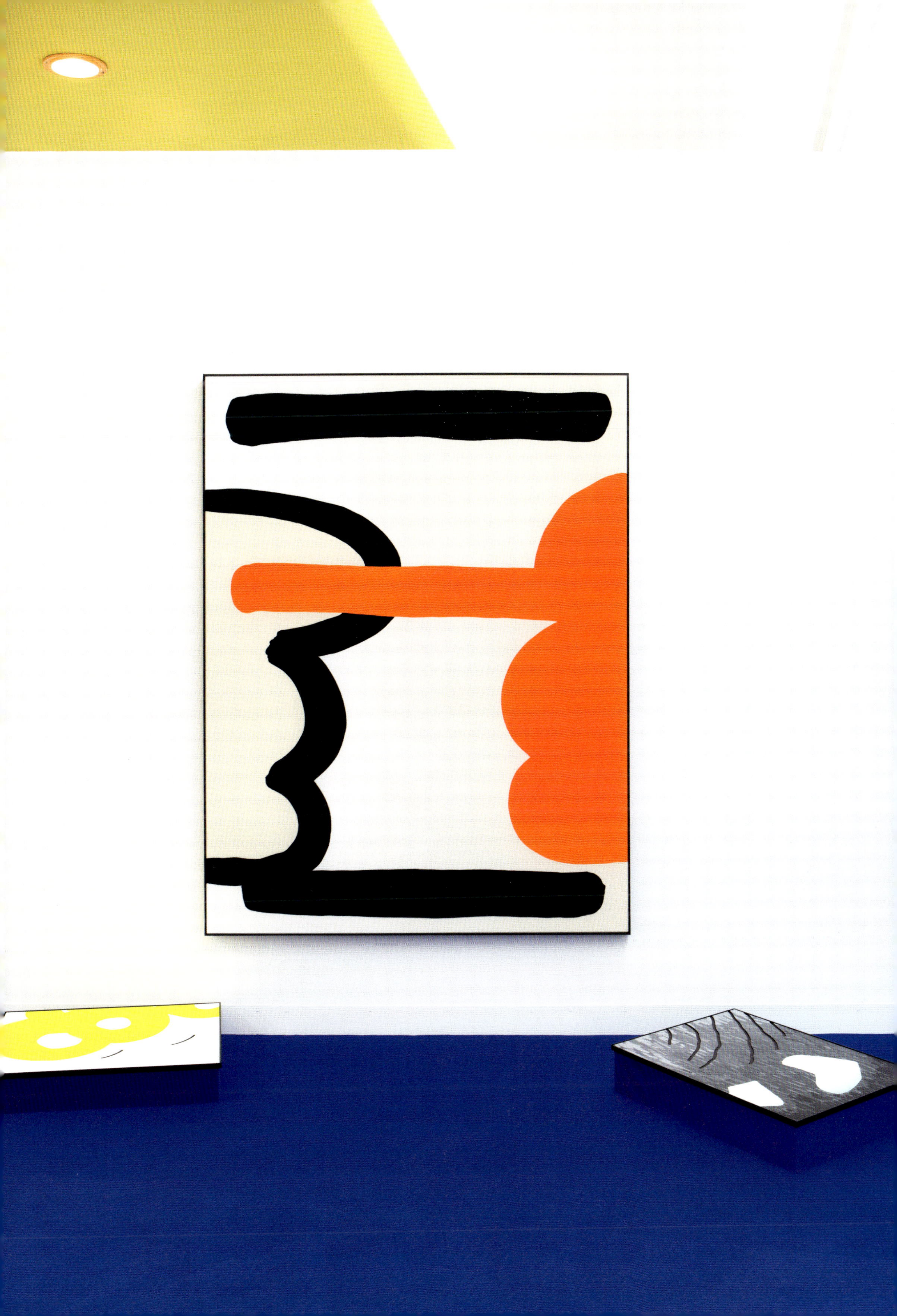

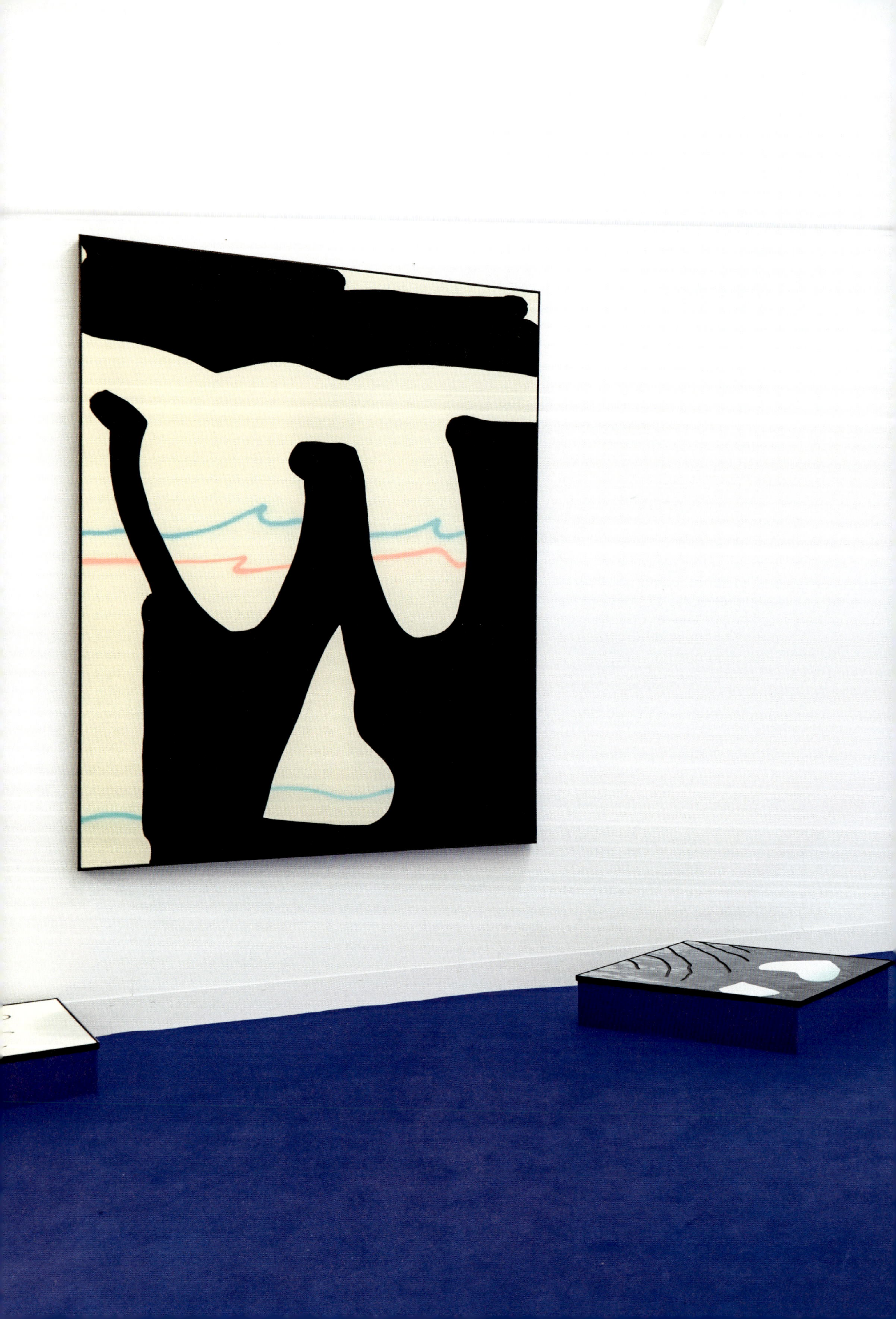

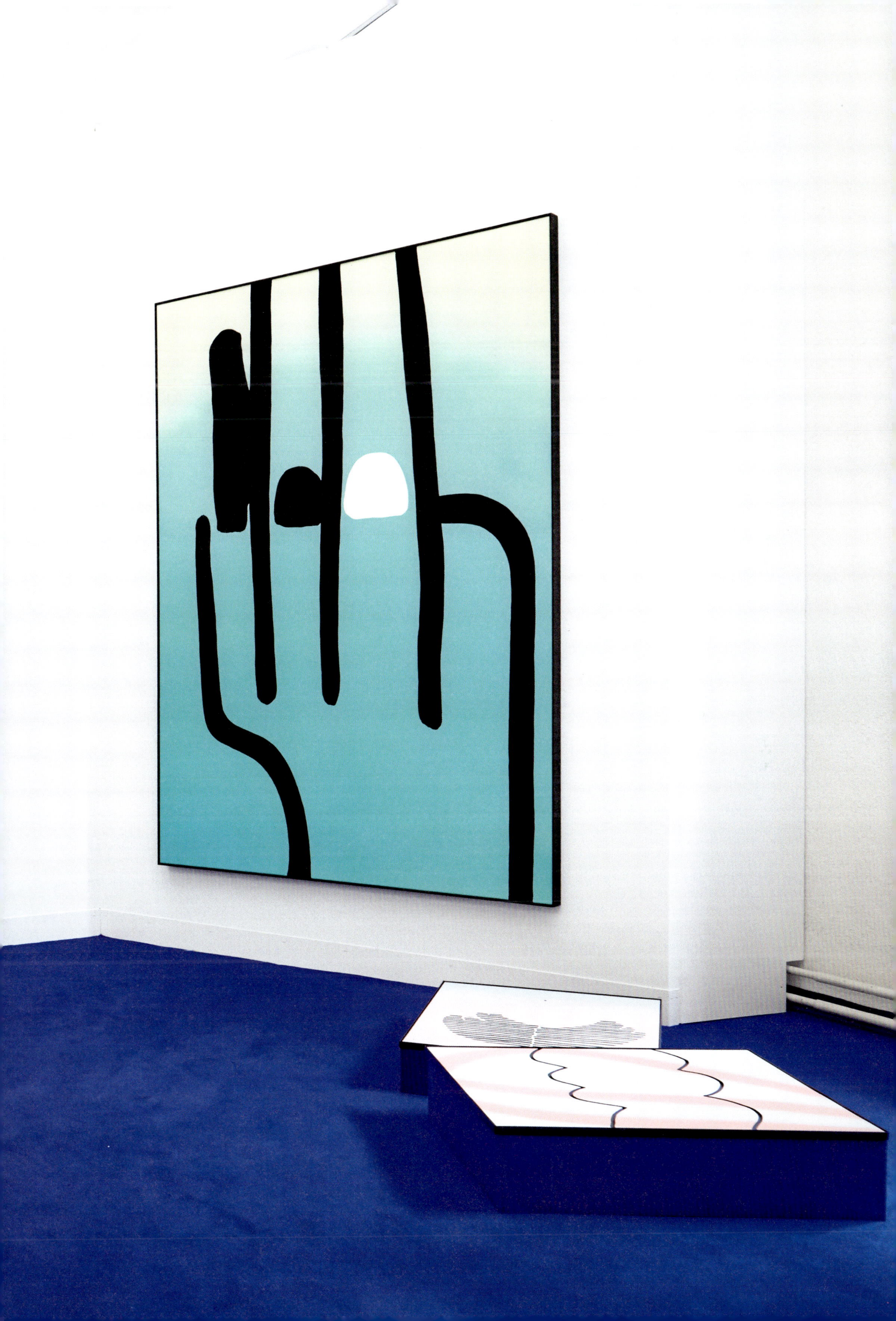

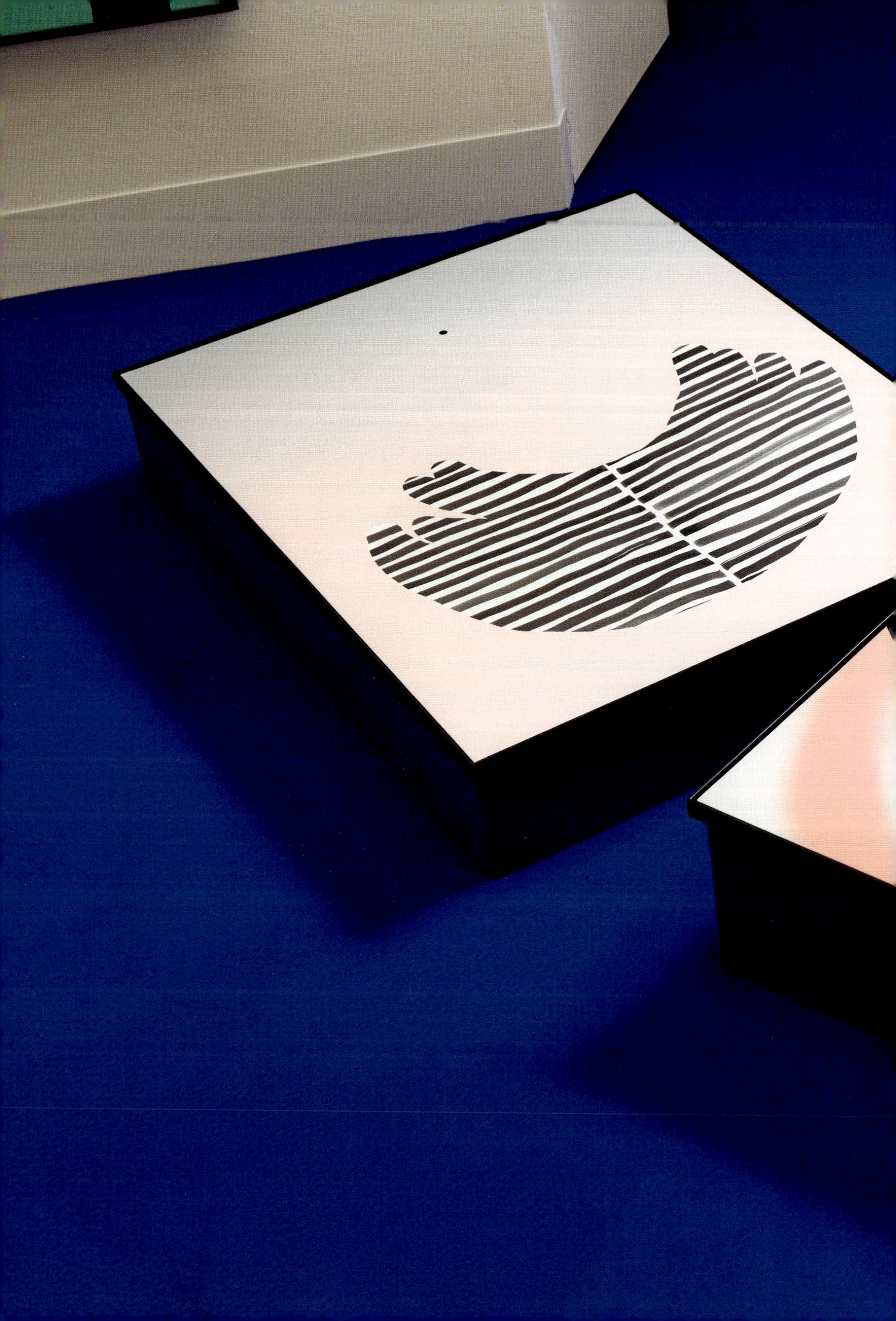

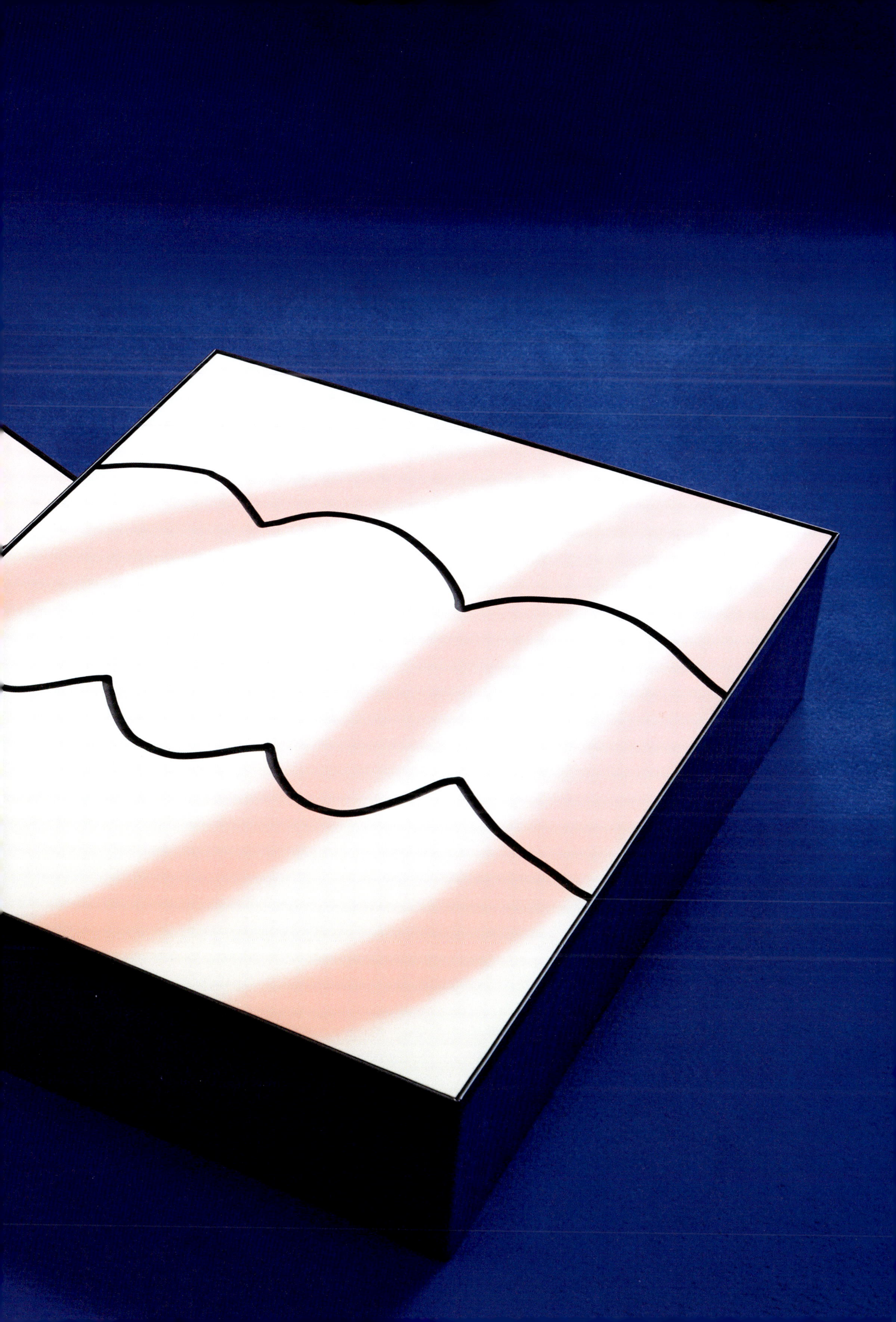

Drunk Octopus wants to fight, Limoncello, London (UK), 2016

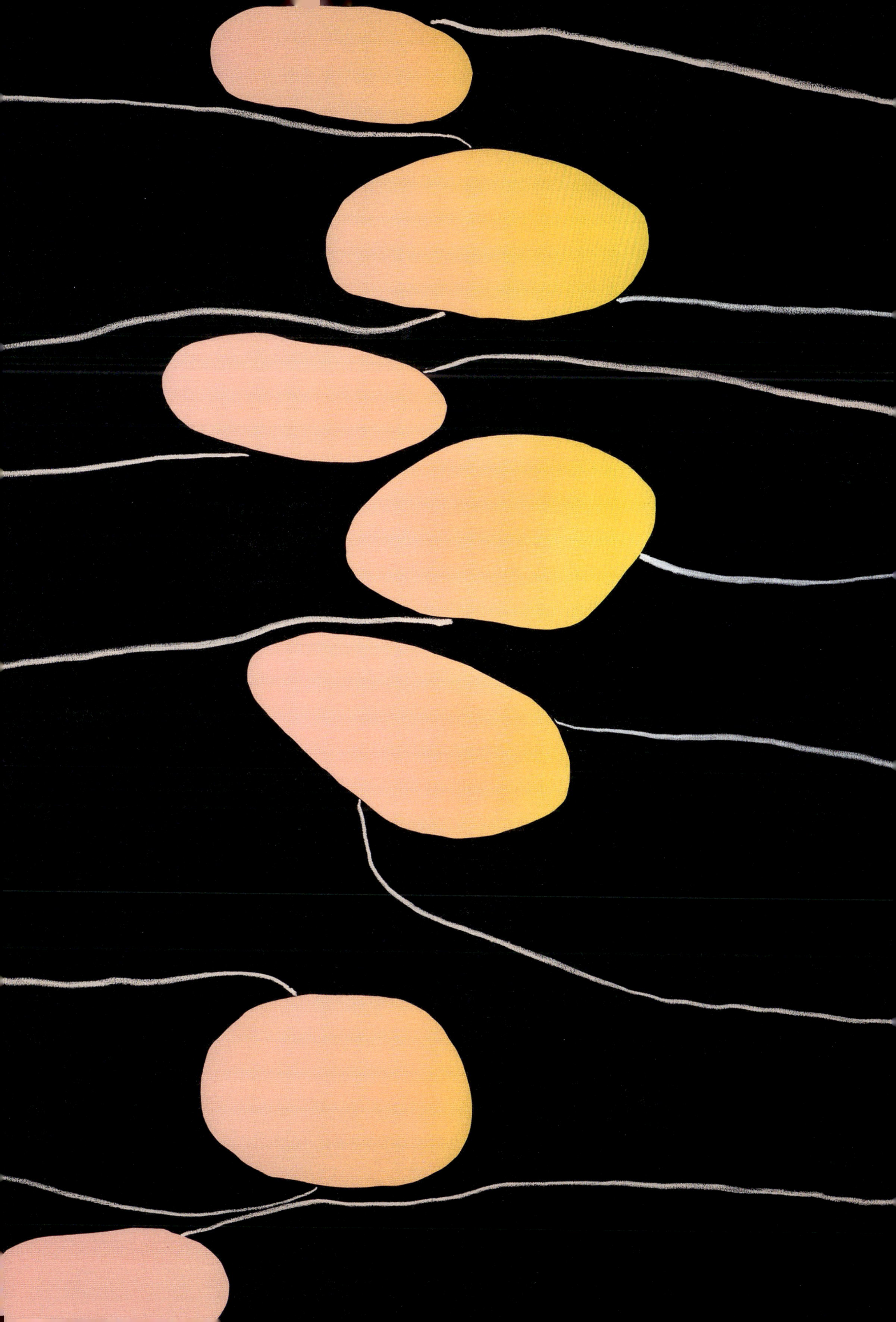

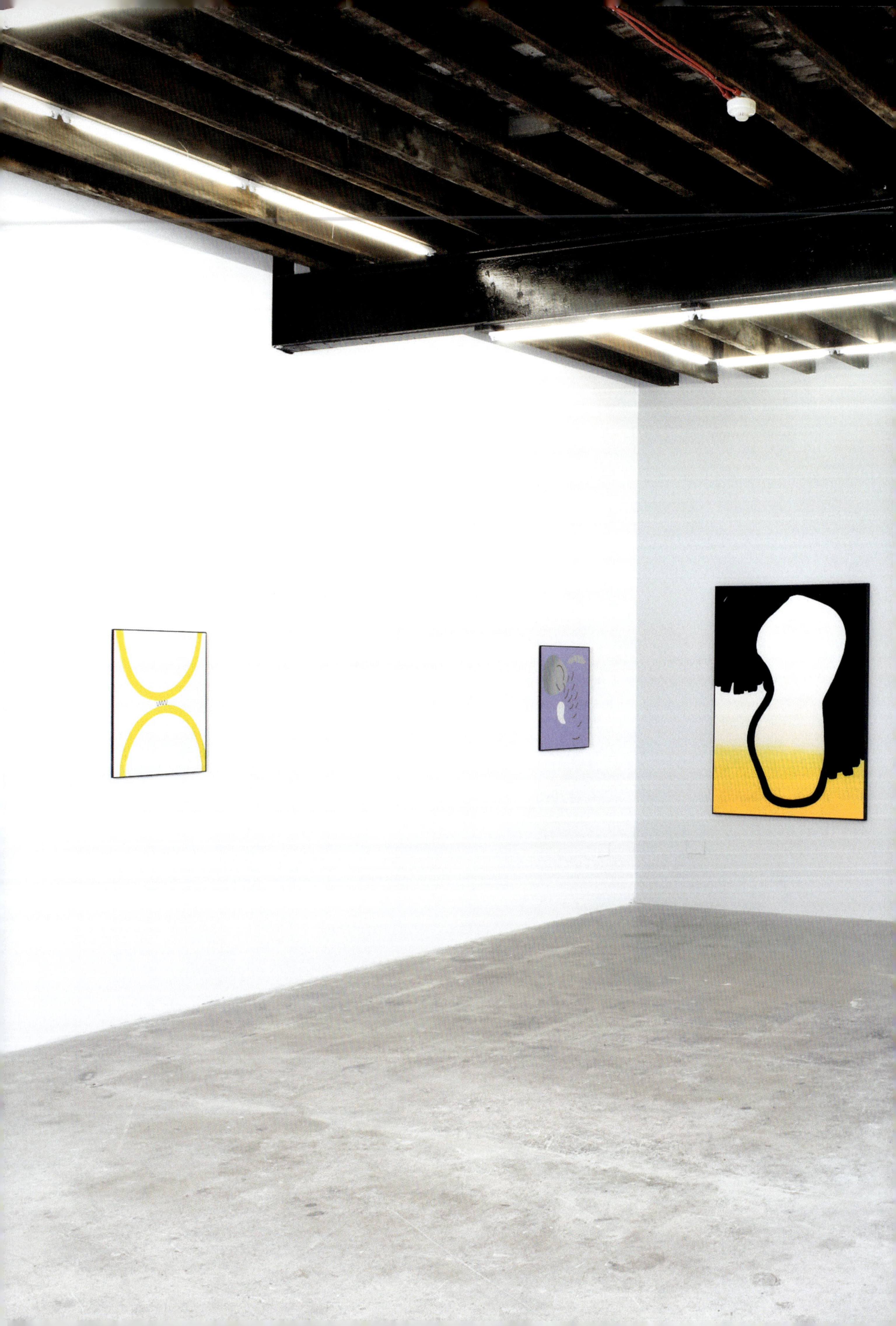

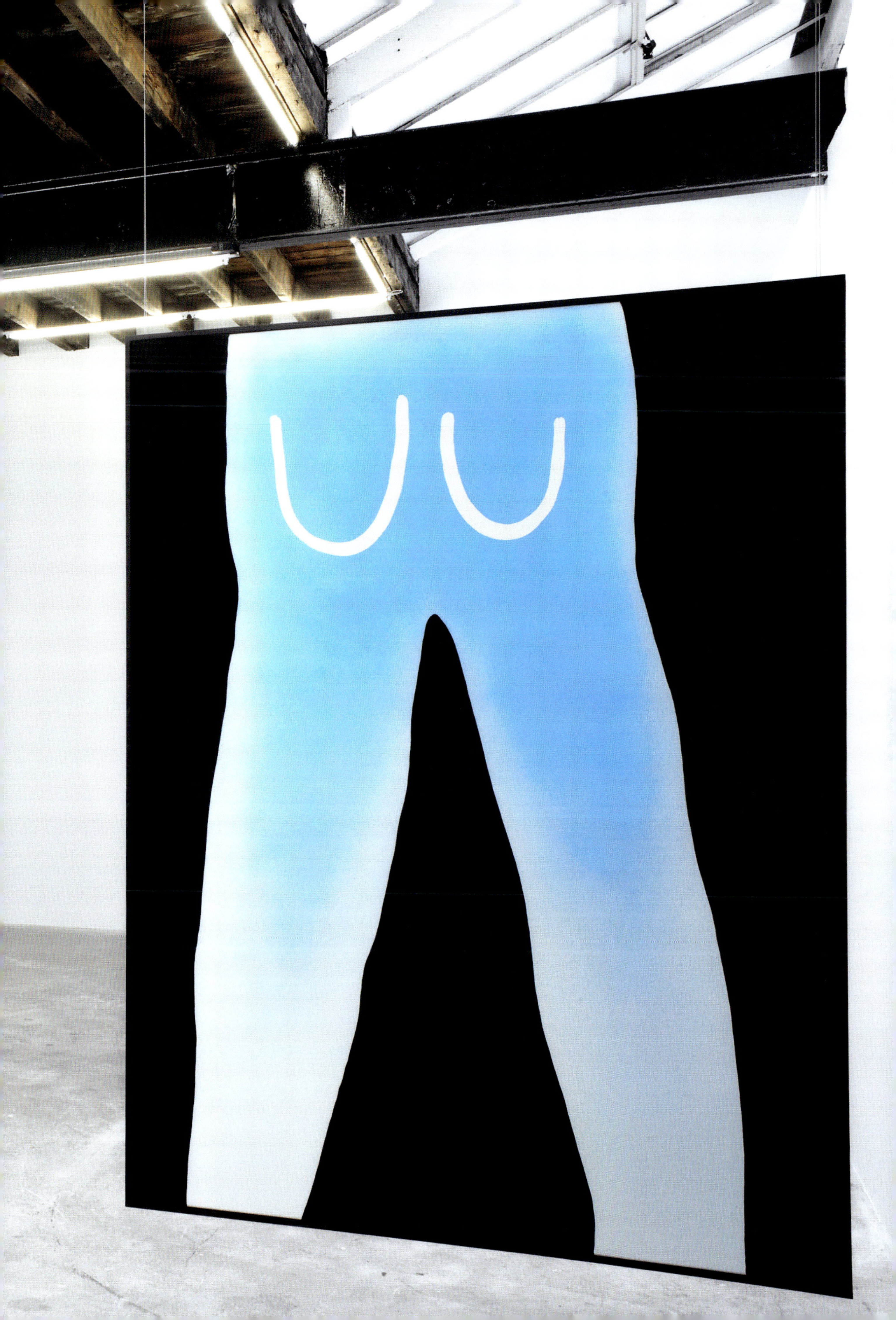

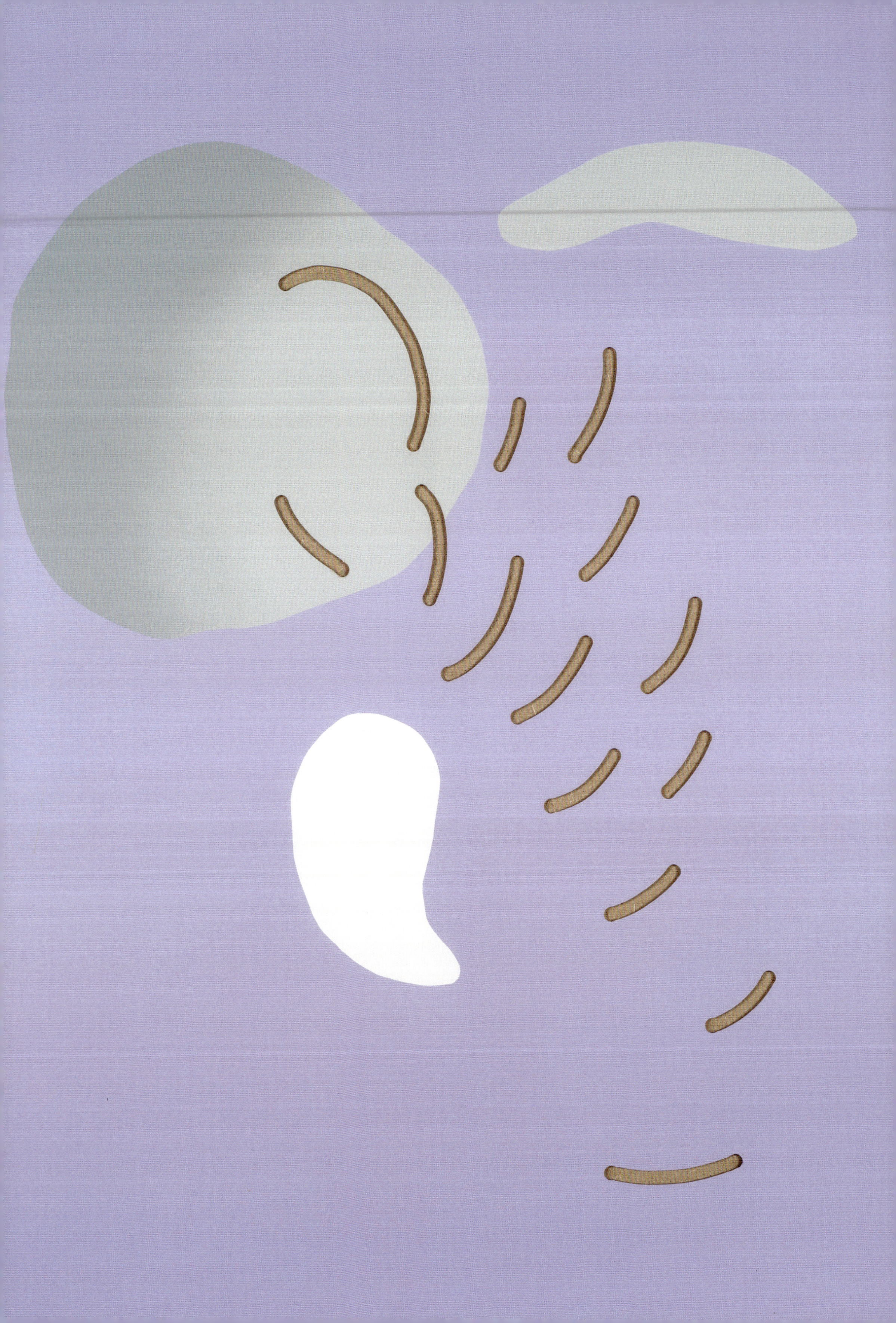

Mission Gallery, Swansea (UK), 2016

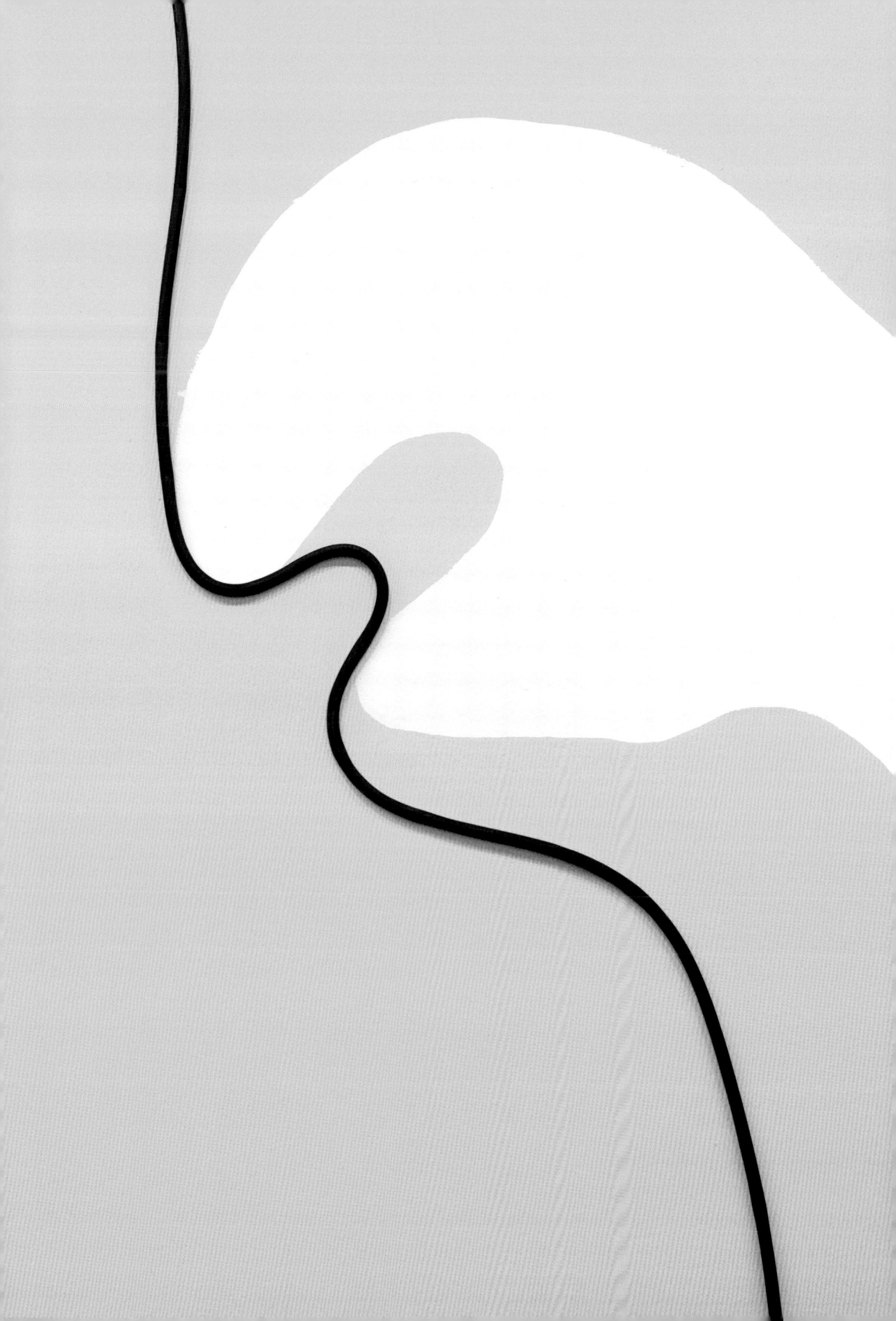

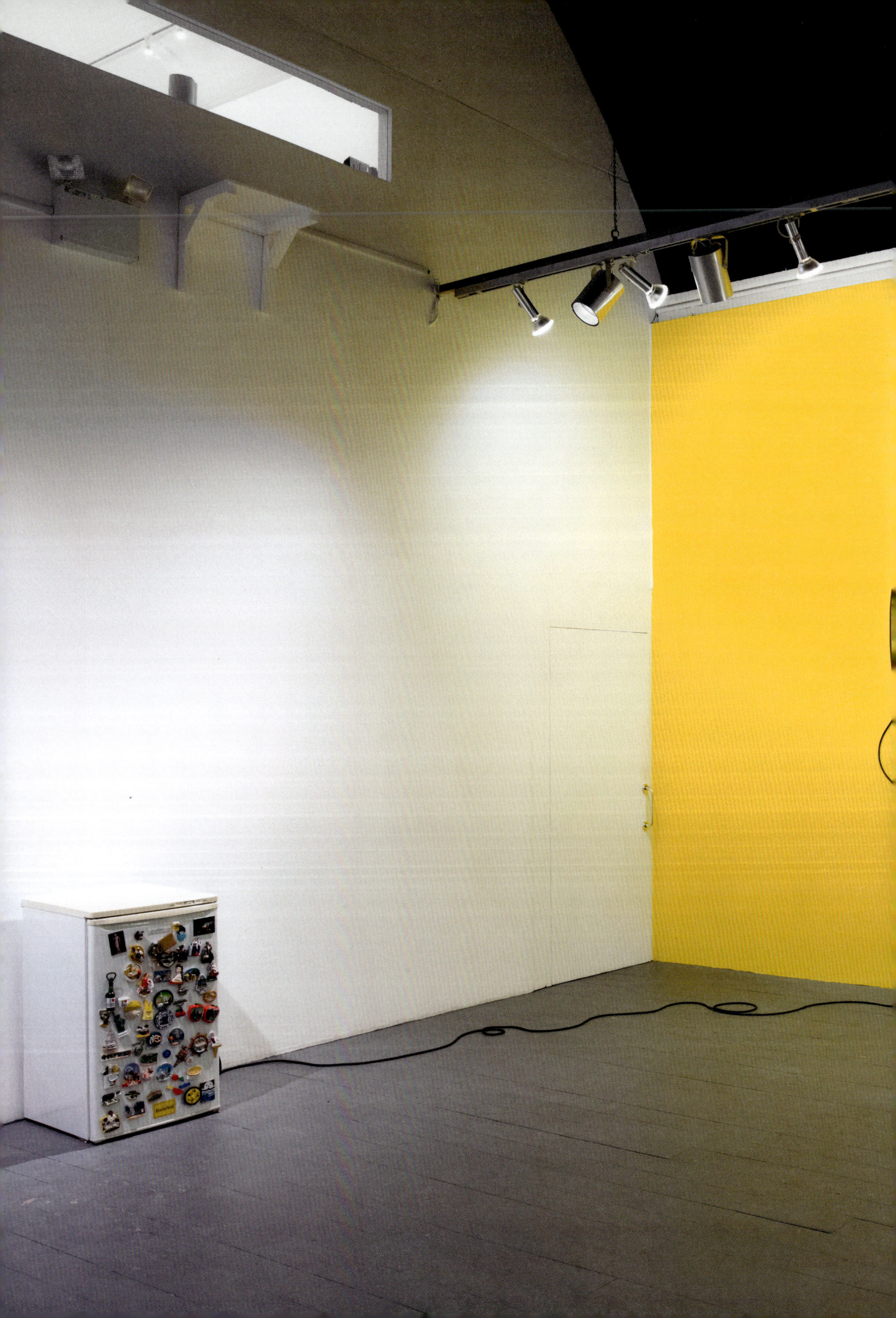

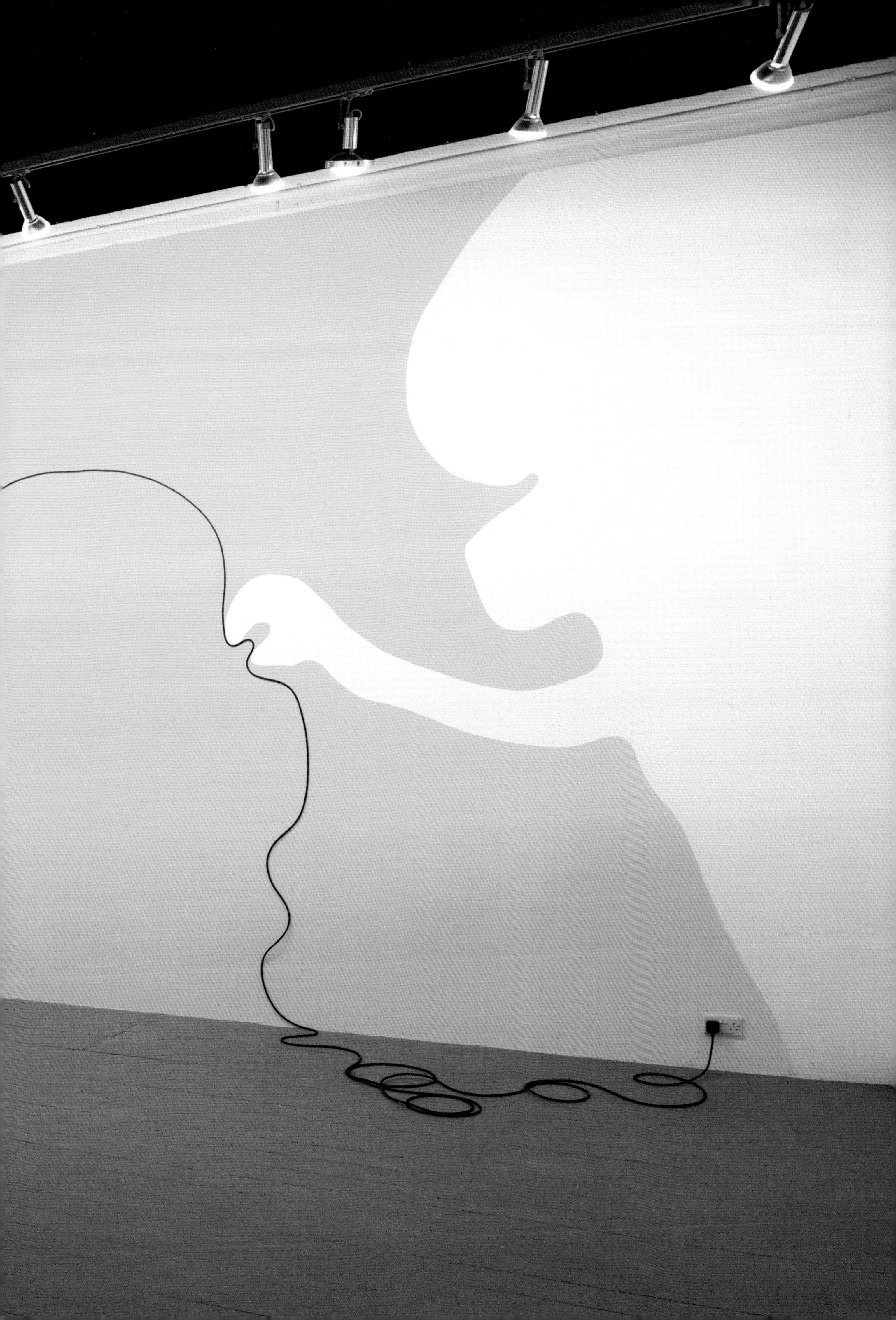

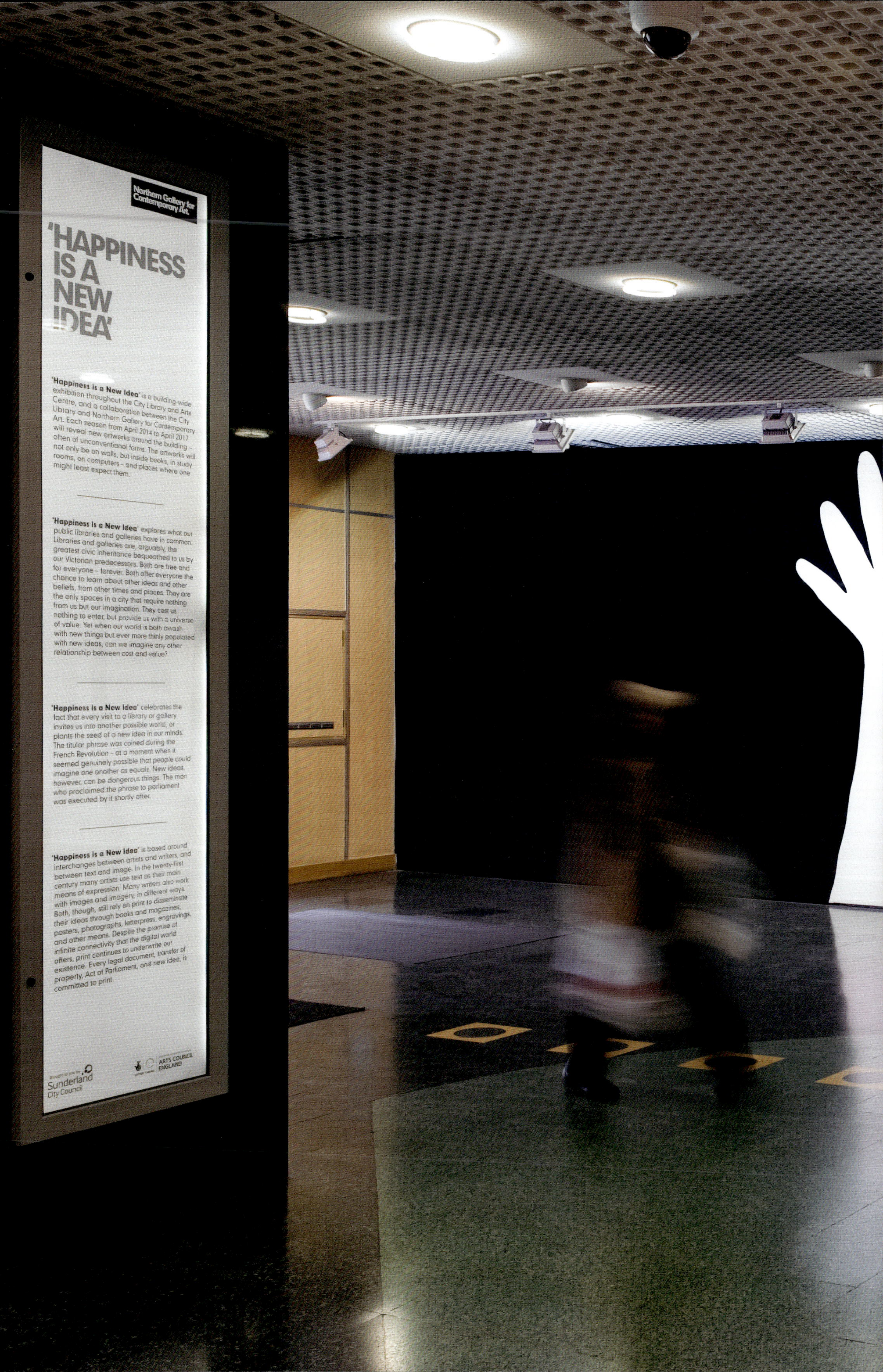
Northern Gallery for Contemporary Art
'HAPPINESS IS A NEW IDEA'
'Happiness is a New Idea' is a building-wide exhibition throughout the City Library and Arts Centre, and a collaboration between the City Library and Northern Gallery for Contemporary Art. Each season from April 2014 to April 2017 will reveal new artworks around the building – often of unconventional forms. The artworks will not only be on walls, but inside books, in study rooms, on computers – and places where one might least expect them.
'Happiness is a New Idea' explores what our public libraries and galleries have in common. Libraries and galleries are, arguably, the greatest civic inheritance bequeathed to us by our Victorian predecessors. Both are free and for everyone – forever. Both offer everyone the chance to learn about other ideas and other beliefs, from other times and places. They are the only spaces in a city that require nothing from us but our imagination. They cost us nothing to enter, but provide us with a universe of value. Yet when our world is both awash with new things but ever more thinly populated with new ideas, can we imagine any other relationship between cost and value?
'Happiness is a New Idea' celebrates the fact that every visit to a library or gallery invites us into another possible world, or plants the seed of a new idea in our minds. The titular phrase was coined during the French Revolution – at a moment when it seemed genuinely possible that people could imagine one another as equals. New ideas, however, can be dangerous things. The man who proclaimed the phrase to parliament was executed by it shortly after.
'Happiness is a New Idea' is based around interchanges between artists and writers, and between text and image. In the twenty-first century many artists use text as their main means of expression. Many writers also work with images and imagery, in different ways. Both, though, still rely on print to disseminate their ideas through books and magazines, posters, photographs, letterpress, engravings, and other means. Despite the promise of infinite connectivity that the digital world offers, print continues to underwrite our existence. Every legal document, transfer of property, Act of Parliament, and new idea, is committed to print.
Sunderland City Council
ARTS COUNCIL ENGLAND

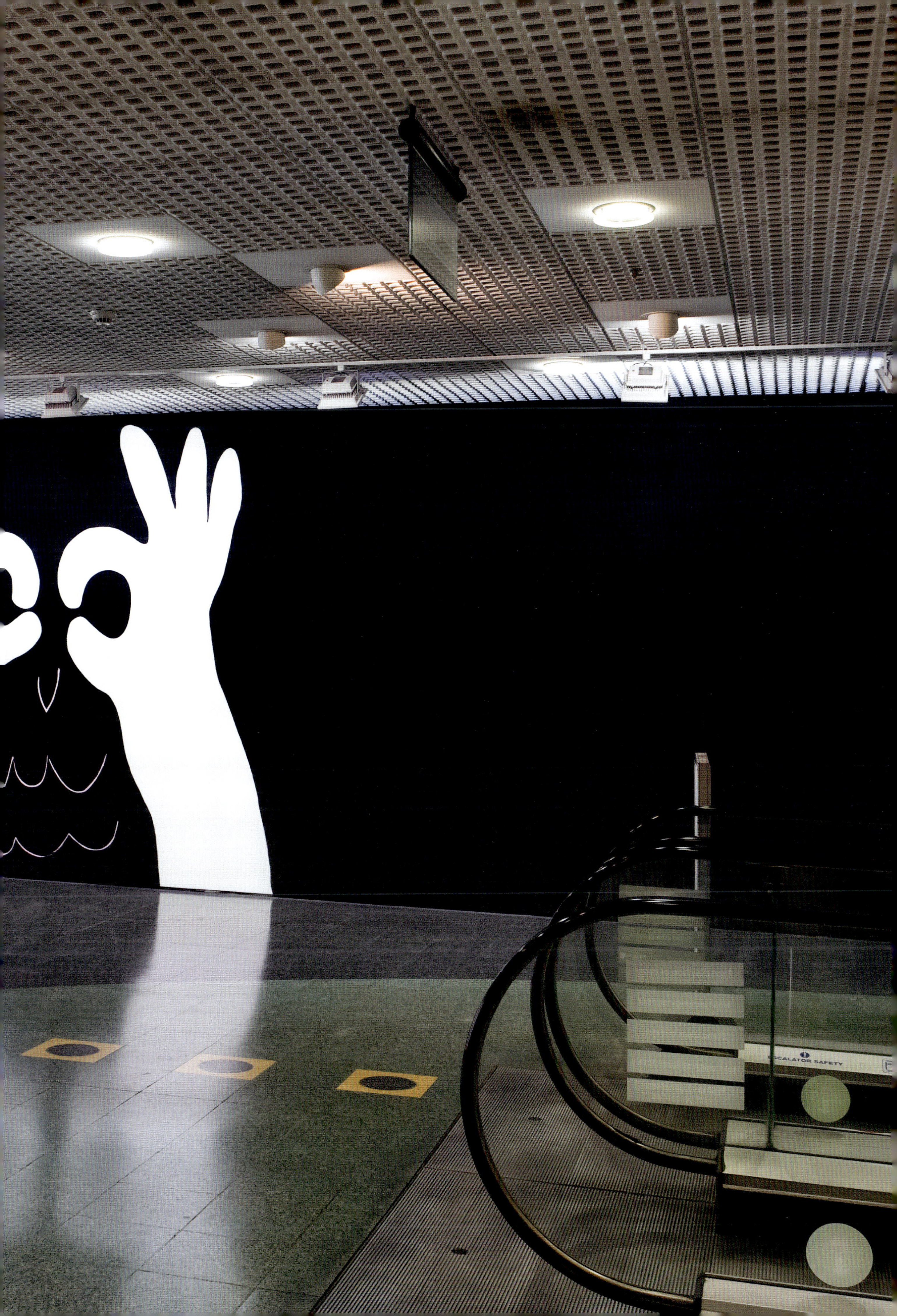
SAFETY

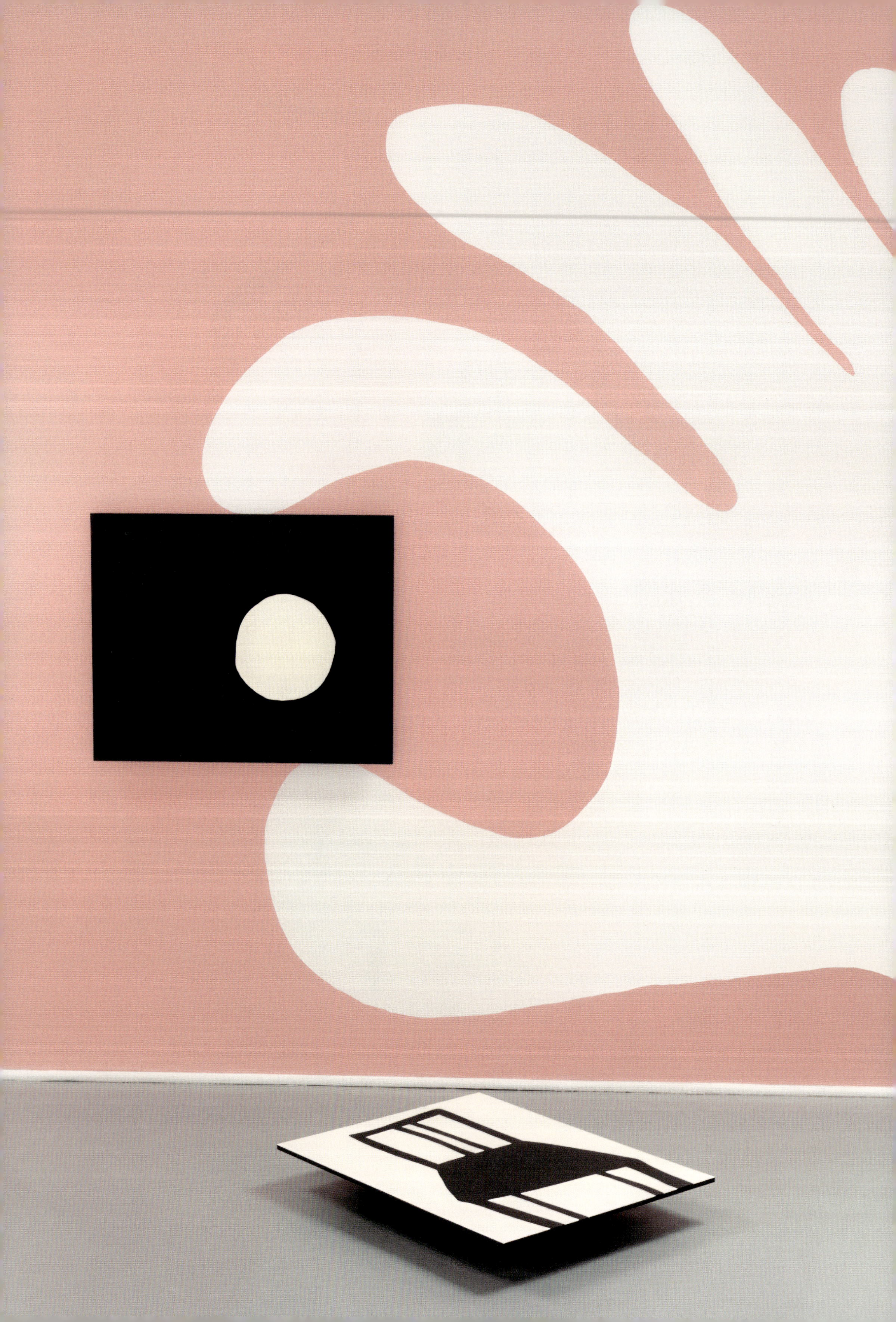

Turner, Northern Gallery for Contemporary Art, Sunderland (UK), 2015

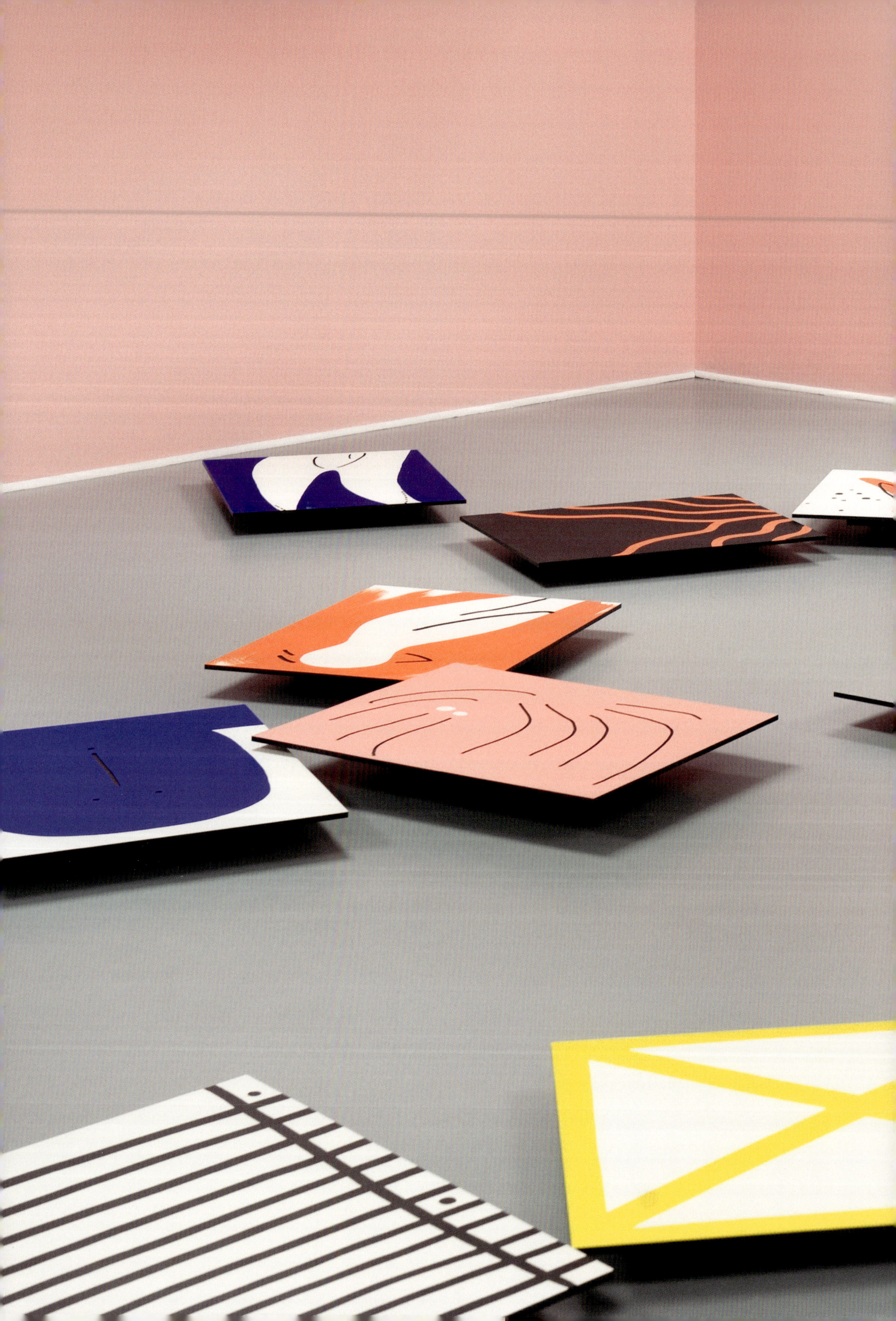

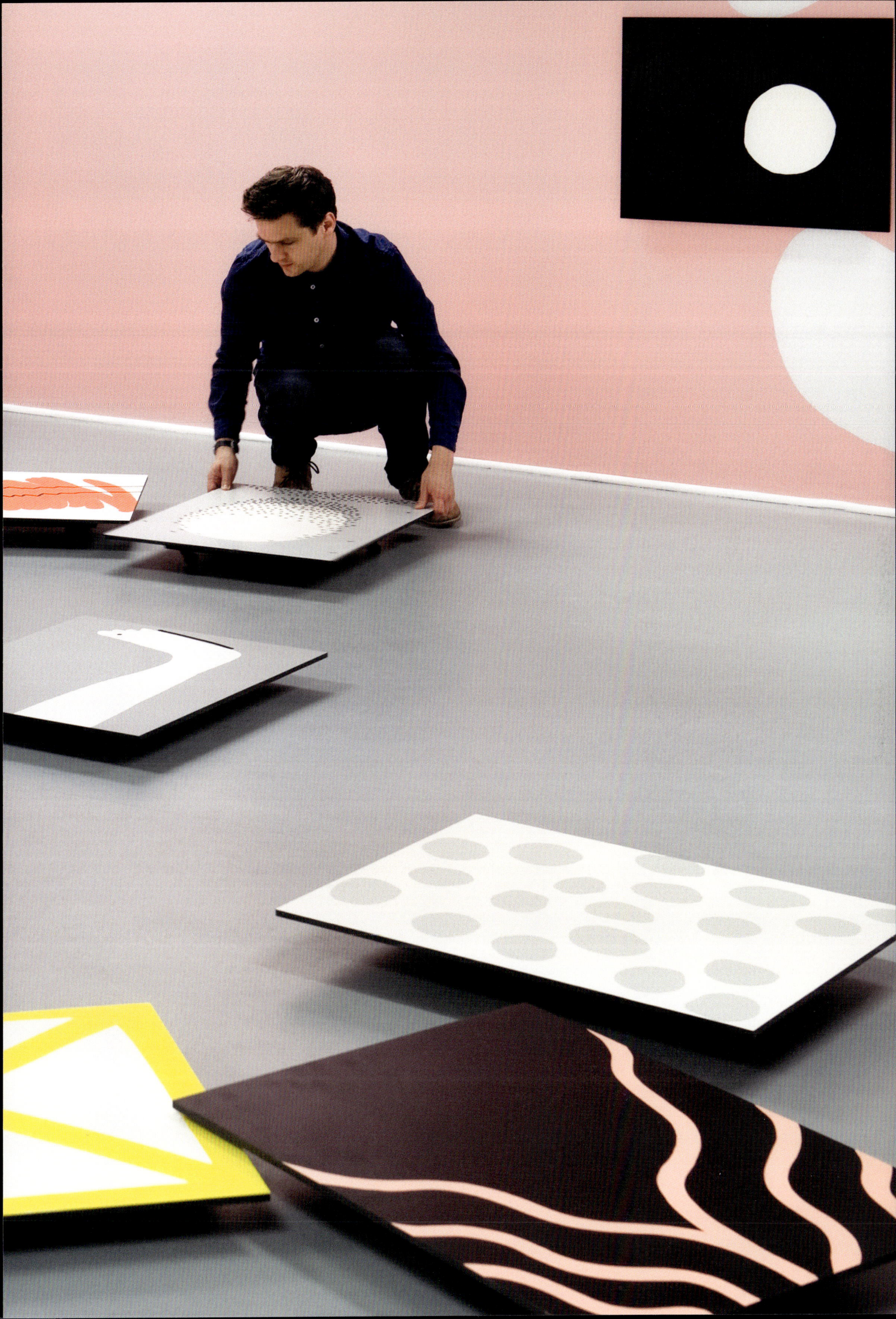

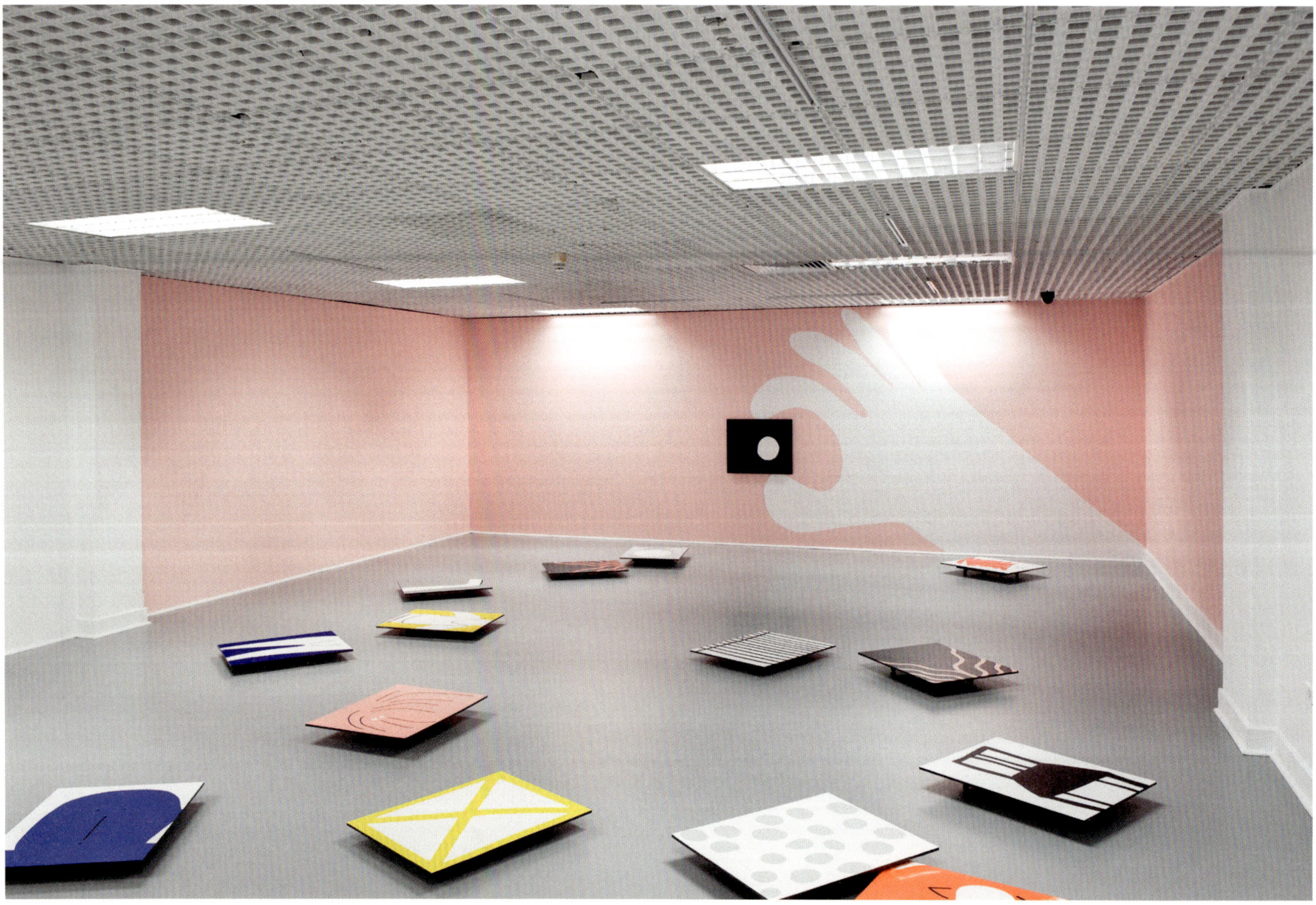

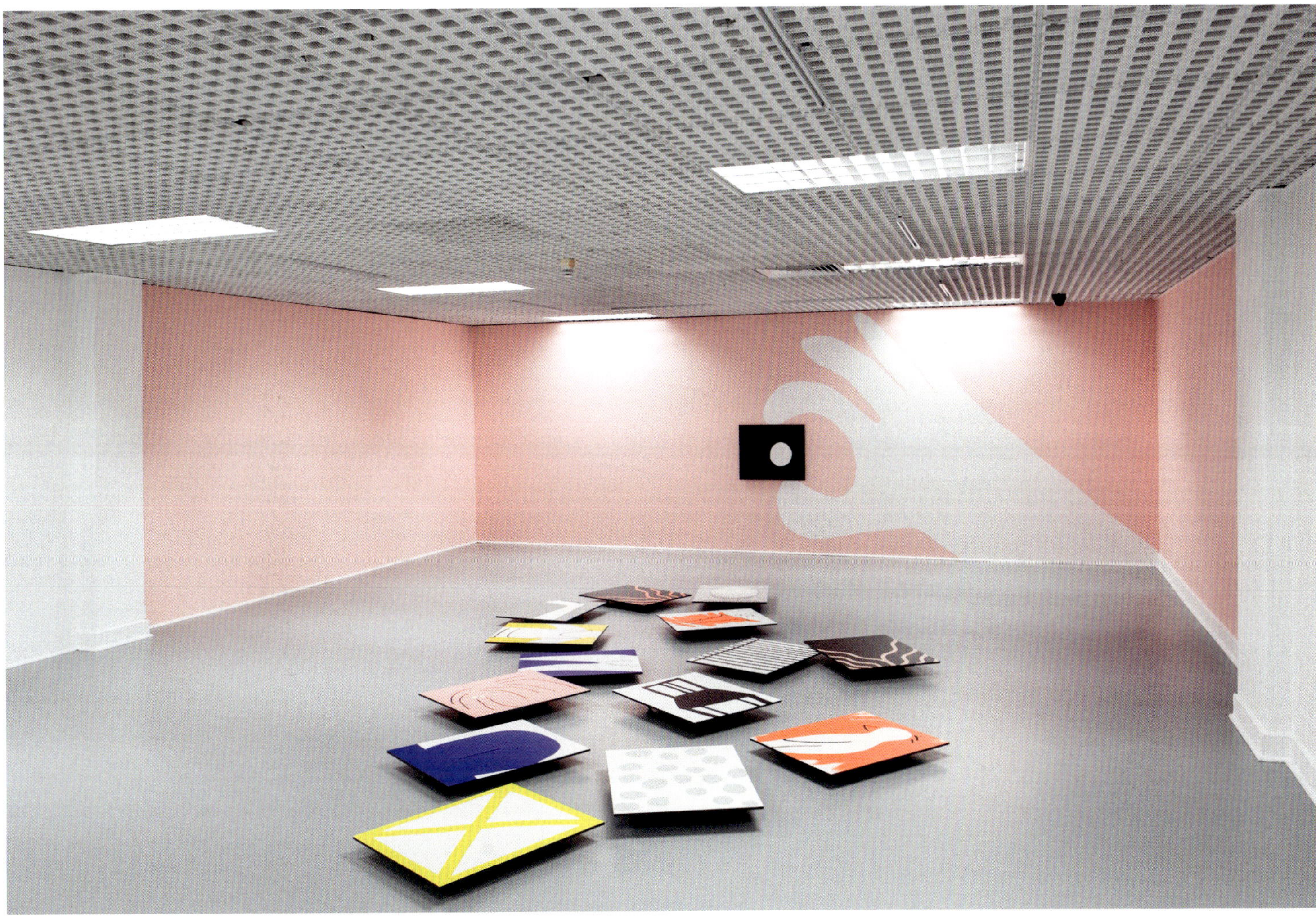

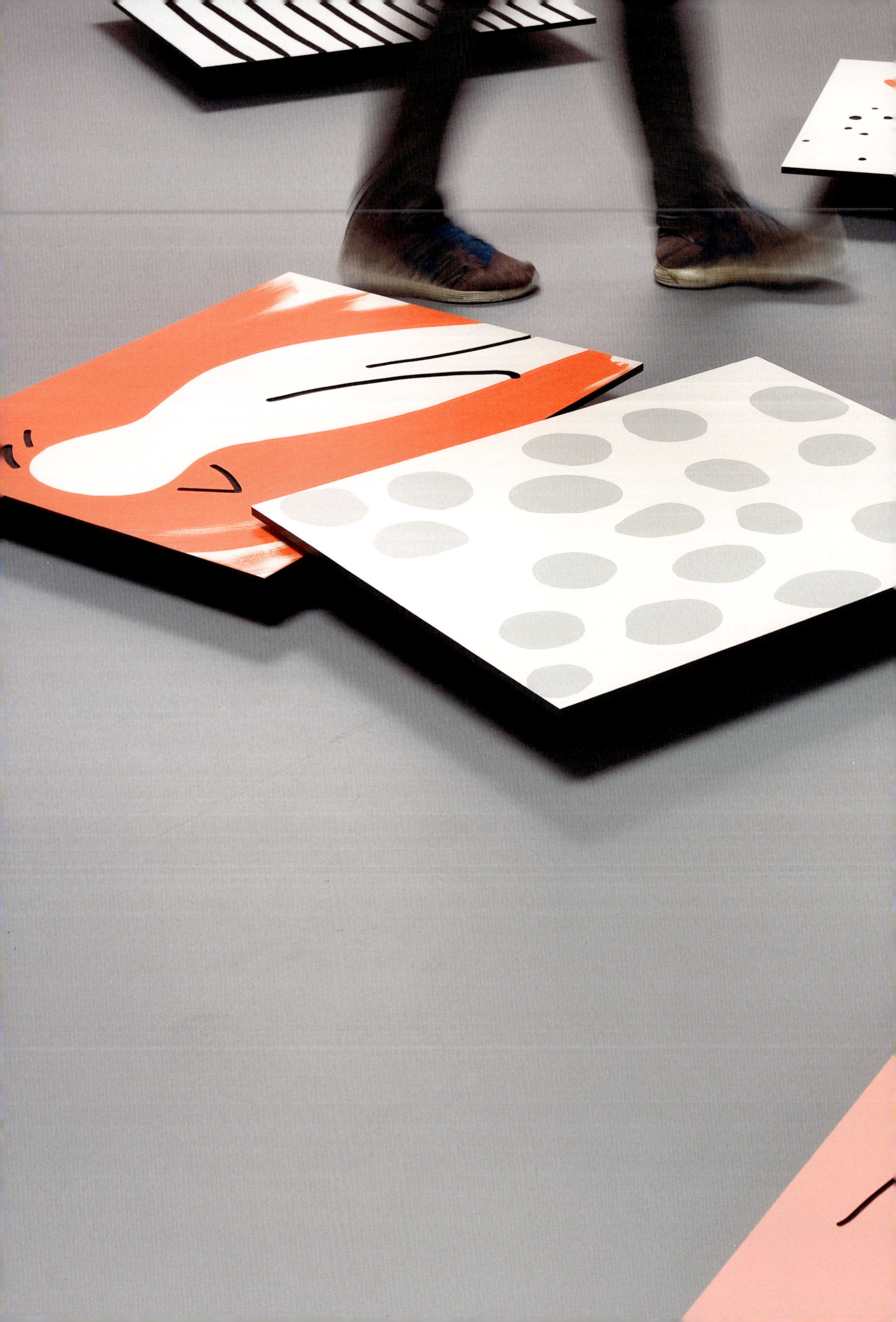

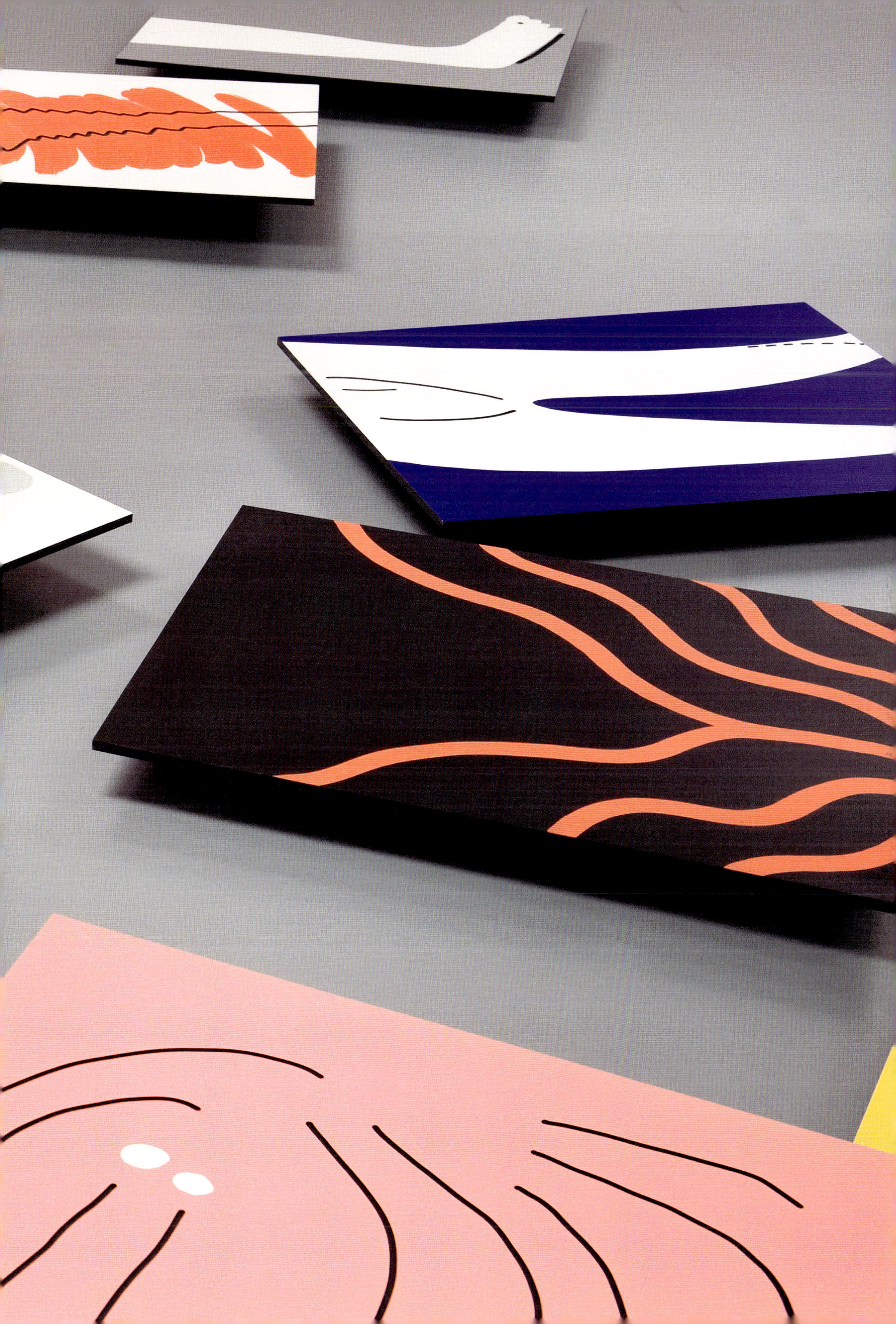

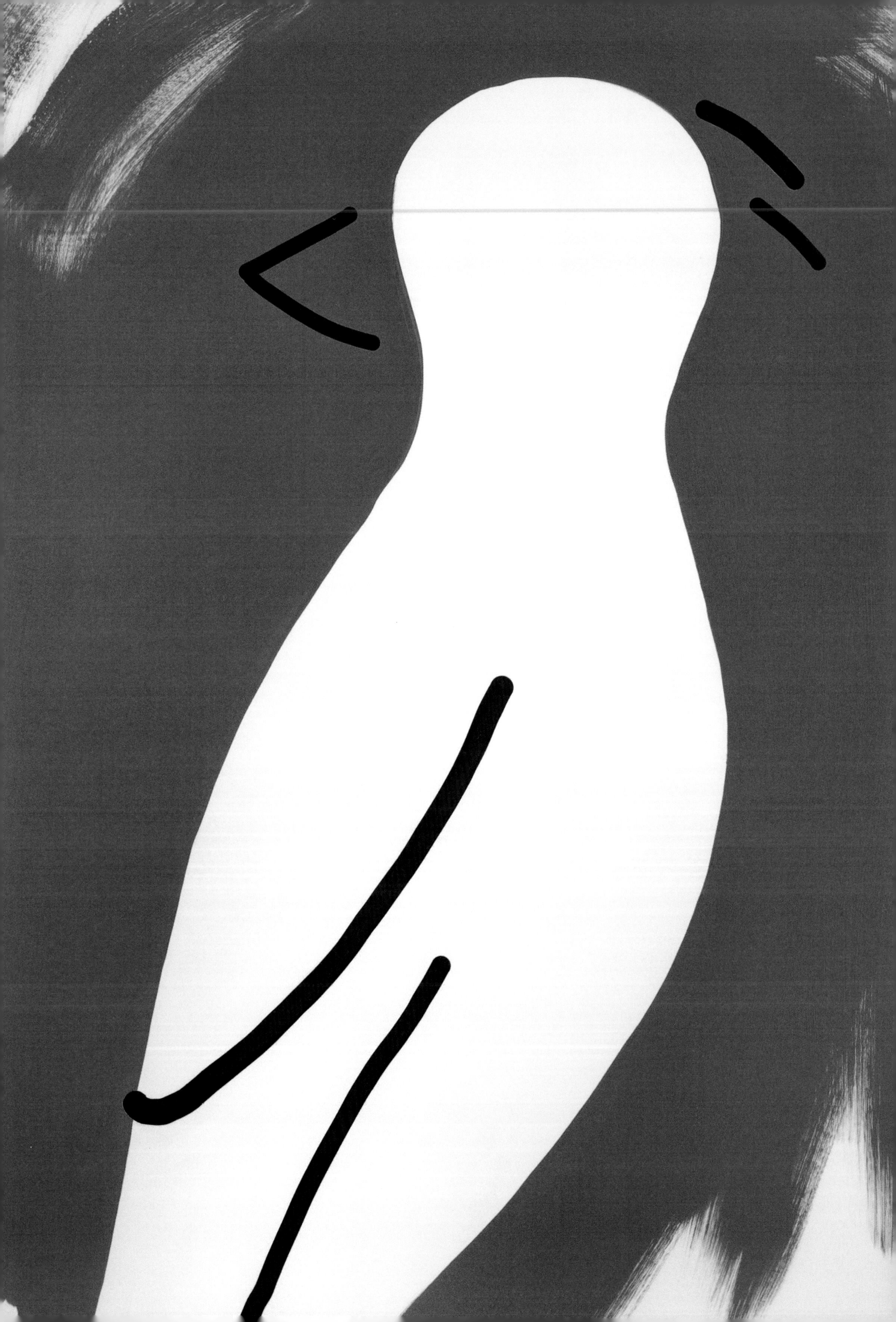

Tiny Dancer, Kunstverein Ulm (DE), 2015

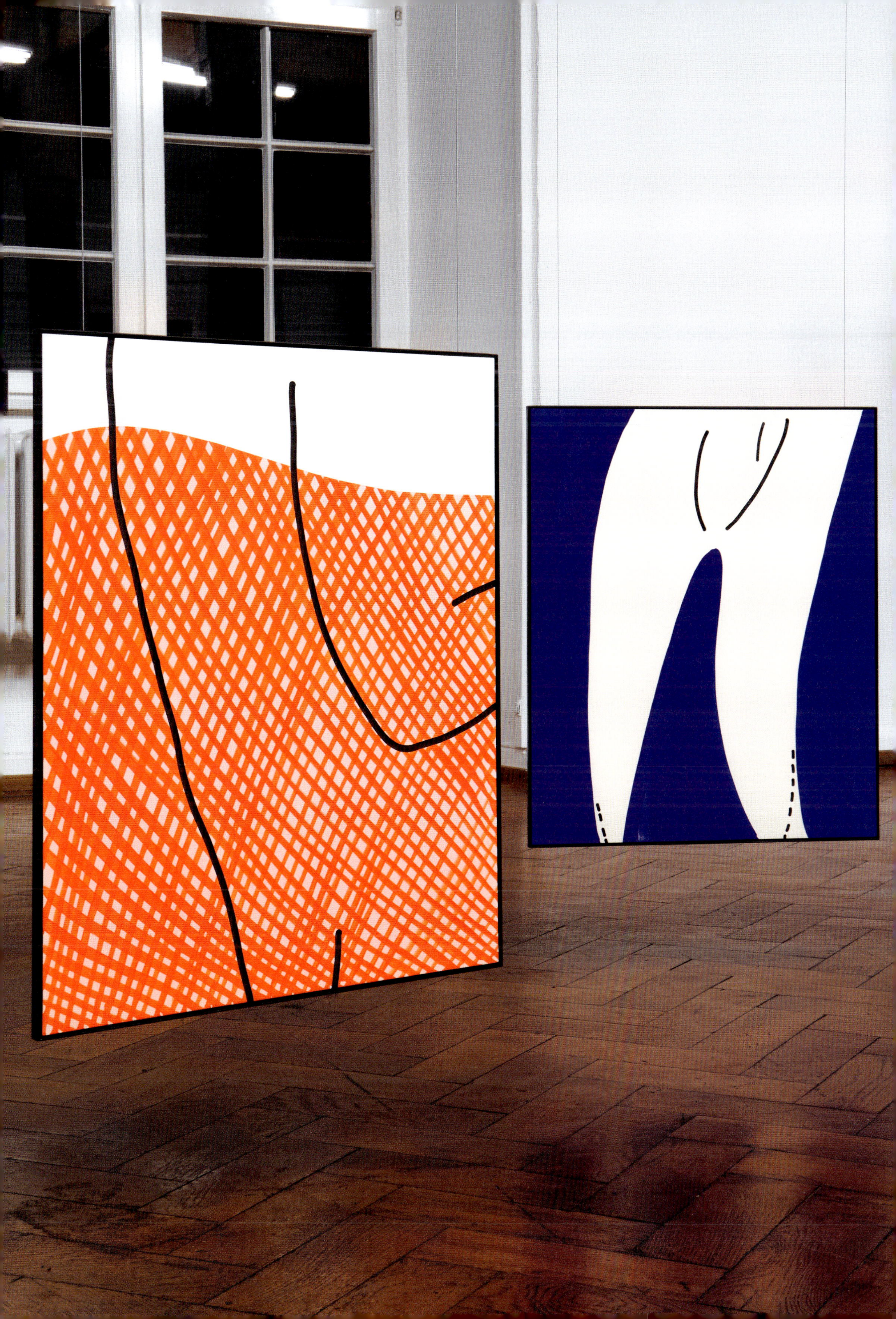

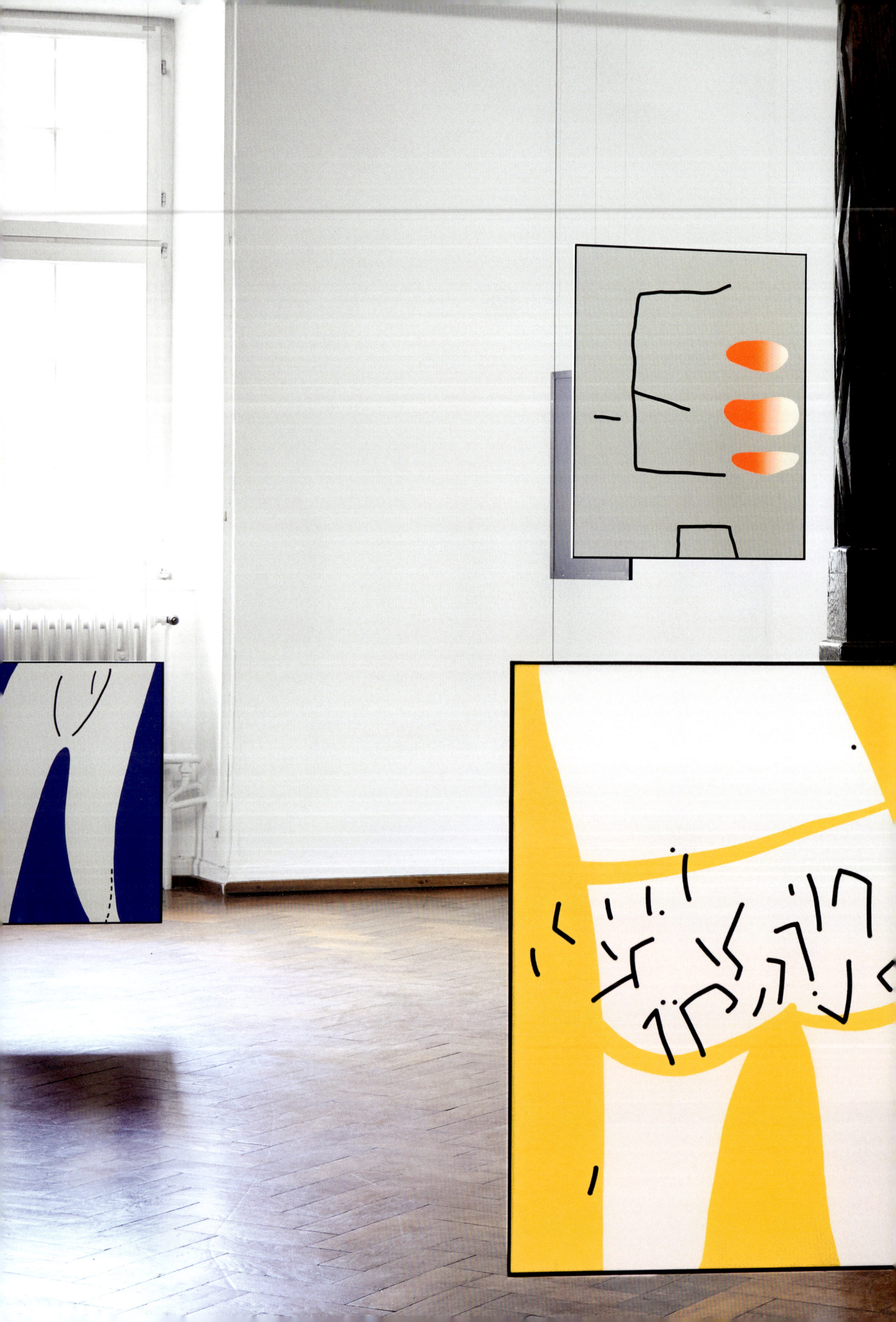

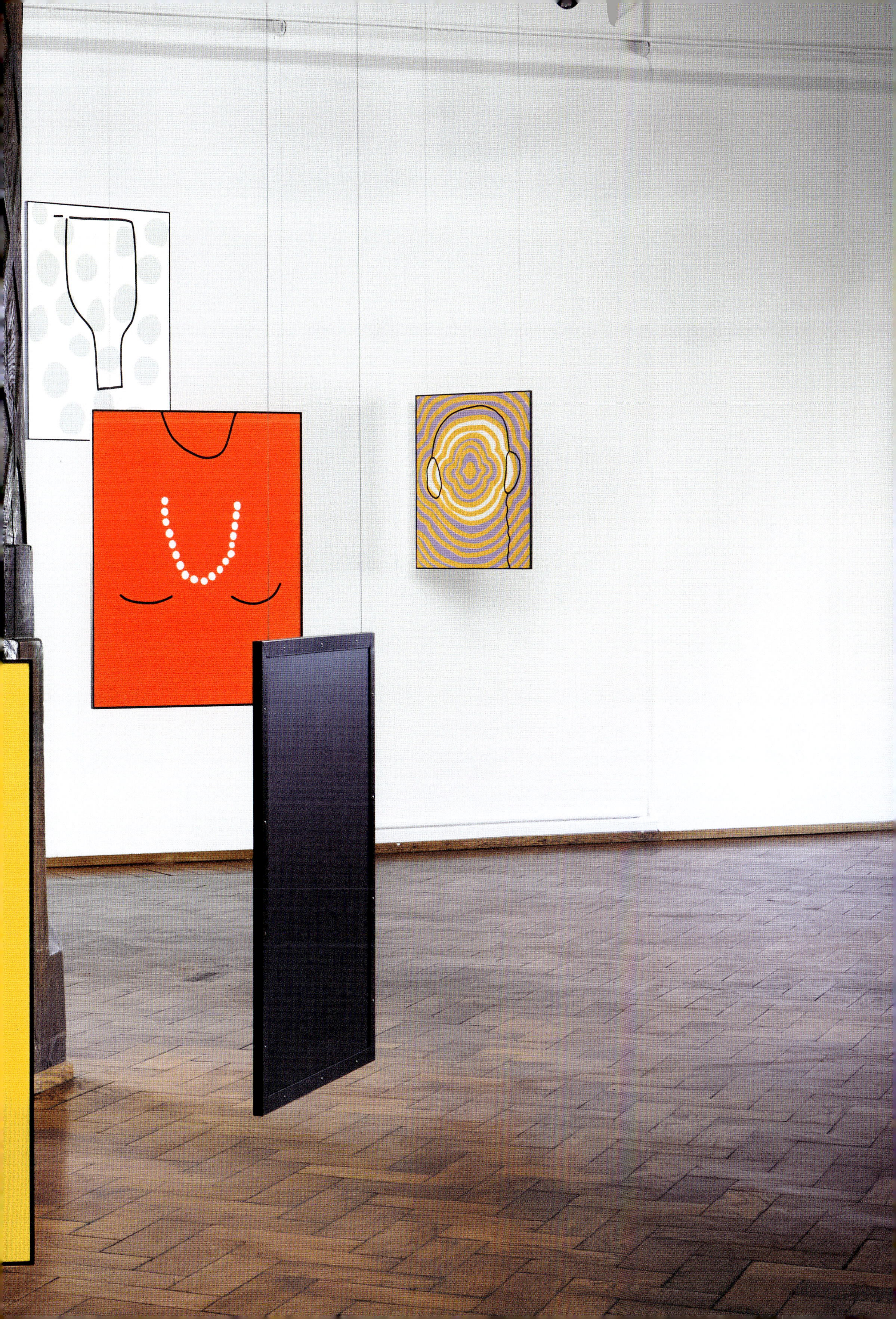

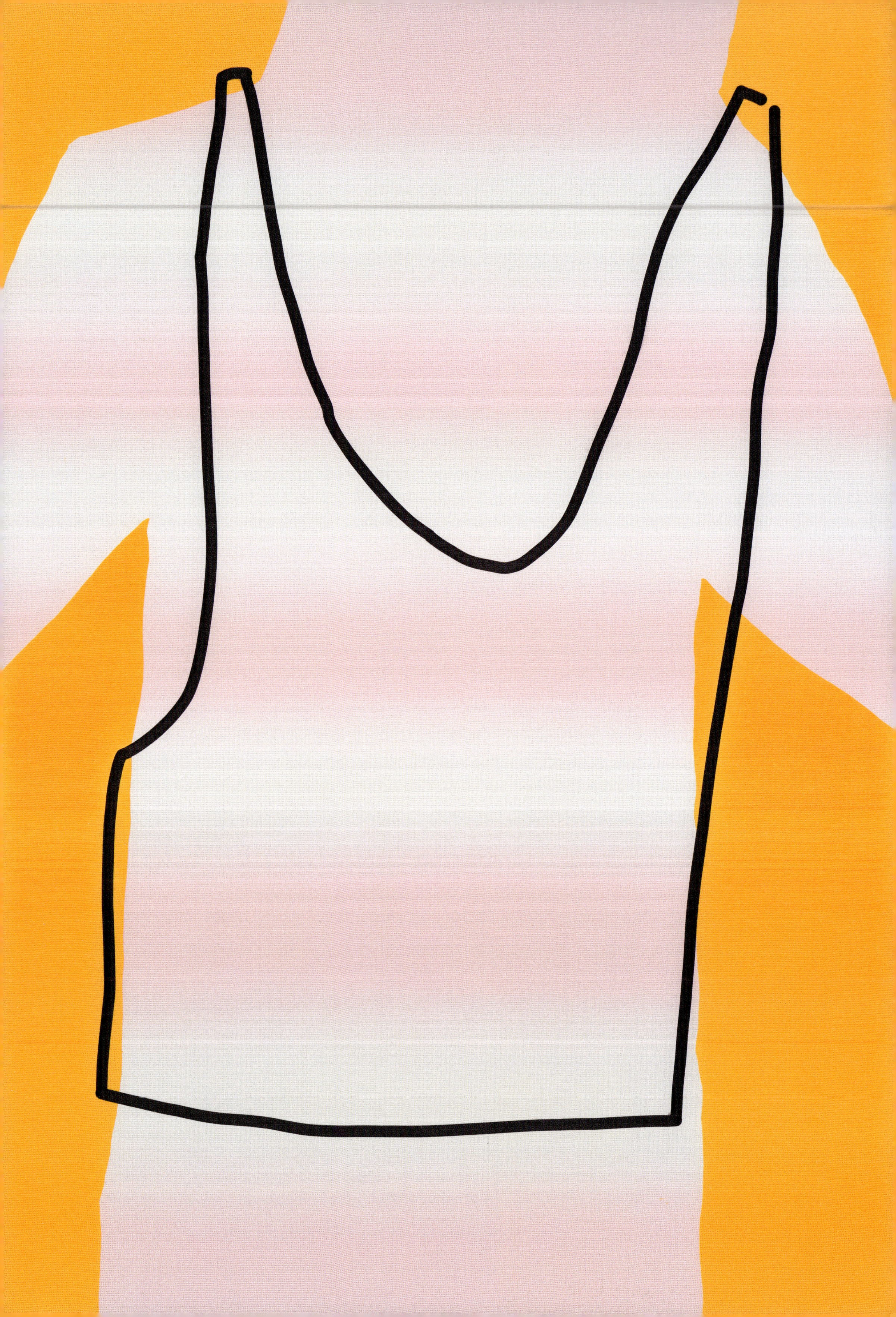

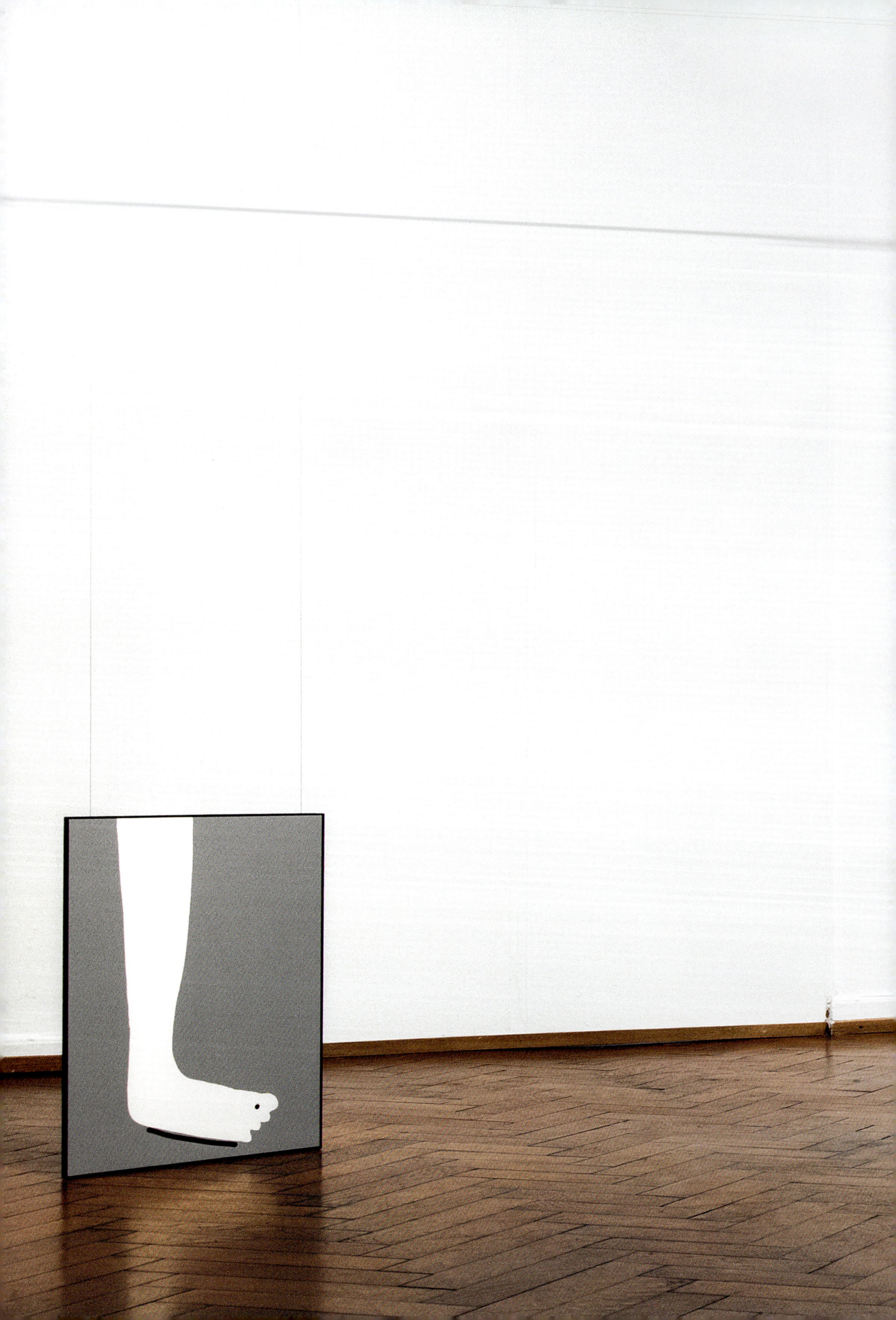

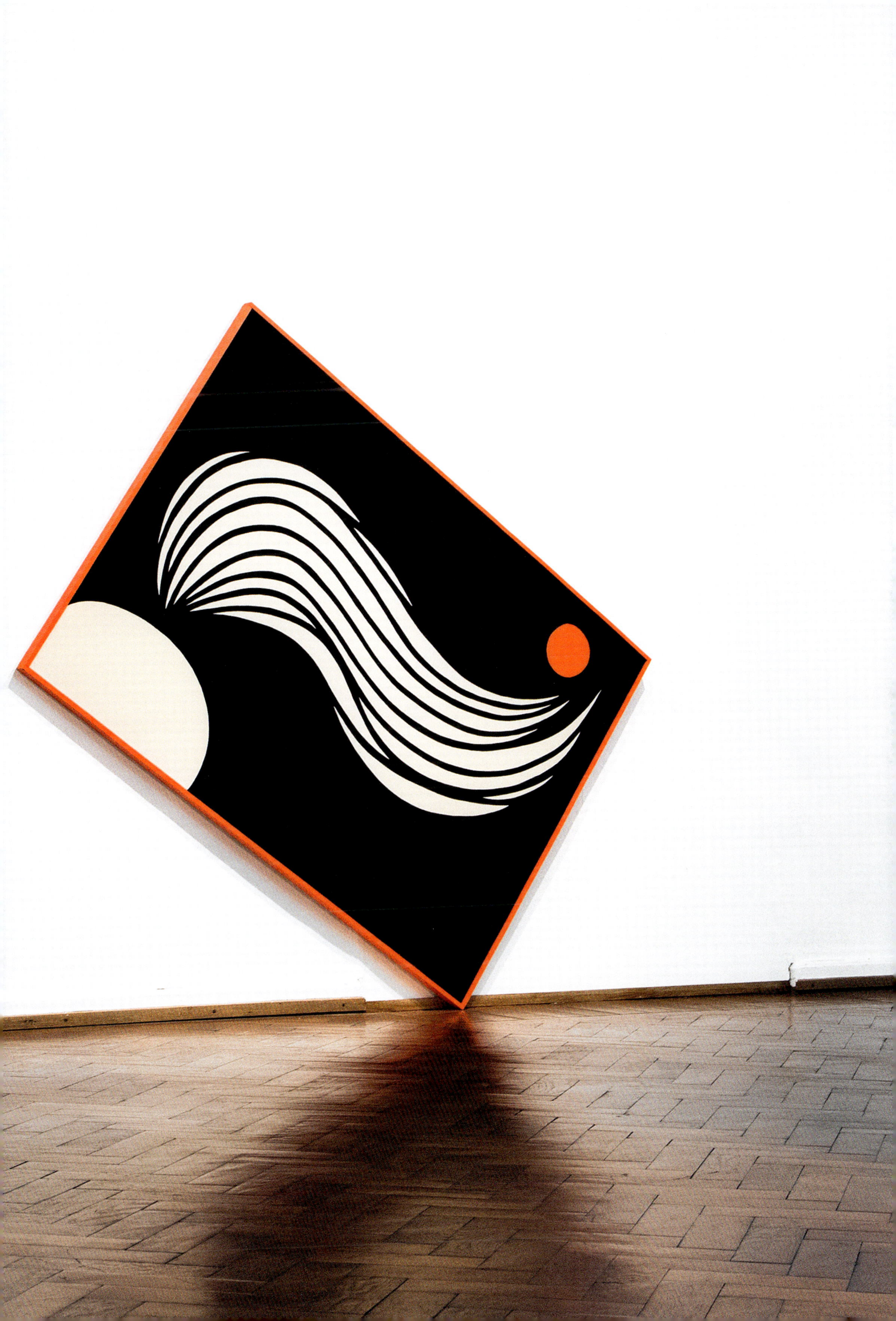

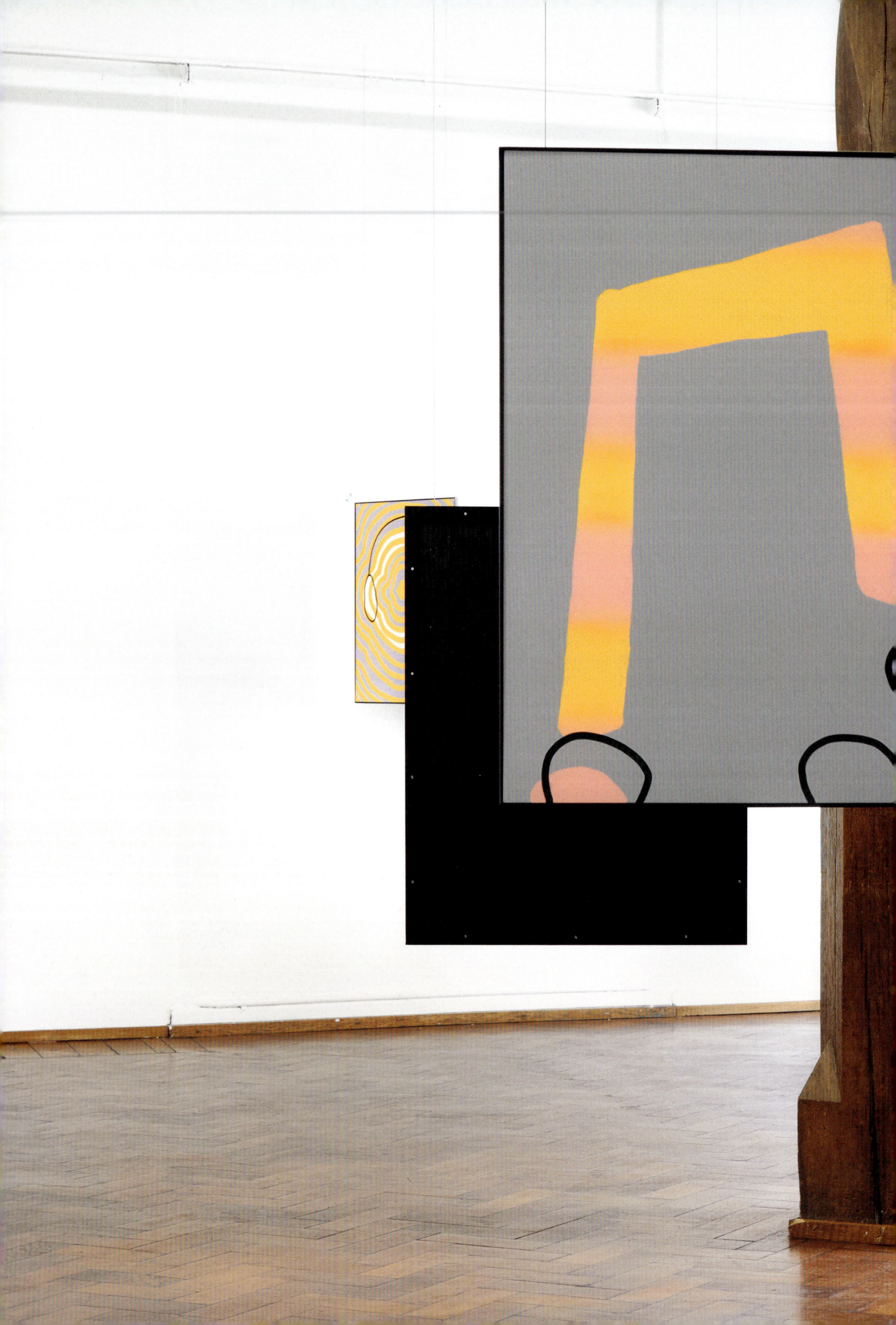

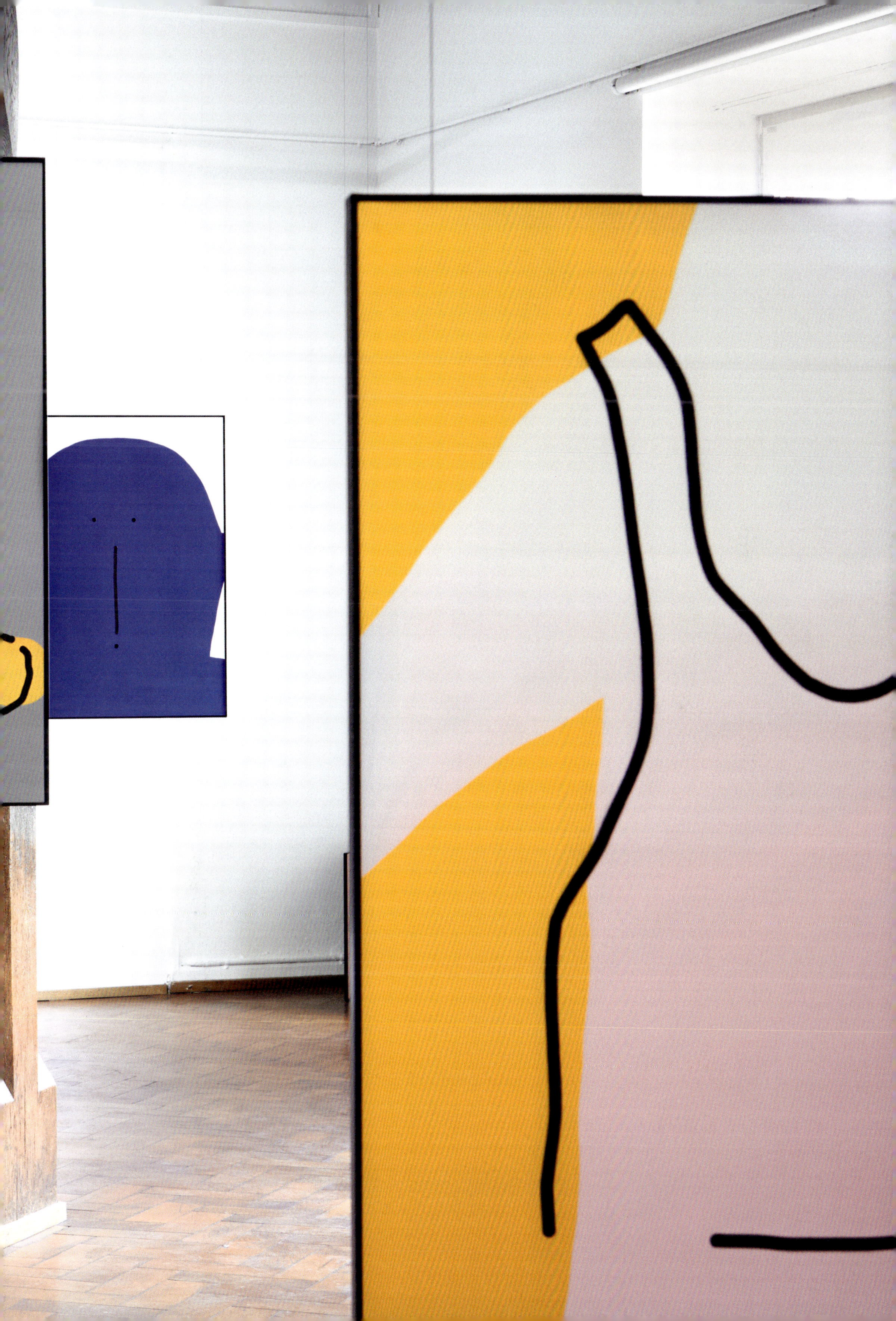

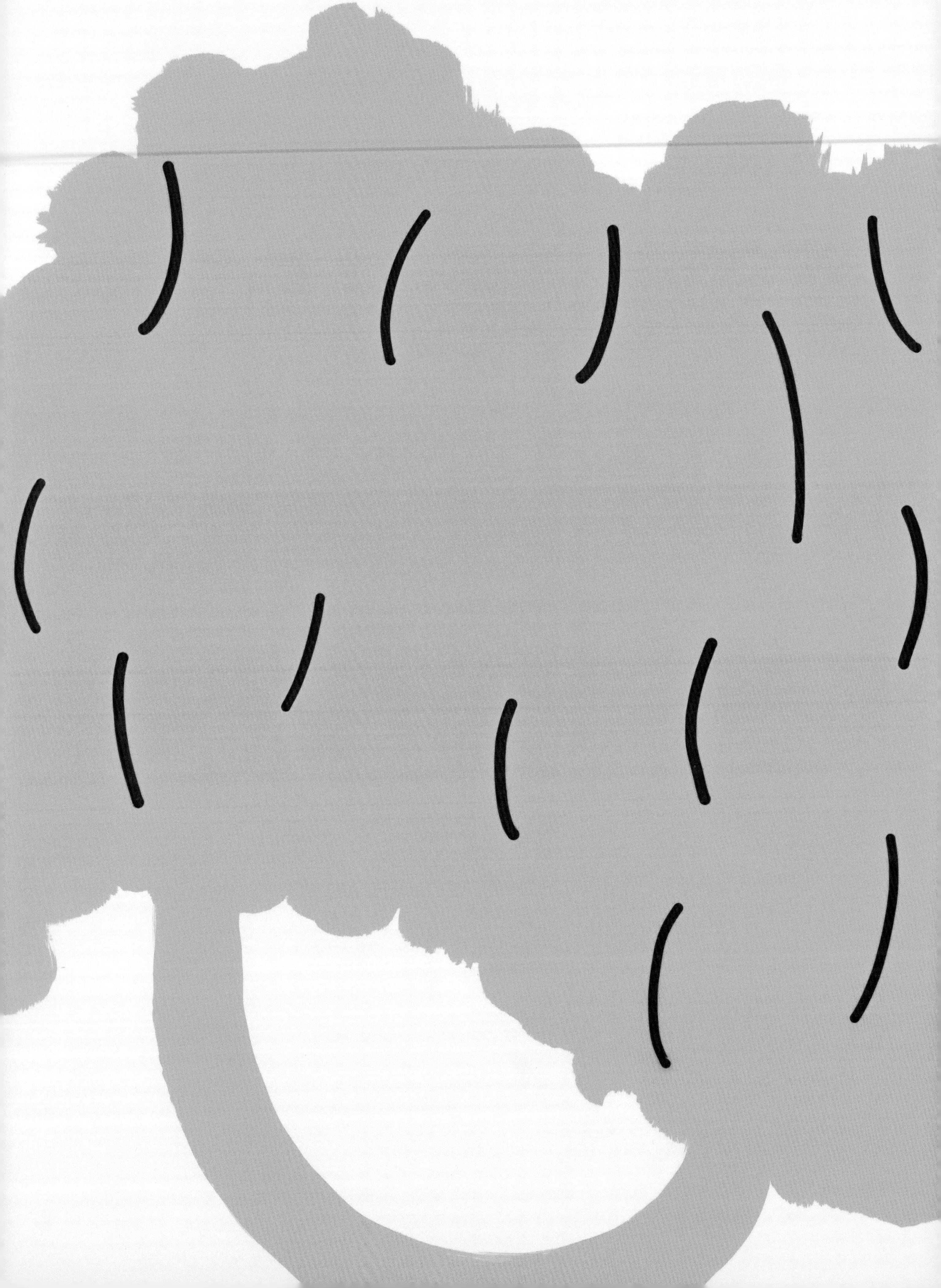

Hanging Out Again, Royal London Hospital (permanent installation), London (UK), 2014

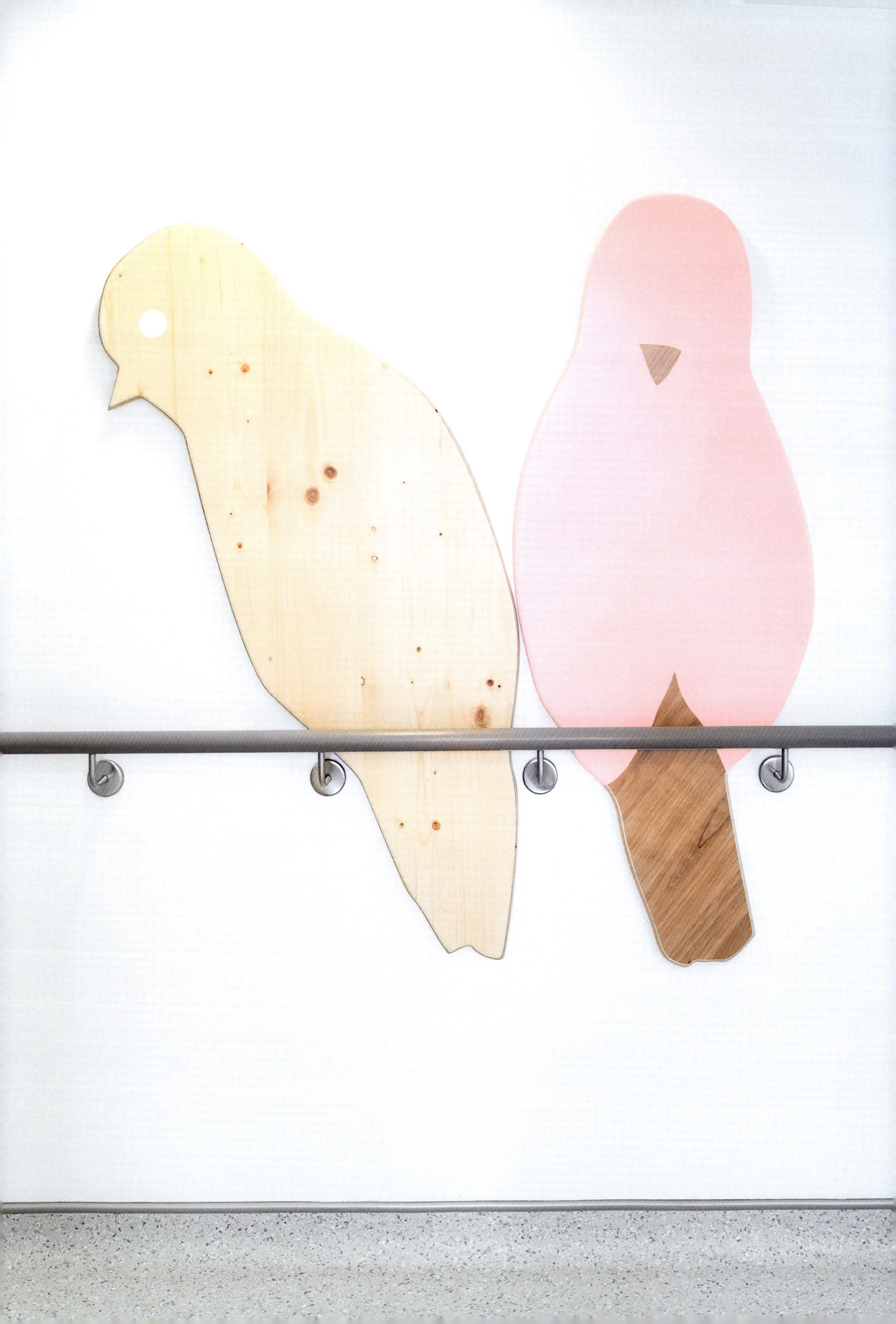

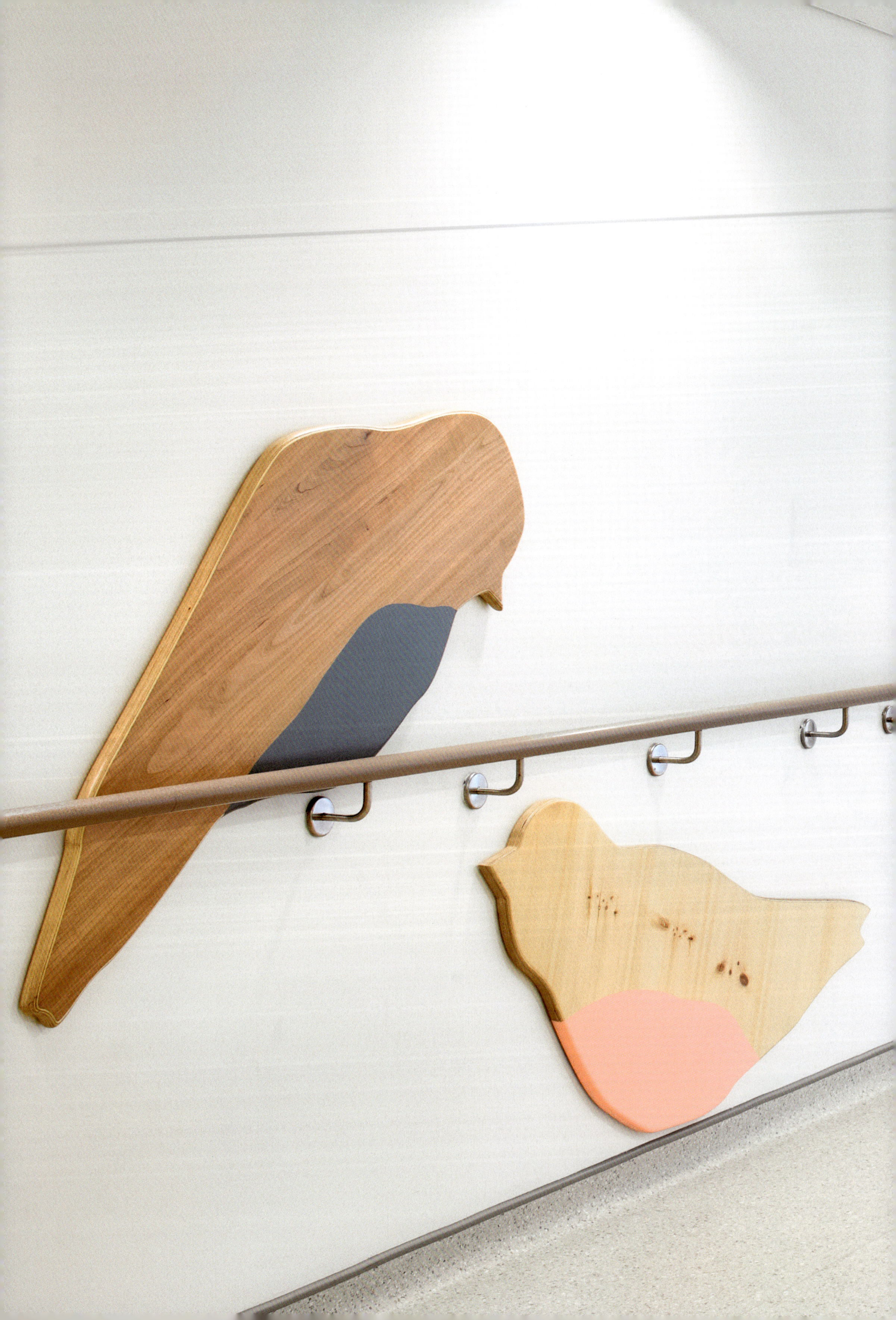

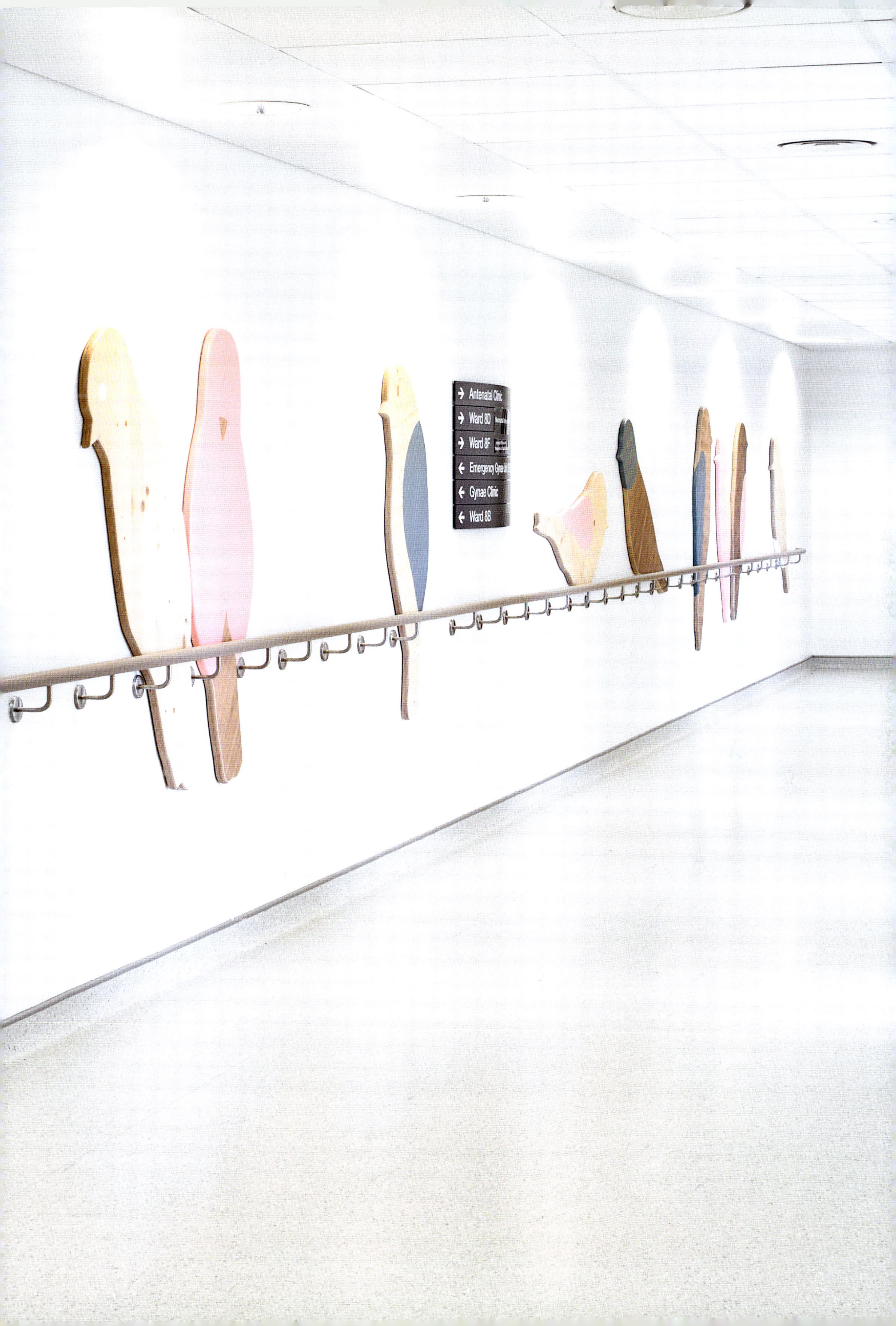
Antenatal Clinic
Ward 8D
Ward 8F
Emergency Gynae
Gynae Clinic
Ward 8B

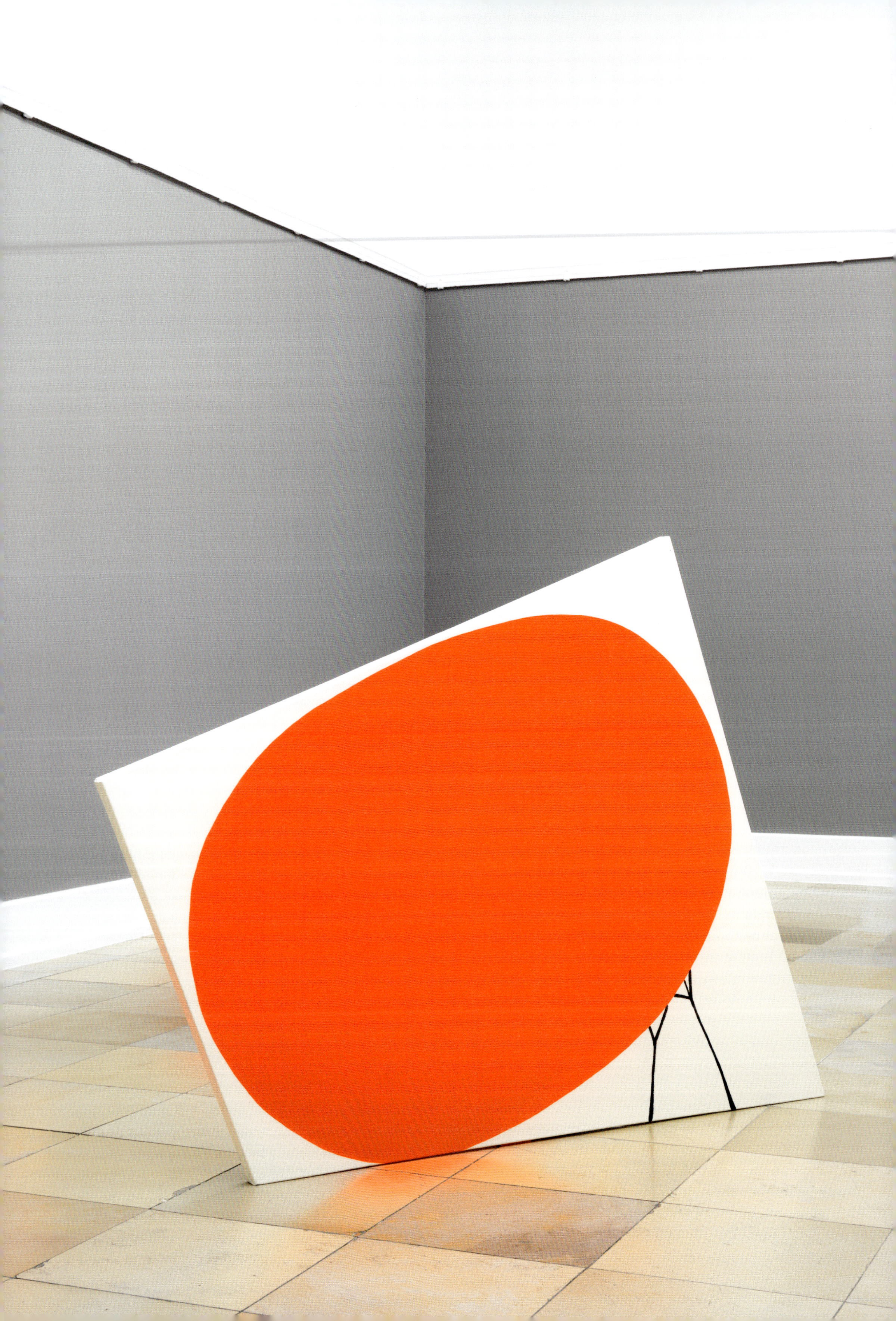

Off the Wall!, Kunsthalle Nürnberg (DE), 2014

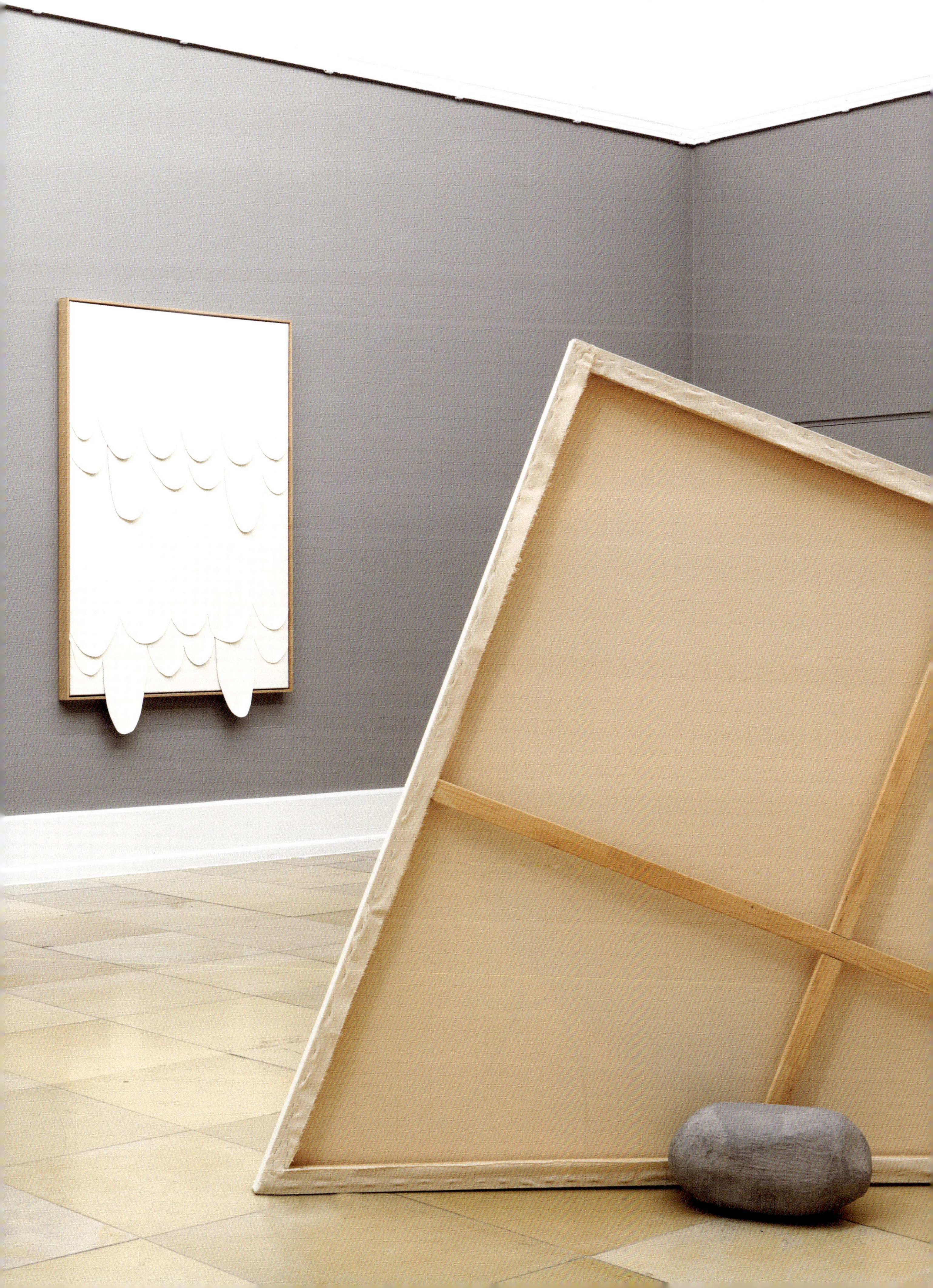

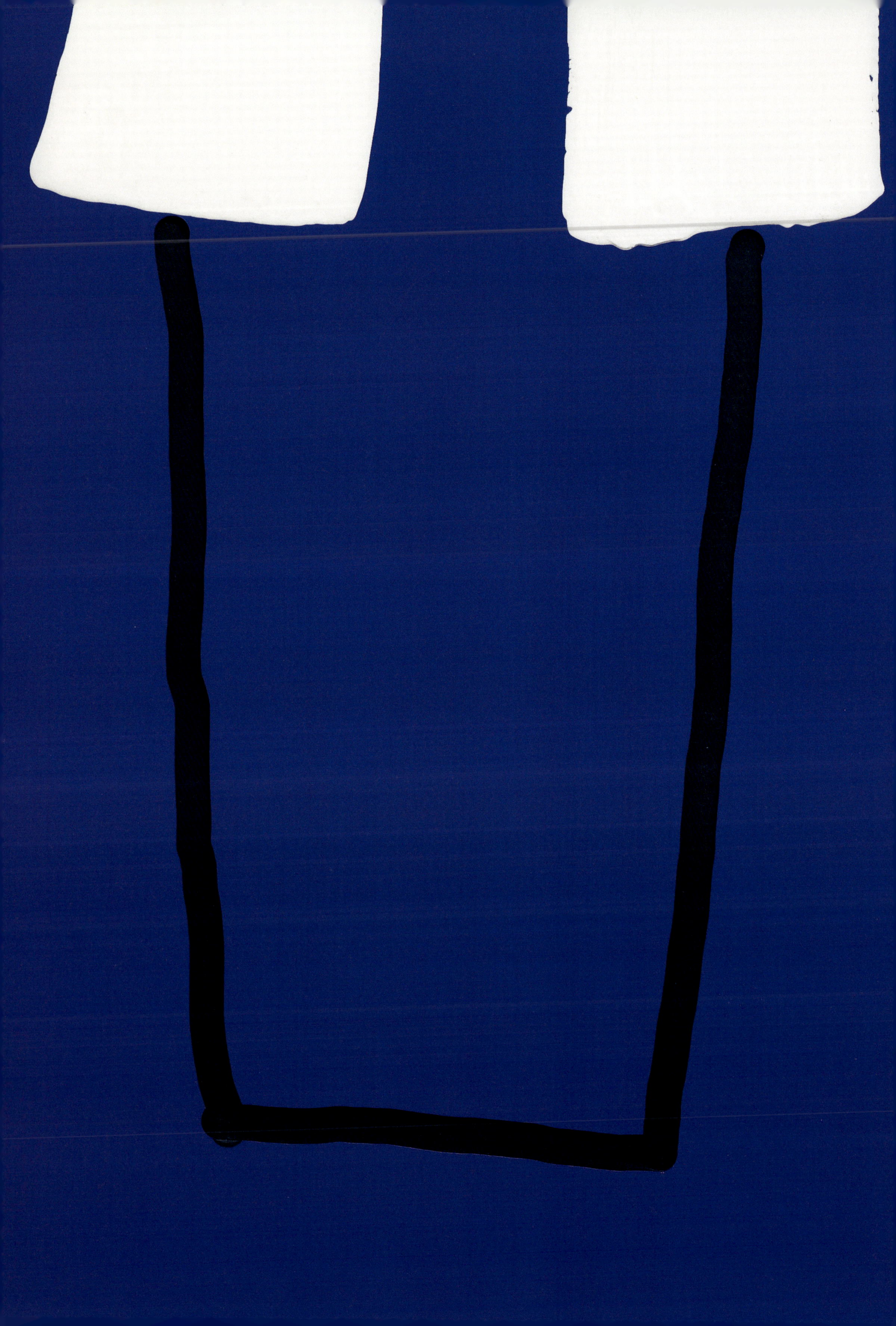

Schnick Schnack Schnuck!, Limoncello, London (UK), 2013

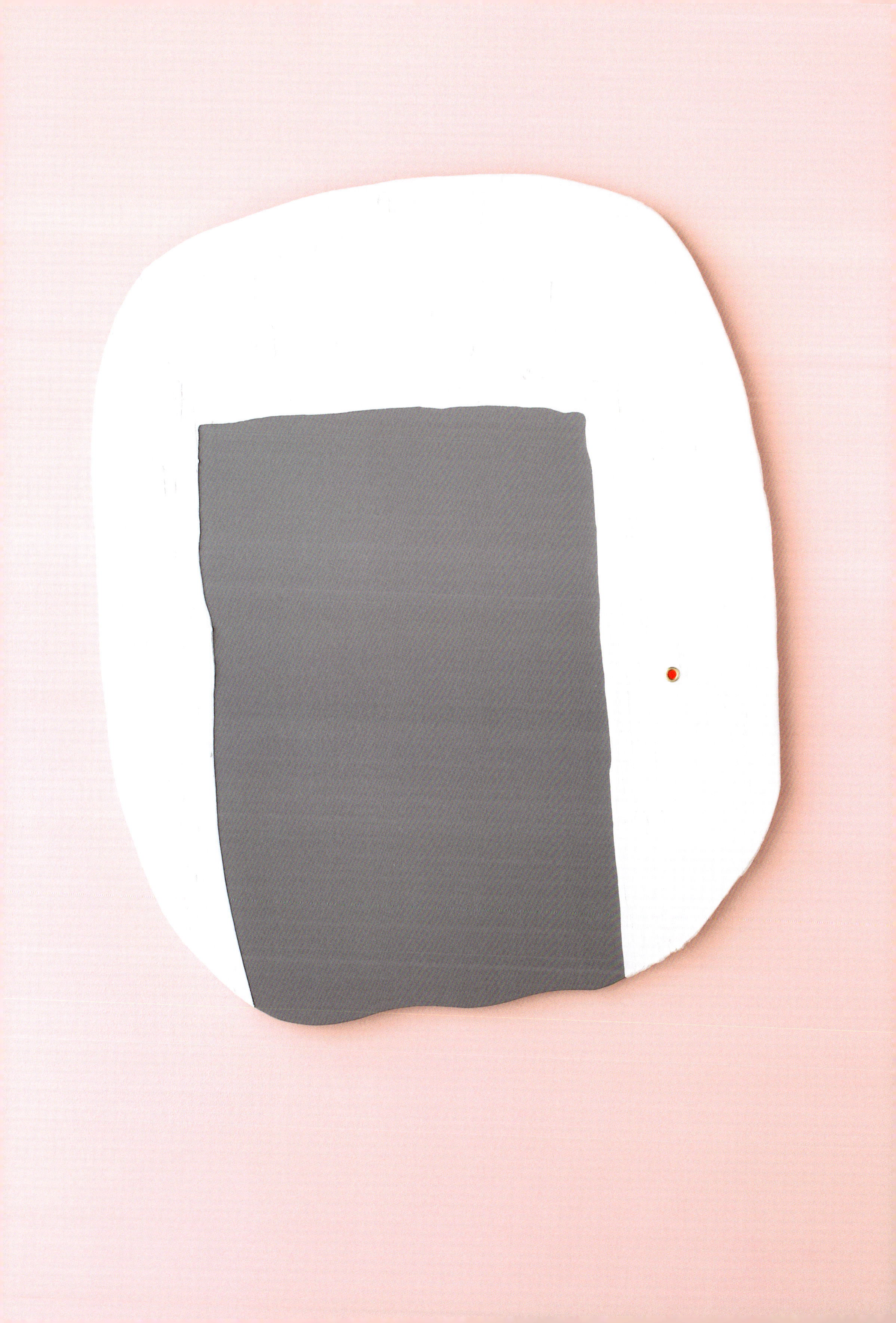

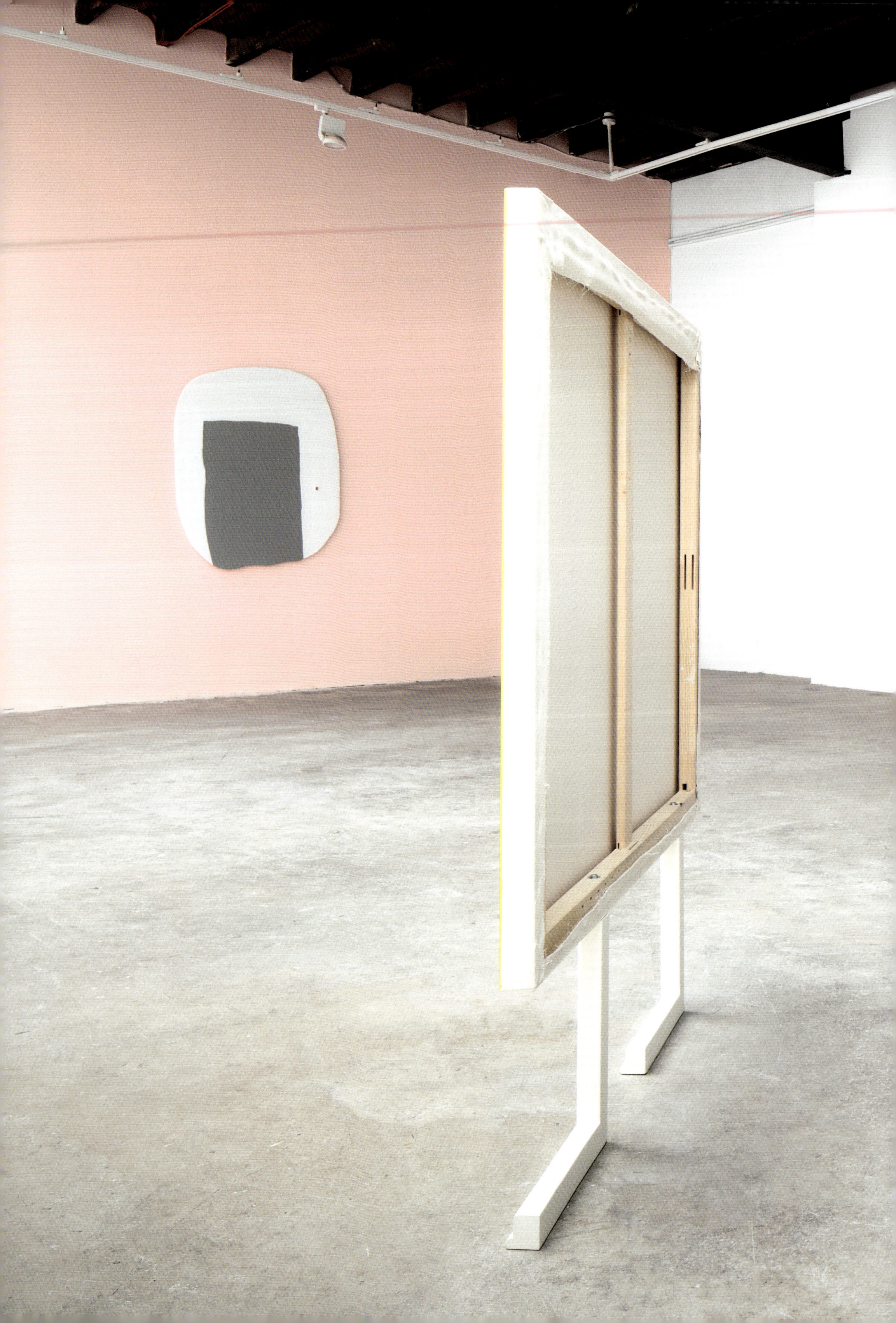

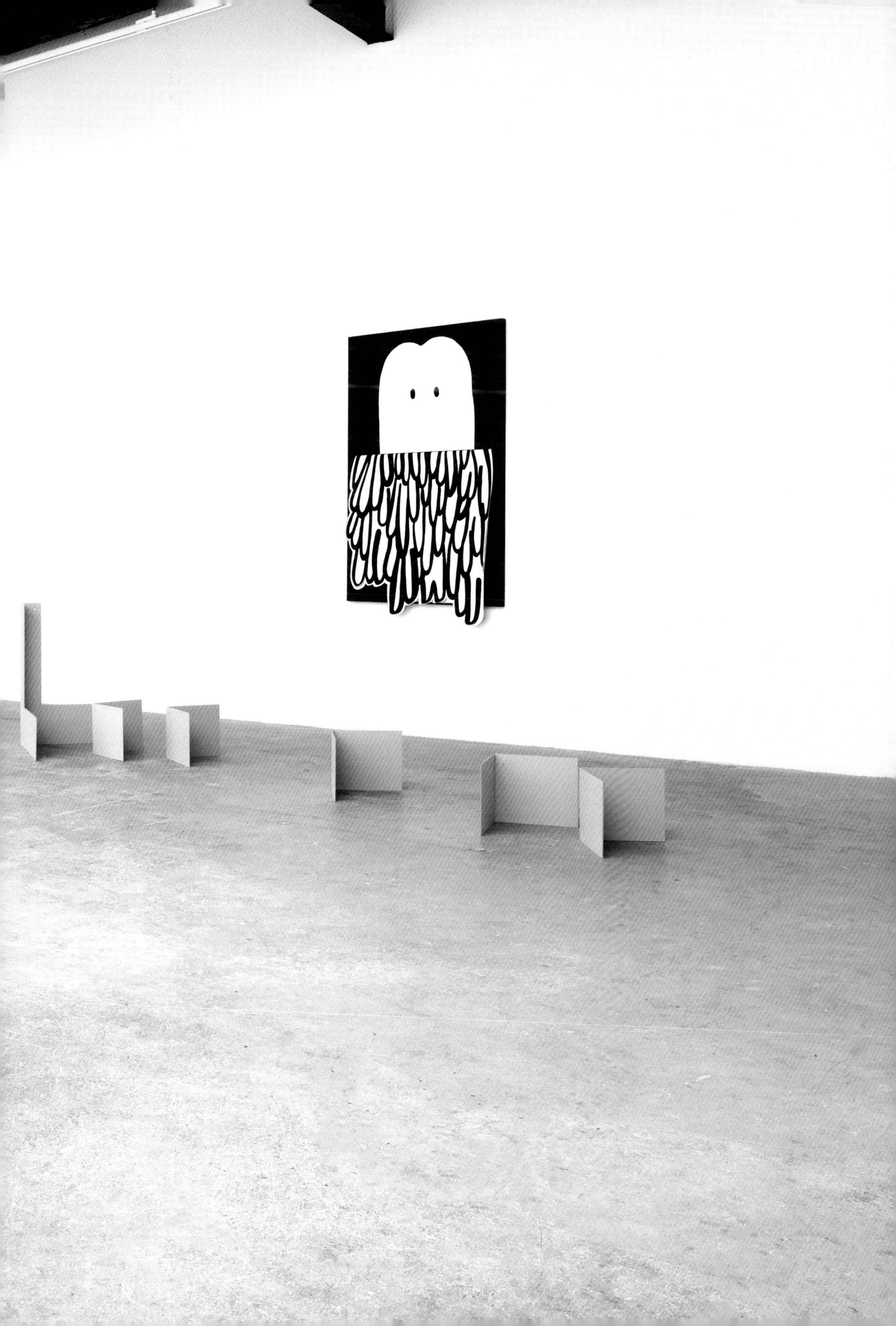

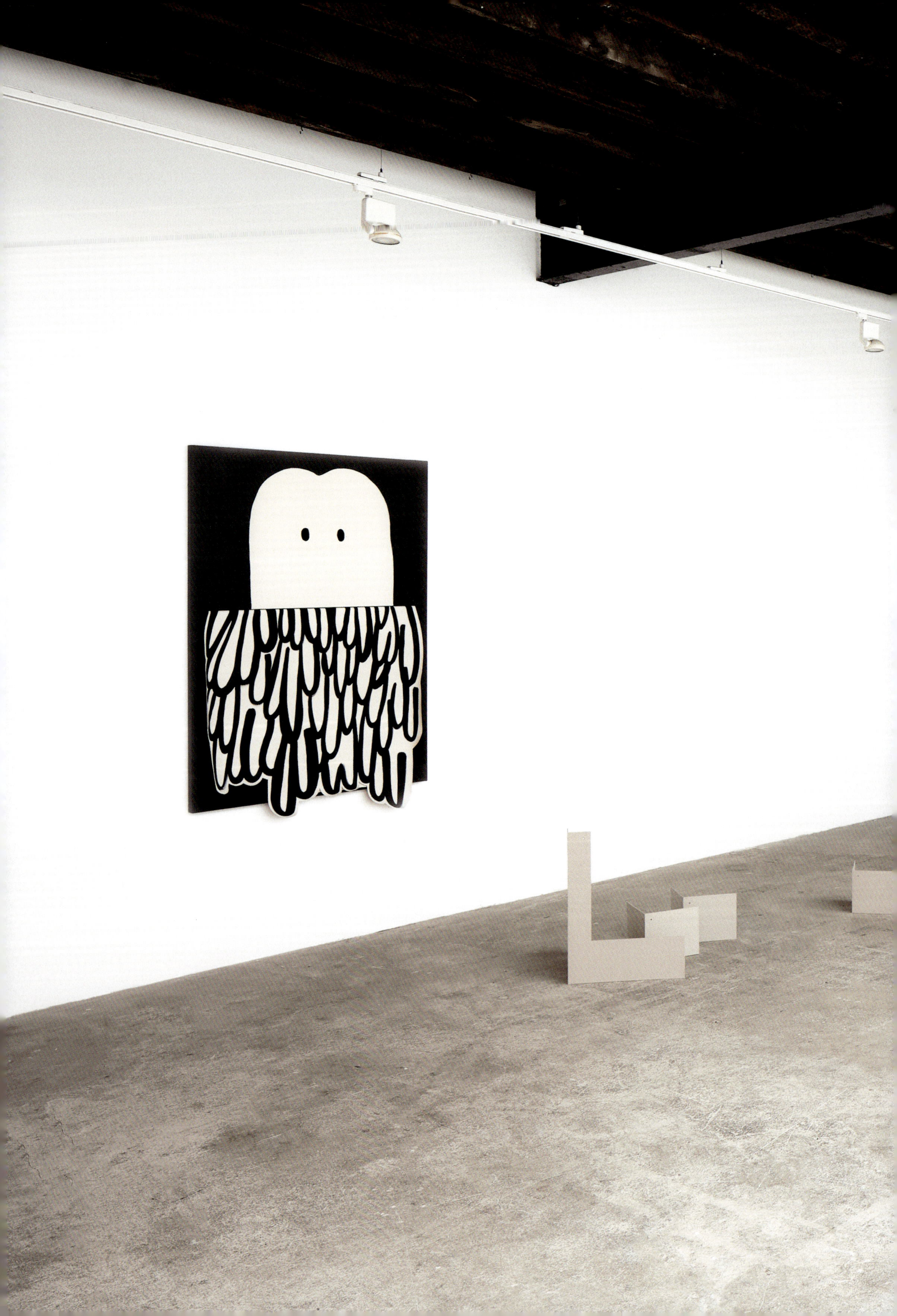

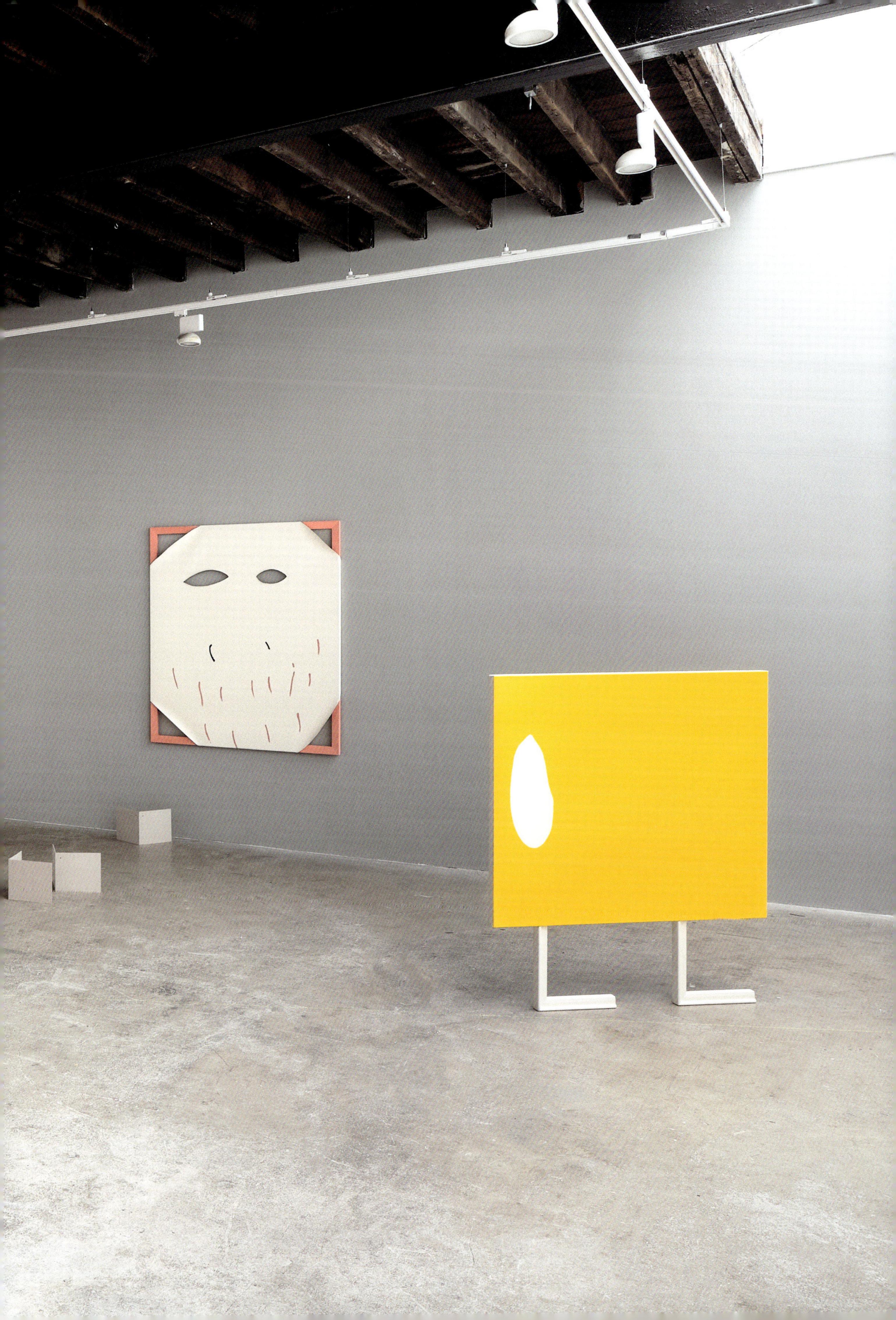

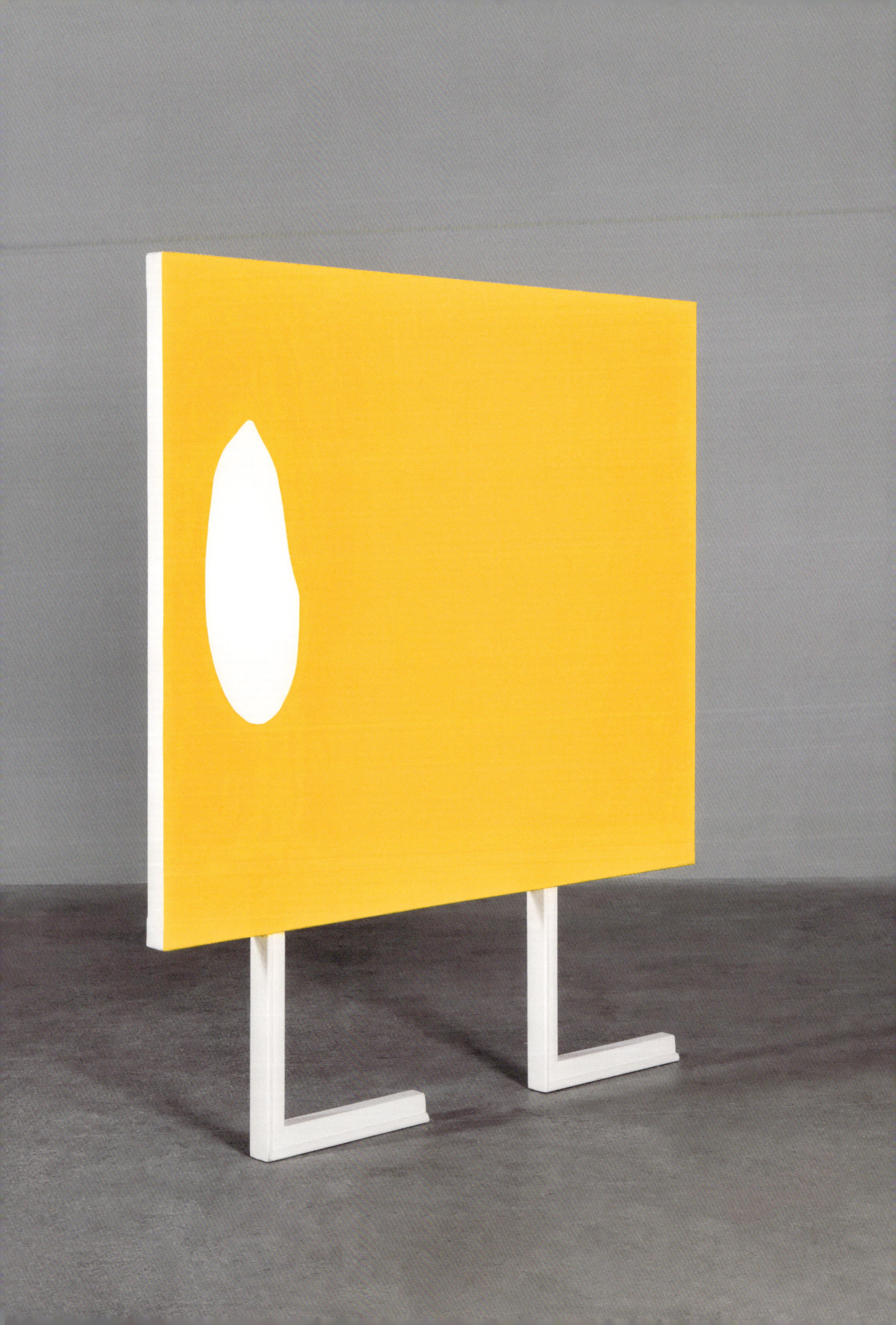

Just What Is Not Is Possible – Painting in Space, Museum Folkwang, Essen (DE), 2013

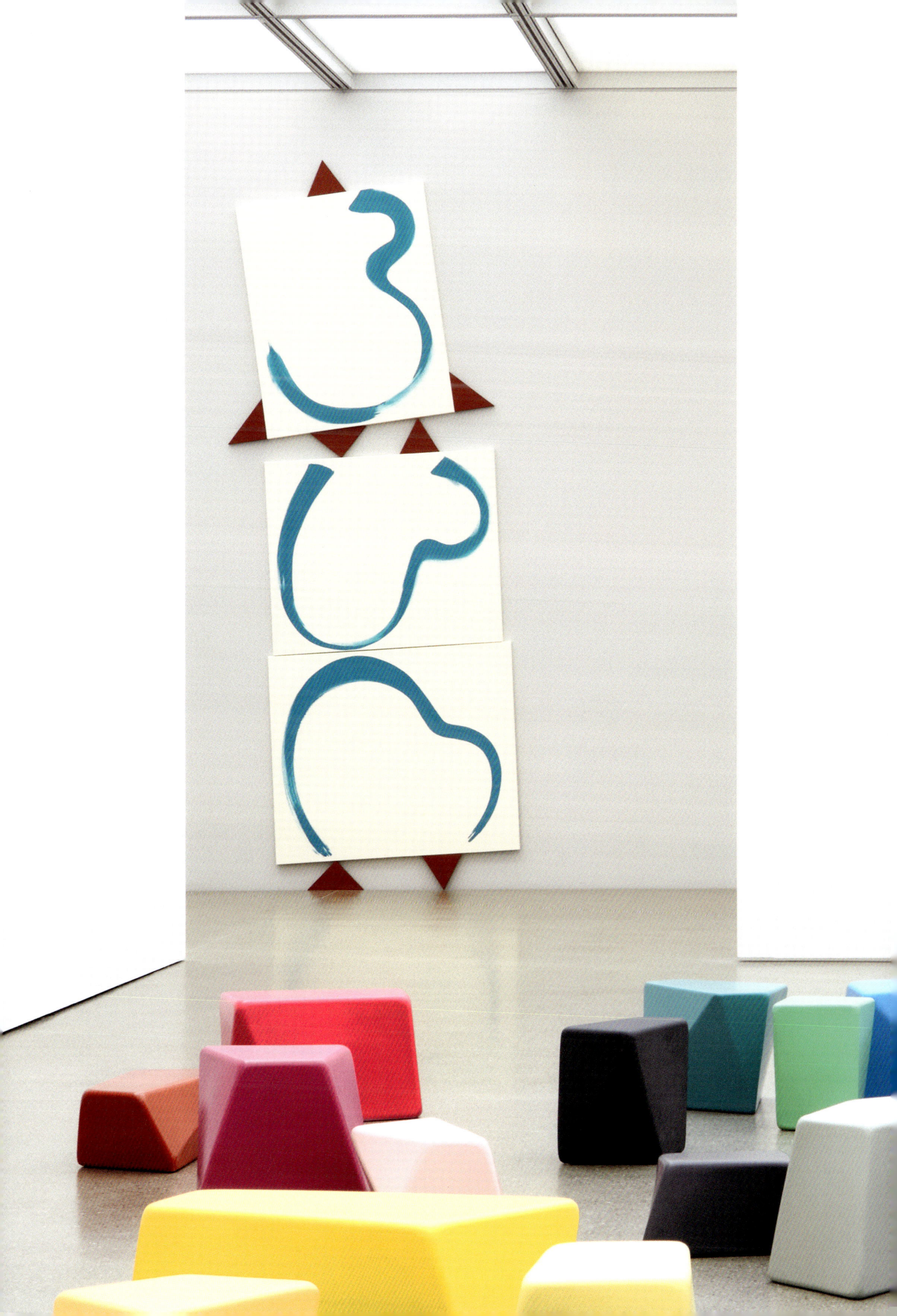

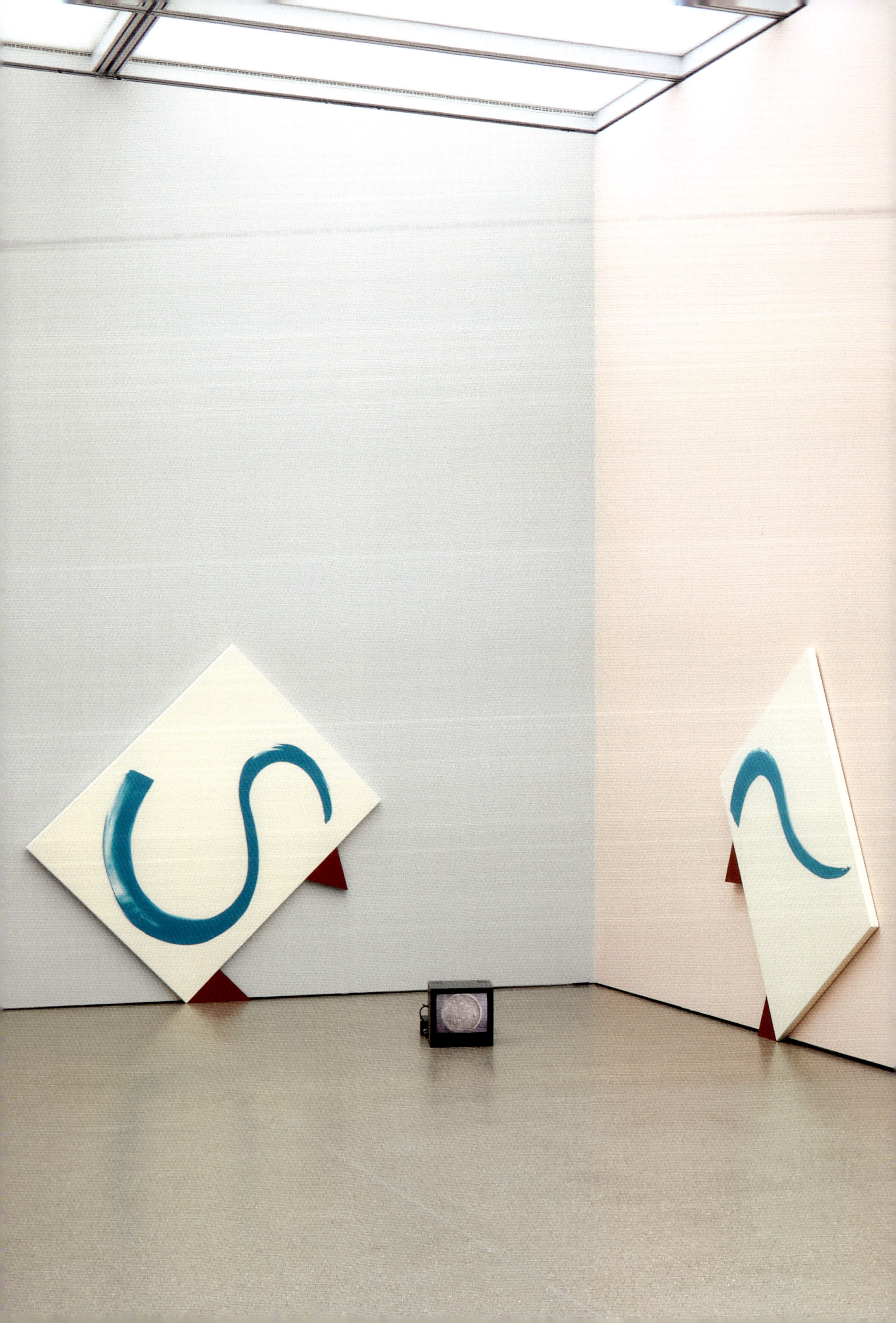

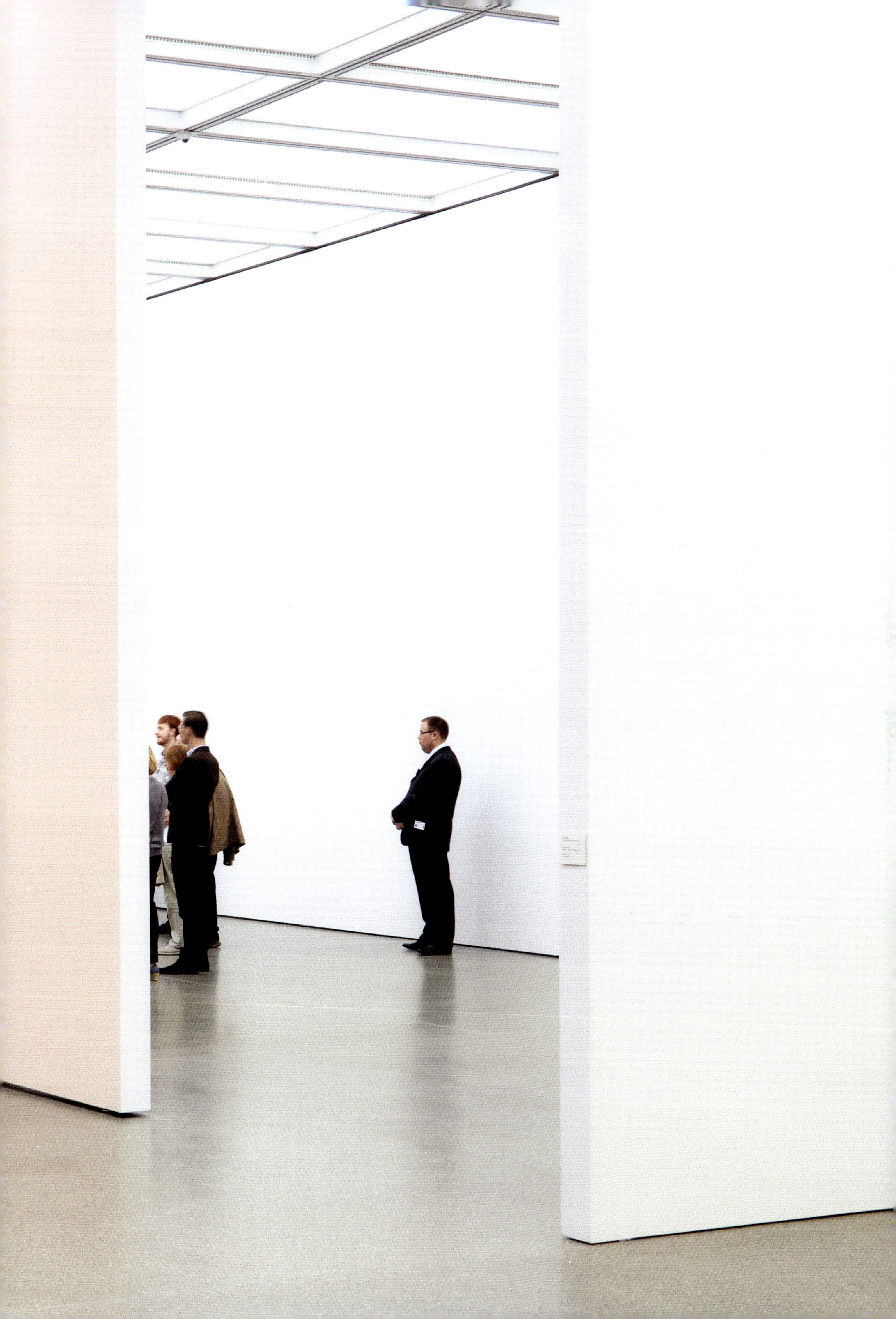

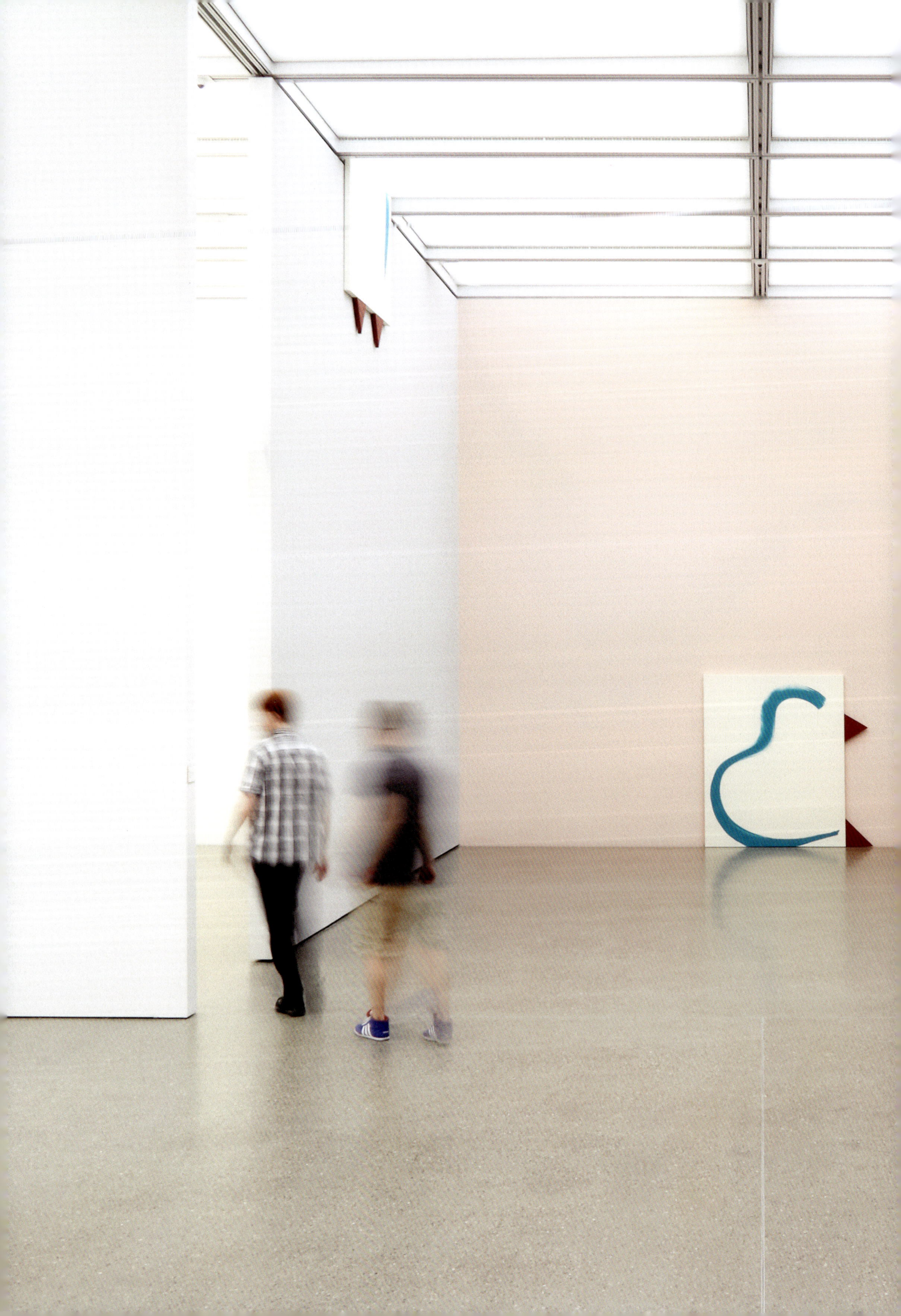

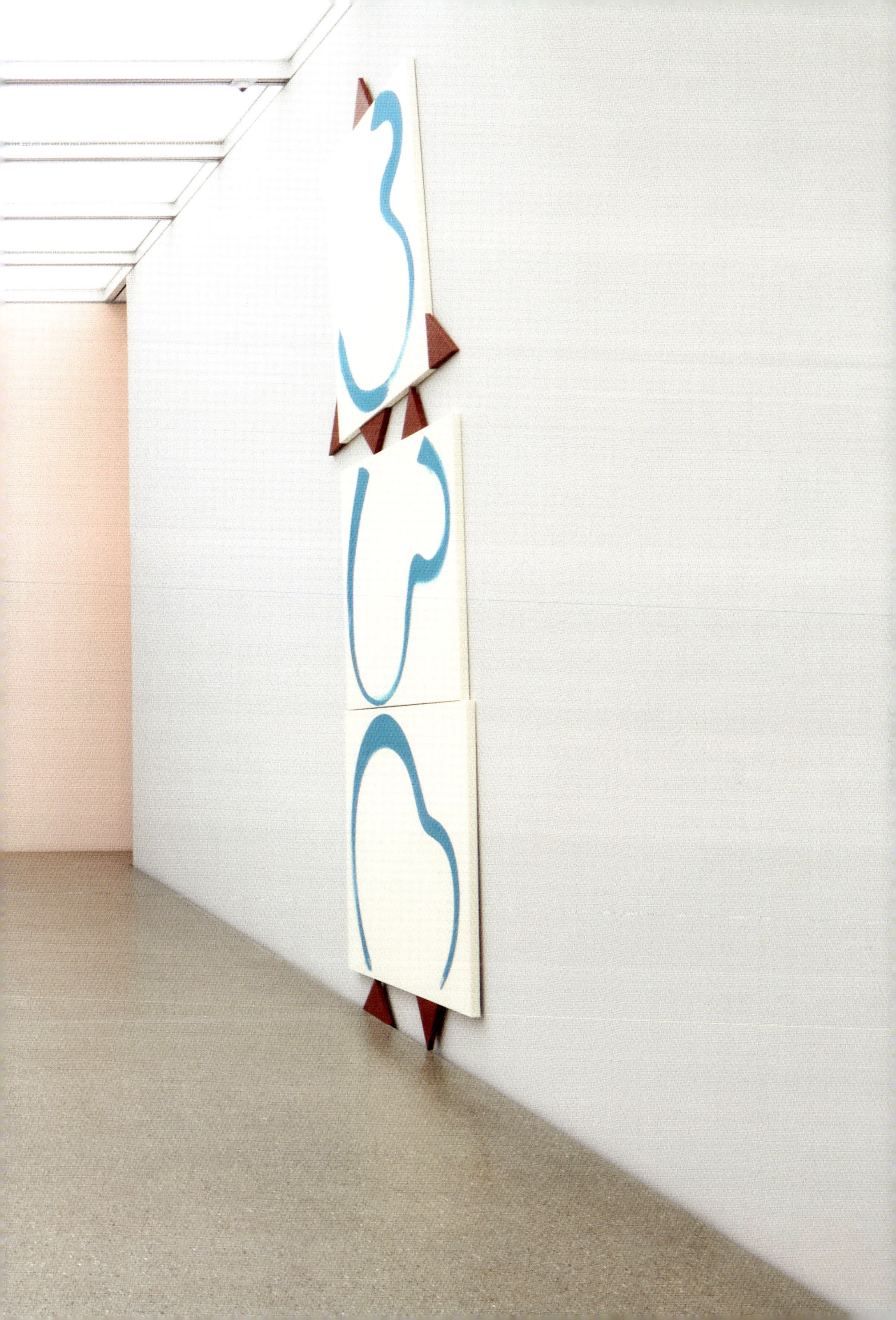

Sunday Art Fair, Limoncello, London (UK), 2012

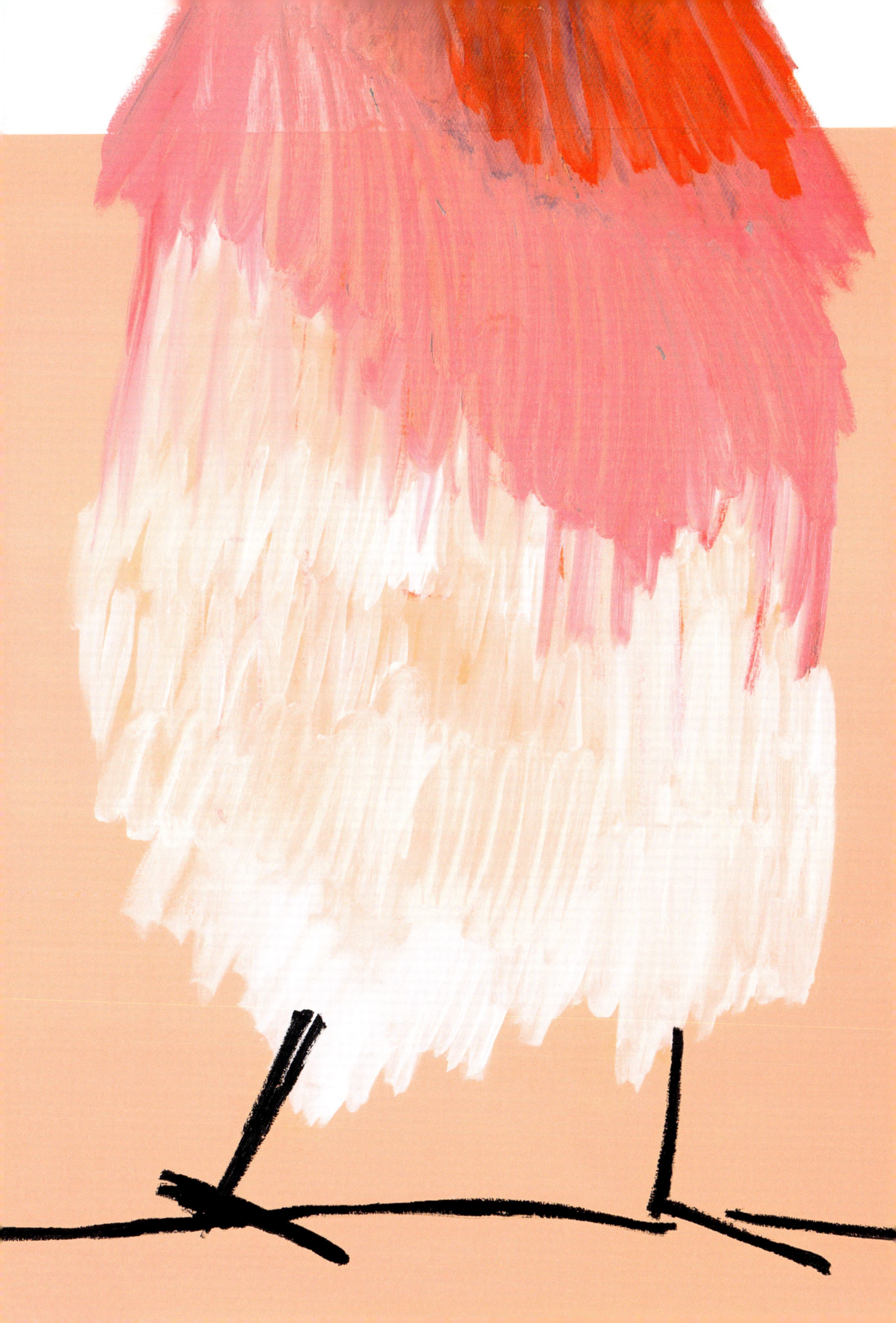

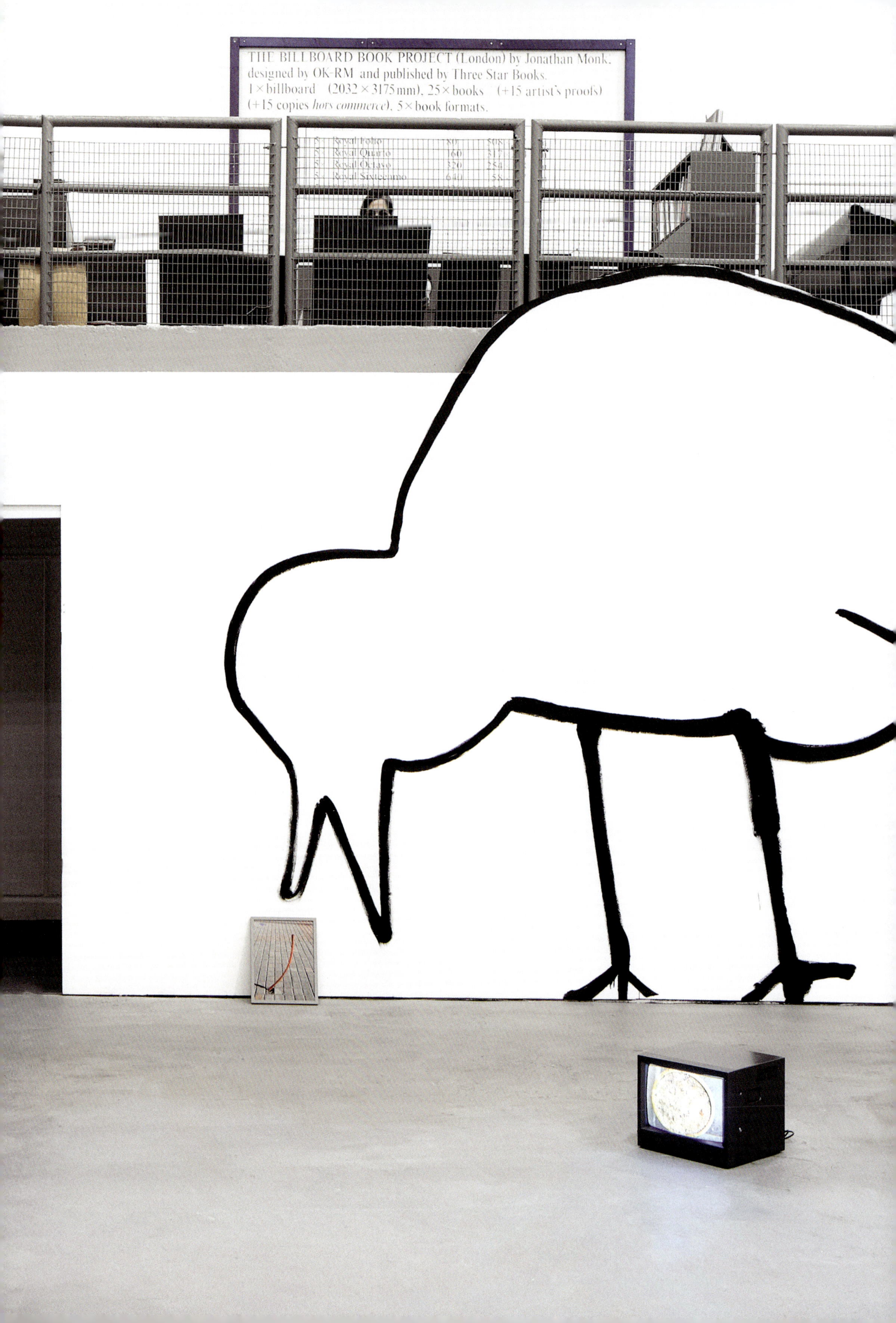
THE BILLBOARD BOOK PROJECT (London) by Jonathan Monk,
designed by OK-RM and published by Three Star Books.
1× billboard (2032 × 3175mm), 25× books (+15 artist's proofs)
(+15 copies hors commerce), 5× book formats.

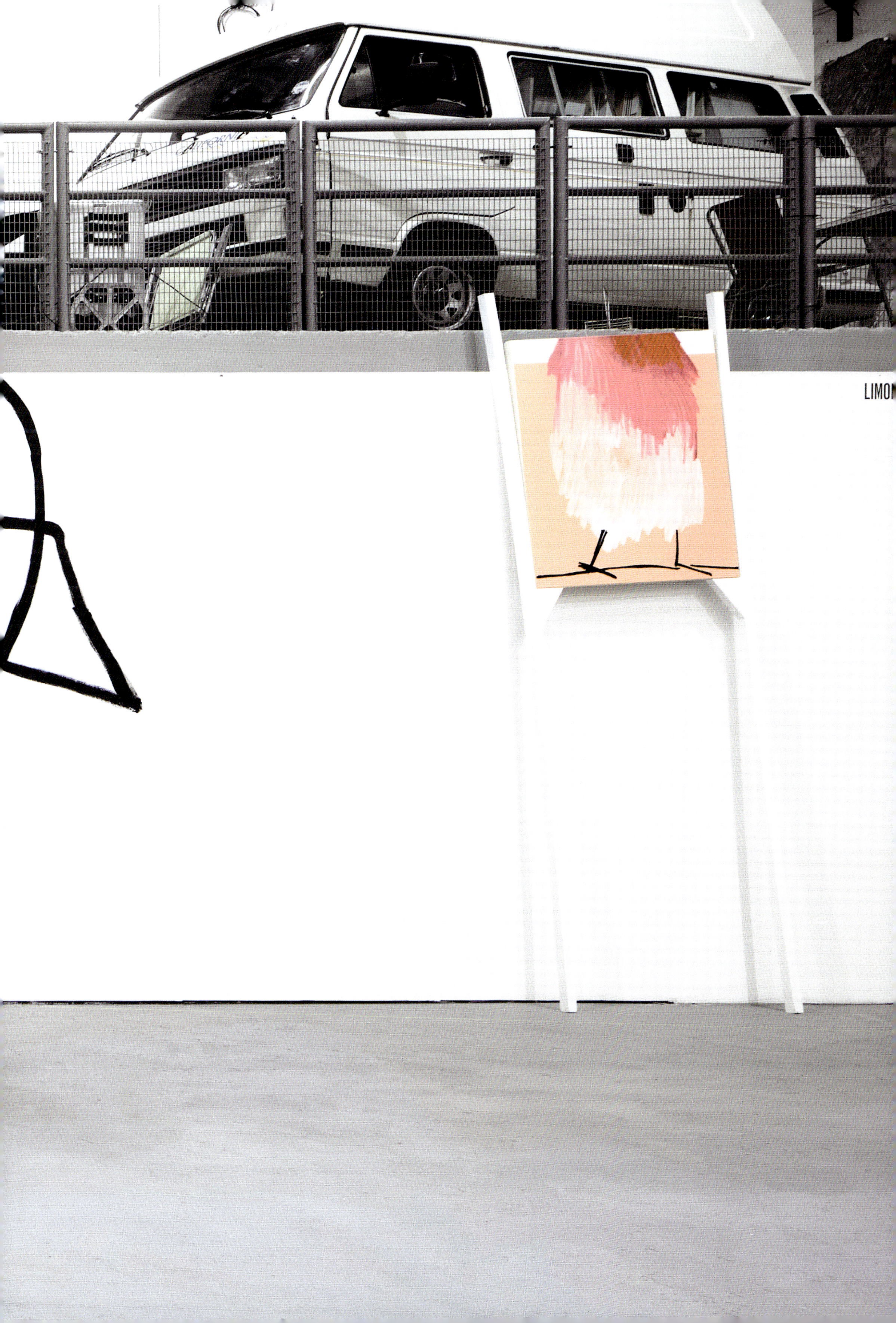
LIMO

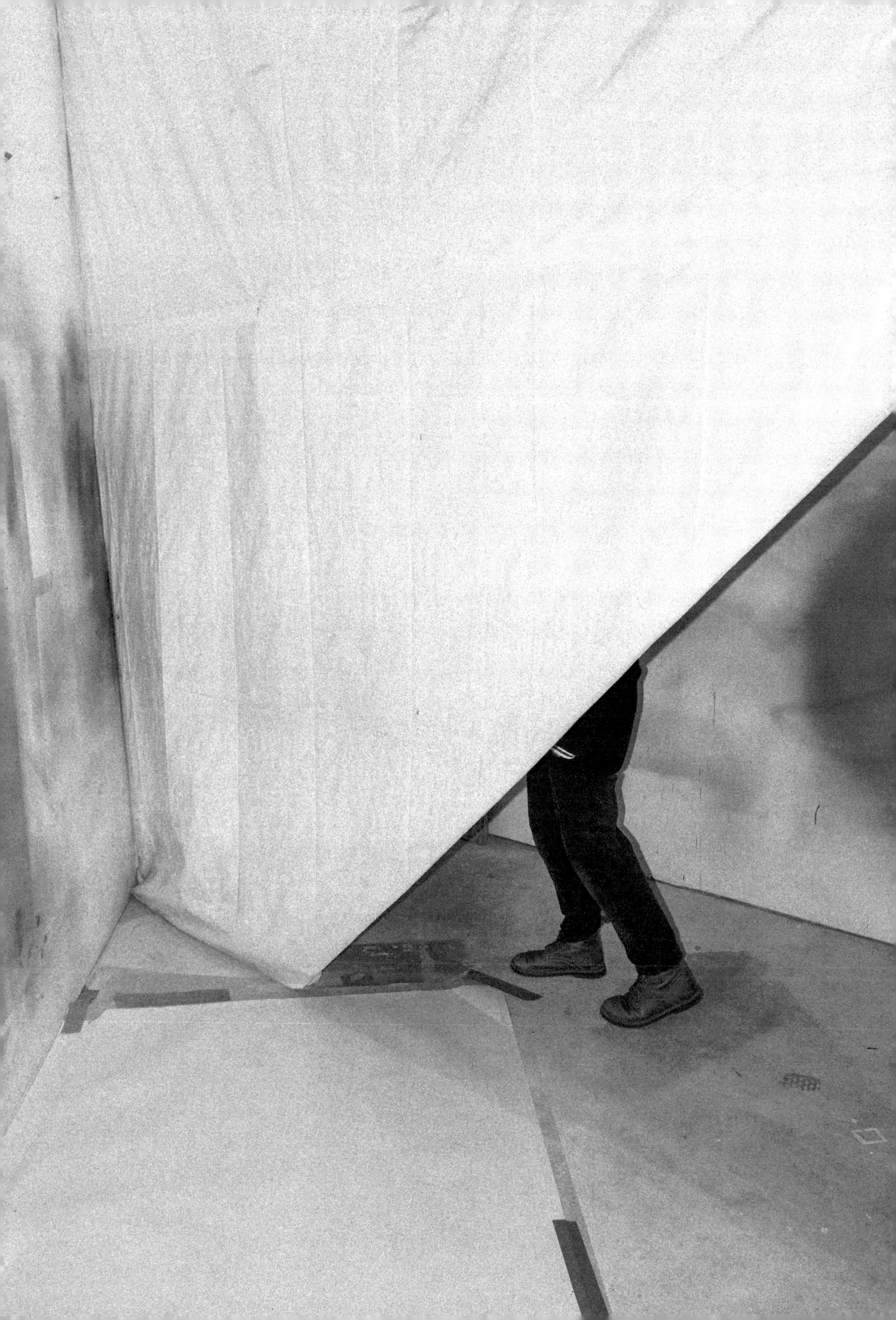

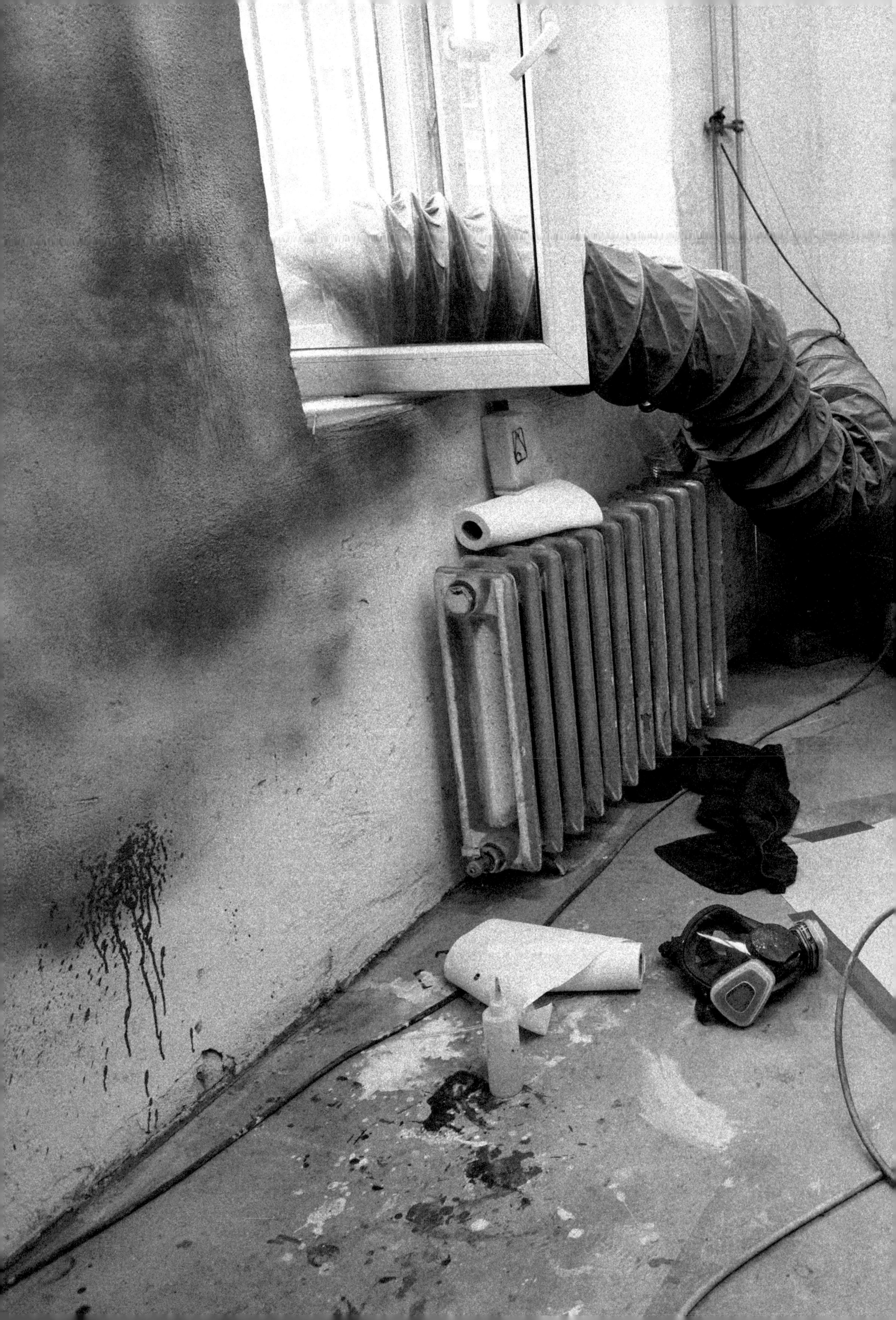

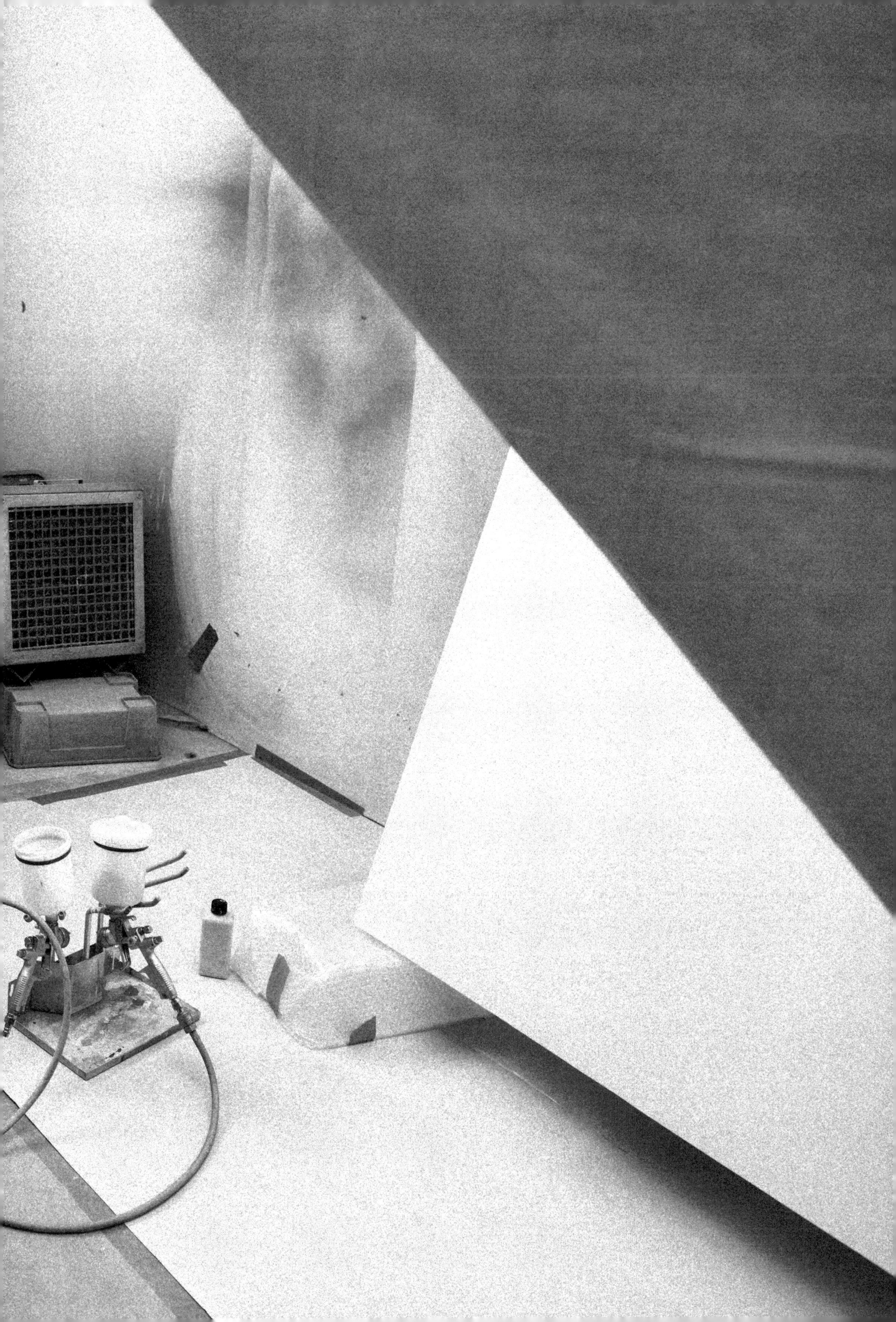

List of Works
Werkverzeichnis

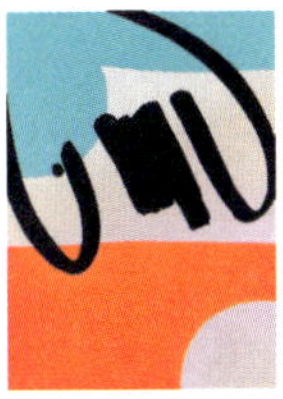

Fla, 2023 (p. 17)
Acrylic on canvas
230 × 170 cm
Collection Hamburger Kunsthalle (DE)

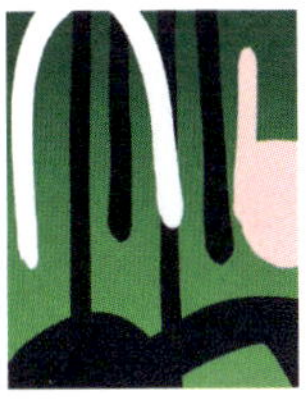

Taa, 2023 (p. 20)
Acrylic on canvas
50 × 40 cm
Private Collection, Brussels (BE)

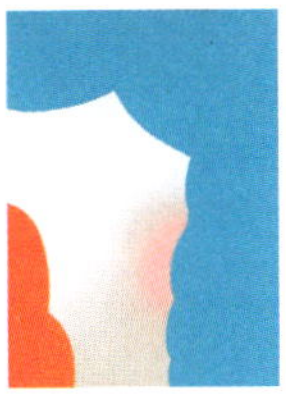

Mina, 2021 (p. 24)
Acrylic on canvas
230 × 170 cm
Private Collection, Berlin (DE)

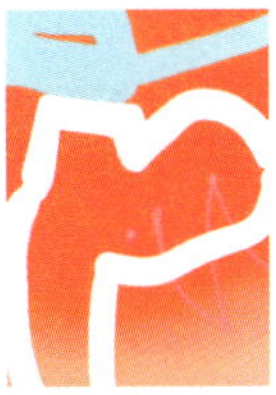

Jag, 2021 (p. 25)
Acrylic on canvas
210 × 150 cm
Private Collection, Berlin (DE)

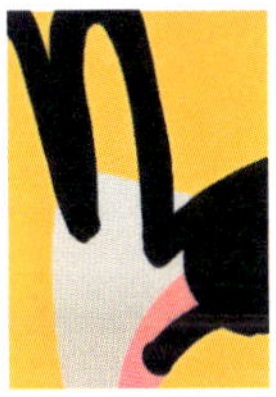

Lik, 2023 (p. 27)
Acrylic on canvas
210 × 150 cm
The A.R.M. Holding Art Collection, Dubai (AE)

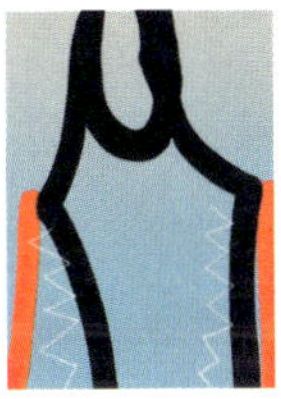

Hon, 2023 (p. 29)
Acrylic on canvas
95 × 70 cm
Private Collection, Stockholm (SE)

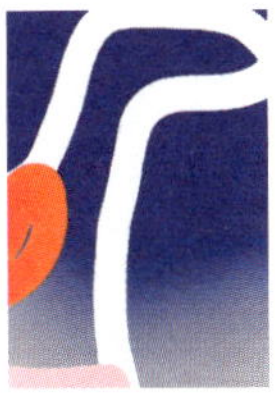

Hob, 2023 (p. 30)
Acrylic on canvas
210 × 150 cm

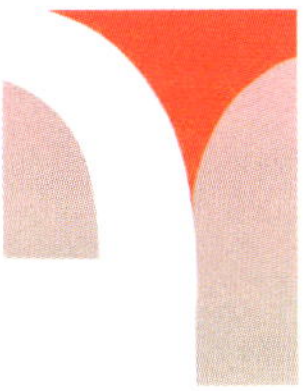

Tja, 2023 (p. 31)
Acrylic on canvas
50 × 40 cm
Private Collection, Stockholm (SE)

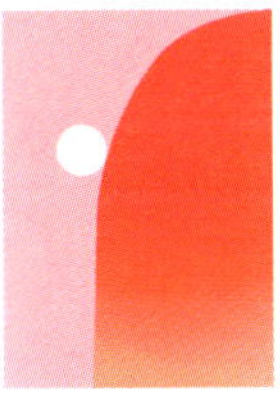

Ehm, 2023 (p. 32)
Acrylic on canvas
190 × 140 cm
The A.R.M. Holding Art Collection, Dubai (AE)

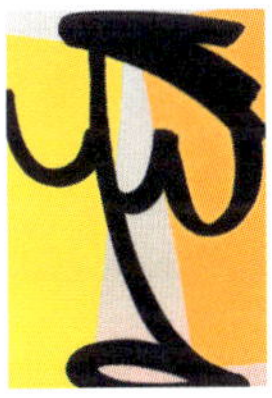

Bup, 2023 (p. 35)
Acrylic on canvas
213 × 152 cm
Private Collection, Fort Worth (US)

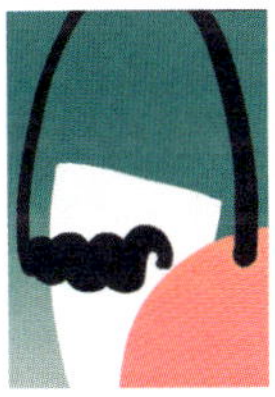

Hup, 2023 (p. 36)
Acrylic on canvas
213 × 152 cm
Private Collection, Fort Worth (US)

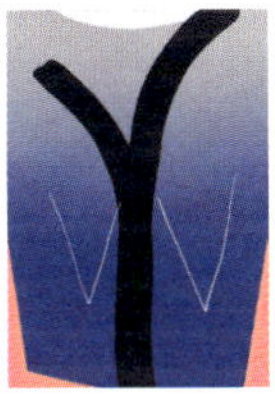

Tup, 2023 (p. 39)
Acrylic on canvas
213 × 152 cm
Private Collection, Fort Worth (US)

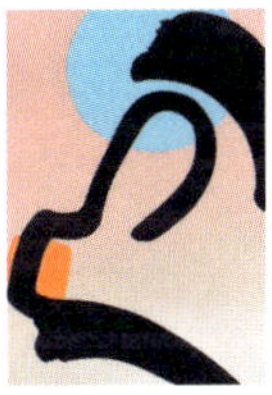

Lup, 2023 (p. 40)
Acrylic on canvas
213 × 152 cm
Private Collection, Fort Worth (US)

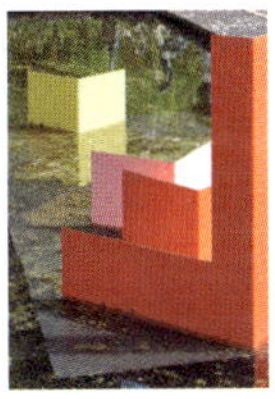

oh-HO, 2022 (p. 43)
Powder-coated steel
97 × 280 × 105 cm

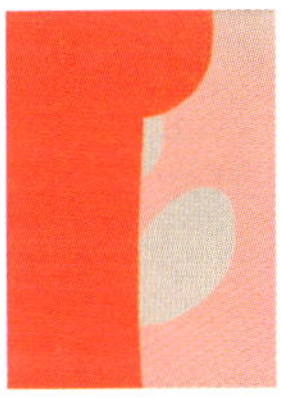

Ray, 2022 (p. 49)
Acrylic on canvas
95 × 70 cm
Private Collection, Brussels (BE)

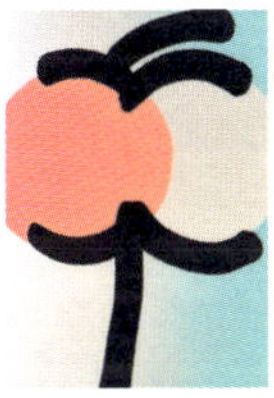

Hrý, 2022 (p. 50)
Acrylic on canvas
210 × 150 cm
Private Collection, Hamburg (DE)

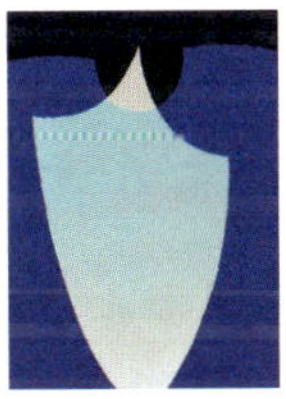

Nmo, 2022 (p. 51)
Acrylic on canvas
160 × 120 cm
Private Collection, Abu Dhabi (AE)

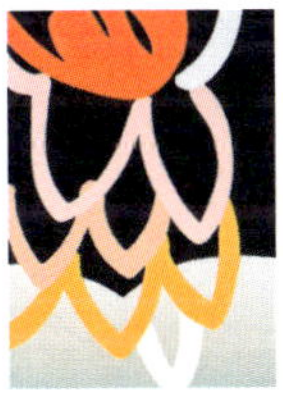

Nom, 2022 (p. 52)
Acrylic on canvas
190 × 140 cm
Private Collection, Dusseldorf (DE)

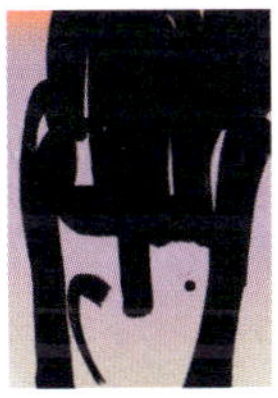

Frý, 2022 (p. 53)
Acrylic on canvas
180 × 130 cm
Private Collection, Brussels (BE)

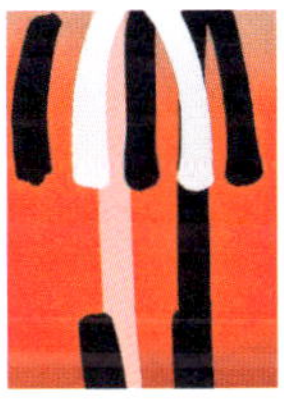

Tet, 2022 (p. 54)
Acrylic on canvas
190 × 140 cm
Private Collection, Abu Dhabi (AE)

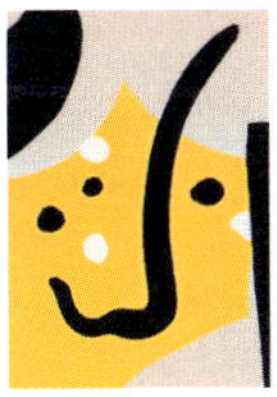

Nem, 2022 (p. 58)
Acrylic on canvas
180 × 130 cm
Private Collection, Salzburg (AT)

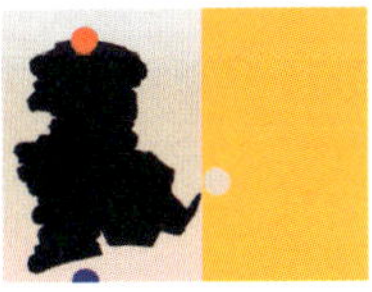

Sko, 2022 (p. 60)
Acrylic on canvas
160 × 120 cm
Private Collection, New York (US)

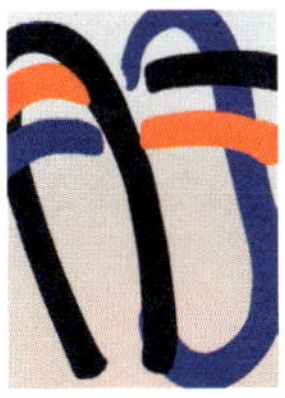

Odi, 2022 (p. 60)
Acrylic on canvas
190 × 140 cm
Private Collection, Los Angeles (US)

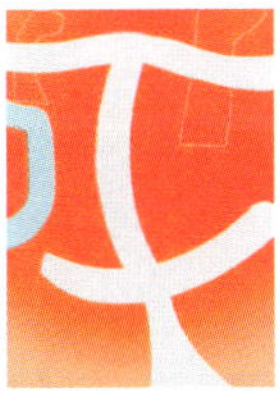

Boo, 2022 (p. 61)
Acrylic on canvas
190 × 140 cm
Private Collection, Tripoli (LB)

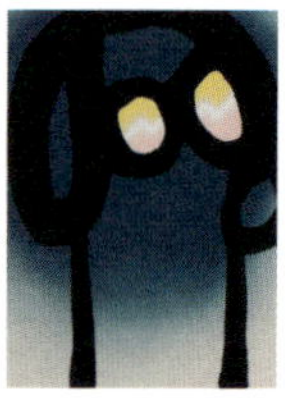

Unn, 2022 (p. 63)
Acrylic on canvas
190 × 140 cm
Private Collection, New York (US)

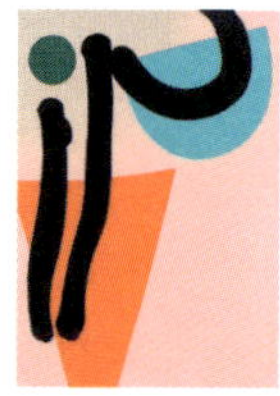

Olm, 2022 (p. 64)
Acrylic on canvas
220 × 160 cm
Private Collection, Dubai (AE)

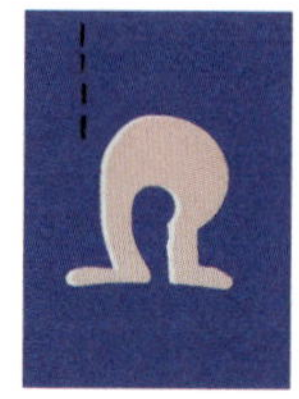

Len, 2022 (p. 66)
Acrylic on canvas
95 × 70 cm
Private Collection, New York (US)

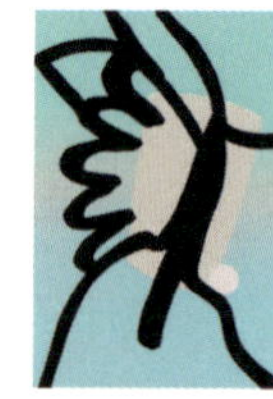

Eld, 2022 (p. 67)
Acrylic on canvas
190 × 140 cm
Private Collection, New York (US)

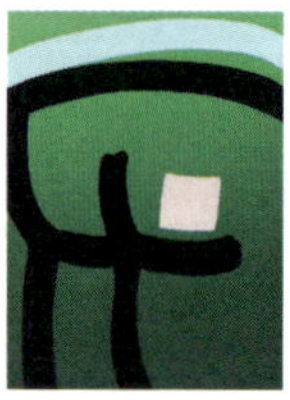

Bom, 2022 (p. 68)
Acrylic on canvas
40 × 30 cm
Private Collection, Los Angeles (US)

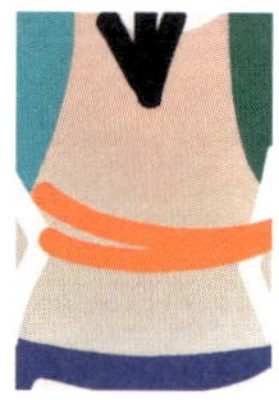

Dud, 2022 (p. 70)
Acrylic on canvas
210 × 150 cm
Private Collection, Liège (BE)

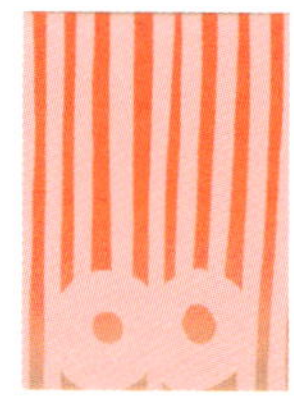

Omn, 2022 (p. 71)
Acrylic on canvas
95 × 70 cm

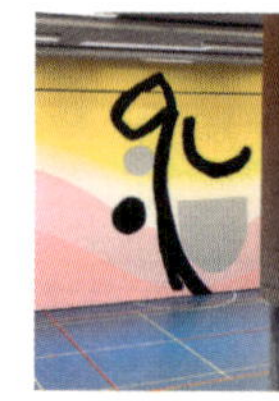

Glen, 2021 (p. 73)
Wall paint and varnish on wall
SOSU Østjylland, Aarhus (DK)

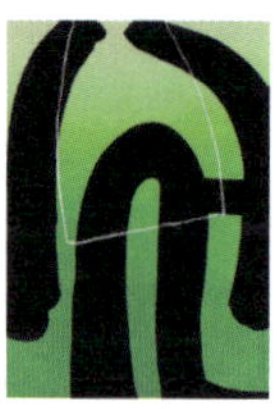

Ko Au, 2021 (p. 77)
Acrylic and oil stick on canvas
180 × 130 cm
Private Collection, Dubai (AE)

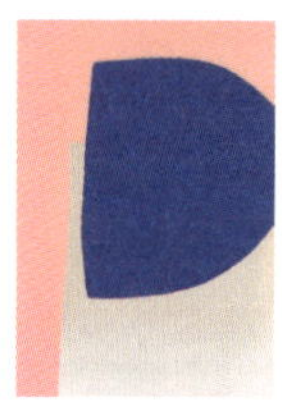

Ek, 2021 (p. 79)
Acrylic on canvas
180 × 130 cm

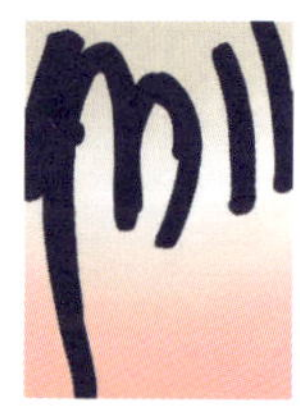

Jeg, 2021 (p. 81)
Acrylic on canvas
230 × 170 cm

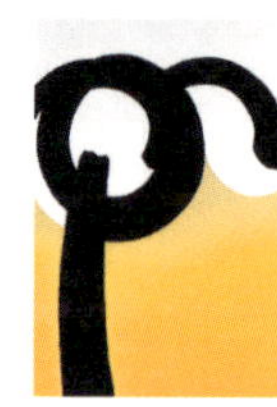

Ako, 2021 (p. 82)
Acrylic on canvas
160 × 120 cm
Private Collection, Singapore (SG)

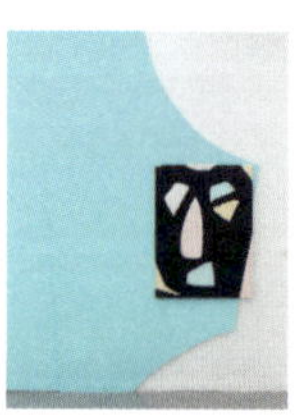

Moi, 2021 (p. 86)
Acrylic on canvas
120 × 90 cm

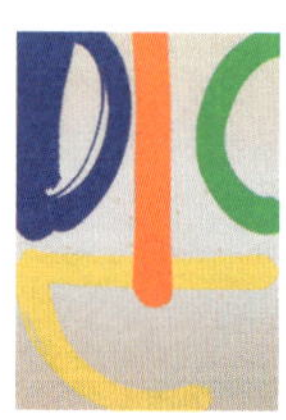

Con, 2020 (p. 89)
Acrylic on canvas
190 × 140 cm

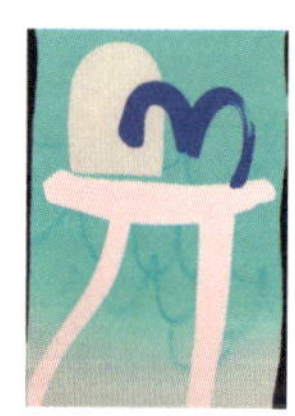

Noy, 2020 (p. 92)
210 × 150 cm
Acrylic on canvas
Private Collection, Birmingham (UK)

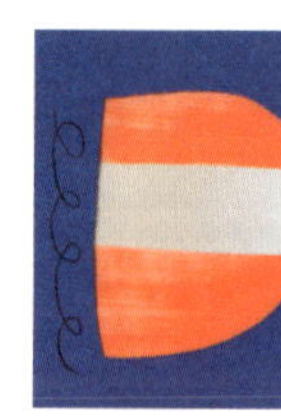

Soy, 2020 (p. 95)
Acrylic and oil stick on canvas
120 × 160 cm
Private Collection, Stockholm (SE)

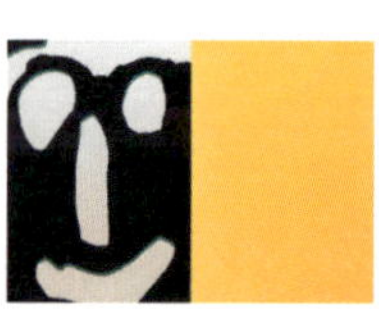

Sig, 2020 (p. 96)
Acrylic on canvas
140 × 200 cm
Private Collection, Atlanta, Georgia (US)

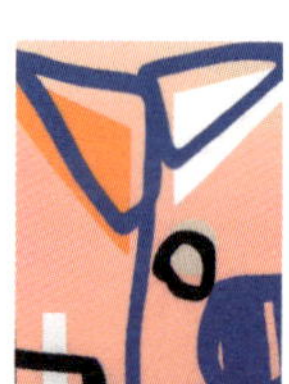

Loy, 2020 (p. 97)
Acrylic on canvas
230 × 170 cm
Private Collection, Vienna (AT)

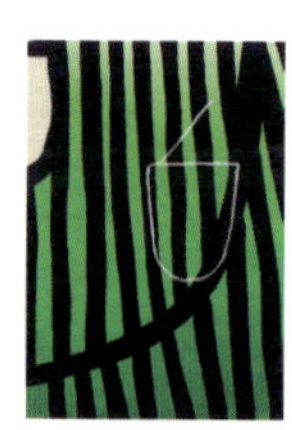

Takk, 2019 (p. 99)
Acrylic and oil stick on canvas
140 × 100 cm
Private Collection, Krefeld (DE)

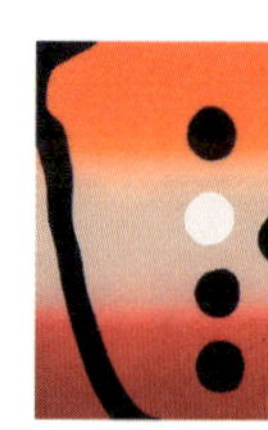

Semm, 2019 (p. 100)
Acrylic on canvas
140 × 100 cm
Private Collection, Nanjing (CN)

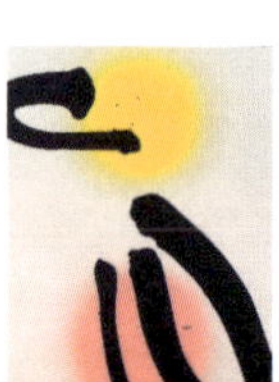

Olgh, 2019 (p. 101)
Acrylic on canvas
210 × 150 cm
Collection Kunsthaus : Kollitsch,
Klagenfurt (AT)

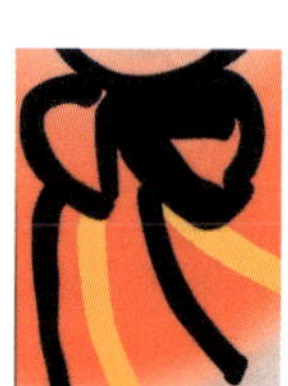

EK, 2018 (p. 103)
Acrylic on canvas
190 × 140 cm
Private Collection, London (UK)

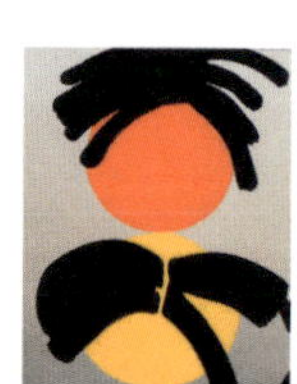

OTT, 2018 (p. 104)
Acrylic on canvas
230 × 170 cm
Private Collection, Stuttgart (DE)

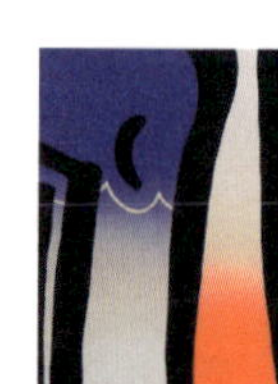

Colm, 2019 (p. 107)
Acrylic on canvas
190 × 140 cm
Private Collection, Nanjing (CN)

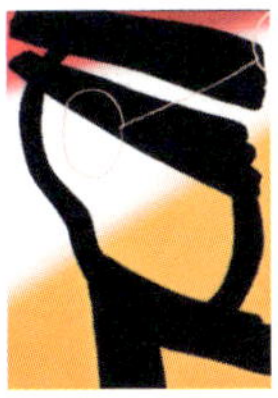

Remu, 2019 (p. 108)
Acrylic and oil bar on canvas
210 × 150 cm
Private Collection, Nanjing (CN)

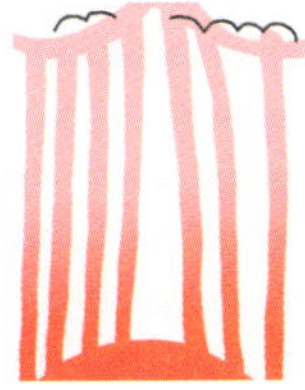

Nic, 2018 (p. 111)
Acrylic on routed black MDF
69 × 55 cm
Collection Soho House London (UK)

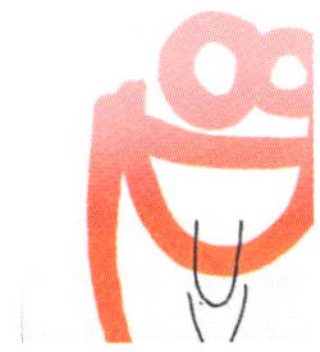

Cec, 2018 (p. 113)
Acrylic on routed black MDF
69 × 55 cm

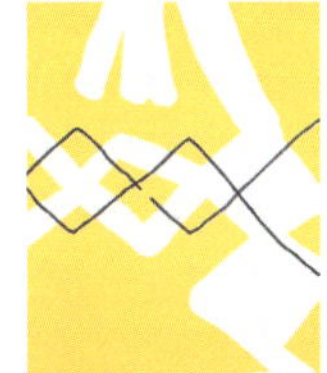

Lark, 2018 (p. 114)
Acrylic on routed black MDF
69 × 55 cm
Private Collection, Berlin (DE)

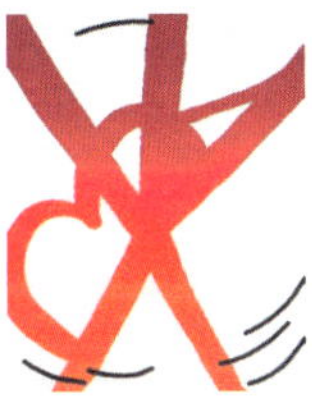

Eme, 2018 (p. 115)
Acrylic on routed black MDF
69 × 55 cm
Collection Soho House London (UK)

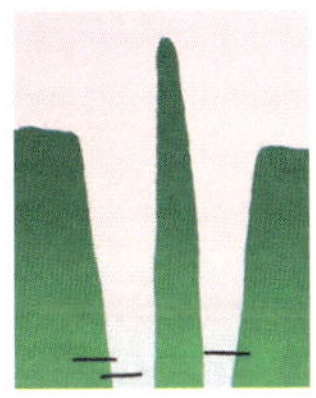

Nel, 2018 (p. 115)
Acrylic on routed black MDF
69 × 55 cm
Private Collection, Rome (IT)

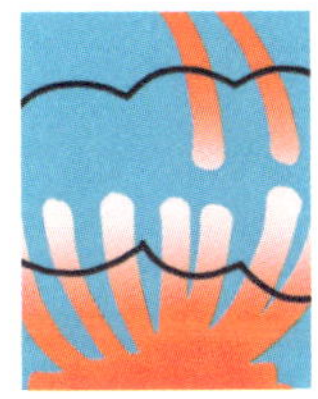

Con, 2018 (p. 116)
Acrylic on routed black MDF
69 × 55 cm
Collection Soho House London (UK)

Val, 2018 (p. 117)
Acrylic on routed black MDF
69 × 55 cm
Private Collection, Rome (IT)

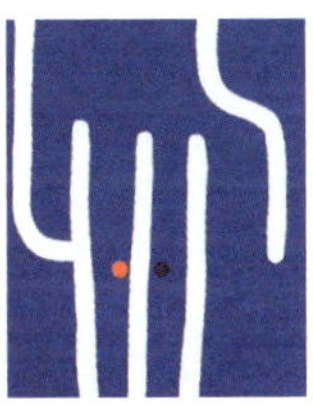

Ell, 2018 (p. 118)
Acrylic on routed black MDF
69 × 55 cm
Private Collection, Berlin (DE)

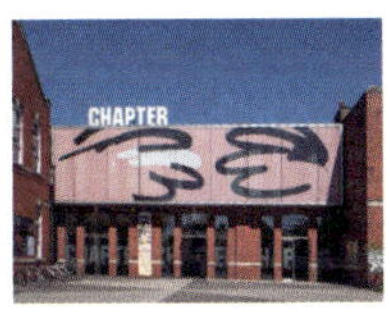

Cue, 2018 (p. 120)
Vinyl banner
Chapter Arts Centre,
Cardiff (UK)

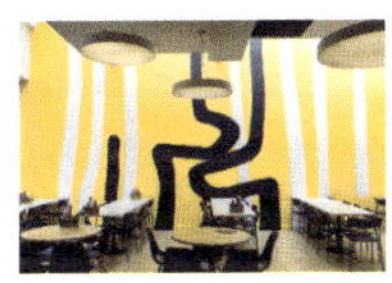

Cue, 2018 (p. 122)
Acrylic on wall
Chapter Arts Centre,
Cardiff (UK)

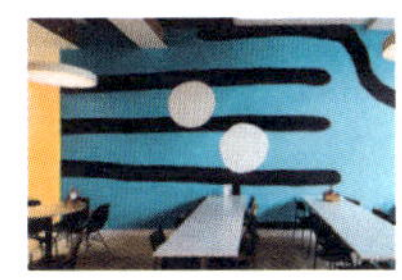

Cue, 2018 (p. 123)
Acrylic on wall
Chapter Arts Centre,
Cardiff (UK)

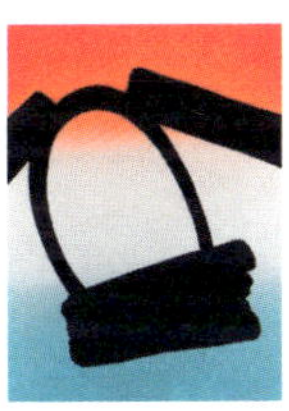

Tjob, 2018 (p. 125)
Acrylic on canvas
230 × 170 cm
Private Collection, Nanjing (CN)

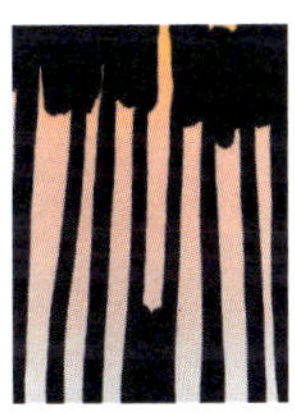

Teek, 2018 (p. 126)
Acrylic on canvas
230 × 170 cm
Private Collection, Zurich (CH)

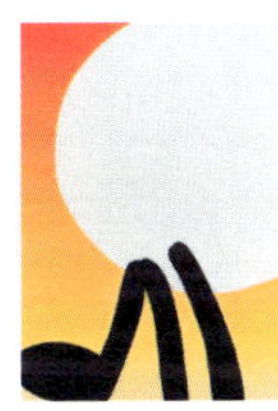

Sinn, 2018 (p. 128)
Acrylic on canvas
190 × 140 cm
Private Collection, Zurich (CH)

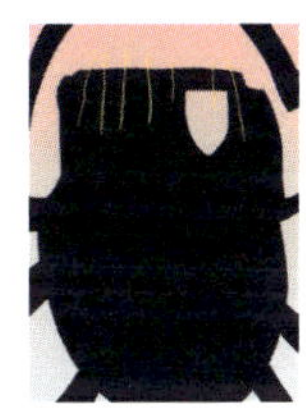

Tibp, 2018 (p. 129)
Acrylic on canvas
190 × 140 cm
Private Collection, Zurich (CH)

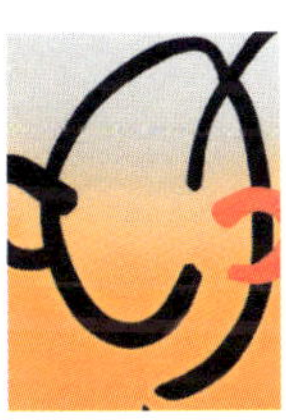

Balb, 2018 (p. 131)
Acrylic on canvas
190 × 140 cm
Private Collection, Zurich (CH)

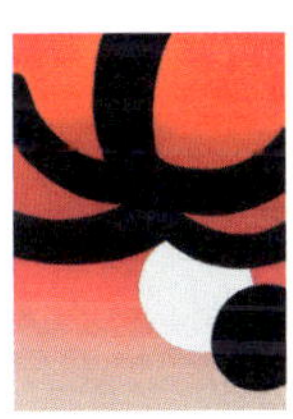

Taam, 2018 (p. 132)
Acrylic on canvas
95 × 70 cm
Private Collection, Los Angeles (US)

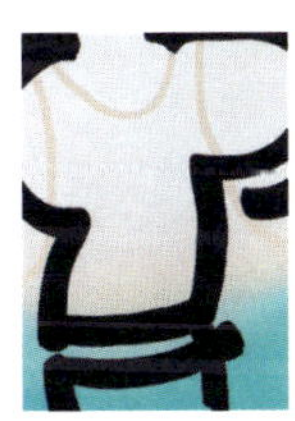

Cody, 2017 (p. 135)
Acrylic on canvas
190 × 140 cm
Private Collection, Singapore (SG)

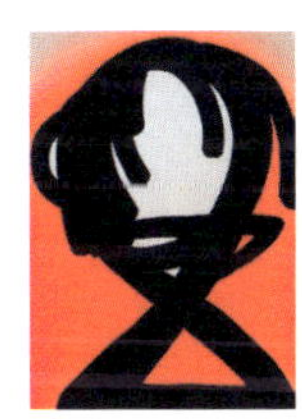

Cooper, 2017 (p. 136)
Acrylic on canvas
190 × 140 cm
Private Collection, London (UK)

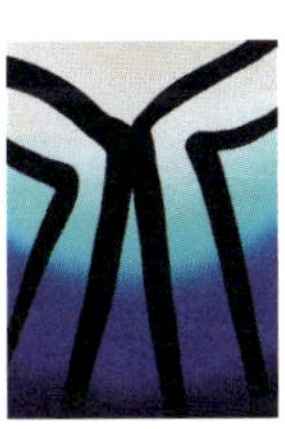

Harper, 2017 (p. 137)
Acrylic on canvas
190 × 140 cm
Private Collection, Miami (US)

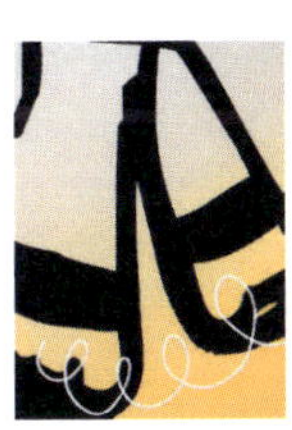

Mario, 2017 (p. 137)
Acrylic on canvas
190 × 140 cm
Private Collection, Florida (US)

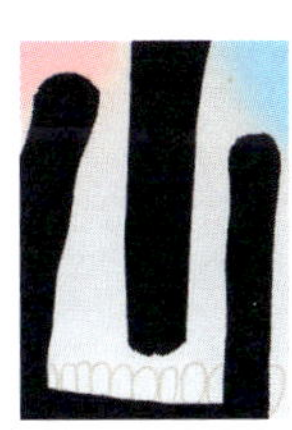

Planck, 2017 (p. 138)
Acrylic on canvas
190 × 140 cm
Private Collection, Istanbul (TK)

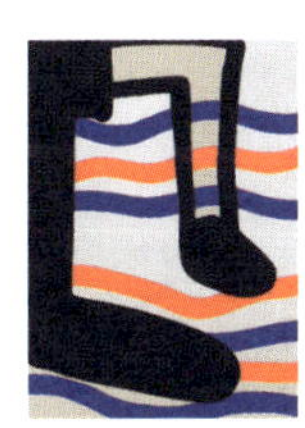

Kenn, 2018 (p. 141)
Acrylic on canvas
190 × 140 cm
Private Collection, Santiago (CL)

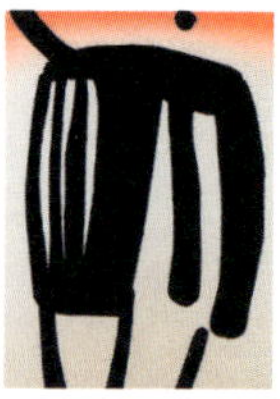

Hopper, 2017 (p. 142)
Acrylic on canvas
190 × 140 cm
Private Collection, Copenhagen (DK)

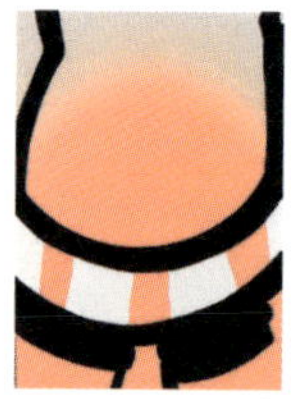

Hobie, 2017 (p. 143)
Acrylic on canvas
190 × 140 cm
Private Collection, Zwevegem (BE)

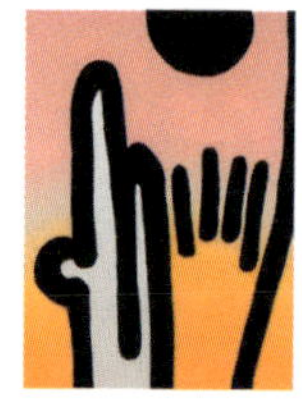

Holden, 2017 (p. 144)
Acrylic on canvas
190 × 140 cm
Private Collection, Miami (US)

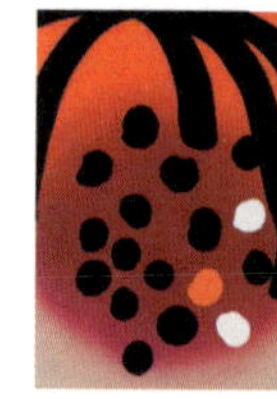

Garner, 2017 (p. 144)
Acrylic on canvas
190 × 140 cm
Private Collection, Washington (US)

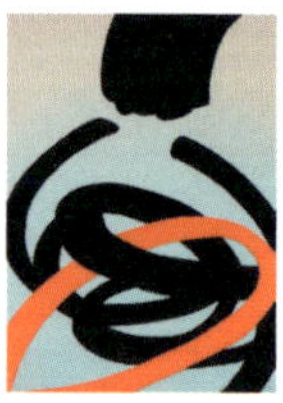

Gayle, 2017 (p. 145)
Acrylic on canvas
190 × 140 cm
Private Collection (CH)

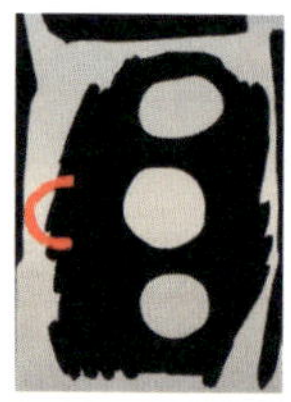

Sol, 2017 (p. 146)
Acrylic on canvas
190 × 140 cm
Private Collection, London (UK)

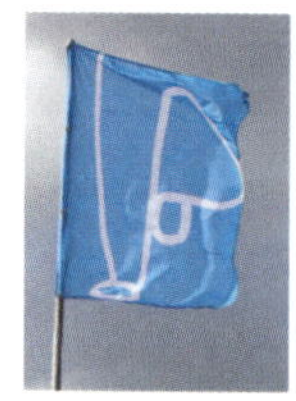

Einbeinstand, 2016 (p. 149)
Digital print on polyester
140 × 110 cm

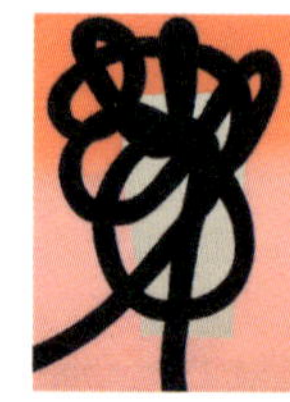

Pink Path Patty, 2016 (p. 150)
Acrylic on canvas
180 × 140 cm
Collection Kunsthaus : Kollitsch, Klagenfurt (AT)

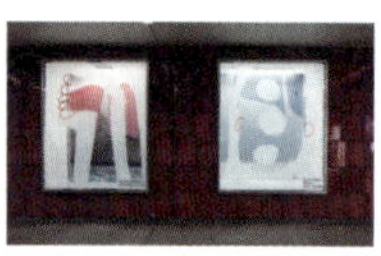

Eclipse, 2016 (p. 152)
Yogurt and acrylic on window, digital print
Projektraum ung5, Cologne (DE)

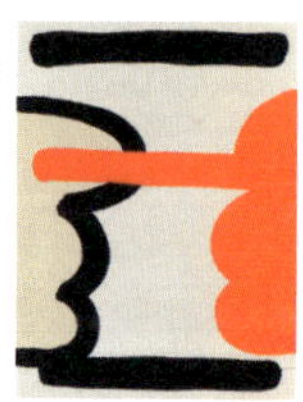

Orange Punch, 2016 (p. 155)
Acrylic on canvas
180 × 140 cm
Private Collection, Leuven (BE)

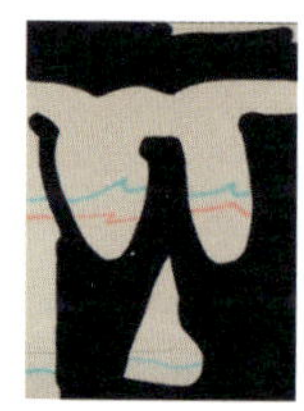

Lizard Dream, 2016 (p. 156)
Acrylic on canvas
160 × 120 cm
Private Collection, Zurich (CH)

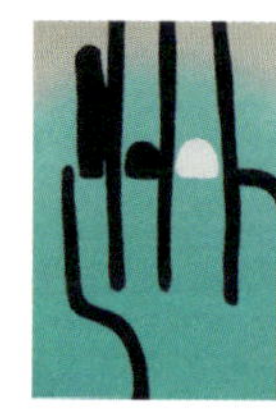

Celeste Bloom, 2016 (p. 157)
Acrylic on canvas
190 × 140 cm
Private Collection, New York (US)

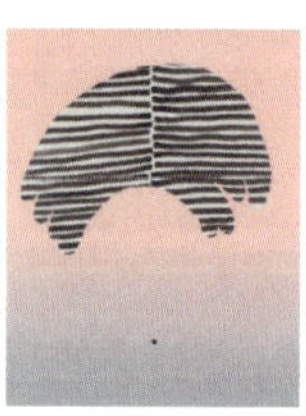

Robert, 2016 (p. 158)
Acrylic on routed black MDF
69 × 55 cm
Private Collection, London (UK)

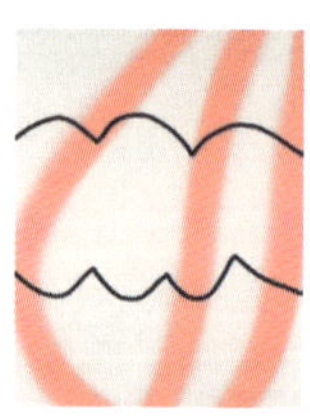

Fluorid, 2016 (p. 159)
Acrylic on routed black MDF
69 × 55 cm

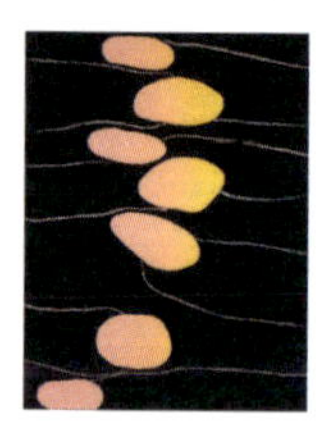

Cindy, 2016 (p. 161)
Acrylic and oil on canvas, artist frame
180 × 140 cm
Private Collection, Paris (FR)

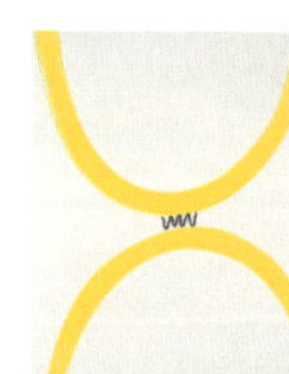

Untitled (Electrolytes), 2016 (p. 162)
Acrylic on routed black MDF
69 × 55 cm
Private Collection, Oxford (UK)

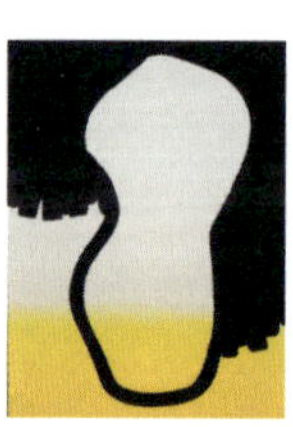

Hendrik, 2016 (p. 162)
Acrylic on canvas, artist frame
160 × 120 cm
Government Art Collection (UK)

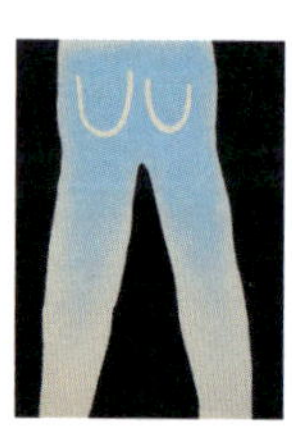

Steve, 2016 (p. 163)
Acrylic on canvas
160 × 120 cm
Collection of the artist

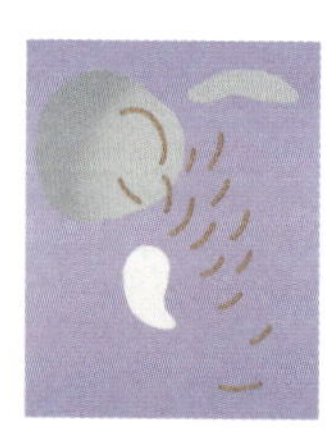

Twinkle, 2015 (p. 164)
Acrylic on routed black MDF
69 × 55 cm
Private Collection, London (UK)

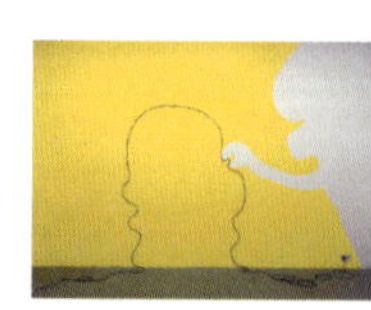

Pinch, 2016 (p. 168)
Acrylic and electric cable on wall
Mission Gallery, Swansea (UK)

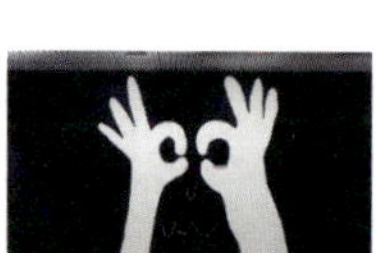

Owl, 2015 (p. 170)
Acrylic on wall
Entrance hall, Northern Gallery for Contemporary Art, Sunderland (UK)

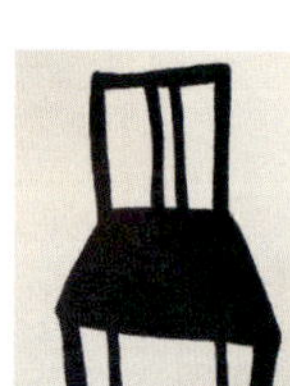

Untitled (Chair), 2015 (p. 172)
Acrylic on routed black MDF
69 × 55 cm
Arts Council Collection, London (UK)

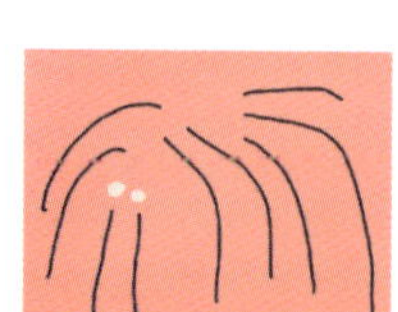

Untitled (Wusel), 2015 (p. 174)
Acrylic on routed black MDF
55 × 69 cm
Private Collection, London (UK)

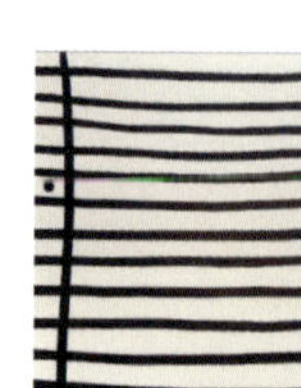

Untitled (Sheet), 2015 (p. 174)
Acrylic on routed black MDF
69 × 55 cm
Private Collection, Berlin (DE)

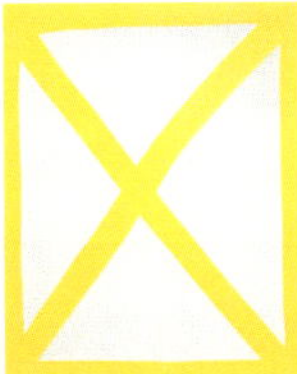

Untitled (Box), 2015 (p. 174)
Acrylic on MDF
69 × 55 cm
Arts Council Collection, London (UK)

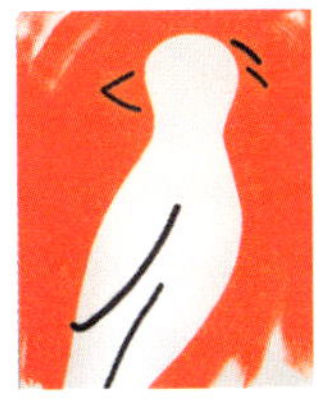

Untitled (Penguin), 2015 (p. 180)
Acrylic on routed black MDF
69 × 55 cm
Arts Council Collection, London (UK)

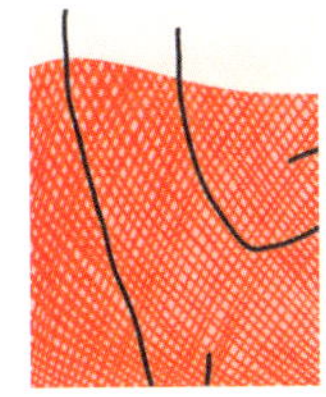

Untitled (Boogie), 2015 (p. 183)
Acrylic on canvas, wood frame
69 × 55 cm

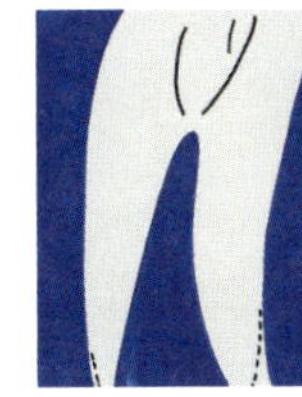

Untitled (Long Johns), 2015 (p. 183)
Acrylic on canvas, wood frame
69 × 55 cm

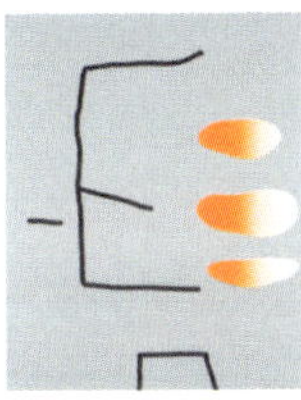

Untitled (Feathers), 2015 (p. 184)
Acrylic on canvas, wood frame
69 × 55 cm
Private Collection, London (UK)

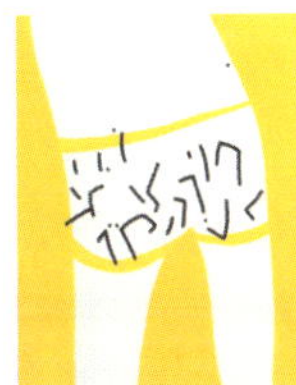

Twiste wo ich swinge I, 2015 (p. 184)
Acrylic on routed black MDF
69 × 55 cm
Private Collection, Berlin (DE)

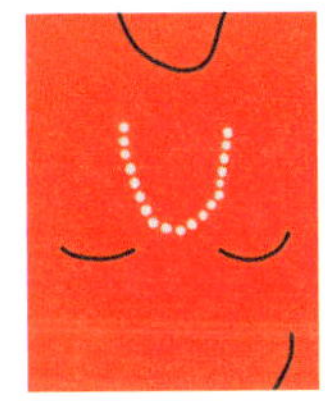

Untitled (Necklace), 2015 (p. 185)
Acrylic on routed black MDF
69 × 55 cm

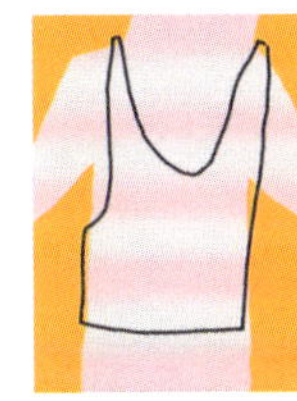

Untitled (Underwear II), 2015 (p. 186)
Acrylic on routed black MDF
69 × 55 cm
Private Collection, Athens (GR)

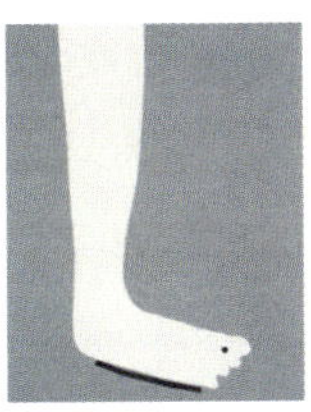

Untitled (Underwear II), 2015 (p. 188)
Acrylic on routed black MDF
69 × 55 cm
Private Collection, Athens (GR)

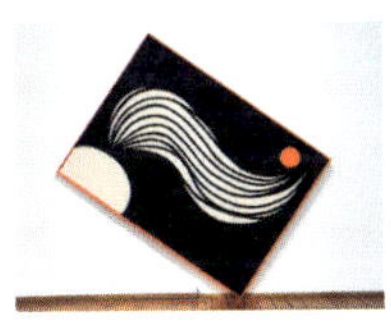

Whipped, 2015 (p. 189)
Acrylic on canvas, artist frame
140 × 190 cm
Private Collection, Monte Carlo (MC)

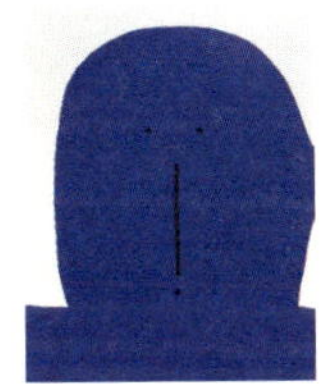

Untitled (Stalker), 2015 (p. 191)
Acrylic on routed black MDF
69 × 55 cm
Arts Council Collection, London (UK)

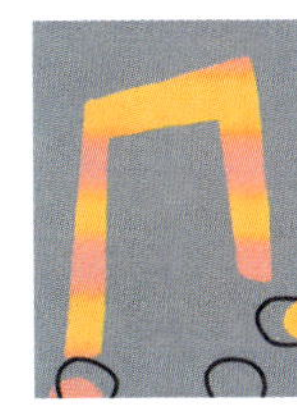

Untitled (Notes), 2015 (p. 192)
Acrylic on routed black MDF
69 × 55 cm

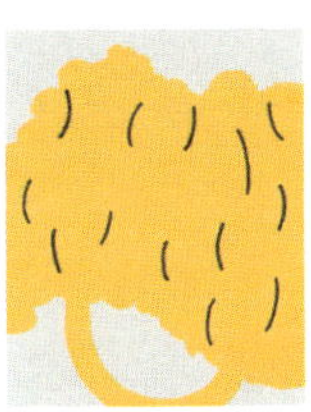

Rodrigo, 2016 (p. 194)
Acrylic on routed black MDF
69 × 55 cm
Private Collection, Milan (IT)

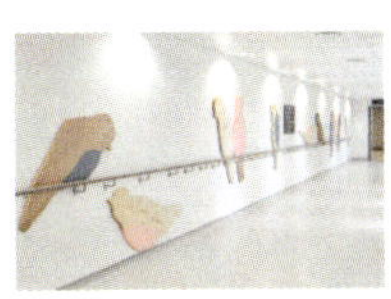

Hanging Out Again, 2014 (p. 198)
Acrylic and varnish on
veneered wood panels, 15 parts
The Royal London Hospital,
Whitechapel, London (UK)

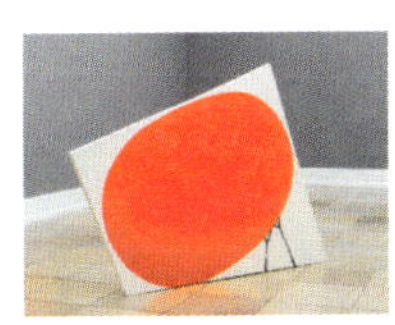

Stoned, 2014 (p. 200)
Acrylic and oil on canvas,
jesmonite on aerated concrete
170 × 220 × 20 cm
Private Collection, Wilnsdorf (DE)

Snowflake, 2014 (p. 203)
Acrylic on canvas, wooden shadow frame
164 × 125 × 6,5 cm
Private Collection, Neu-Isenburg (DE)

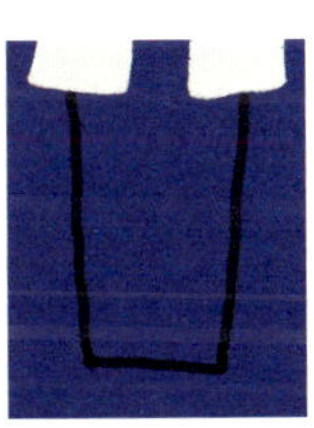

Nightshift, 2014 (p. 204)
Acrylic on routed black MDF
69 × 55 cm
Private Collection, Wilnsdorf (DE)

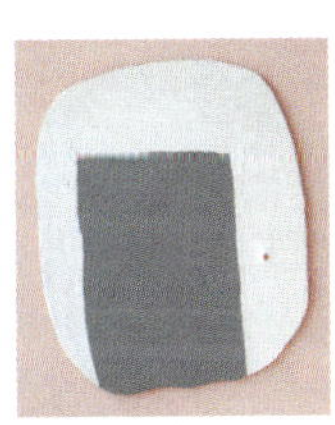

Girl with a Pearl Earring, 2013 (p. 207)
Oil, acrylic, eyelet on canvas and board
120 × 103 cm
Private Collection, London (UK)

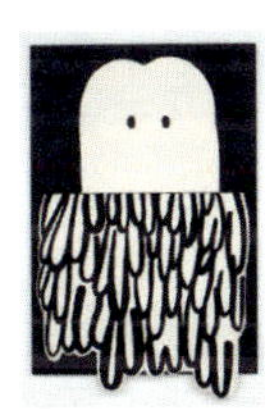

Ghostowl, 2013 (p. 209)
Acrylic on canvas and board
168 × 110 cm
Private Collection, London (UK)

Deep Thought, 2013 (p. 211)
Oil and acrylic on canvas
148 × 138 cm

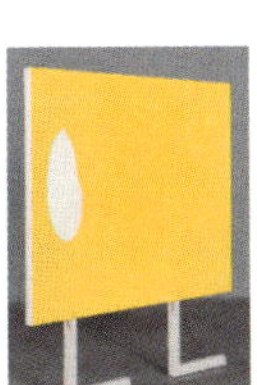

Dingbats, 2013 (p. 212)
Acrylic on canvas and wood
120 × 135 cm
Private Collection, Neu-Isenburg (DE)

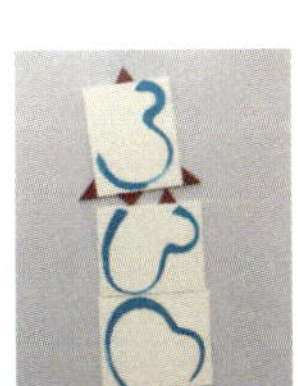

Hanging Out, 2013 (p. 215)
Acrylic on canvas and wood (nine parts)
Private Collection, Neu-Isenburg (DE)

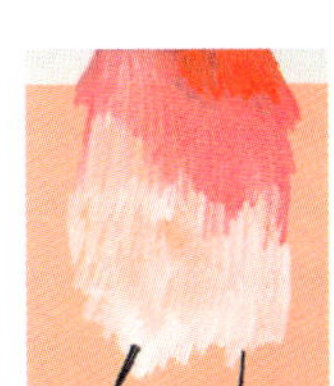

Headless Chicken, 2012 (p. 221)
Oil and acrylic on canvas
120 × 100 cm
Private Collection, London (UK)

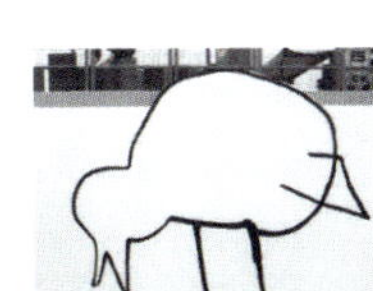

CooCoo, Headless Chicken, 2012 (p. 222)
Acrylic on wall
Sunday Art Fair, London (UK)

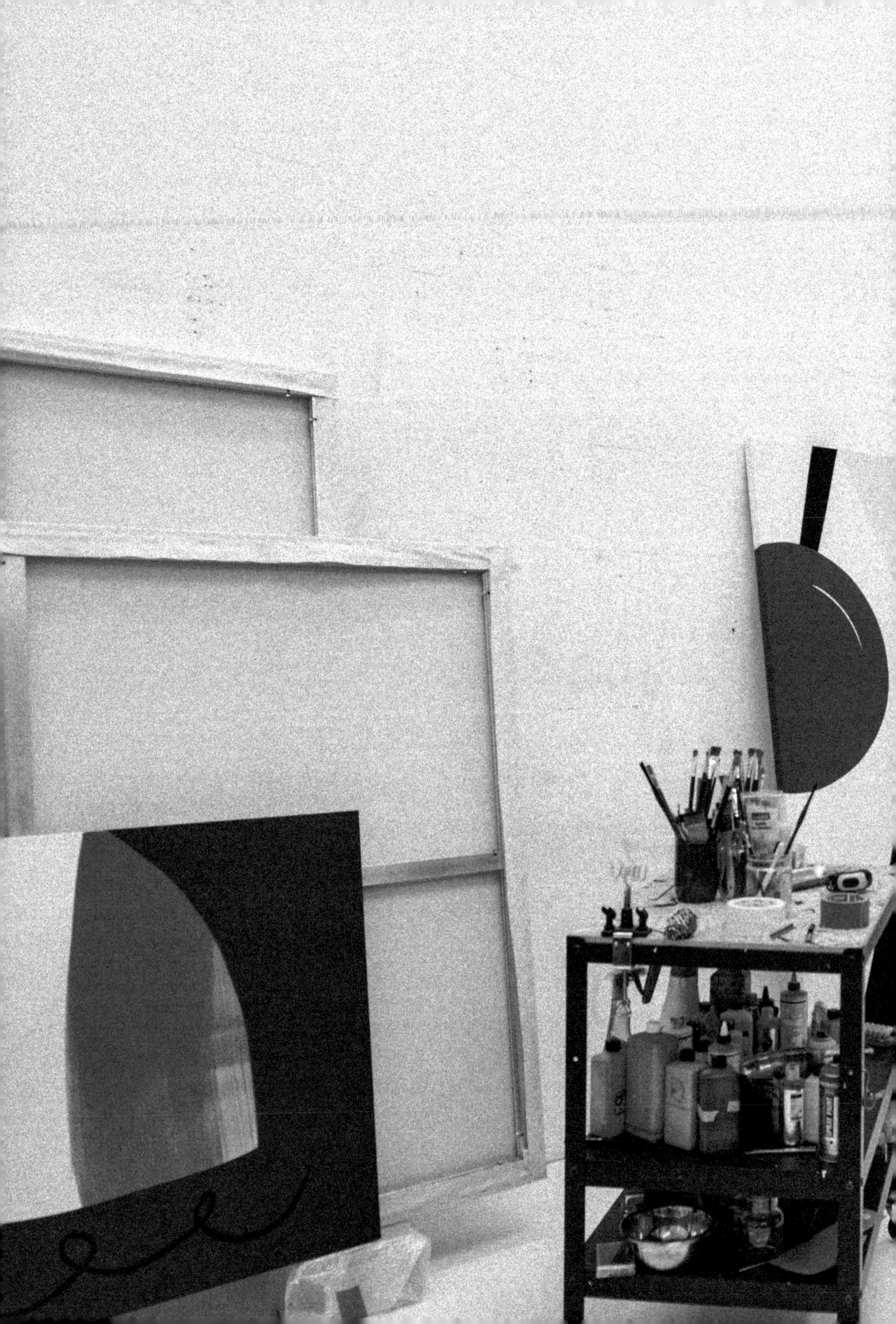

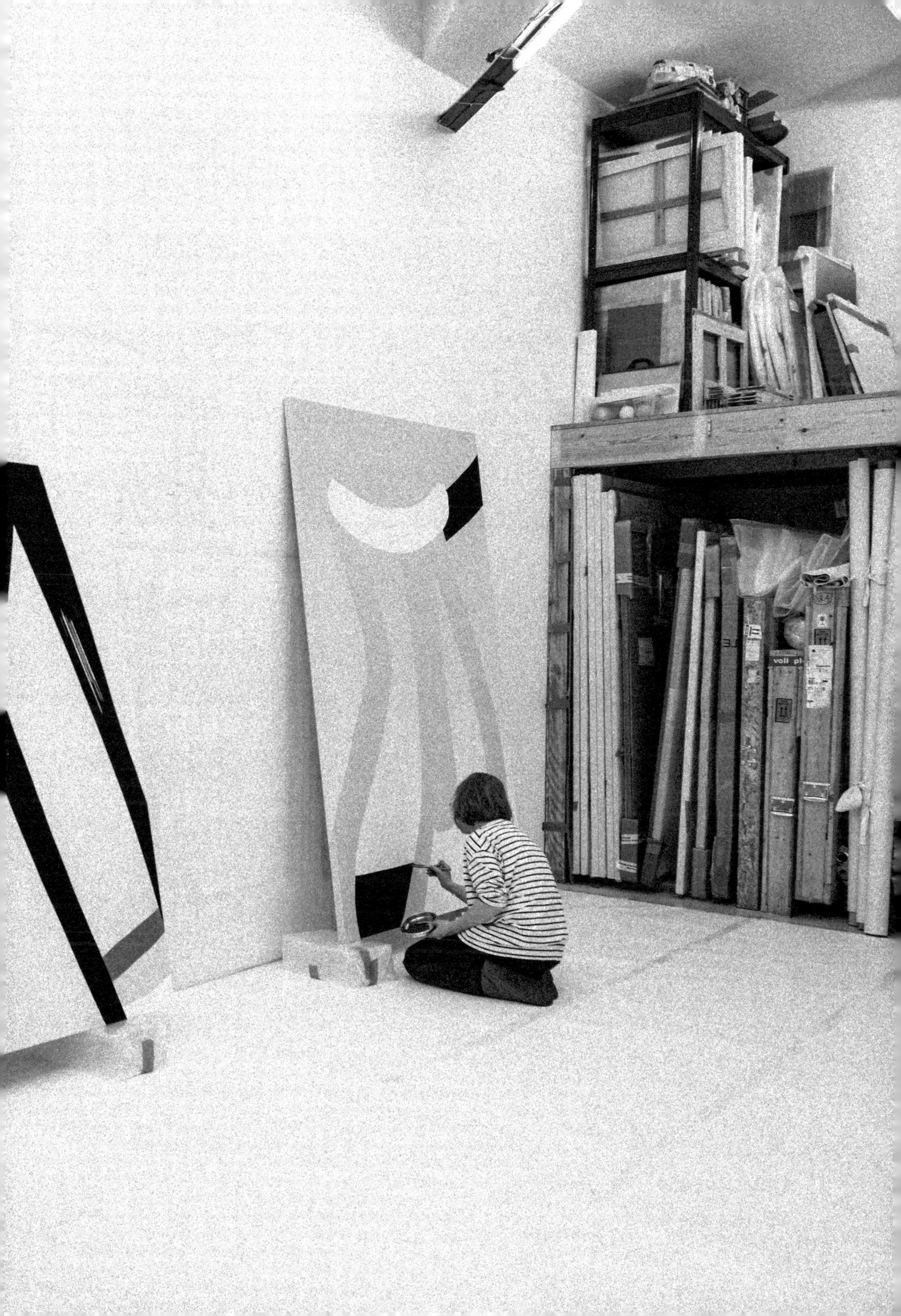

CV

Cornelia Baltes
* 1978 in Mönchengladbach (DE)
lives and works in Berlin (DE)

EDUCATION

2009 – 2011
(MFA) Slade School of Fine Art, London (UK)
2003 – 2006
(Diploma) Folkwang University of the Arts, Essen (DE)
2000 – 2003
Bergische Universität Wuppertal (DE)

SELECTED SOLO EXHIBITIONS

2023
Hub Bub, Andréhn-Schiptjenko, Stockholm (SE)

2022
Waggle Dance, rodolphe janssen, Brussels (BE)
Lazybones, Nino Mier Gallery, Los Angeles (US)

2021
Eigenbrötler, EIGEN + ART Lab, Berlin (DE)

2020
Tit for Tat, Galleri Nicolai Wallner, Copenhagen (DK)

2018
Teamwork, Frutta, Glasgow (UK)
Lightbox, Chapter Arts Center, Cardiff (UK)
Mingle Mime, BolteLang, Zurich (CH)

2017
CAPRI, Galleri Nicolai Wallner, Copenhagen (DK)

2016
Eclipse, Projektraum ung5 (curated by KubaParis), Cologne (DE)
Gone Fishing, Centrum, Berlin (DE)
Drunk Octopus wants to fight, Limoncello, London (UK)
Liste (solo presentation with Limoncello), Basel (CH)

2015
Turner, Northern Gallery for Contemporary Art, Sunderland (UK)
Tiny Dancer, Kunstverein Ulm (DE)

2013
Schnick Schnack Schnuck!, Limoncello, London (UK)
There's a light and a whistle for attracting attention, DREI, Cologne (DE)

2012
HOOLOOVOO, Aspex Gallery, Portsmouth (UK)

2010
The Great Loop Forward, Tank Gallery, London (UK)

SELECTED GROUP EXHIBITIONS

2024

Giants, rodolphe janssen, Brussels (BE)

2023

No Illusions – Painting in Space, Hamburger Kunsthalle, Hamburg (DE)
BOTTOM UP, Kühlhaus Berlin, Berlin (DE)
7th Garden Edition, Contemporary Sculpture Fulmer, Buckinghamshire (UK)
BEACH (curated by Danny Moynihan), Nino Mier Gallery, New York (US)
Schau…9, Kunsthaus : Kollitsch, Klagenfurt (AT)

2022

State of Play (curated by Brooke Benington), Canary Wharf, London (UK)
Trio Feminin, Christine König Galerie, Vienna (AT)
Girl Meets Girl, Vestfossen Kunstlaboratorium, Oslo (NO)
Nine Positions of Young Painting, Landesmuseum Detmold (DE)

2021

Jahresgaben, Kunstverein Reutlingen (DE)
Schau…7, Kunsthaus : Kollitsch, Klagenfurt (AT)

2020

Cadmium Lemon (curated by Cristina Anglada), Galeria Pelaires, Palma (ES)
You can do better – Bad Painting (curated by Laura Helena Wurth), Elektrohalle Rhomberg, Salzburg (AT)
Now! Painting in Germany Today, Deichtorhallen Hamburg (DE)

2019

Now! Painting in Germany Today, Kunstmuseum Bonn, Museum Wiesbaden, Kunstsammlungen Chemnitz (DE)

2018

The Everyday and Extraordinary, Birmingham Museum and Art Gallery / Towner Art Gallery, Eastbourne (UK)

2017

Schau…4, Kunsthaus : Kollitsch, Klagenfurt (AT)
An eyeful of wry, Government Art Collection, Hull (UK)
You see me like a UFO, Marcelle Joseph Projects, London (UK)
Jump, Galleri Nicolai Wallner, Copenhagen (DK)
Home is not a place (curated by Marlene von Carnap, Coraly von Bismarck), German Embassy London (UK)
Every Line tells its own story, Galerie Nathalie Halgand, Vienna (AT)
31 women, Breese Little, London (UK)
Jump ball, Dio Horia, Mykonos (GR)
Cinque Mostre, American Academy in Rome (IT)
Jokes on Painting, Schau Fenster, Berlin (DE)

2016

Catherine Biocca, Cornelia Baltes, Rosalie Schweiker (curated by Louise Hobson), Mission Gallery, Swansea (UK)
Double Acts (curated by Marcelle Joseph), At Home Salon, London (UK)
Alice in Crisis, Dio Horia, Mykonos (GR)
New Adventures in Vexillology 2 (curated by Valeska Hageney), Kunstverein Amrun (DE)
Life Eraser (curated by Domenico de Chirico), Brand New Gallery, Milan (IT)
Your Swath, My Jab, DREI, Cologne (DE)
Inflatable Aesthetics, Hawaii-Lisbon, Lisbon (PT)
True Love Over Physics, Coma Gallery, Sydney (AU)
Wilhelm Screams, The Landing Strip, Berlin (DE)
Gestalt and Werden, FeldbuschWiesnerRudolph, Berlin (DE)

2015

Women's Art Society II, MOSTYN, Wales (UK)
Oh, of course, you were berry picking, DREI, Cologne (DE)
Feel the discourse (curated by Christina Ramos), Guest Projects, London (UK)

2014

100 Painters of tomorrow, Christie's /Beers Contemporary London (UK)
Off the Wall!, Kunsthalle Nürnberg (DE)
East London Painting Prize, Bow Arts, London (UK)
Apples and Pears, DREI, Cologne (DE)

2013

Curiosity and Method, Less Is More Projects, Paris (FR)
Carousel, Aspex Gallery, Portsmouth (UK)
Just What Is Not Is Possible – Painting in Space, Museum Folkwang, Essen (DE)
Zero Gravity, Less Is More Projects, Paris (FR)

2012

Chimera Q.T.E., Cell Project Space, London (UK)
P/N/7 The summary show, Project Number, London (UK)
Summer Exhibition, Royal Academy London (UK)
Young British Art II (curated by Ryan Gander and Christina von Rotenhan), Dienstgebäude, Zurich (CH)

2011

Bloomberg New Contemporaries 2011: In the Presence ICA, London (UK)
Postgraduate Printmaking Exhibition 2011, Clifford Chance, London (UK)
Helter Skelter, UCLH Arts, London (UK)
Jealous Graduate Print Prize, Jealous Gallery, London (UK)
Bloomberg New Contemporaries 2011, Site Gallery/S1 Artspace, Sheffield (UK)

2010

John Moores Painting Prize, Walker Art Gallery, Liverpool (UK)
Istanbul was Constantinople, Hush Gallery, Istanbul (TR)
Threads, Tank Gallery, London (UK)
Exhibitionism, East Wing 9, The Courtauld Institute of Art, Somerset House, London (UK)

PRIZES

2023
Publication Grant, Kunstfonds Bonn e.V. (DE)
2020
Working Grant, Kunstfonds Bonn e.V. / Neustart-Kultur (DE)
2016
Working Grant, Kunstfonds Bonn e.V. (DE)
2015
Project Grant, Kunststiftung NRW (DE)
2014
Marianne Defet Painting Fellowship, Kunsthalle Nürnberg (DE)
2011
Graduate Printmaking Prize Winner, Jealous Gallery, London (UK)
2010
Finalist, John Moores Painting Prize, Liverpool (UK)
2009 – 2011
Scholarship, Hartmut and Lore Schuler-Stiftung, Wuppertal (DE)
2006
Scholarship, Pentiment Academy, Hamburg (DE)

BIBLIOGRAPHY (SELECTION)

Girl Meets Girl, Vestfossen Kunstlaboratorium, 2022, pp. 12-17
Cornelia Baltes Shows Us How to Play Among Paintings, Martin Herbert, *ArtReview*, 05/2021, p. 91
Mehr Berlin, *Tagesspiegel*, 02/2020
Frische Farbe; Jetzt! Der große Überblick zur jungen Malerei in Deutschland, *Art – Das Kunstmagazin* 09/2019, pp. 46-48
Now! Painting in Germany Today, Hirmer Verlag, 2019, pp. 38-41
Critics' Picks, Nicolas John Jones, *Art Forum Online*, 02/2016
Cornelia Baltes' Drunk Octopus wants to fight, Louisa Elderton, *Flash Art*, no. 307, vol. 49, 03-04/2016
Womens Art Society II, Mostyn Publishing, 2015, pp. 11-14
Oui! Cornelia Baltes, Marianne-Defet-Malerei-Stipendium, Hrsg. Institut für moderne Kunst, 2015
Off the Wall!, Kunsthalle Nürnberg, Verlag für Moderne Kunst, 2014, pp. 68-87
100 Painters of Tomorrow, Thames & Hudson, 2014, pp. 36-37
Just What Is Not Is Possible – Painting in space, Edition Folkwang/Steidl, 2013, pp. 92-101
Starter – die neuen Künstler, *Art – Das Kunstmagazin*, 08/2013, p. 64
24 Artists to Watch, *Modern Painters*, 12/2012, p. 82
Bloomberg New Contemporaries, In the Presence, 2011, pp. 33-34
John Moores 26 Contemporary Painting Prize 2010, Walker Art Gallery, 2010, p. 24

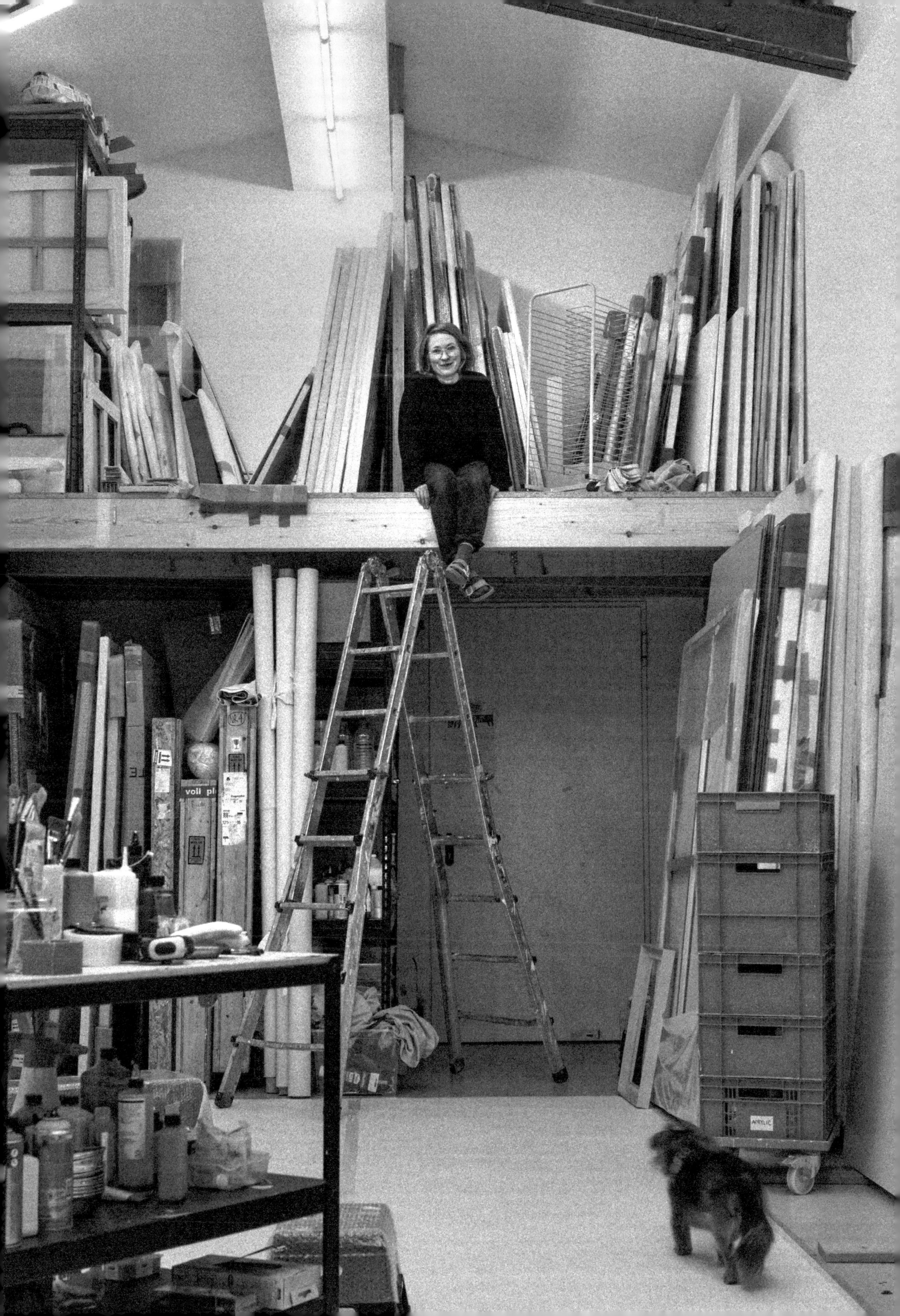

Imprint Impressum

Concept Konzeption
Cornelia Baltes & Jan Motyka

Design Gestaltung
Jan Motyka

Texts Texte
Larissa Kikol
Alexander Klar
George Vasey

Translation Übersetzung
Richard Humphrey

Copy editing Lektorat
Uta Grosenick

Photography Fotografie
Joe Clark, pp. 17-20, 22-25, 27, 35-36, 39-40, 48, 64, 68, 77-84, 86-87, 89, 92, 95, 99, 103, 104, 108, 114, 117, 118, 125, 131, 135, 138, 141, 146, 150, 161, 164, 180, 186, 191, 194, 197-199, 207-212, 215-219, 221-223
Jean-Baptiste Béranger, pp. 28-32
Corey Bartle-Sanderson, pp. 43-46
Hugard & Vanoverschelde, pp. 49-54, 57
Dawn Blackman, pp. 58-63, 66-67
Studio GRAYSC, pp. 70-71
Joakim Züger, pp. 73-75
Anders Sune Berg, pp. 90-91, 96-97, 136-137, 142-145
Henning Rogger, pp. 100-101
David Ertl, pp. 106-107
Stefan Jaeggi, pp. 126-129, 132-133
Sandra Hermannsen, p. 149
Hermes Villena, pp. 152-153
Andy Keate, pp. 162-163
Justin Meeke, p. 155
Ben Westoby, pp. 156-159
Colin Davison, pp. 172, 174-179
Annette Kradisch, pp. 200, 203
Johanna Ruebel, pp. 225-227, 234-235, 239

Image editing Lithografie
Jan Motyka

Supported by Gefördert durch

STIFTUNG**KUNSTFONDS**

Die Beauftragte der Bundesregierung
für Kultur und Medien

This book was made possible by the generous support of:
Dieses Buch wurde ermöglicht durch die großzügige Unterstützung von:
Andréhn-Schiptjenko, Stockholm/Paris
rodolphe janssen, Brussels
Nino Mier Gallery, Los Angeles/Brussels/New York
Galleri Nicolai Wallner, Copenhagen

This publication is listed in the German National Bibliography by the German National Library. Detailed bibliographic data are available at http://dnb.d-nb.de.
Die Deutsche Nationalbibliothek verzeichnet diese Publikation in der Deutschen Nationalbibliografie; detaillierte bibliografische Daten sind im Internet über http://dnb.dnb.de abrufbar.

Distribution and marketing Vertrieb und Marketing
DCV
sales@dcv-books.com

Production management Produktion
DCV

Printing and binding Gesamtherstellung
L&C Printing Group, Kraków

ISBN 978-3-96912-182-5
Printed in Poland

Published by Erschienen bei
DCV
www.dcv-books.com

DCV

Many thanks to all those who have supported my work and this publication.
Vielen Dank an alle, die meine Arbeit und diese Publikation unterstützt haben.